INDIAN

of the

AMERICAN SOUTH

1610 - 1858

A guide for

GENEALOGISTS & HISTORIANS

MICHAEL A. PORTS

CLEARFIELD

ISBN 978-0-8063-5849-9

Table of Contents

Table of Contents...1

Introduction 7

Part One History of the Southern Indian Wars...11

    Early Colonial Wars...13

        Powhatan Wars, 1610-1646 13

        Chowanoac Wars, 1666, 1675-1677 16

        Bacon's Rebellion, 1676 17

        Westo War, 1679-1680 19

        Queen Anne's War, 1702-1713...21

        Chitimacha War, 1707–1718..23

        Natchez Wars, 1716-1731 24

        Chickasaw War, 1736-1739 27

        Places of Interest...29

        Further Reading 32

    Tuscarora War, 1711-1715...37

        Background...37

        Campaigns 38

        Aftermath...40

        Places of Interest...41

        Further Reading 45

    Yamasee War, 1715-1716...46

        Background...46

        Campaigns 47

        Aftermath...49

        Places of Interest...50

        Further Reading 53

    French and Indian War, 1754-1763..55

        Background...55

Campaigns 56

Aftermath 58

Places of Interest 59

Further Reading 63

First Cherokee War, 1758-1761 67

Background 67

Campaigns 68

Aftermath 70

Places of Interest 71

Further Reading 75

Pontiac's War, 1763 77

Background 77

Campaigns 78

Aftermath 79

Points of Interest 80

Further Reading 82

Lord Dunmore's War, 1774 83

Background 83

Campaigns 84

Aftermath 85

Places of Interest 86

Further Reading 90

Revolutionary War, 1775-1783 92

Background 92

Campaigns 93

Aftermath 97

Places of Interest 98

Further Reading 105

Second Cherokee War, 1776-1795 108

Background 108

Campaigns 110

Aftermath 121

Places of Interest 122

Further Reading 128

First Creek War, 1813-14 134

Background 134

Campaigns 136

Aftermath 140

Places of Interest 141

Further Reading 151

First Seminole War, 1817-1818 155

Background 155

Campaigns 157

Aftermath 160

Places of Interest 161

Further Reading 166

Second Seminole War, 1835-1842 168

Background 168

Campaigns 169

Aftermath 174

Places of Interest 175

Further Reading 181

Second Creek War, 1836-1837 183

Background 183

Campaigns 184

Aftermath 187

Places of Interest 188

Further Reading 193

Third Seminole War, 1855-1858 194

Background 194

Campaigns 195

Aftermath 196

Places of Interest 197

Further Reading 201

    Removal to the Indian Territory, 1830-1838..202

        Cherokee Removal...203

        Chickasaw Removal...205

        Choctaw Removal..206

        Creek Removal 207

        Seminole Removal...208

        Places of Interest..210

        Further Reading 221

Part Two Records of the Southern Indian Wars 223

    Federal Repositories..225

        National Archives and Records Administration.................................225

        Army Center of Military History..250

        Army Heritage and Education Center 251

        Naval History and Heritage Command 252

        National Museum of the Marine Corps..253

        Coast Guard Museum...254

        Library of Congress 255

    State Archives..262

        Alabama..263

        Florida..265

        Georgia 267

        Kentucky..270

        Louisiana 273

        Mississippi...275

        North Carolina 280

        South Carolina 286

        Tennessee...290

        Virginia..293

        West Virginia...299

    Native American Tribes and Archives 301

        Alabama..301

        Florida..304

Georgia 305

Louisiana 306

Mississippi..308

North Carolina 309

Oklahoma..312

South Carolina 315

Virginia...318

The Draper Manuscript Collection..323

Other Significant Repositories and Sources 329

National 329

Alabama...333

Florida..337

Georgia 344

Kentucky..349

Louisiana 353

Mississippi...357

Oklahoma...360

North Carolina 365

South Carolina 369

Tennessee...374

Virginia..379

West Virginia...384

Hereditary Societies..386

Miscellaneous Libraries, Archives, and Foundations...391

General Publications 395

Reenactment Organizations 397

5

Introduction

Soon after the founding of the first English settlement in the New World at Jamestown, armed conflict arose between the settlers and the Native Americans. From the onset of the First Powhatan War in 1610 through the end of the Third Seminole War in 1858, there were no less than twenty-seven separate and distinct Indian wars in or involving the American South. This research guide chronicles those wars and presents the surviving records needed to document your ancestor's participation in those conflicts. Of course, other ambushes, attacks, raids, and skirmishes occurred in between the various named wars, all too numerous and small to be included here. This guide focuses on the four southern colonies of Virginia, North Carolina, South Carolina, and Georgia, the states that were formed from their original territory, Alabama, Kentucky, Mississippi, Tennessee, and West Virginia, and the states of Florida and Louisiana, which were so inextricably linked to the other southern states. The numerous early armed conflicts between the native tribes and the Spanish in Florida prior to the establishment of the Providence of Carolina in 1663 are not addressed here. Similarly, only the armed conflicts in French Louisiana in which American Southerners participated or in which they were directly impacted are addressed here. And, finally, the various armed conflicts that were solely between opposing tribes, with no involvement of the white settlers, also are not addressed.

The spelling of the names of many of the various tribes changed over time. For example, Yamasee also was spelled Yemessee, Yamassee, etc. Throughout the guide, the modern generally accepted spellings are adopted. The Lenni Lenape, or sometimes just the Lenape, are also called the Delaware. The guide adopts the modern name Delaware for the tribe. Similarly, the Creek often are called the Muskogee. The guide adopts the generally accepted name Creek. Hopefully, these adoptions will help avoid confusion.

The first part of the guide chronicles the various Indian wars, more or less in chronological order. The discussion of each war is presented in three parts, first the background presents the causes of the conflict and the event or events that triggered it, the second presents the campaigns, and the third discusses the aftermath. The discussions concentrate on the military aspects of the wars, not the political, social, or cultural aspects. Whenever possible, the names of the commanding officers, names of the military units, troop strengths, battle locations, numbers of casualties, and dates are included. The date and name of the treaty ending each war and its significant terms are included. Unfortunately, for some of the earlier wars, precious little specific detailed information about the conflicts and who participated in them has survived. More unfortunately, many of the records documenting military service in the earlier wars either were never made or have been lost over time. Following the discussions of the various wars is a section called Points of Interest and another called Further Reading. The Points of Interest section includes selected national, state, and local parks and historical sites, museums, monuments, historical markers, and tombstones that commemorate the people, events, and places that were part of the wars. The Further Reading section is not meant to be a comprehensive bibliography, but rather is a list of selected published works that have more detailed histories of the wars and who fought in them. Some of the listed publications appear in more than one list; however, many more could be. Those publications that cover most, if not all, of the Indian wars or are of a general nature are listed under Miscellaneous Resources at the end of the guide. Following the war chronicles is a discussion of the removal of the Five Civilized Tribes from their ancestral homes in the South to the Indian Territory west of the Mississippi River.

The second part of the guide is a discussion of the surviving records that document the military and civilian participation in the wars. The first section deals with the important national repositories of the National Archives, Army Center of Military History, Army Heritage and Education Center, and the Library of Congress. The next section deals with the archives of the subject eleven states and provides some insight into genealogical research in those states. The third section deals with the archives, libraries, and museums of the Five Civilized Tribes. The fourth section presents the Draper Manuscript Collection, one of the most important record collections. The last section presents other significant repositories, arranged geographically, including genealogical and historical societies, museums, public and university libraries, manuscript collections, hereditary societies, and a few other miscellaneous sources. When one begins genealogical research in the Indian wars, it will be evident that many of the records, as well as indexes and guides to the records, are widely available on microfilm and online at both free and subscription websites. The scope and scale of what is available online continuously changes at a fairly rapid rate. Thus, to avoid immediately becoming outdated and obsolete, the guide concentrates on the surviving original records and where they are housed.

If your ancestor lived on, or even near, the Southern frontier, the chances are good that he fought in a conflict or he and his family were affected by it. For example, if your ancestor settled in the Shenandoah Valley of Virginia in the 1750s, it is likely that he or his family were part of the French and Indian War or the ensuing First Cherokee War. As a general rule of thumb, when researching someone's Indian war participation, begin by reading about the war to gain an overall understanding of who participated in it, where they lived, and where they served. Take note of the records cited and references listed in the footnotes and bibliographies. Then consult those sources and repeat the process until the published sources are exhausted. One also should consult state, regional, county, and local histories both where the subject lived and where the subject served. The history of the place where your subject lived may include a roster of the volunteers who went off to fight in the war. The history of the place where a battle or skirmish happened or where a fort or other installation was established may include an account of the engagement, description of the fort, or even a mention of the militia company or other units that were there.

If the war occurred prior to the Revolution, begin at the pertinent state archives. Start by consulting the databases and finding aids. Most of the surviving colonial muster rolls and other records documenting military service have been published and many are available online. However, one should always look at the original records, or at least facsimile copies, noting any differences in spelling, transcription errors, and any additional information that may not have been included in the published transcription, abstract, or electronic database. Usually, the muster rolls and other records concern a particular militia company identified by the name of the captain commanding it. Most of the colonial military engagements were small, often involving only one militia company. However, if more than one militia company was involved, the names of the other captains as well as the names of the officers commanding the battalion, regiment, or other larger unit should be noted. Using the names of the officers, both online and offline published sources should be searched for more detailed accounts of the engagement and possible mention of the soldier one is researching. Also, consider searching the records of the colonial governors and legislatures for mention of the subject officers.

For the Revolutionary War and all conflicts thereafter, begin at the national archives. Look for military service records, pension application files and payment records, and bounty-land warrant records. Most of the primary records, indexes to or abstracts of them, as well as research guides and other finding aids are widely available on microfilm and online. For records documenting military service, look beyond just the compiled military service records. Consider searching medical and hospital records, regimental returns, military post returns, and court martial records. After searching the national archives, repeat the process previously suggested for the pertinent state archives. Some states offered pensions or bounty-land for Revolutionary War service. In addition to the records of the state adjutant general or other military department, gubernatorial papers may include muster rolls, military appointments, discussion of troop deployments, descriptions of battles, descriptions of Indian depredations, and correspondence to or from veterans.

County court records also should be searched for references to the militia captains, as well as other officers, both during the colonial period and after statehood. Both state and county historical and genealogical societies should be consulted and searched as they often hold unique finding aids, compiled service records, published abstracts, manuscript collections, local histories describing the wars, and other materials found nowhere else. Whenever visiting a research facility, whether it is a local, county, state, or even national facility, it is a good idea to spend some time politely engaging the archivist, curator, or librarian there, explaining the overall object of your research and asking questions. Often, they can direct you to specific records to search or introduce you to a local expert on your particular subject. When they cannot provide a positive suggestion, they sometimes can confirm that you have searched all the available records. In short, their advice can be definitive and helpful.

In addition, to the federal, state, and county records, manuscript collections are a valuable source of material. If the subject of one's research was a private or other low ranking soldier, the probability that his private papers are in a manuscript collection is low, but not impossibly so. However, the personal papers of his militia captain, other commanding officers, his governor, or even the president may include muster rolls, rosters, accounts of engagements, maps, correspondence, and other materials naming the subject soldier or his military unit. Of course, locating a set of personal papers can be a daunting task; but, a patient search can yield extraordinary results. For example, my own ancestor, who was a veteran of the Virginia militia during the French and Indian War, many years later asked his former commanding officer for a character reference. Tucked away in the collection of his personal correspondence, is a letter from George Washington recommending his former sergeant and commenting on his high moral character.

Start by searching the *National Union Catalog of Manuscript Collections*, available on the Library of Congress webpage. Recognize that not all manuscript collections are covered by the catalog and many of the collections that are covered are imperfectly cataloged. Search the manuscript collections at the state archives, university libraries, and historical societies where your subject lived and died. Most manuscript collections, especially the larger ones, have extensive and detailed finding aids, many of them online. Be creative by searching on more than just the names of military officers. Use keywords such as the name of a fort or other military post, name of a battle, name of the war, name of the tribe, name of an Indian town, name of a county, or name of a town or city. It is important to note that the original personal papers of one individual may reside in more than one manuscript collection.

Newspapers also are a valuable source of information. Often vivid accounts of the battles, with direct quotations from the participants, were published soon after the event. For example, reading the Columbus, Georgia *Enquirer*, situated as it was at the epicenter of the Second Creek War, provides a detailed almost day-by-day chronicle of the conflict in the Chattahoochee River

Valley. Newspapers published far from the scenes of a conflict may report the gruesome details of an Indian massacre, or may note that someone raised a company of local volunteers, the company marched off to the conflict, or the company returned from the conflict, sometimes even listing the names of the volunteers or describing their participation. As more and more historic newspapers are digitized and placed online, be creative in selecting the newspapers and the keywords for your search. Spectacular events, such as Braddock's Defeat, the victory at Point Pleasant, the massacre at Fort Mims, and the victory at Horseshoe Bend, were widely reported in newspapers far from the scenes of action. In a similar way, monuments erected at the scene of an event may list the names of those who were killed or taken prisoner. Such monuments may have been erected on the grounds of the local county courthouse, commemorating the residents from the county who participated in an event far away. Other monuments, not just tombstones, were erected in cemeteries, often over or near mass graves, that commemorate the fallen.

Another important source of information is hereditary societies. Most hereditary societies have published or online databases of the ancestors that their members used to qualify for membership. The ancestor's military or civilian service may have been documented and proven by unusual, rare, or otherwise obscure records that one may not have considered or known about. Some hereditary societies maintain libraries and manuscript collections, preserve and maintain historical sites, and erect monuments and historical markers. In addition, there are groups of modern reenactors who specialize in an individual military unit or tribe. Often, the groups have collected substantial material concerning the history of the unit or tribe they have adopted as well as the men who served in it.

The guide is dedicated to the memory of Drury Puckett, an early settler on the waters of the Clinch River, in what later became the New Garden section of Russell County, Virginia, veteran of the French and Indian War, Lord Dunmore's War, and Revolutionary War, and one of the author's numerous Southern ancestors who were veterans of almost every Indian conflict, from the Powhatan Wars through the Indian Removals. Many thanks are offered to Joe Garonzik, of the Genealogical Publishing Company, for suggesting the project and his professional advice and counsel throughout the process of producing it. Thanks also are offered the author's mother, Ouida J. Ports, for first suggesting the inclusion of the Points of Interest. Special thanks are offered Marcia Tremonti for her encouragement and patience during this very challenging endeavor.

Part One
History of the Southern Indian Wars

Early Colonial Wars

Powhatan Wars, 1610-1646

The early English settlers of the Virginia Colony fought a series of three wars against the Indians of the Powhatan Confederation in the early seventeenth century. At the founding of Jamestown in 1607, Wahunsenacawh, the principal chief of the Powhatan Confederation ruled thirty Algonquian tribes, each in turn ruled by a local chief called a weroance. Wahunsenacawh, commonly called Powhatan by the Virginians, mostly ruled from his capital Werowocomoco, on the northern bank of the York River. The thirty tribes held sway over the Virginia Tidewater region, east of the fall line. The First Powhatan War began in 1610 and ended with a peace settlement in 1614, the second was fought between 1622 and 1626, and the third began in 1644, ending when Chief Opechancanough was captured and killed in 1646. That last war resulted in a boundary being defined between the Indian and English lands that could only be crossed for official business with a special pass. This situation would last until 1677, when the Treaty of the Middle Plantation established Indian reservations following Bacon's Rebellion.

In November 1609, Powhatan invited John Ratcliffe, Council President of the Jamestown Colony, to their new capital at Orapakes, on the Paumnkey River. There the Powhatan killed all the Englishmen that came ashore, including Ratcliffe, while those on board their ship safely returned to Jamestown. The following year, the tribe attacked Jamestown, killing many colonists. On August 9, 1610, Thomas West, the 3rd Baron De La Warr, governor-for-life and captain-general of the Colony of Virginia, sent George Percy with 70 men to attack the Paspahegh capital near Jamestown, burning the houses, destroying their cornfields, killing about 70, and capturing one of Chief Wowinchopunk's wives and her children. During their return, the English savagely murdered the children, but waited until they reached Jamestown to execute the queen. The Paspahegh never recovered from the attack, and abandoned their town. A second small force, under the command of Samuel Argall, set out against the Warraskoyak tribe, discovered that they had fled, then destroyed their village and cornfields. In retaliation, later that autumn, a party of Englishmen were ambushed at Appomattoc. Soon thereafter, Baron De La Warr established a company of men at the falls of the James River to protect the scattered settlements. In February 1611, Chief Wowinchopunk was killed in a skirmish near Jamestown. A few days later, some of his tribe enticed a few colonists out of the Jamestown stockade and killed them in revenge.

Illness caused Lord De La Warr to return to England in the spring of 1611. The new governor, Sir Thomas Dale, arrived in May and immediately started looking to establish new settlements. Dale seized an island in the James River from the Arrohattoc and established a fortified settlement he named Henricus. Late in 1611, Dale seized the Appomattoc town at the mouth of their river, quickly erecting a stockade across the neck of land, renaming it New Bermudas.

In December 1612, Sir Samuel Argall made peace with the Patawomeck tribe. In April of the following year, Japazaws, the brother of the Patawomeck weroance, delivered Pocahontas, the daughter of the powerful Chief Powhatan, to the governor. Holding her ransom to guarantee peace caused an immediate halt of the Powhatan raids on the English, thereby allowing the settlers to expand southward at City Point, now Hopewell, Virginia.

In early 1609, Jamestown Island was the only territory under colonial control, but by 1613, the Powhatan Confederation had lost much of their riverfront property along the James River; the

Kicoughtan and Paspehegh tribes had been destroyed; and, the settlers had encroached significantly into the lands of the Weyanoke, Appomattoc, Arrohattoc, and Powhatan tribes. The Arrohattoc and Quiockohannock tribes dispersed or merged with other chiefdoms. Peace negotiations dragged on for nearly a year, but in March 1614, Dale concluded peace with Powhatan at his new capital Matchcot, consummated by the marriage of Pocahontas to the colonist John Rolfe, ushering in a brief period of peaceful relations with the Indians. Another peace treaty was concluded the same year with the autonomous Chickahominy tribe, making them honorary Englishmen and subjects of King James I.

In 1616, after Governor Dale had returned to England with Pocahontas, the Chickahominy refused to pay their corn tribute to the new governor, George Yeardley, rejected their alliance with the English, and instead allied themselves with Chief Powhatan's Confederation. Following Powhatan's death in 1618, his younger brother Opechancanough assumed full power. Opechancanough maintained a friendly face to the colony, even giving the appearance of his imminent conversion to Christianity. On March 22, 1622, his subjects, planted among the settlements, suddenly attacked at least 31 scattered settlements and plantations, mostly along the James River, without warning, in what is now known as the Indian Massacre of 1622, killing 347 inhabitants in one day, one third of the colony, capturing twenty women, and marking the start of the Second Powhatan War.

Opechancanough did not continue his offensive, preferring to wait and see what would happen, hoping that the English would abandon their settlements and move elsewhere. However, the colonists retaliated, marching out every summer for the next ten years to make assaults on the Powhatan settlements. The Accomac and Patawomeck, allied with the English, provided them corn, while the English plundered the villages and cornfields of the Chickahominy, Nansemond, Warraskoyack, Weyanoke and Pamunkey. In 1623, Opechancanough sued for peace. The colonists arranged to meet to discuss a peace agreement, but poisoned their wine, then attacked them, killing about 250 in revenge for the massacre. The English then attacked the Chickahominy, Powhatan, Appomattoc, Nansemond, and Weyanoke.

In 1624, both sides were itching for a major and decisive victory. The Powhatan assembled 800 warriors to face just 60 Englishmen in the act of destroying Powhatan cornfields. When the Englishmen succeeded in burning the fields, the bowmen gave up the fight and retreated. A shortage of gunpowder delayed any English offensive moves in 1625 and 1626. However, the summer of 1627 saw renewed assaults against the Chickahominy, Appamattoc, Powhatan, Warraskoyak, Weyanoke and Nansemond. Peace was declared in 1628, but did not last, as hostilities resumed in March 1629 and continued until peace finally was reached on September 30, 1632. The English then continued to expand their settlements in Virginia. By 1634, the colonists completed a stockade across the Virginia Peninsula, about 6 miles long, providing some protection from Indian attacks.

After twelve years of peace, the Third Powhatan War began on March 18, 1644, as a last-ditch effort by the remnants of the Powhatan Confederation, still under Chief Opechancanough, to destroy the English settlements. About 500 colonists were killed, nearly one tenth the total colonial population. The English retaliated in July by attacking the Pamunkey, Chickahominy, and Powhatan, and south of the James River, the Appomattoc, Weyanoke, Warraskoyak, and Nansemond, as well as two Carolina tribes, the Chowanoac and Secotan.

In February 1645, the governor ordered the construction of three forts to protect the frontier: Fort Charles at the falls of the James River, Fort James on the Chickahominy River, and Fort Royal at the falls of the York River. In August, Governor William Berkeley stormed Opechancanough's stronghold, capturing him and deporting all the male captives over 11 years old to Tangier Island, in the Chesapeake Bay. Opechancanough, around 92 years old, was taken to Jamestown where he was shot by a guard, his death resulting in the disintegration of the Powhatan Confederation. The English continued to attack the splintered tribes and, in 1646, erected a fourth fort, Fort Henry, at the falls of the Appomattox River.

The Third Powhatan War came to a close with the peace treaty of October 1646. The new weroance, Necotowance, and the tribes formerly in the Confederation, each became subjects of the King of England. The treaty delineated a formal boundary between Indian and English settlements, with members of each group forbidden to cross to the other side, except by special pass obtained at one of the newly erected border forts. The end of the wars ushered in thirty years of relative peace between the colonists and the Powhatan, shattered only by the attacks of Bacon's Rebellion in 1676. Today, eight tribes, who trace their lineage to the Powhatan Confederation, are recognized officially by the state of Virginia.

Chowanoac Wars, 1666, 1675-1677

The Chowanoac, sometimes called the Chowanoke, Chowanook, or Chowan, an Algonquian tribe, lived in northeastern North Carolina, along the Chowan River, in modern Bertie, Chowan, Gates, and Hartford counties. They may have migrated from the north sometime before European settlement, but by the turn of the 17th century probably the most powerful tribe in the region.

By 1666, the Chowanoac began to feel the deleterious effects from colonial encroachment onto their lands. In response to the encroachment, war parties began raiding the colonial settlements west of the Chowan River. The settlers organized their defenses and quelled the short rebellion, after which the Chowanoac ceded their claim to the lands west of the Chowan River. There were several killed on both sides. A peace was established that lasted for a decade, and settlement expanded rapidly onto the former Chowanoac lands.

By 1675, Chowanoac war parties again began raiding the colonial settlements, part of the general native uprising that touched off Bacon's Rebellion. By the end of 1677, the settlers had banded together and completely subdued the Chowanoac, reducing their numbers to no more than about two hundred, and forcing the survivors onto a reservation of twelve square miles in modern Gates County. Like many other coastal native tribes, the Chowanoac began to accept living among the colonials. George Fox, a Quaker, and other missionaries met with some success in converting many to Christianity. The tribe suffered from continued white encroachment and European diseases, including a smallpox epidemic in 1696.

At the outbreak of the Tuscarora War, the Chowanoac had declined to the point they could contribute only fifteen warriors to join the British in fighting the Tuscarora. Chief John Hoyter begged the Carolina government to protect his people. Their numbers continued to decline and their reservation shrank in size, as the tribe sold off more land. By the middle of the 18th century, for all intents and purposes, the Chowanoac ceased to exist as a functioning tribe.

Bacon's Rebellion, 1676

The immediate cause of the rebellion was the refusal of Governor Sir William Berkeley to retaliate for a series of Indian attacks on frontier settlements of Virginia and North Carolina. In addition, many colonists wished to push westward to claim Indian land, but the governor denied permission. Other contributing factors were mostly economic in nature. Recent storms and a hurricane wreaked havoc on the local economy, already struggling against growing competition from the adjoining colonies of Maryland and the Carolinas, falling prices for tobacco, and rising prices for manufactured goods imported from England. Scholars long have held that the rebellion represented the first overt evidence of revolutionary spirit in the colonies, some one hundred years before Lexington and Concord. However, more recent scholars have come to believe that the rebellion was more a result of a clash between two strong headed men. The elderly Berkeley was a scholar, veteran of the English Civil Wars, experienced Indian fighter, and a favorite of King Charles II. His cousin by marriage, Nathaniel Bacon, Jr., was a born trouble maker, whose father had banished him to his kinsman's colony. In early 1675, Berkeley welcomed the youthful Bacon with a generous grant of land and a seat on the council.

When colonial settlement began in the Northern Neck of Virginia, circa 1650, members of the Doeg, Patawomeck, and Rappahannock tribes also moved into the area. The tribes resented the new settlements, but their complaints fell on deaf ears. By 1670, the expanding settlements had forced most of the Doeg across the Potomac River into Maryland. The Doeg, however, continued to harass the Northern Neck settlements. In July 1675, a Doeg raiding party crossed the Potomac and stole some hogs from Thomas Mathew, in retaliation for his not paying them for trade goods. Mathew and a few of his neighbors pursued the party, killing a few of them. The Doeg retaliated by attacking the Mathew plantation, killing his son and two servants. As tensions mounted, a group of settlers attacked a Susquehannock village, killing fourteen, and touching off a general uprising of most of the tribes against the settlers in Virginia and the Carolinas. Wanting to avoid further bloodshed, Berkeley arranged for peace talks between the settlers and the tribes. The angry colonists murdered some of the chieftains, further fanning the flames. Berkeley continued to call for peace, asking the colonists to be patient and friendly toward the tribes. Bacon, for one, ignored the pleas and seized a few friendly Appomattoc for stealing corn. Berkeley openly reprimanded Bacon, causing further consternation among many colonists.

Berkeley wanted to cultivate and preserve the loyalty and friendship of the local tribes and convince the settlers that the tribes were peaceful. To that end, he confiscated the powder and lead from the local tribes, with promises of protecting them. In March 1676, he convinced the assembly to declare war on the hostile tribes and to authorize a strong defense. To pay for raising an army and conducting war, taxes were raised. The assembly also passed strict regulations governing all trade with the tribes, restricting trade to a few favored traders, all friends of Berkeley. The obvious corruption, compounded by high taxes, further aggravated the colonists. Bacon resented his cousin, because his trading business was curtailed and he was refused a commission in the militia. Promising to finance their campaign, Bacon convinced a group of volunteers to elect him as their leader.

Bacon first led his men against the Pamunkey driving them from their homes. Berkeley, at the head of 300 loyal militia, rode to confront Bacon at Henrico, his headquarters. Bacon, with about 200 of his followers, fled into the surrounding wilderness. Berkeley then formally declared Bacon a rebel, but pardoned his followers, provided they desist and return home peaceably. Bacon was to be apprehended and tried for his rebellion. In defiance, Bacon and his men raided a friendly Occoneechee village, on Occoneechee Island, in the Roanoke River, near modern Clarksville, destroying three forts, killing more than 100 warriors and many women and children, and confiscating their supply of valuable beaver pelts.

Berkeley, in an effort to keep peace, offered to forgive Bacon, provided he surrendered himself and return to England for trial. The House of Burgesses balked at Berkeley's offer, insisting that Bacon confess his transgressions and ask forgiveness from the governor. In June 1676, the newly elected Bacon attempted to take his seat in the House of Burgesses. Bacon immediately was arrested and taken before the governor and council to apologize. Berkeley pardoned him and allowed him to take his seat. In the middle of a heated debate over the Indian issue, Bacon left the assembly and returned with about 500 of his armed followers. Bacon then demanded that Berkeley give him a commission to lead his militia against the Indians. Governor Berkeley refused. Bacon then ordered his men to aim their muskets at Berkeley, who responded by opening his shirt and baring his breast, daring Bacon to shoot him. Seeing that the Governor could not be moved, Bacon then had his men take aim at the assembled burgesses, who quickly granted Bacon his commission. While Bacon was at Jamestown with his small army, eight colonists were killed by Indians on the frontier in Henrico County.

On July 30, 1676, Bacon and his army issued their *Declaration of the People of Virginia*, criticizing Berkeley's administration, accusing him of levying unfair taxes, appointing friends to high positions, and failing to protect the frontier settlements from Indian attack. After months of conflict, Bacon's small army, then numbering about 300 to 500 men, moved to Jamestown. They burned the colonial capital to the ground on September 19, 1676. Greatly outnumbered, Berkeley and his men retreated across the river. Before an English naval squadron could arrive to aid Berkeley and his forces, Bacon died abruptly from natural causes on October 26, 1676. John Ingram took over leadership of the rebellion, but many followers drifted away. Berkeley resumed control of the colony, launched a series of successful raids against the rebels, and defeated the small pockets of remaining insurgents scattered across the Tidewater. Berkeley ordered the execution of twenty-three rebel leaders and confiscated rebel property without any trial. After the king relieved him, Berkeley returned to England, where he died in July 1677.

Westo War, 1679-1680

The Westo tribe first established a harmonious relationship with their neighbors, the English colonists in Virginia, principally by trading native slaves for firearms. Later, the Westo migrated south to live along the Savannah River, where they wielded their martial power by raiding other tribes and seizing slaves, particularly in Spanish Florida. In 1661, a Westo war party raided down the Altamaha River, destroying Santo Domingo de Talaje, a Spanish mission situated at the mouth of the river, near modern Darien, Georgia. Alonso de Aranguiz y Cortés, the governor of Spanish Florida, ordered soldiers to present-day St. Simons, Georgia, to defend against further Westo raiding parties.

While the Westo had been friendly with the Virginians, they were not necessarily friendly with the Carolina settlers, at least at first. In 1673, the Westo began raiding the coastal tribes, seizing slaves. They also began raiding the outlying white settlements in Carolina, who had relied upon the Catawba to defend them against other tribes. In 1674, however, a party of Westo leaders met with Dr. Henry Woodward to make peace with the Carolinians. Woodward, the first British colonist in Carolina, was instrumental in establishing relationships with many of the native tribes and initiating trade, mostly in deerskins and slaves, with them. The Westo hosted Woodward at their towns on the Savannah River, offered peace and friendship, and bestowed gifts on him. As a result, trade thrived for the next half decade, Carolina traders providing arms, ammunition, and other goods, with the Westo providing deerskins and native slaves. The Westo captured slaves from the tribes in Spanish Florida, as well as the Cherokee, Chickasaw, and other smaller tribes who eventually would ally themselves with the Muscogee people to form the Creek Confederation.

Because of their constant slave raiding, all the other tribes in the region were natural enemies of the Westo. Due to their strong alliance with the Westo, Carolina could not develop good relationships with the other tribes, whose members were taken as slaves. During this period, a band of Shawnee moved into the Savannah River area. When Dr. Woodward was at the Westo towns, he witnessed the first meeting of the Shawnee and Westo chiefs. The Shawnee warned that the other tribes were conspiring to attack them in retaliation for their slave raiding, thereby earning Westo gratitude.

Carolina traders understood the value of establishing good relationships with the other tribes, both in maintaining peace and widening trade. The Shawnee met independently with Woodward to establish friendly relations. In 1679, war broke out between Carolina traders and the Westo. In 1680, with the Shawnee as their ally, the traders destroyed the Westo. The Shawnee then moved onto the Westo lands and assumed their role as Carolina's principal trading partner. Most of the surviving Westo were enslaved and shipped to the West Indies to work on sugar plantations. Some other survivors lived at a town on the Ocmulgee River, upriver from the mouth of the Towaliga River, near the important Lower Creek town of Coweta. Like many other survivors from tribes defeated in the never-ending Indian wars who sought refuge among the Creek people, the Westo gradually were absorbed into the emergent Creek Confederation.

In 1684, 148 Scot Covenanter settlers established Stuarts Town on the Port Royal Sound, near modern Beaufort, South Carolina. The Scots quickly established trading relationships with the Yamasee and other nearby tribes, arming them and encouraging them to raid the tribes in Spanish Florida. The Scots also frequently led attacks against the Spanish tribes and raided the Timucuan village at Santa Catalina de Guale, the Spanish mission on Sapelo Island. The raid yielded only a few slaves, but garnered the wrath of the Spanish governor. In retaliation, the Spanish sent three galleys with 150 soldiers and allied Indians to attack Stuarts Town in August 1686, destroying the town and scattering its survivors.

Queen Anne's War, 1702-1713

Queen Anne's War, from 1702 to 1713, was the North American theater of the War of the Spanish Succession, as it was known in Europe, and was the second in a series of French and Indian wars fought between France and Britain, for control of the North American continent. In addition to the two main combatants, the war also involved numerous Indian tribes allied with each nation, as well as Spain, allied with France.

The war was fought on two primary fronts. The first, in the north, pitted English colonists against the French and their Indian allies, the northern front beyond the scope of this guide. The second front was in the south, with Spanish Florida and English Carolina attacking each other, and the English engaging the French based at Mobile, in what was essentially a proxy war involving allied Native Americans on both sides. Even though the southern war did not result in significant territorial changes, it left the Indian population of Spanish Florida, as well as the southern portion of modern Georgia, nearly wiped out. The war also destroyed the intricate Spanish network of Catholic missions.

Even at the beginning of the eighteenth century, both the French and English realized future expansion, settlement, and trade would depend upon controlling the Mississippi River. The French explorer Pierre Le Moyne d'Iberville developed his *Projet sur la Caroline*, proposing to nurture French relationships with the Indians in the Mississippi River watershed and then leveraging those relationships to push the English off the continent, or at least limit them to coastal areas. Toward that end, he established Fort Maurepas in 1699, at Old Biloxi, now modern Ocean Springs, Mississippi. From there, as well as from Fort Louis de la Mobile, he started relationships with the local Choctaw, Chickasaw, Natchez, and other tribes.

English traders, mostly from Carolina, already had established a substantial trading network across the southeastern part of the continent, extending all the way to the Mississippi River. Carolina's leaders, who had little respect for the Spanish in Florida, understood the threat posed by the arrival of the French on the coast, expressing visions of expanding to the south and west at the expense of French and Spanish interests.

To convert the native population to Christianity and keep them peaceful, the Spanish established a network of Catholic missions. By 1680, there were fourteen missions in the Apalachee Province, roughly the modern Florida Panhandle and southwestern Georgia, populated by 8,000 natives, mostly Apalachee. By 1700, the region was the primary source of food for both Pensacola and St. Augustine. Forced to labor for both the military garrisons and plantation owners, the Apalachee, Guale, Timucua, and other tribes in Florida chafed against Spanish rule, the previous century witnessing numerous armed uprisings. Because firearms were prohibited, the Apalachee had to rely upon their cruel Spanish masters for protection against their Creek enemies, who were armed by the English. As a result, some Apalachee left Florida to settle in Carolina.

In 1702, before the war broke out in Europe, Iberville recommended that the Spanish arm the Apalachee and send them against the Carolina traders. The Spanish organized an expedition under Captain Francisco Romo de Uriza of some 800 Apalachee warriors that left San Luis de Apalachee in August for the trading centers of the Carolina backcountry. The traders, under the leadership of Anthony Dodsworth, with nearly 500 Apalachicola warrior allies, having been warned, organized their defense at the head of the Flint River, by arranging empty sleeping blankets by their campfires and hiding in the surrounding woods. The Apalachee attacked at dawn, firing into the blankets, but before they could reload, the Creeks attacked, routing the invaders and leaving more than 500 Spanish and Apalachee killed or captured, in what became known as the Battle of the Blankets.

After receiving formal notice of the start of war, Carolina Governor Moore organized and led a force against Spanish Florida. In the 1702 Siege of St. Augustine, 500 English soldiers and militia with 300 allied Indians captured and burned the town of St. Augustine. Unable to capture the main fortress, Castillo de San Marcos, they withdrew when a Spanish fleet arrived from Havana. While the expedition was not successful in driving out the Spanish, it did destroy the missions along the southern Georgia coast. Florida Governor José de Zúñiga y la Cerda ordered the remaining missions to move closer together and consolidate, making them easier to defend. In 1703, Creek war parties raided three mission communities, taking as many as 500 captives as slaves.

In 1704, Governor Moore led about 50 volunteers and 1,000 Creek warriors to attack the Apalachee towns, on January 25th reaching Ayubale, one of the more important mission towns. Moore's force captured the mission, killing many Apalachee, while his Creek allies scrounged the small villages in the vicinity, killing and capturing many more. Captain Juan Ruíz de Mexía, at the head of 30 Spanish cavalrymen and 400 Apalachee, attacked Moore at Ayubale, but was soundly defeated, losing 200 Apalachee killed or captured, three Spanish killed, and eight Spanish captured, Mexia among them. The battles at Ayubale often are called the Apalachee Massacre. Moore continued attacking the villages in the region, plundering along the way, destroying the missions, and taking many prisoners. In his official report, Moore claimed that his expedition killed more than 1,100 men, women, and children, removed 300 more into exile, and captured as slaves more than 4,300 people, mostly women and children.

In August 1704, the Creek attacked two missions and the following year attacked a third Apalachee town. In 1706, the Creek attacked two more towns. In these later raids, many Apalachee were killed or captured as slaves, and many more were driven into exile. In 1706, Carolina successfully repulsed an attack on Charleston by a combined Spanish and French force sent from Havana. By the end of 1706, the Spanish had lost or abandoned their missions and plantations, their only presence in Florida limited to Pensacola and St. Augustine. In 1707, the Creek, with English help and support, twice laid siege to Pensacola, but were not successful.

Britain and France declared a truce in 1712 and formally ended the war by signing the Treaty of Utrecht the following year. Spanish Florida did not recover from the war, having lost their system of missions, as well as most of their forced native labor. The tribes who had been resettled along the Atlantic coast chafed under British rule, as did those allied to the British in the war. In 1715, their discontent erupted into the Yamasee War, a threat to the very existence of South Carolina. In 1732, King George II granted a charter for the new colony of Georgia, partly to establish a buffer between Carolina and Spanish Florida.

Chitimacha War, 1707–1718

The Chitimacha, comprised of four subtribes, the Chawasha, Chitimacha, Washa, and Yagenachito, inhabited much of the Atchafalaya Basin in south central Louisiana, establishing their unfortified villages in the relative safety of the swamp. By circa 1700, the Chitimacha population had been greatly reduced by European diseases, especially measles, smallpox, and typhoid, contracted by contact with other tribes who had traded with them, reducing their numbers by as much as one half. Less than about 10,000 Chitimacha lived in fifteen or so villages.

French women were very reluctant to migrate to Louisiana and suffer the difficulties of life on the frontier, creating a severe shortage of feminine companionship in the colony. To solve their problem, French traders and trappers occasionally raided Chitimacha villages, abducting the women. Louisiana Governor John Baptiste Le Moyne Sieur de Bienville was horrified and ordered the men to stop, but with little effect. In 1706, the Taensa captured several Chitimacha families to sell to the French as slaves. In retaliation, the following year, the Chitimacha sent a war party to attack the offending Taensa village. However, before locating any Taensa, the war party came across the camp of the Jesuit missionary Father Jean Francois Buisson de St. Cosme, slaying the entire party of four, but setting the native slave free.

Upon hearing of the murders, Bienville declared war on the Chitimacha and arranged an alliance of the Acolapissa, Bayougoula, Biloxi, Chawasha, Choctaw, Houma, Natchitoches, Pascagoula, and Taensa to fight the Chitimacha. In March 1707, a party of 20 Bayougoula, 15 Biloxi, 40 Chawasha, four Natchitoches, and seven Frenchmen attacked a Chitimacha village, killing 15 and wounding 40 men, women, and children. They brought many prisoners back to Mobile, including one of the party who had killed St. Cosme. M. de St. Denis led another expedition, comprised of fifteen Frenchmen and eighty Acolapissa and Natchitoches. They encountered a party of Chitimacha, who immediately dispersed, the expedition managing only to capture twenty women and children.

For more than a decade, the war raged on, the French and their allied tribes driving the Chitimacha deep into the swamps of southern Louisiana. The outnumbered Chitimacha continued to fight, but were nearly annihilated. Many warriors were killed defending their homes and families, their women and children sold into slavery. The raids gradually diminished in frequency and intensity, but continued into 1718.

After seeing the establishment of New Orleans, the Chitimacha realized they could not win the war and sued for peace. The eastern Chitimacha were forced to settle on land on the Mississippi River near the entrance to Bayou Lafourche, where they live today. Eventually, significant numbers of Chitimacha intermarried with the local French Acadians, becoming acculturated into their culture and society and converting to Catholicism. In the mid-nineteenth century, the federal government formally established a reservation in St. Mary Parish, making them the only tribe in Louisiana still living on their ancestral lands.

Natchez Wars, 1716-1731

The First Natchez War took place in 1716, the second occurred from 1722 to 1724, and the third erupted in 1729 and lasted until 1731. From 1682, when Robert de la Salle first encountered them, the French believed the Natchez were both civilized and friendly. By 1720, the Natchez population, residing in nine villages in modern southwestern Mississippi, had been decimated by European diseases to number no more than 2,000. From the turn of the 18th century, the Natchez allowed French missionaries to live among them and benefited from trading with the French.

From 1707 to 1718, the Chitimacha fought the French, headquartered in Mobile and Biloxi, and their several allied tribes, losing very badly, almost to the point of extinction. In 1718, Jean Baptiste Le Moyne, Sieur de Bienville founded New Orleans, 130 miles upstream from the mouth of the Mississippi River. Bienville immediately employed the captured and enslaved Chitimacha to dig the drainage canals and level the ground for his new city.

In 1716, Louisiana Governor Antoine Laumet de La Mothe, Sieur de Cadillac passed through the Natchez territory, but neglected to renew or even acknowledge the Natchez alliance. The offended Natchez retaliated against the perceived slight by killing four French traders. The governor sent Jean-Baptiste Le Moyne, Sieur de Bienville to chastise the Natchez. Bienville requested the Natchez headmen to come talk to him, then ambushed their party, and kidnapped them, forcing the tribe to hand over the killers in exchange for their headmen. Upon executing the culprits, Bienville negotiated peace with the Natchez, ending the First Natchez War. The tribe provided labor and material to construct Fort Rosalie, intended to pacify the Natchez, protect and serve new French settlements, and counter British incursions into French territory.

In 1717, to bolster their trade and friendship with the Creek and their allied tribes, the French built a fort and trading post, called Fort Toulouse, at the confluence of the Tallapoosa and Coosa rivers, at modern Wetumpka in Elmore County, Alabama. Usually garrisoned by two to four dozen French marines, many of whom married Creek and Alabama women and took up farms nearby. Overall, relations between the French and the Creek and Alabama living near the fort were excellent. Due primarily to their general lack of quality trade goods, the French were frustrated at their inability to cement close relations with the many other tribes throughout New France. The British, with their superior and more plentiful trade goods, established and maintained strong trade relations with numerous tribes over a vast portion of the territory claimed by France.

Over the next five years, the French established numerous plantations and smaller farms, on land obtained from the Natchez, in the vicinity of Fort Rosalie, situated at modern Natchez, Mississippi. Overall relations between the French and Natchez were peaceable and friendly. While many Frenchmen married Natchez women, helping to ease relations, tensions mounted as French settlers abused their Natchez neighbors, encroaching on their lands, impressing their labor, and cheating them in trade.

The Second Natchez War, from 1722 to 1724, was characterized by numerous small skirmishes. In 1723, Bienville attacked and destroyed Pomme Blanche, a Natchez village, in retaliation for perceived harassment by the settlers. He also seized and enslaved several villagers. In 1724, a settler murdered the son of a Natchez chief, the Natchez retaliating by killing a Frenchman. Bienville sent a contingent of French soldiers to subdue the Natchez, who immediately sued for peace. The governor and Tattooed Serpent, the Natchez war chief, negotiated a peace.

In spite of the negotiated peace, tensions between the French and Natchez continued to fester. The death of Tattooed Serpent, a firm French ally, in 1725, further obstructed good relations. The French believed that Great Sun, the chief of the Grand Village, ruled over all the other Natchez villages; but, he did not, as each village was ruled by a local chief, only two of which were allied with him and his followers at Grand Village. Three other villages were pro-British. When Great Sun died in 1728, he was succeeded by his young and inexperienced nephew, the three pro-British villages grew stronger than the pro-French villages at Natchez.

By 1729, the estimated population of the French settlement at Fort Rosalie included 28 soldiers, and about 200 male colonists, 80 female colonists, 150 children, and 280 slaves. Sieur de Chépart, the new commander at Fort Rosalie, demanded that the Natchez abandon Pomme Blanche so that a plantation could be established there. The Natchez naturally refused the demand, as their holy temple holding the remains of their royal ancestors was situated there. Believing they had no other alternative, the Natchez attacked the French settlements, on November 29, 1729, by some accounts, killing 144 men, 35 women, and 56 children, and capturing more women, children, and slaves. The Natchez captured and executed Chépart, but kept two of their prisoners alive, a drayman, to carry their plunder back to the Great Village, and a tailor, to fit the stolen clothing to the new owners. They burned the fort, trading post, and all the homesteads. They also beheaded the dead Frenchmen and delivered the heads to Great Sun as tribute.

A party of Yazoo, who witnessed the massacre, were inspired by the Natchez. When the party returned to their village at the Yazoo trading post, they attacked and destroyed Fort Saint Pierre, killing 17 French soldiers and a Jesuit priest. Four Jesuit priests, from the seminary at Quebec, led by Reverend Francis de Montigny, established Fort Saint Pierre as a trading post in 1719, on modern Snyder's Bluff, near present-day Redwood, in Warren County, Mississippi. By 1729, the settlements around the fort had grown to include sixteen nearby farms. The fort was abandoned after all but four of its inhabitants were killed on December 31, 1729.

When news of the massacre reached New Orleans, the city panicked, dependent as they were on grain and other supplies from the Illinois country, and fearing attacks on shipping up and down the Mississippi River. Governor Étienne Périer ordered French troops and some slaves to kill everyone in a Chaouacha village, situated on the east bank of the Mississippi River a short distance below New Orleans, who had played no part in the uprising, as a warning to the Natchez. He also ordered the reconstruction of Fort Rosalie. Jean-Paul Le Sueur and Henri de Louboëy led two expeditions, one in December 1729 and one in January 1730, attacking Natchez fortifications near Grand Village, killing about 80 warriors, capturing 18 women, and recovering a few French women who had been taken prisoner at the massacre. The Tunica and Choctaw, allies of the French, attacked the Natchez. In one raid, the Choctaw killed about 100 Natchez warriors and captured many women and children. Both tribes turned over their captives to the governor, who sold most of them as slaves, while publicly torturing and executing several.

In late February 1730, Chevalier de Louboëy led a force of about 500 Choctaw against the Natchez. Louboëy rescued most of the remaining captives and laid siege to the fortified Natchez village. The Natchez made their escape at night, crossed the Mississippi River, and retreated to Sicily Island in modern Catahoula Parish. One year later, the French attacked them again, killing many, the survivors fleeing to Natchitoches. In the fall of 1731, the French tracked down the survivors and attacked, capturing 387 and selling them as slaves at Saint Domingue. By the start of 1732, most Natchez were dead or enslaved on sugar plantations in the French Caribbean. Most

25

of the few hundred survivors sought refuge in the Chickasaw towns, while other small groups went to live among the Creek, Cherokee, and Cusabo.

In 1732, displeased with the governor's performance, King Louis XV recalled Périer and appointed Bienville, who was more experienced in dealing with the natives, to replace him. After losing their largest and most successful settlement, the Company of the Indies gave up their trading monopoly in French Louisiana. As a result, the French crown assumed jurisdiction over all trade in the colony, opening the way for traders to operate freely on their own account. Bienville continued to seek the final destruction of the Natchez who were living among the Chickasaw, setting the stage for the Chickasaw War.

Chickasaw War, 1736-1739

Both the Chickasaw and Natchez were hostile to French rule in the lower Mississippi River Valley. Subjugating the tribes would facilitate French settlement and provide unfettered passage along the river, firmly connecting New Orleans to Canada. The French cultivated an alliance with the Choctaw, supplying them with arms and other supplies and convincing them to wage war against the Natchez. By 1736, the Choctaw had substantially reduced the Natchez to a few scattered remnant bands, many seeking refuge among their Chickasaw neighbors. Jean Baptiste LeMoyne, Sieur de Bienville, Governor of Louisiana, believed "It is absolutely necessary that some bold and remarkable blow be struck, to impress the Indians with a proper sense of respect and duty toward us." To accomplish his ends, Bienville planned a two-pronged offensive. One prong from the north led by Major Pierre d'Artaguette, commander of the Illinois District. The second prong from the south under his personal command. The two forces were to meet at the Chickasaw Bluffs, at present-day Memphis, then proceed together against the fortified Chickasaw towns.

D'Artaguette departed Fort de Chartes, on the east bank of the Mississippi River in modern Randolph County. Illinois, at the head of 130 French regulars and militia, 38 Iroquois, 28 Arkansas, and about 300 Miami and Illinois warriors. They arrived at Chickasaw Bluffs at the appointed time, but Bienville and his forces were not there. After a short wait, d'Artaguette proceeded into Chickasaw territory, only to be told by a courier that Bienville was late and he should do as he thought best. D'Ataguette proceeded to the fortified town Ogoula Tchetoka, at modern Tupelo, Mississippi, on Sunday, March 25, 1736. He attacked immediately, but was repulsed. The Chickasaw counterattacked and routed the retreating French forces. Led by Chief Mingo, the Chickasaw suffered about 50 casualties, while most of the French were killed, 21 were captured, only a few managing to escape. Nineteen of the captured were burned at the stake, including the wounded d'Artaguette.

At Mobile, Bienville assembled his force of 544 regulars, militia, Swiss, and 45 Africans. On April 23, they reached Fort de Tombecbé, a stockade fort on the Tombigbee River, about 270 miles upriver from Mobile, where they were joined by about 600 Choctaw warriors. At modern Amory, Mississippi, they constructed a fortified camp to protect the supplies and boats they would need for their return. Thus, the hostile Chickasaw remained a thorn in the side of the French, discouraging French settlement and navigation on the Mississippi River. Armed, supplied, and encouraged by the French, the Choctaw continued their campaign against the Chickasaw, ambushing hunting and trading parties, burning crops, and killing livestock. However, those efforts alone were not enough to subdue the Chickasaw, protected as they were in their fortified towns. Early in 1739, the French began planning for another strike.

Bienville ordered the erection of a supply depot on the west bank of the Mississippi River, near the mouth of the St. Francis River, and, directly across the river, Fort de l'Assumption, on the Chickasaw Bluffs. There Bienville began assembling his men and supplies for the coming campaign. In August, militia and 200 Illinois warriors from Fort de Chartres, a detachment from New Orleans, and Pierre Joseph Céleron, Sieur de Blainville with a company of cadets from Canada and a large number of northern Indians, arrived at the Chickasaw Bluffs. In November, Bienville arrived, at the head of an assembled force of about 1,200 French and 2,400 Indian allies. Preparations for the campaign, including the construction of a road to transport their artillery, were plagued by disease, short rations, desertion, and general discontent.

In March, frustrated with the delays, Céleron led his cadets, 100 regulars, and more than 400 warriors, mostly Choctaw, to the Chickasaw towns. When they arrived at their target, Céleron directed his Choctaw to attack. They kept up a constant, but ineffective, fire for several days. The Chickasaw, fearing the French preparations at Chickasaw Bluffs and the pressure from the Choctaw, agreed to peace talks. After they handed over a few Natchez warriors and their French prisoners, all agreed to peace. The British continued to arm and supply the Chickasaw, who remained defiantly hostile to the French, as they lived comfortably safe inside their fortified towns.

Places of Interest

Historic Jamestowne
1368 Colonial Pkwy
Jamestown, Virginia 23081

(757) 856-1250

http://historicjamestowne.org/

Visitors can explore the James Fort site with an archeologist who has troweled the site, a park ranger who has studied the stories, or an educator who can bring the past to life. The Archaearium Museum exhibits over 2,000 artifacts. Special interpretative programs are offered throughout the year.

Colonial Williamsburg
101 Visitor Center Drive
Williamsburg, Virginia 23185

(877) 671-1754

http://www.history.org/

The largest living history museum in the world, the historic area recreates Virginia's colonial capital as an authentic, live, working, and complete city, including the original capital building, residences, shops, restaurants, and lodging. Special historical programs are provided every day.

Fort de Chartres State Historic Site
1350 Illinois Route 155
Prairie du Rocher, Illinois 62277

618-284-7230

https://www2.illinois.gov/ihpa/Experience/Sites/Southwest/Pages
/Fort-de-Chartres.aspx

The site has a partially rebuilt eighteenth-century fort, with bastions, gatehouse, musket ports, embrasures for cannon, and restored powder magazine. The King's Storehouse is home to the Piethman Museum, which uses items discovered during archaeological research near the fort, other artifacts, and exhibits to interpret life in Illinois during the colonial period. The East Barracks and the Government House have been outlined by wood frames, a technique called ghosting, to provide a sense of their original size and form. An annual two-day Rendezvous is held the first weekend in June and features shooting competitions, military drills, dancing, music, food, and traders of eighteenth-century style goods.

Fort Toulouse National Historic Park
2521 West Fort Toulouse Road
Wetumpka, Alabama 36093

(334) 567-3002

https://fttoulousejackson.org/

The Park contains the recreated 1751 Fort Toulouse, Creek Indian houses, and a 1,000-year-old Indian mound. There is a visitor center, museum, and book store. The park hosts monthly living history events, as well as the annual Alabama Frontier Days celebration.

Castillo de San Marcos National Monument
1 South Castillo Drive
Saint Augustine, Florida 32084

(904) 829-6506

https://www.nps.gov/casa/index.htm

The monument consists of the 20.5-acre site of the original fort, including a reconstructed section of the walled defense line surrounding the city of St. Augustine, incorporating the original city gate. The fort, the object of the 1702 siege, did not surrender to the Carolina attackers. The site has a small visitors center with gift shop and bookstore.

Meherrin-Chowanoke Nation
P. O. Box S
Winton, North Carolina 27986

(252) 301-6081

MeherrinChowanokeServices@gmail.com

http://meherrin-chowanoke.com/Home.php

The tribe sponsors its three-day-long Annual Pow-Wow in April, featuring Native American crafts, food, cultural exhibits, music, and dancing.

Natchez Trace Parkway
2680 Natchez Trace Parkway
Tupelo, Mississippi 38804

(800) 305-7417

https://www.nps.gov/natr/index.htm

There are numerous sites along the parkway of historical significance.
One such site is the Chickasaw Village at milepost 261.8, an
archaeological site that represents the village that once occupied the area.
There are no structures surviving, but there is an outline of a Chickasaw winter home, summer
home, and fort. A nature trail gives more information on native uses of plants in the area. Nearby
is the Ackia Battleground National Monument.

Fort Christanna Historical Marker
Boydton Plank Road and
Christanna Highway, in
Brunswick County, Virginia

Nearby to the south stood Fort Christanna, a wooden
structure built in 1714 under the auspices of Alexander
Spotswood and the Virginia Indian Company. Members of
the Meiponsky, Occaneechi, Saponi, Stuckenock, and Tutelo
Indian tribes lived within the fort and built a nearby
settlement. The fort included a frontier trading post and the
English operated a school to educate and convert the Indians
to Christianity there. The Virginia Indian Company
dissolved in 1717; funding for the garrison ceased the next year. By 1740, the Indian groups no
longer lived at the fort but had migrated to other areas nearby in the region.

Battle of the Blankets Historical Marker
Georgia Florida Parkway and Jones Place, near
Oakfield, in Worth County, Georgia

In 1702 a decisive battle took place along the nearby Flint
River. Nine hundred Apalachees, in league with the
Spanish, fought here against English traders and five
hundred of their Creek allies. Forewarned of an impending
attack, the Creeks arranged empty sleeping blankets by their
campfires and hid in the surrounding woods. The Spanish
Apalachees attacked at dawn, firing into the blankets, but
before they could reload their muskets, were themselves
attacked by the Creeks. The Battle of the Blankets diminished Spanish influence in North
America and served as a prelude to Queen Anne's War.

Further Reading

Albrecht, Andrew C., "Indian-French Relations at Natchez." *American Anthropologist*, New Series, Volume 48, Number 3, Arlington County, Virginia: American Anthropological Association, 1946.

Arnade, Charles W., *The Siege of St. Augustine, 1702.* University of Florida Monographs, Social Sciences, Number 3, Gainesville, Florida: University Press of Florida, 1959.

_____, "The English Invasion of Spanish Florida, 1700–1706." *The Florida Historical Quarterly*, Volume 41, Number 1, July 1962, pages 29–37.

Atkinson, James R., *Splendid Land, Splendid People: The Chickasaw Indians to Removal.* Tuscaloosa, Alabama: University of Alabama Press, 2004.

Barnett, James F. Jr., *The Natchez Indians: A History to 1735.* Jackson, Mississippi: University Press of Mississippi, 2007.

Billings, Warren M., "The Causes of Bacon's Rebellion: Some Suggestions." *Virginia Magazine of History and Biography*, Volume 78, Number 4, 1970, pages 409–435.

Bowne, Eric E., "The Rise and Fall of the Westo Indians." *Early Georgia: Journal of the Society for Georgia Archaeology*, Volume 28, Number 1, 2000, pages 56–78.

_____, *The Westo Indians: Slave Traders of the Early Colonial South.* Tuscaloosa, Alabama: University of Alabama Press, 2005.

Cave, Alfred A., *Lethal Encounters: Englishmen and Indians in Colonial Virginia.* Lincoln, Nebraska: University of Nebraska Press, 2011.

Cooper, William James, Jr. and Tom E. Terill, *The American South: A History.* New York, New York: Knopf, 1990.

Covington, James, "Migration of the Seminoles into Florida, 1700–1820." *The Florida Historical Quarterly*, Volume 46, Number 4, 1968, pages 340–357.

Crane, Verner W., "The Southern Frontier in Queen Anne's War." *The American Historical Review*, Volume 24, Number 3, 1919, pages 379–395.

Crane, Verner W. and Steven C. Crane, *The Southern Frontier 1670-1732.* Tuscaloosa, Alabama: The University of Alabama Press, 2004.

Cullen, Joseph P., "Bacon's Rebellion." *American History Illustrated*, Volume 3, Number 8, December 1968, page 4.

Cushman, Horatio Bardwell, *History of the Choctaw, Chickasaw, and Natchez Indians.* Greenville, Texas: Headlight Printing House, 1899.

Dunn, Caroline and Eleanor Dunn, *Indiana's First War.* Indianapolis, Indiana: W. B. Burford, Printer, 1924.

Fausz, J. Frederick, "The Barbarous Massacre Reconsidered: The Powhatan Uprising of 1622 and the Historians." *Explorations in Ethnic Studies, Journal of the National Association for Interdisciplinary Ethnic Studies*, Volume 1, January 1978.

_____, "An Abundance of Blood Shed on Both Sides: England's First Indian War, 1609–1614." *The Virginia Magazine of History and Biography*, Volume 98, Number 1, January 1990.

French, Benjamin F., *Historical Memoirs of Louisiana: From the First Settlement of the Colony to the Departure of Governor O'Reilly in 1770: With Historical and Biographical Notes Forming the Fifth of the Series of Historical Collections of Louisiana*. New York, New York: Lamport, Blakeman & Law, 1853.

Gallay, Alan, Editor, *Colonial Wars of North America 1512–1763, An Encyclopedia*. New York, New York: Routledge, Taylor, & Frances Group, 2015.

Gayarre, Charles, *Louisiana: Its Colonial History and Romance*. New York, New York: Harper and Brothers, 1851-1852.

_____, *History of Louisiana: The French Domination*. New York, New York: Redfield, 1854.

Grenier, John, *The First Way of War, American War Making of the Frontier, 1607-1814*. New York, New York: Cambridge University Press, 2005.

Higginbotham, Jay, *Old Mobile: Fort Louis de la Louisiane, 1702–1711*. Tuscaloosa, Alabama: University of Alabama Press, 1977, 2nd Edition, 1991.

Hoffman, Paul, *Florida's Frontiers*. Bloomington, Indiana: Indiana University Press, 2002.

Hudson, Charles M., *Four Centuries of Southern Indians*. Athens, Georgia: University of Georgia Press, 1975.

King, Grace, *Jean Baptiste Le Moyne, Sieur de Bienville*. New York, New York: Dodd, Mean & Company, 1892.

Leckie, Robert, *A Few Acres of Snow: The Saga of the French and Indian Wars*. New York, New York: John Wiley & Sons, 1999.

Liebersohn, Harry, *Aristocratic Encounters: European Travelers and North American Indians*. Cambridge, England: Cambridge University Press, 2001.

McCartney, Martha W. and Helen C. Rountree, *Powhatan Indian Place Names in Tidewater Virginia*. Baltimore, Maryland: Genealogical Publishing Company, 2017.

Mooney, James, "The End of the Natchez." *American Anthropologist*, New Series. Volume 1, Number 3, Arlington County, Virginia: American Anthropological Association, 1899.

Neville, John Davenport, *Bacon's Rebellion. Abstracts of Materials in the Colonial Records Project*. Jamestown, Virginia: Jamestown-Yorktown Foundation, 1985.

Oberg, Michael Leroy, *Samuel Wiseman's Book of Record: The Official Account of Bacon's Rebellion in Virginia, 1676–1677*. Lanham, Maryland: Lexington Books, 2006.

Peckham, Howard, *The Colonial Wars, 1689–1762*. Chicago, Illinois: University of Chicago Press, 1964.

Price, David A., *Love and Hate in Jamestown: John Smith, Pocahontas, and the Start of a New Nation*. New York, New York: Alfred A. Knopf, 2003.

Rice, James D., "Bacon's Rebellion in Indian Country." *Journal of American History*, Volume 101, Number 3, December 2014, pages 726–750.

Rountree, Helen, *Pocahontas's People: The Powhatan Indians of Virginia*. Norman, Oklahoma: University of Oklahoma Press, 1990.

Tarter, Brent, "Bacon's Rebellion, the Grievances of the People, and the Political Culture of Seventeenth-Century Virginia." *Virginia Magazine of History & Biography*, Volume 119, Number 1, 2011, pages 1–41.

Thompson, Peter, "The Thief, the Householder, and the Commons: Languages of Class in Seventeenth-Century Virginia." *William & Mary Quarterly*, Volume 63, Number 2, 2006, pages 253–280.

Tucker, Spencer C., James R. Arnold, and Roberta Wiener, *The Encyclopedia of North American Indian Wars, 1607–1890: A Political, Social, and Military History*. Santa Barbara, California: ABC-CLIO, 2011.

Usner, Daniel H., Jr., *American Indians in the Lower Mississippi Valley*. Lincoln, Nebraska: University of Nebraska Press, 1998.

Waselkov, Gregory A., and M. Thomas Hatley, *Powhatan's Mantle: Indians in the Colonial Southeast*. Lincoln, Nebraska: University of Nebraska Press, 2006.

Washburn, Wilcomb E., *The Governor and the Rebel: A History of Bacon's Rebellion in Virginia*. Chapel Hill, North Carolina: Published for the Institute of Early American History and Culture at Williamsburg by the University of North Carolina Press, 1957.

Webb, Stephen Saunders, *1676, The End of American Independence*. Syracuse, New York: Syracuse University Press, 1995.

Weber, David, *The Spanish Frontier in North America*. New Haven, Connecticut: Yale University Press, 2009.

Wells, Mary Ann, *Native Land: Mississippi, 1540-1798*. Jackson, Mississippi: University Press of Mississippi, 1994.

Wertenbaker, Thomas Jefferson, *Torchbearer of the Revolution: The Story of Bacon's Rebellion and its Leader*. Princeton, New Jersey: Princeton University Press, 1940.

Wetmore, Ruth Y., *First on the Land: The North Carolina Indians.* Winston-Salem, North Carolina: John F. Blair Publisher, 1975.

Wright, J. Leitch, Jr., *Anglo-Spanish Rivalry in North America.* Athens, Georgia: University of Georgia Press, 1971.

Tuscarora War, 1711-1715

Background

Of Iroquois stock, the Tuscarora left the Great Lakes region centuries before, settling in what later would become North Carolina. At the turn of the eighteenth century, Chief Tom Blount led the northern group of Tuscarora, who lived along the Roanoke River in Old Bertie County; and King Hancock, headed the southern group, resident at Catechna, south of the Pamlico River. The Tuscarora War in North Carolina pitted the British, Dutch, and German settlers against the Tuscarora tribe. The settlers enlisted the Yamasee and Cherokee as allies against the Tuscarora, in the bloodiest Indian war in that colony.

For more than five decades, the early settlers of North Carolina mostly lived peacefully with their indigenous neighbors, at a time when nearly every other American colony suffered through active warfare with Native Americans. Gradually, the settlers drew the enmity of the Tuscarora, who had three primary grievances. The settlers often cheated the natives when trading, sometimes stealing from them, or even killing them for their goods or land. Slavers increasingly impressed individual natives into bondage. Moreover, the introduction of European diseases depleted the native population. While the principal threats against the settlers emanated from the powerful Tuscarora, the first armed conflicts involved the smaller tribes who lived south of the Neuse River. In 1703, North Carolina declared the Coree and Nynee tribes to be public enemies. The records of this conflict, sometimes called the Coree War, have been lost; but, because the tribes later moved onto Tuscarora territory further west, they apparently were defeated.

The Tuscarora generally favored riverbanks when establishing their villages, locations coveted by the settlers seeking fertile soil and ready access to waterborne transportation. A significant clash between cultures arose as the colony imposed European concepts of land ownership. The Tuscarora believed that the land and the animals that lived on it were not property, but freely available to all. On the other hand, the Tuscarora respected the concept of ownership when applied to crops that an individual planted. Settlers resented the theft of their livestock, as well as the destruction of valuable timber and farmland, set afire by the natives in rituals performed prior to their annual hunts.

Attempts to maintain peace ultimately proved futile, the settlers often ignoring the provisions of the signed peace treaties intended to protect Tuscarora lands and control trade. The Tuscarora attempted to emigrate to Pennsylvania in 1710, but the colonial government there turned down their request. In the eyes of Chief Hancock, the continual encroachment onto their lands left them with no other alternative but open warfare. Chief Blount did not join him in the ensuing war.

Campaigns

In mid-September 1711, John Lawson, an early settler of the town of Bath, and Christopher de Graffenreid, the leader of the Swiss and Palatine settlers at New Bern, in the company of two Negro slaves and two friendly Indians from New Bern, traveled up the Neuse River to explore the distant territory. A party of sixty warriors captured the explorers and took them to Catechna, where King Hancock decreed that they be held and tried before a war council. At first, the council decided that the men could go free. But, after Lawson and Cor Tom, chief of Coree Town, argued vociferously, the council condemned Lawson to death. They let Graffenreid go free, because they feared immediate reprisal if the colonial official were harmed.

Determined to attack and drive the settlers out of Carolina, Chief Hancock forged alliances with the nearby Coree, Cothechney, Mattamuskeet, and Pamlico tribes. He organized a force of 500 warriors to attack the settlements and plantations along the Neuse, Roanoke, and Trent rivers. Small bands of warriors began their surprise attacks at dawn on the morning of September 22, 1711, killing everyone who did not flee -- men, women, and children alike -- often savagely mutilating their bodies and impaling many of their victims on stakes. They even killed and mutilated the slaves. The warriors also burned the houses and barns, slaughtered or drove off the livestock, trampled the crops, destroying everything they could, leaving the countryside in ashen ruins.

The settlers who survived the first wave of attacks fled to the relative safety of Bath Town, New Bern, and the fortified plantation of William Brice on the Trent River. After three long days of violence, the warriors returned to their villages, with their plunder and captives, mostly women and children. They killed at least 130 settlers, wounded many more, and took two or three dozen women and children prisoners. Some of the survivors fortified their homes, determined to defend themselves. In the coming days and weeks, the Tuscarora attacked and destroyed these small isolated homesteads. The inhabitants erected a fort on high ground in the center of Bath Town, where more than 300 widows and orphans sheltered. By the end of October, the settlers had constructed eleven forts across old Bath County.

Governor Edward Hyde mobilized the militia and requested the assistance of the neighboring colonies of South Carolina and Virginia. Major General Thomas Pollock, of Chowan Precinct, raised 150 volunteers to mount a counter offensive against the Tuscarora and proceeded to Bath. Captain William Brice, led about five dozen volunteers up the Neuse River to an abandoned Tuscarora village, intending to rendezvous with Pollock there. The soldiers at Bath refused to leave the safety of the town, leaving Brice and his men vulnerable. Brice continued moving upriver, until he was attacked by 300 warriors, forcing him to withdraw to his fortified plantation.

Virginia Governor Alexander Spotswood refused to send troops, but did send some gunpowder. Spotswood also encouraged Chief Tom Blunt's Tuscarora to join the fight against Hancock's followers. South Carolina responded by sending the experienced Indian fighter, Colonel John Barnwell, in command of 33 mounted militia and nearly 500 warriors from the Appalachee, Congaree, Pee Dee, Wateree, Waxhaw, and Yamasee tribes.

In January 1712, after marching more than 200 miles in the harsh winter weather, and reinforced by a contingent of North Carolina militia, Barnwell turned his attention to the southern Tuscarora and their allies. On January 29, his force reached the fortified Tuscarora town of Narhantes. He attacked immediately, killing 52 and taking 30 prisoners. Barnwell then swept across Tuscarora territory killing his foes, destroying their crops, and burning their towns as he went. On February 6th, while Barnwell and his men were crossing the Pamlico River, more than fifty Tuscarora attacked. After driving them off, Barnwell continued his march, reaching Bath Town on February 11th, his remaining forces only 25 white volunteers and 178 Indians.

On February 27, reinforced by 67 local volunteers, Barnwell headed his force to Hancock's fort near Catechna. When he attacked the fort, he and his men discovered that Hancock held many white prisoners, who he began to torture. Barnwell called off the attack and began to negotiate with Hancock, who agreed to surrender his prisoners, provided Barnwell would withdraw his forces. They also agreed to meet near New Bern on March 19th to discuss peace terms. After Hancock failed to appear for the peace talks, Barnwell built a fort across the Pamlico River from Bath Town. He then constructed Fort Barnwell on the Neuse River, about thirty miles upriver from New Bern, where he planned a second attempt to take Hancock's fort.

On April 7, 1712, Barnwell attacked Hancock's fort with 153 militia and 128 Indian allies. After a siege lasting ten full days, Barnwell allowed the fort to surrender, under very generous terms. In spite of the Tuscarora surrender, Barnwell's victory was seen as disappointing, South Carolina expecting payment in return for its assistance, and North Carolina expecting a decisive defeat, if not annihilation, of the Tuscarora. The South Carolina officers exacerbated the situation by keeping their prisoners to sell as slaves, a clear violation of the law, fomenting more Tuscarora discontent and directly leading the next summer to another round of vicious attacks.

That summer, a yellow fever epidemic swept through the colony, claiming Governor Hyde, on September 9th, as one of its many victims. Thomas Pollack then assumed command as president of the council. In December, Colonel James Moore at the head of 33 militia volunteers and about 900 warriors, mostly Cherokee and Yamasee, arrived from South Carolina. Delayed by heavy snow, Moore left Fort Reading on the Pamlico River, early in February 1713, and headed for the fortified Tuscarora town of Neoheroka, on Contentnea Creek. He surrounded Neoheroka in early March and maintained his siege for more than three weeks. Finally, on March 23rd, all resistance collapsed. In all, more than 950 Tuscarora men, women, and children were killed or captured, effectively ending any further threat from the Tuscarora.

While Moore laid siege to Neoheroka, Coree and Machapunga warriors attacked settlements on the Pungo River. In June 1713, Moore brought more than 120 of his Indians to the Pamlico region to punish the last remaining hostiles. Moore returned to South Carolina in September, after quelling much of the remaining resistance. In the spring of 1714, small war parties again began to attack isolated settlements, keeping all of Bath County in a constant state of terror.

The remaining Tuscarora signed a treaty with North Carolina in 1715, granting them a reservation on a tract of 56,000 acres of land on the Roanoke River in what is now Bertie County. This was the area already occupied by Tom Blount, who was recognized by the Legislature of North Carolina as King Tom Blount. The remaining southern Tuscarora were removed from their homes on the Pamlico River and forced to the reservation, officially called Indian Woods. Over the next several decades, the remaining Tuscarora lands continually diminished as the tribe sold off their land to speculators who designed the deals to take advantage of the Tuscarora.

Aftermath

Most of the surviving southern Tuscarora migrated to New York, where they formally joined the Five Nations of the Iroquois Confederation. At the outset, large groups, even whole villages, packed up and moved, followed by other sporadic migrations. In 1722, there were 300 warriors and their families on the reservation in Bertie County. In 1755, only 100 warriors and their families remained. In 1804, the last group of Tuscarora migrated north to join their people in New York, leaving only ten to twenty old families.

At the close of the war, as many as 1,500 southern Tuscarora sought refuge in the colony of Virginia. Although a few accepted their status in Virginia, the majority ultimately continued north to New York. In 1715, seventy of the southern Tuscarora went to South Carolina to fight against the Yamasee. Those warriors later asked permission to have their wives and children join them, and settled near Port Royal, South Carolina.

In 1802, the last Tuscarora still living at *Indian Woods* negotiated a treaty with the government, by which land would be held for them that they could lease. Because the government never ratified the treaty, the Tuscarora viewed the treaty as null and void. In 1831, they sold most of their remaining rights to their lands, reducing their original 56,000 acres to 2,000 acres. Although without a reservation, some Tuscarora descendants remained in the southern portion of the state, intermarrying with others and gradually assimilating. In 2010, the descendants were formally recognized as the Tuscarora Nation One Fire Council.

The smaller tribes allied with the Tuscarora (the Coree, Machapunga, Mattamuskeet, and Pamlico) were reduced to remnant bands. Most were moved to a reservation, about 36 square miles in size, on Lake Mattamuskeet, in modern Hyde County. There the different bands gradually merged, intermarried with their neighbors, both white and free persons of color, assimilating into American society. As early as 1731, they began to sell portions of the reservation, completing the dissolution of the reservation with a final sale in 1761. Some surviving Coree gradually merged with the Tuscarora on their *Indian Woods* reservation, while others remained in isolated villages in modern Carteret County.

Places of Interest

Fort Barnwell Historical Marker
On State Highway 55
near Belltown and Biddle Roads
in Craven County

Constructed by Colonel John Barnwell of South Carolina in
campaign against the Tuscarora Indians in April, 1712. Remains
are 2 mi. N. E.

Colonel John Barnwell Grave
Saint Helena's Episcopal Church
505 Church Street
Beaufort, South Carolina 29902

(843) 522-1712

John Barnwell, ca1675-1724, led an army against
the Tuscarora in 1712 and an expedition against the
Yamesee in 1715. Barnwell also was instrumental
in founding Beaufort, South Carolina.

Catechna Indian Village
Grifton Museum
P. O. Box 85
437A Creekshore Drive
Grifton, North Carolina 28530

252-524-0190

Catechna Indian Village, on the banks of Contentnea Creek is a scaled-down replica of a
Tuscarora village located just across the street from the Grifton Museum. During annual festivals
like John Lawson Days, volunteers demonstrate lifestyle skills of the Native Americans who lived
here. The precise location of the actual Catechna village inhabited by the Tuscarora is unknown
but the artifacts recovered here indicate that the town was very near this site.

41

Nooherooka Historical Marker
State Route 58 and Fort Run Road
Snow Hill, North Carolina

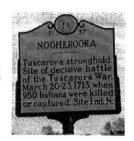

Tuscarora stronghold. Site of decisive battle of the Tuscarora War, March 20-23, 1713, when 950 Indians were killed or captured. Site 1 mi. N.

Boochawee Hall Historical Marker
on a Lake Greenview Park walking trail
near East Pandora Drive, in Goose Creek South Carolina

Boochawee Hall, created in 1683 by a 2,400-acre grant, was owned by two colonial governors, father and son. James Moore (d. 1706), a trader and planter, served on the Grand Council and later led "the Goose Creek Men," an anti-proprietary faction. Appointed governor in 1700, Moore commanded an expedition to Florida, burning St. Augustine in 1702. Moore, replaced as governor by Sir Nathaniel Johnson in 1703, returned to the council and held a seat there until his death.

James Moore, Jr. (d. 1724) served three terms in the Commons House of Assembly and as an officer in the Tuscarora War (1711-13) before commanding the provincial forces in the Yemassee War (1715). Moore was appointed governor when the proprietary government was overthrown in 1719. He was essentially a caretaker until he was succeeded by provisional royal governor Francis Nicholson in 1721. Moore was Speaker of the House in the first Royal Assembly at his death.

Historic Bath
P. O. Box 148
207 Carteret Street
Bath, North Carolina 27808

(252) 923-3971

bath@ncdcr.gov

http://nchistoricsites.org/bath/

The district consists of the historic heart of North Carolina's first town and has a visitor center, several historic structures, trails, monuments, and an outdoor exhibit.

Indian Woods Historical Marker
U. S. Route 17, south of
Windsor, North Carolina

Indian Woods

Reservation established in 1717 for Tuscaroras remaining in N. C.
after war of 1711-1713. Sold, 1828. Five miles N.W.

Mattamuskeet Historical Marker
U. S. Route 264, at
State Route 94, south of Lake Mattamuskeet

Mattamuskeet

Largest natural lake in N.C. Center of an Indian reservation,
established 1715. Twice drained and farmed. Wildlife refuge since
1934. One mile N.

Robert Gibbes Memorial Monument
Park at Meeting Street and
Broad Street, behind City Hall
Charles, South Carolina

Robert Gibbes, 1644-1715. Early Barbadian supporter of the
settlement of South Carolina. Colonial Governor 1710-1712.
Proprietor's Deputy Chief Justice of South Carolina. Member of 1st
Assembly. Colonel South Carolina Militia, sent South Carolina
Militia to aid North Carolinians against the Tuscarora Indians.

Further Reading

Cain, Robert J., Editor, *The Colonial Records of North Carolina [Second Series] Volume VII: Records of the Executive Council 1664-1734*. Raleigh, North Carolina: Department of Cultural Resources, Division of Archives and History, 1984.

Johnson, F. Roy, *The Tuscaroras: History, Traditions, Culture*. Murfreesboro, North Carolina: Johnson Publishing Company, 1968.

Patrick Keith, *Through Colonialism and Imperialism: The Struggle for Tuscarora Nationhood in Southeastern North Carolina*. MA thesis, 2005, University of Arizona, Tucson, Arizona.

La Vere, David, *The Tuscarora War: Indians, Settlers, and the Fight for the Carolina Colonies*. Chapel Hill, North Carolina: University of North Carolina Press, 2016.

Lee, E. Lawrence, *Indian Wars in North Carolina, 1663-1763*. Raleigh, North Carolina: North Carolina Office of Archives and History, 1963.

Powell, William S., *North Carolina: A History*. Chapel Hill, University of North Carolina Press, 1977, Reprinted 1988.

Seaman, Rebecca M., "John Lawson, the Outbreak of the Tuscarora War, and Middle Ground Theory." *Journal of the North Carolina Association of Historians*, Volume 18, April 2010, page 9.

Wallace, Anthony F. C., *Tuscarora: A History*. Albany, New York: SUNY Press, 2012.

Todd, Vincent H., Editor, *von Graffenried's Account of the Founding of New Bern*. New Bern, North Carolina, John P. Sturman, Bern Bear Gifts, November 2003.

Yamasee War, 1715-1716

Background

Strictly speaking, the Yamasee were not a tribe; instead, they were an amalgam of earlier tribes and chiefdoms, first appearing in the disputed territory between Spanish Florida and South Carolina in the 17th century. By the turn of the 18th century, the Yamasee migrated northward to the lands around Port Royal Sound and the mouth of the Savannah River.

By 1715, the profitability of rice planting encouraged many settlers to covet the Yamasee lands they considered ideal for rice plantations. After the Tuscarora War, the Yamasee were faced with dwindling opportunities to sell captured rivals into slavery. Many Yamasee, after the British took a census of their population, feared they would be captured and enslaved. As the demand for deerskins increased, the deer population plummeted, making it more difficult for the Yamasee to feed themselves. Further increasing Yamasee discontent was their growing indebtedness to British traders, who supplied them with goods on credit.

Military collaboration among the various tribes that helped South Carolina in the Tuscarora War brought the tribes of the region into close contact and strengthened their intercommunication. Moreover, they witnessed the bickering among the colonies over the war. Just a couple of years later, all the tribes that had helped South Carolina during the war, the Yamasee, and their allies, the Apalachee, Apalachicola, Cape Fear, Catawba, Cheraw, Cherokee, Congaree, Creek, Pee Dee, Savannah River Shawnee, Waxhaw, Yuchi, and others, joined the attack against South Carolina. Each of the tribes had their own reasons for war, some combination of land encroachment, trader abuses, Indian slave trade, the scarcity of deer, and growing rice plantations. Friendly relations with Spanish Florida and the French in Louisiana offering an alternative to British traders further encouraged Indian discontent. By early 1715, friendly Indians warned of impending hostilities from the Ochese Creek.

South Carolina acted swiftly after word of the possible uprising, sending a delegation, consisting of Samuel Warner and William Bray, from the Board of Commissioners; Thomas Nairne and John Wright, two important traders; Seymour Burroughs; and, an unknown South Carolinian, to Pocotaligo, the main village of the Upper Yamasee. The men wanted the Yamasee to help arrange an immediate meeting with the Ochese Creek leaders. On April 14, 1715, the delegation spoke to a group of Yamasee, promising to redress Yamasee grievances and explaining that Governor Charles Craven was in route to the village. Later that night, the Yamasee discussed what they should do and made their decision. They woke the sleeping delegation and attacked them, killing Warner, Bray, Nairne, and Wright. Seymour Burroughs and the unknown man managed to escape. The murderous events in the early morning hours of Good Friday, April 15, 1715, marked the start of the Yamasee War.

Campaigns

The Yamasee immediately organized two parties of several hundred warriors, one to attack the settlements at Port Royal and the other to attack Saint Bartholomew's Parish. The alarm was raised in Port Royal, when the escaping Seymour Burroughs reached the nearby plantation owned by John Barnwell. When the Yamasee arrived, they found hundreds of settlers on board a ship in the harbor, many others having already fled. In St. Bartholomew's Parish, many plantations were sacked and burned, numerous captives taken, and more than a hundred settlers and slaves murdered. Within one week, a large war party was preparing to fight a contingent of militia then heading their way.

Several hundred Yamasee warriors attacked about 240 militia, commanded by Governor Craven, near the Indian village of Salkehatchie. The fighting on open terrain was fierce, but after several warrior leaders were slain, the Yamasee disengaged and retreated into the nearby swamps. In spite of the almost even number of casualties, about two dozen on each side, the battle was a clear victory for the militia. Other militia units attacked various groups of Yamasee, winning a series of small victories and boosting morale in general.

Alexander MacKay, an experienced Indian fighter, commanding a force of militia, attacked about 200 Yamasee, who were in a stockade fort, killing many of the warriors, the survivors slipping away into the surrounding forest. Later that summer, in what became known as the Daufuskie Fight, a scouting crew ambushed a party of Yamasee and killed 35 of them, but received only one casualty. After suffering so many defeats and loosing so many warriors, the Yamasee decided to move south to the Altamaha River, just north of Spanish Florida.

At the start of the war, about 100 traders, mostly from South Carolina, were operating throughout present-day Georgia, Alabama, and Mississippi. Within the first few weeks of the war, more than 90 were killed by members of several tribes. Further to the north, the Catawba and Cherokee were killing the traders they found in their territory.

By May 1715, about 400 Catawba and 70 Cherokee warriors moved south to attack the scattered settlers living on the South Carolina frontier. In June, Captain Thomas Barker led 90 cavalrymen to retaliate. The war party ambushed Barker and his men, killing all. Another band of Catawba and Cherokee attacked Benjamin Schenkingh's plantation, killing all twenty of the people who had sheltered there. George Chicken assembled a force of militia, who, on June 13, 1715, ambushed a band of Catawba, and chased them back to their main war party. Chicken immediately attacked, defeating and scattering them in the Battle of the Ponds. The Catawba sent emissaries to Virginia, stating they wanted to make peace and would join the settlers in fighting the other hostile tribes.

That summer, smaller tribes, including the Apalachee, Apalachicola, Savannah River Shawnee, and Yuchi, attacked settlements in South Carolina. After the settlers launched successful counterattacks, the smaller tribes fled their homes in the Savannah River region, many going to live among the Ochese Creek. South Carolina traders had made the Creek people dependent upon their goods. The Creek considered trading with the French and Spanish, but found their goods unsatisfactory in both quality and quantity, especially the arms and munitions needed to wage war. While the Upper Creek declined to join their Ochese Creek brethren in attacking South Carolina, the Yamasee War strengthened their ties to the French and the Spanish.

Like the Creek, the Cherokee also were divided. The Overhill Cherokee preferred an alliance with South Carolina and waging war against the Creek, while the Lower Cherokee, who lived closer to South Carolina, preferred war against the colonists.

In 1715, two traders convinced the Cherokee to send a delegation with them to Charleston, where plans were made to attack the Creek. Late that year, South Carolina dispatched more than 300 militia to visit the important Lower, Middle, and Overhill Cherokee towns. The division among the Cherokee immediately became evident to the South Carolinians. Caesar, a Middle Cherokee chief, spent that winter traveling throughout the Cherokee territory, trying to persuade the others to wage war on the Creek. Other Cherokee chiefs opposed war, while some Lower Creek leaders preferred peace with South Carolina and war against the Yuchi and Savannah River Shawnee tribes.

In January 1716, the Lower Cherokee invited many Creek and Cherokee leaders to confer with the South Carolinians at Tugaloo Town, near where the Tugaloo River meets the Keowee River to form the Savannah River. While the details remain rather murky, the South Carolina delegation arrived to discover that the Cherokee had killed all the Creek chiefs. Creek historians recall 32 dead chiefs, while the official white history records only eleven or twelve. The Tugaloo Massacre touched off the Creek Cherokee War that lasted nearly four decades.

While the Creek, left leaderless by the massacre, did not join the attacks against South Carolina, violence continued for the rest of 1716. When the militia attacked villages in retaliation, they killed or enslaved all the residents, with the Yamasee and other smaller tribes suffering increasingly severe losses. While most of the Creek and other Muskogee tribes signed peace treaties by the end of 1717, the Apalachicola, Creek, and Yamasee continued to attack isolated settlements and plantations through most of the next decade.

After the Yamasee and Catawba retreated, the militia reoccupied their abandoned settlements to provide security for the frontier, fortifying several plantation homes in the process. While the militia were successful when on offence, they were less than effective in protecting the scattered frontier settlements against the marauding bands of Indians. Moreover, the militia suffered from desertion, as some men feared for their own families and others simply decided to leave South Carolina altogether.

By August 1715, Governor Craven disbanded the militia and created a professional army, consisting of about 600 of its citizens, 400 black slaves, 170 friendly Indians, and 300 men from North Carolina and Virginia. The army, however, was unable to provide effective security, the Indians refusing to fight large battles, preferring instead to rely on scattered raids and ambushes in waging their war. After peace with the Cherokee was reached in 1716, Craven disbanded his army.

Aftermath

The Yamasee War, one of the most disruptive conflicts of colonial America, also was one of the most serious challenges to European colonization. South Carolina faced the prospect of total annihilation, losing roughly seven percent of its white population. The war brought about new Indian confederations, like the Muscogee Creek and Catawba.

There was no definitive conclusion to the war. Some considered the war essentially over after the first few critical weeks or months. Some believed the war effectively over when peace with the Cherokee came in early 1716. Still others thought the war over when peace treaties were signed with the Creek and other tribes in late 1717. However, some tribes never agreed to peace. Insecurity remained a problem, even after the Yamasee and Apalachicola moved further south, as their sporadic attacks on the frontier of South Carolina continued.

Many South Carolinians disliked their proprietary government and their discontent grew overwhelming as the Yamasee War began. This prompted the Crown to remake both North Carolina and South Carolina as crown colonies in 1729 and hopefully bringing added royal protection. Another outgrowth of the war was King George II granting a royal charter to James Oglethorpe for the colony of Georgia, to serve as a buffer between South Carolina and Spanish Florida. Oglethorpe negotiated with the Yamacraw, as the few remaining Yamasee were known, for the rights to establish Savannah, his new capital.

The war also brought great suffering to the Yamasee, who lost one-fourth of their population and were forced to flee southward. Dividing into two factions, about one third of the survivors opted to move to Creek lands, where they became part of the new Creek Confederation. The remainder moved with the Apalachicola to the St. Augustine area, both continuing their sporadic raids against South Carolina. The Yamasee continued to decline in population, power, and influence, through warfare, disease, and other factors, eventually becoming absorbed by the Seminole.

The Ochese Creek, together with refugees from the Apalachee, Apalachicola, Yamasee, and other tribes, settled in the Chattahoochee River valley and became known as the Lower Creek. Elements of the Cheraw, Congaree, Pee Dee, Santee, Waccamaw, Wateree, and Winyah joined the Catawba Confederation, the strongest group in the Piedmont region.

Places of Interest

Old Tugaloo Town Historical Marker
U. S. Route 123 at Tugaloo River on the
South Carolina boundary

North of this marker, in the center of the lake, once stood
an important Indian town. The area now marked by a
small island was settled around 500 A. D. and occupied by
Cherokee Indians around 1450. Traders were coming to
the town by 1690. In 1716, while Col. Maurice Moore
treated with Charity Hague, Cherokee Conjuror, a group of
Creek ambassadors arrived. The Creek Indians, who
supported Spain and France, wished to drive the British
from the Carolinas in the Yamassee War. The Cherokees killed the Creek ambassadors and
joined the British. By 1717, Col. Theophilus Hastings operated a trading center at Tugaloo where
gunsmith, John Milbourne cared for Cherokee firearms. Indian agent, George Chicken visited
Tugaloo in 1725 and described it as "…the most ancient town in these parts." Tugaloo remained
a principal Cherokee town until destroyed by American patriots fighting these allies of the British
in 1776.

Catawba Cultural Center
1536 Tom Steven Road
Rock Hill, South Carolina 29730

(803) 328-2427

http://catawbaindian.net/about-us/our-culture/catawba-cultural-center/

The Cultural Center provides an overview of the rich culture and history of the Catawba Indian
Nation through exhibits. There is also a craft store in the center that features crafts from many of
our native artisans.

The Yamasee War at Goose Creek, 1715 Historical Marker
adjacent to Goose Creek Primary School,
200 Foster Creek Road
Goose Creek, South Carolina

In April 1715 Yamasee warriors killed government agents and traders
who had come to meet with them at Pocotaligo, in present-day
Beaufort County. Others killed colonists and raided plantations and
farms at Port Royal, initiating the Yamasee War. Catawbas and
Cherokees soon launched raids on other white towns and settlements,
and many whites in Goose Creek fled to Charleston or barricaded
themselves in their houses. Capt. Thomas Barker, who lived 1.5 mi. N,
left Goose Creek on May 15 with 102 militia, intending to meet the Congarees near the Santee
River. He and 26 men were killed in an ambush on May 16. On June 13 Capt. George Chicken
and 120 cavalrymen of the Goose Creek militia ambushed a war party 20 mi. W near

Wassamassaw, killing 40-60 and scattering the rest. The Catawbas would not threaten Goose Creek again.

First Fort Historical Marker
Bay Street, near Scott Street
Beaufort, South Carolina

On or near this site in the settlement known as Stuart Town stood the "Tight Watch House" erected in 1683-4. After the destruction of the town by the Spanish in 1686 it was replaced by a fort, approximately 100 feet square defended by "9 Great Guns" known as the Beaufort Fort after 1710. It was the main defense of the area until Fort Frederick was erected in 1735.

Further Reading

Crane, Verner, *The Southern Frontier, 1670-1732.* Durham, North Carolina: Duke University Press, 1928.

Gallay, Alan, *The Indian Slave Trade: The Rise of the English Empire in the American South 1670-1717.* New Haven, Connecticut: Yale University Press, 2002.

Oatis, Steven J., *A Colonial Complex: South Carolina's Frontiers in the Era of the Yamasee War, 1680–1730.* Lincoln, Nebraska: University of Nebraska Press, 2004.

Ramsey, William L., *The Yamasee War: A Study of Culture, Economy, and Conflict in the Colonial South.* Lincoln, Nebraska: University of Nebraska Press, 2008.

Worth, John, *Prelude to Abandonment: The Interior Provinces of Early 17th-Century Georgia.* [Place of publication not identified.]: Society for Georgia Archaeology. 1993.

French and Indian War, 1754-1763

Background

While the French and Indian War was fought principally outside of the region covered by this guide, it is included here because so many of the participants were from southern colonies. Officially part of the Seven Years War, between France and England, it essentially was a struggle to control the interior of North America and its lucrative fur trade.

The French, with a long presence along the Mississippi River and in the Great Lakes region, coveted the lands south of the Great Lakes all the way to Mobile and the Gulf. The British colonies along the Atlantic coast claimed the lands west of their borders all the way to the Mississippi River and beyond. Both sides attempted to control the vast region by establishing alliances with the various tribes living there, but neither side was successful. The French lived principally in Canada, with scant presence in the upper Ohio territory. However, in 1749, the French governor ordered Pierre Joseph Céloron de Blainville to compel the scattered trading houses to remove the British flags they flew and the traders, who the French considered trespassers, to stay east of the Appalachian Mountains. His orders were not obeyed; thus, in 1752, the French destroyed the British trading post at Pickawillany on the Great Miami River and killed every British trader they and their Indian allies could find, threatening both Pennsylvania and Virginia.

Virginia claimed that the lands in the upper Ohio region were hers, according to their 1609 colonial charter, superseding the French claim founded on La Salle's later exploratory journey down the Mississippi River. Moreover, Virginia had issued grants to more than 2,000 acres of land in the contested area. Lieutenant Governor Robert Dinwiddie sent George Washington to the French Fort LeBouef, at what is now Waterford, Pennsylvania, to tell the French that they were intruding on Virginia soil. After Washington's effort failed to dislodge the French, the Ohio Company of Virginia, ordered a fort erected at the confluence of the Monongahela and Allegheny rivers, under the belief that Virginia troops would support them.

In early 1754, William Trent, with a party of about 40 men, began construction of the small fort. Claude Pierre Pecaudy de Contrecœur, commanding 500 French soldiers from Fort Venango, met Trent's party on April 16th. He allowed Trent to withdraw his men peacefully, purchased their tools, and then built Fort Duquesne. Meanwhile, Dinwiddie ordered Washington to bring reinforcements to Trent, but Washington was too late. Hearing of Trent's withdrawal, he diverted his course to meet with Tanaghrisson, a Mingo chief, who told Washington that a party of French soldiers were nearby. On May 28th, Washington, Tenaghrisson, and their men attacked the scouting party, killing many of them, including their commander Joseph Coulon de Jumonville, in the first battle of the French and Indian War.

In March, 1756, the Virginia legislature authorized the erection of a chain of forts to defend the settlements along the western frontier. Colonel George Washington, commander of the Virginia Regiment, was tasked with overseeing the effort. The long chain extended from the head of the Ohio River, eastward to Fort Cumberland on the Potomac River at Wills Creek, then southward along the Allegheny Mountains to the North Carolina border. Over the next decades, many were attacked, some the scenes of tragedy with numerous lives lost, primarily on the waters of the South Branch of the Potomac River.

Campaigns

After the Battle of Jumonville Glen, Washington withdrew his men southward several miles, there hastily constructing a defensive structure he dubbed Fort Necessity. On July 3rd, 1754, Jumonville's brother, Louis Coulon de Villiers, commanding a body of French soldiers and a number of Delaware, Mingo, and Shawnee warriors, attacked. Given the overpowering forces facing him, Washington surrendered, but managed to negotiate a safe withdrawal for his men.

After the news reached London, the government appointed Major General Edward Braddock to take Fort Duquesne. On May 29, 1755, Braddock led a large force, setting out from Fort Cumberland in Maryland, on a 110-mile journey over the heavily wooded Allegheny Mountains to the forks of the Ohio. His force consisted of the British 44th (East Essex) and 48th (Northamptonshire) Regiments of Foot, the Virginia Regiment, and militia mostly from Virginia and Maryland, but including 85 North Carolina militia under Captain Edward Brice Dobbs. In order to get his large column, with their equipment, provisions, and artillery, to their destination, Braddock constructed a road as they progressed. Splitting his command in two, a column of 1,300 under his command leading the way, and another group of 800 with the baggage train following behind. Small bands of French and Indians harassed both columns as they made their way forward along the Braddock Road.

French and Indian scouts alerted Contrecœurt, the commander at Fort Duquesne, to the approaching British, who decided to ambush Braddock before he could bring his cannon to bear on his wooden stockade. On July 9, 1755, after the main army crossed the Monongahela River about ten miles from their destination, the advance guard of 300 regulars and militia stumbled upon the French and Indians, the opening skirmish the start of the Battle of the Monongahela.

The advance guard withdrew in some confusion, colliding with the main column advancing along the narrow road. With the French regulars advancing down the narrow road in their front and their Indian allies firing into their flanks from the cover of the adjacent woods, Braddock's entire force fell into disorder. The British regulars attempted to form into regular battle order, but could not do so effectively on such a narrow road. The militia moved into the woods and began firing at the Indians. After hours of fierce fighting, Braddock was shot and unhorsed and all resistance dissolved. Washington assumed command and immediately formed a rear guard to cover their retreat.

The defeated British force fled back over the road they had built, Braddock dying from his wounds along the way. Of the 1,300 men who fought that day, 456 were killed and 422 wounded. Officers were prime targets, suffering 26 killed and 37 wounded, out of 86. The French suffered eight killed and four wounded and their Indian allies fifteen killed and twelve wounded. The French chose not to pursue the defeated and demoralized British. When the retreating remnants of Braddock's army reached their supply train, Colonel Dunbar assumed overall command, ordering the destruction of most of the supplies, wagons, and artillery, before continuing their retreat back to Fort Cumberland.

After Braddock's defeat, the Shawnee and other tribes raided the settlements in the Virginia backcountry. In July 1755, a Shawnee war party attacked the settlement on Draper's Meadow, on the present site of Blacksburg, in Montgomery County, Virginia, killing at least five and wounding at least one. They took five or six women and children back to their villages in Ohio. One of the captives, Mary Draper Ingels later escaped and walked more than 300 miles over the mountains back home to Drapers Meadow. Other settlements were attacked that summer, leaving the Virginia backcountry virtually abandoned by the settlers.

In 1758, Brigadier General John Forbes commanded an army of more than 6,000 soldiers in another expedition intended to retake Fort Duquesne. Because Forbes was ill, his second in command, Lieutenant Colonel Henry Bouquet, commander of a battalion of the American Regiment, effectively led the expedition. The army included Virginians under the command of Colonel George Washington, as well as North Carolinians led by Major Hugh Waddell. Forbes ordered the construction of a military road from Carlisle, Pennsylvania, through the Allegheny Mountains, to their objective, erecting a series of small forts along the route and storing supplies in each. As the expedition approached its ultimate target, a reconnaissance party, led by Major James Grant, was defeated at the Battle of Fort Duquesne. The French then attacked one of the small supply forts, but the men of Fort Ligonier repulsed them.

In October, the Delaware, Mingo, and Shawnee abandoned their French allies after the Treaty of Easton, leaving the French in the upper Ohio region vulnerable. In November, with the expedition approaching within a few miles, the French destroyed Fort Duquesne and retreated to other forts to the north and northwest. Under Washington's orders, Major Waddell's scouts moved forward and entered the smoldering ruins on November 24th.

Henry Bouquet ordered the fort rebuilt and named the new outpost Fort Pitt, after the prime minister, William Pitt. The other battles and campaigns of the war took place in the northern British colonies and Canada, with little or no participation from the southern colonies. By 1760, after the British capture of Fort Niagara, Quebec, and Montreal, hostilities in North America were over. The Seven Years War, however, continued in Europe and India, ending in 1763 with the Treaty of Paris.

Aftermath

The Treaty of Paris provided for France ceding Canada and that portion of the Louisiana Territory east of the Mississippi River to the British and that portion of the Louisiana Territory west of the Mississippi River to Spain, in return for Spain ceding Spanish Florida to the British. In gratitude for the services of his Indian allies and to protect their territory from encroachment, King George III issued his Royal Proclamation of 1763, forbidding all settlement west of a line drawn along the crests of the Allegheny Mountains. Many colonials detested the proclamation, wanting to settle the fertile lands west of the line and contributing to their distrust and dislike of British rule that erupted into revolution the following decade.

The fruits of the British victory sowed the seeds of unrest among the American colonies. Because the expensive war strained the British treasury, the government attempted to impose various taxes to refill their coffers. Such attempts only fueled colonial resentment to the rule of King George III and his Parliament.

During the French and Indian War there were more than eighty frontier forts built in Virginia, extending from the Potomac River to North Carolina, 54 of which were in old Frederick and Hampshire counties. The forts were intended to defend against attacks from the French and their Indian allies in the Ohio country. The line of forts was anchored by Fort Loudon, at modern Winchester, in Frederick County, the largest of the fortifications. Colonel George Washington supervised its construction and made his headquarters there. As the commander of the Virginia Regiment, he was responsible for the overall defense of the Virginia frontier.

Places of Interest

Fort Necessity National Battlefield
1 Washington Parkway
Farmington, Pennsylvania 15437

(724) 329-5512

The park includes a visitor center, with an introductory movie, book store, and historical displays, Great Meadows and Fort Necessity, the grave of General Braddock, and Jumonville Glen. The park also provides talks, tours, and weapons demonstrations during the summer.

Point State Park
601 Commonwealth Place
Pittsburgh, Pennsylvania 15222

(412) 281-9284

Situated at the confluence of the Allegheny and Monongahela rivers, the park has numerous monuments, plaques, and markers commemorating events and people of historical importance, including a delineation of Fort Duquesne. The Fort Pitt Museum presents the history of western Pennsylvania in the French and Indian War. The Fort Pitt Blockhouse, built in 1764, is the only remaining bastion of Fort Pitt.

Fort Ligonier
Intersection of U. S. Route 30 and State Route 711
200 South Market Street
Ligonier, Pennsylvania 15658

(724) 238 – 9701

Eight acres of the original site of Fort Ligonier have been preserved, with the subsurface features restored and the above-ground elements reconstructed. The inner fort is 200 feet square, with four bastions. Inside is the officers' mess, barracks, quartermaster, guardroom, underground magazine, commissary, and officers' quarters. Immediately outside the fort is General Forbes's hut. An outer retrenchment, 1,600 feet long, surrounds the fort. Opening in the Spring of 2017 is the new Center for History Education, including a large museum.

Fort Cumberland Historical Marker
At Washington and Cumberland Streets,
in Cumberland, Maryland

The storehouses of the Ohio Company were first located near this
point. In 1754 the first fort (called Mt. Pleasant) was built. Gen'l
Edward Braddock enlarged the fort in 1755 and renamed it after his
friend the Duke of Cumberland.

Brigadier General John Forbes Memorial
Christ Episcopal Church
Philadelphia, Pennsylvania

John Forbes (1710-1759), a brigadier general, commanded the 1757
expedition against Fort Duquesne, constructing the Forbes Road, a
wagon road across the Allegheny Mountains, later a major
migration route west. In 1758, Forbes accepted the French
surrender. The fort was rebuilt and renamed Fort Pitt, and
eventually the settlement grew into what is now Pittsburgh.

Daniel Boone Grave
Frankfort Cemetery
Frankfort, Kentucky

Daniel Boone (1734-1820) began his illustrious career as teamster in the
ill-fated Braddock Expedition. He went on to serve in the North Carolina
militia during the First Cherokee War, the Virginia militia in Lord
Dunmore's War, with George Rogers Clark in the Illinois Expedition, and
in the defense of Kentucky during and after the Revolution.

Fort Le Boeuf Historical Marker
South High Street, just south of 1st Street
in park opposite Fort Le Boeuf Museum,
Waterford, Pennsylvania

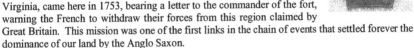

This monument marks the site of Fort Le Boeuf, erected by the French in 1752. George Washington as a major representing the governor of Virginia, came here in 1753, bearing a letter to the commander of the fort, warning the French to withdraw their forces from this region claimed by Great Britain. This mission was one of the first links in the chain of events that settled forever the dominance of our land by the Anglo Saxon.

Fort Loudon
419 North Loudon Street
Winchester, Virginia 22601

(703) 574-6110

fiwf.dsg@comcast.net

http://frenchandindianwarfoundation.org/

From 1756-1758, George Washington designed and supervised the construction of the fort, built of horizontal logs filled with earth and rubble, with four bastions, barracks for 450 men, and a well sunk 103 feet into limestone. The fort was headquarters for Washington and his Virginia Regiment. The site is owned and maintained by the French and Indian War Foundation, headquartered in an antebellum house on the property. The foundation hosts the annual Fort Loudon Day celebration.

Museum of the Shenandoah Valley
901 Amherst Street
Winchester, Virginia 22601

(888) 556-5799

visit@theMSV.org

The museum interprets the art, history, and culture of the great valley for which it is named. The complex includes an historic house dating to the 18th century, six acres of spectacular gardens, and a museum open year-round. The house and gardens are open April through October.

61

George Washington's Office Museum
32 West Cork Street
Winchester, Virginia 22601

(540) 662-4412

http://winchesterhistory.org/george-washingtons-office/

George Washington used a little log building, now the middle room of George Washington Office Museum, as a military office from September 1755 to December of 1756 while Fort Loudoun was being constructed at the north end of town. The museum features exhibits highlighting Washington's connections to Winchester and the history of the local area.

Cartmill's Gap Historical Marker
Arcadia Road, near
Lee Highway, near Greyledge, in
Botetourt County, Virginia

This gap, just west, is named for Henry Cartmill who acquired land nearby on Purgatory Creek. During the French and Indian War (1754-1763), conflicts between Indians and settlers increased in this area. In 1757, Indians laid waste to several nearby farmsteads, including the Robert Renick settlement a few miles north, near present-day Natural Bridge. Renick was killed, while his wife and children (William, Robert, Thomas, Joshua, and Betsy) were taken captive. A neighbor, Hannah Dennis, also was made prisoner; Joseph Dennis, her husband, and their child were among those killed. The Indians escaped south through Cartmill's Gap.

Audley Paul's Fort Historical Marker
Lee Highway, south of
Plank Road, near Harvey, in
Botetourt County, Virginia

Nearby stood Capt. Audley Paul's fort, built in 1757 during the French and Indian War (1754-1763) as one in a series of fortifications to protect Virginia's frontier. Paul served as a lieutenant in Maj. Gen. Edward Braddock's ill-fated expedition against the French at Fort Duquesne in 1755. He soon joined Col. William Preston's ranger company as first lieutenant and served in the 1756 expedition against the Shawnee at Sand Creek. In 1761, Paul's fort sheltered settlers fleeing their homesteads in anticipation of Indian attacks. Paul later served in Dunmore's War and fought in the Battle of Point Pleasant, 10 Oct. 1774.

Further Reading

Anderson, Fred, *Crucible of War: The Seven Years War and the Fate of Empire in British North America, 1754–1766.* New York, New York: Knopf, 2000.

Axtell, James, *The Invasion Within.* New York, New York: Oxford University Press, 1985.

Bailey, Kenneth P., *Christopher Gist: Colonial Frontiersman, explorer, and Indian Agent.* Hampton, Connecticut: Archon Books, 1976.

Borneman, Walter R., *The French and Indian War: Deciding the Fate of North America.* New York, New York: Harper Collins, 2006.

Brumwell, Stephen, *Redcoats: The British Soldier and War in the Americas, 1755-1763.* Cambridge, England: Cambridge University Press, 2006.

Calloway, Colin G., *The Scratch of a Pen: 1763 and the Transformation of North America.* Oxford, England: Oxford University Press, 2006.

Cubbison, Douglas R., *The British Defeat of the French in Pennsylvania, 1758: A Military History of the Forbes Campaign Against Fort Duquesne.* Jefferson, North Carolina: McFarland, 2010.

Cave, Alfred A., *The French and Indian War.* Westport, Connecticut, London: Greenwood Press, 2004.

Drake, Samuel, *Tragedies of the Wilderness.* Boston, Massachusetts: Antiquarian Bookstore and Institute, 1844.

Ellis, Joseph J., *His Excellency George Washington.* New York, New York: Vintage Books, 2004.

Fowler, William M., *Empires at War: The French and Indian War and the Struggle for North America, 1754-1763.* Vancouver, Canada: Douglas & McIntyre, 2005.

Freeman, Douglas Southall, *George Washington, Volume I, Young Washington, 1732-1754.* New York, New York: Charles Scribner's Sons, 1948.

Gipson, Lawrence H., *The Great War for the Empire: The Years of Defeat, 1754–1757.* New York, New York: Knopf, 1948.

_____, *The Great War for the Empire: The Victorious Years, 1758–1760.* New York, Knopf, 1949.

Hale, John P., Harold J. Dudley, Editor, *Trans-Allegheny Pioneers: Historical Sketches of the First White Settlements West of the Alleghenies, 1748 and After.* Radford, Virginia: Roberta Ingles Steele, 1886, Third Edition, 1971.

Harrison, Fairfax, "With Braddock's Army: Mrs. Browne's Diary in Virginia and Maryland." *The Virginia Magazine of History and Biography*, Volume XXXII, Number 4, 1924.

Hough, Walter, S., *Braddock's Road through the Virginia Colony*. Winchester-Frederick County Historical Society. Strasburg, Virginia: Shenandoah Publishing Company, 1970.

Jennings, Francis, *Empire of Fortune: Crowns, Colonies, and Tribes in the Seven Years' War in America*. New York, New York: W. W. Norton and Company, 1988.

Kegley, F. B., *Kegley's Virginia Frontier: The Beginning of the Southwest, The Roanoke of Colonial Days, 1740-1783*. Baltimore, Maryland: Genealogical Publishing Company, 1938, Reprinted 2003.

Kopperman, Paul E., *Braddock at the Monongahela*. Pittsburgh, Pennsylvania: University of Pittsburgh Press, 1977.

Laycock, John Kennedy, "Braddock Road." *The Pennsylvania Magazine of History and Biography*, Volume XXXVII, Number 1, 1914.

Lowdermilk, Will H., *History of Cumberland (Maryland} from the time of the Indian Town, Caiuctucuc, in 1728, up to the present day. Including Major General Braddock's Orderly Book from February 26 to June 17, 1755*. Baltimore, Maryland: Regional Publishing Company, 1971.

Marston, Daniel, *The Seven Years' War*. Chicago, Illinois and London, England: Fitzroy Dearborn, 2001.

McCardell, Lee, *Ill-Starred General: Braddock of the Coldstream Guards*. Pittsburgh, Pennsylvania: University of Pittsburgh Press, 1958.

Nester, William R., *The First Global War: Britain, France, and the fate of North America, 1756–1775*. Westport, Connecticut: Praeger, 2000.

_____, *The French and Indian War and the Conquest of New France*. Norman, Oklahoma: University of Oklahoma Press, 2014.

Nicholas, Franklin T., *The Braddock Expedition*. PhD dissertation, Harvard University, 1946.

O'Meara, Walter, *Guns at the Forks*. Englewood Cliffs, New Jersey: Prentice Hall, 1965.

Peckham, Howard H., *The Colonial Wars, 1689-1762*. Chicago, Illinois: University of Chicago Press, 1964.

Pendleton, William Cecil, *History of Tazewell County and Southwest Virginia: 1748-1920*. Richmond, Virginia: W. C. Hill Printing Company, 1920

Preston, David L., *Braddock's Defeat: The Battle of the Monongahela and the Road to Revolution*. Oxford, England and New York, New York: Oxford University Press, 2015.

Russell, Peter, "Redcoats in the Wilderness: British Officers and Irregular Warfare in Europe and America, 1740 to 1760." *The William and Mary Quarterly*, Volume 35, Number 4, 1978, pages 629–652.

Salley, A. S., *The Independent Company from South Carolina at Great Meadows*. Bulletins of the Historical Commission of South Carolina, Number 11, Columbia, South Carolina: The State Company, 1932.

Sargent, Winthrop, Editor, *The History of an Expedition Against Fort Du Quesne, in 1755*. Philadelphia, Pennsylvania: Lippincott, Grambo, & Company, for the Historical Society of Pennsylvania, 1855.

Schwartz, Seymour, *The French and Indian War 1754-1763*. New York, New York: Simon & Schuster, 1994.

Steele, Ian, *Betrayals*. New York, New York: Oxford University Press, 1990.

Waddell, Louis M. and Bruce D. Bomberger, *The French and Indian War in Pennsylvania: Fortification and Struggle During the War for Empire*. Harrisburg, Pennsylvania: Pennsylvania Historical and Museum Commission, 1996.

Wahll, Andrew J., *Braddock Road Chronicles, 1755*. Bowie, Maryland: Heritage Books, Inc., 1999.

White, Richard, *The Middle Ground*. Cambridge, England: Cambridge University Press, 1991.

First Cherokee War, 1758-1761

Background

The First Cherokee War was known by several different names, the Cherokee calling it the War with those in the Red Coats or the War with the English, and the colonials calling it the Cherokee War, Cherokee Uprising, or Cherokee Rebellion. By whatever name, the war pitted the British colonists against the Cherokee. While it was fought during the French and Indian War, strictly speaking, it was not technically part of that conflict.

In the Tuscarora War, the Cherokee allied themselves with North Carolina against the Tuscarora. In the Yamasee War, the Cherokee at first fought with the Yamasee against South Carolina, later changing sides and joining South Carolina to defeat the Yamasee. Continuing their alliance with the British colonies, the Cherokee joined in the British campaign to seize Fort Duquesne in 1754 and other fights with the Shawnee in Ohio. In 1755, at the request of their Iroquois allies, one band of Cherokee, led by Chief Ostenaco, established a fortified town at the mouth of the Ohio River.

In the 1750s, French traders from Fort Toulouse visited the Overhill Cherokee, on the Hiwassee and Tellico rivers, strengthening their relationships. Chiefs Mankiller of Tellico Plains, Old Caesar of Chatuga, and Raven of Hiwassee were very pro-French, as was the "First Beloved Man" Stalking Turkey and his nephew, Kunagadoga, who succeeded him at his death in 1760. In 1759, Big Mortar and his Creek band reoccupied the old Coosa site, in support of the pro-French Cherokee at Great Tellico and Chatuga.

At the start of the French and Indian War, the British sought an alliance with the Cherokee to oppose the French and their Indian allies. Fearing the French were planning to establish forts in the Cherokee territory, the British quickly built Fort Prince George near Keowee near the Lower Towns in South Carolina and Fort Loudoun, near Chota at the mouth of the Tellico River in 1756. The Cherokee then provided 700 warriors to fight in western Virginia. Another large group was to fight the French at Fort Toulouse.

In all, almost 1,000 Cherokee warriors waged war with their British allies. By 1758, the French effectively had been defeated in America. British relations with their Cherokee allies, however, soured. Upset at their meager compensation for aiding the British, bands of Cherokee attacked scattered settlements in the western Virginia backcountry. The settlers retaliated and hostilities quickly spread into the Carolinas, erupting into all out open warfare.

Campaigns

In 1758, the First Cherokee War began in the Virginia backcountry. When traveling home after having helped Forbes take Fort Duquesne, a Cherokee party commandeered some horses they believed were rightly theirs, having been promised material aid for their participation, but not understanding when or where that aid would be provided. Virginia militia attacked Chief Moytoy of Citico, believing the Cherokee guilty of stealing the horses, killing and scalping more than thirty of them. Later, the Virginians claimed the scalps as those of Shawnees and collected bounties for their trophies. In retaliation, Moytoy led attacks against settlements along the Catawba and Yadkin rivers. Some chiefs argued against war, while others continued to lead attacks against the backcountry settlements. In 1759, the war hawks won the argument and the Cherokee formally declared war against the British.

South Carolina Governor William Henry Lyttelton ordered traders to stop providing gunpowder and lead to the Cherokee. He also raised an army of 1,100 men to attack the Lower Towns. When the Cherokee sent a delegation of chiefs to talk, the chiefs were taken hostage and sent to Fort Prince George. While Lyttelton thought holding the hostages would halt the Cherokee raids, his action had the opposite effect, as the Cherokee continued their attacks against the settlements. In February 1760, in an attempt to free the hostages, a large Cherokee force attacked Fort Prince George. The attacks were successfully repulsed, the Cherokee breaking off their siege after all 29 hostages were killed. Simultaneous Cherokee assaults against Fort Ninety Six also were unsuccessful. Other smaller outposts across the South Carolina frontier were overrun and destroyed by Cherokee war parties.

In response to the attacks, a group of about 150 settlers from the Long Cane Creek settlement, in South Carolina, loaded their wagons and headed to the safety of Augusta. On February 1, 1760, one hundred Cherokee warriors ambushed the refugees. The wagons, becoming mired in the boggy soil, hindered their escape, resulting in dozens killed, fourteen captured, and nine children scalped, but alive. A mass grave at the scene holds the remains of 23 victims.

The Cherokee then turned their attention to the North Carolina backcountry, attacking Fort Dobbs, on February 27, 1760. While General Hugh Waddell successfully repelled the onslaught, smaller, scattered settlements across the Carolina backcountry continued to fall prey to Cherokee raids. Field Marshall Jeffrey Amherst, the British military commander in North America, answered South Carolina's plea for help by dispatching a battalion from the Royal Scots Regiment, the 77th Regiment of Foot (Montgomerie's Highlanders), seven troops of Carolina rangers, 100 local militia, and about four dozen Catawba, in all more than 1,300 men, under the command of Lieutenant Colonel Archibald Montgomerie, to subdue the Cherokee. Montgomerie managed to destroy several Cherokee Lower Towns, including Keowee, Estatoe, and Sugar Town, but was severely beaten at Echoee Pass, forcing his retreat to Fort Prince George, before returning to Charleston and sailing to New York with his troops.

In 1761, after the Cherokee laid siege to Fort Loudon, situated on the high ground along the Little Tennessee River, about five miles below the Cherokee capital town of Chota, Captain Demeré surrendered his command. The fort was woefully low on food and other supplies due to Montgomerie's failure to relieve them the previous year. The Cherokee allowed the men to keep their arms and sufficient ammunition to affect their return to South Carolina, but insisted they leave the remaining arms and ammunition behind. The Cherokee entered the fort only to find the ammunition buried and the small arms and cannon thrown in the river. The incensed Cherokee decided to seek revenge, attacking the retreating column the following day and capturing 120 of them.

The Cherokee remained optimistic, despite their losses from smallpox, lack of ammunition, and a disappointing corn harvest. Amherst, wanting "to chastise the Cherokees [and] reduce them to the absolute necessity of suing for pardon," chose Major James Grant for the task. Grant led an army comprised of the 1st (Royal Scots), 17th (Royal Leicestershire), and 22nd (Cheshire) Regiments; a large contingent of militia commanded by Colonel Thomas Middleton; and, a party of Catawba, Chickasaw, Mohawk, and Stockbridge warriors, amounting to 2,800 in all. Tended by dozens of slaves, 600 laden packhorses and a herd of cattle supported the army.

On June 10, 1761, the Cherokee ambushed Grant's column at Echoee, but withdrew after a few hours of skirmishing as their ammunition dwindled. Grant then utterly destroyed fifteen Middle Towns, burning their crops, and leaving thousands of the Cherokee to starve. Amherst's goal was reached, when the Cherokee sued for peace that August.

Aftermath

The Cherokee made peace with Virginia by signing the Treaty of Long Island on the Holston in July 1761 and with South Carolina by signing the Treaty of Charleston five months later, in December. The Cherokee never returned to their destroyed towns, some moving further west to the Little Tennessee River to live among the Overhill Cherokee.

Henry Timberlake led a delegation of chiefs to London for an audience with King George III. Many South Carolinians resented the warm reception the chiefs received, considering it an indication of royal favor at the expense of the colonists; another insult, the Proclamation of 1763, forbidding settlement west of the mountains, followed. Such resentments of royal rule gradually grew to foment revolution.

The Treaty of Hard Labour, signed October 14, 1768, required the Cherokee to renounce all their claims to the territory west of the Allegheny Mountains and south and east of the Ohio River, encompassing most of what is now the state of West Virginia, southwestern Pennsylvania, eastern Kentucky, and southwestern Virginia.

Places of Interest

Fort Loudon State Historical Park
338 Fort Loudon Road
Vonore, Tennessee 37885

(423) 884-6217

Fort Loudoun State Historic Park is 1,200-acres and one of
the earliest British fortifications on the western frontier. Built
in 1756, the fort was reconstructed during the Great
Depression and was designated a National Historic Landmark
in 1965. In addition to living history and monthly interpretive programs, the park and the Fort
Loudoun Association host several popular seasonal events such as, the 18th Century Trade Faire in
October and Christmas at Fort Loudoun.

Fort Dobbs State Historic Site
438 Fort Dobbs Road
Statesville, North Carolina 28625

(704) 873-5882

http://www.fortdobbs.org/

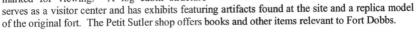

The original site of Fort Dobbs and its well are
marked for viewing.   A log cabin structure
serves as a visitor center and has exhibits featuring artifacts found at the site and a replica model
of the original fort. The Petit Sutler shop offers books and other items relevant to Fort Dobbs.

Ninety Six National Historic Site
1103 Highway 248
Ninety Six, South Carolina 29666

(864) 543-4068

https://www.nps.gov/nisi/index.htm

The park is unique, both historically and archeologically.
Named by Charleston traders after the number of miles to the
Cherokee village of Keowee, in the upper South Carolina foothills, the town was situated
strategically at the intersection of twelve roads and paths. Cherokee warriors attacked the fort,
constructed to defend the nearby settlers, on more than one occasion.

Long Cane Massacre Monument
Off West Charleston Road, west of
Troy, South Carolina

On the National Register, the Long Cane Massacre Site is
significant to the history of exploration and settlement in South
Carolina, for its association with the First Cherokee War, and
the Calhoun settlement of Long Cane. The property includes
the gravestone which marks the place where twenty-three of
the settlers were killed in a bloody massacre by the Cherokee
on February 1, 1760. Among those killed was Catherine
Calhoun, matriarch of the Calhoun family, who figured
prominently in the settlement of upcountry South Carolina.

Keowee Town Historical Marker
on Nimmons Bridge Road, at
Keowee Town Landing Road, near
Salem, South Carolina

Keowee Town, which means "mulberry grove place," was the largest and most important of the
Cherokee "Lower Towns" in what is now S.C. It was 1 mi. E on the Keowee River, and was
already considered a significant Cherokee town when the British took a census of the Lower
Towns in 1721. Keowee was also a major town on the main trading path between the British and
the Cherokees.

Most Cherokees left Keowee by 1752 amid conflict with the Creeks but asked the British to build
Fort Prince George across the river in 1753-54. Keowee was abandoned in 1760, during the
Cherokee War, but later resettled. In 1776, during the Revolution, Maj. Andrew Williamson's
S.C. militia burned it and other Lower Towns. The town and fort sites were covered by Lake
Keowee in 1971.

Fort Prince George Historical Marker
Keowee Baptist Church Road,
at the entrance to Mile Creek Park, near
Six Mile, South Carolina

Fort Prince George, covered by Lake Keowee since 1968,
was built nearby in 1753, near the unofficial boundary
between Cherokee lands and white settlements. Across the
Keowee River from the Cherokee Lower Town of Keowee,
it was built to protect whites and Cherokees from the
Creeks or other enemies and had been promised to the Cherokee "headmen" by Gov. James Glen
since 1748.

The fort, a palisaded earthwork with bastions on the corners, was manned by about 25 men.
Conflict between its officers and Cherokees helped bring on the Cherokee War of 1760-61. Fort
Prince George was abandoned in 1768 as relations between Great Britain and the colonies
worsened. Archaeologists excavated the fort site in 1966-68 before Duke Power Company
flooded the valley in 1968.

Cherokee Villages Historical Marker
State Route 360 and U. S. 411
Vonore, Tennessee

Along the south side of the Little Tennessee River for about
thirteen miles were ten villages of the Overhill Cherokees.
They were Mialaque, Tuskegee, Tomotley, Toquo,
Tennessee, Chota, Citico, Halfway Town, Chilhowee, and
Talassee. White encroachments began upon this site in the
1790's.

Long Island of the Holston Historical Marker
on Netherland Inn Road, near the intersection of
Ridgefields Road, in Kingsport, Tennessee

Its west end seen here in the river, the Long Island of the
Holston is four miles long. Tennessee's first National
Historic Landmark, it was the site of numerous
Revolutionary War events. It served as a sacred Cherokee
Indian island until ceded to Whites in 1806, long after the
Cherokee had ceded all land around it. The end of the first
wagon road to the Southwest, it was the point of origin for the state's earliest western expansion
and the starting point for Boone's Wilderness Road into Kentucky. In 1777, the first July 4
celebration west of the mountains was held on this island near the trading post home of Col.
Joseph Martin.

Battle of Round Mountain Historical Marker
West Mills Street, in
Columbus, in
Polk County, North Carolina

In Commemoration of the 1776 Battle of Round Mountain
(located Northwest of here) in which Captain Thomas
Howard with his brave followers and faithful Indian guide,
Skyuka, won the battle against the Cherokee.

Tamassee Town Historical Marker
Tamassee Knob Road and Cheohee Valley Road
near Tamassee, in
Oconee County, South Carolina

Near this site once stood the Cherokee "lower town" of
Tamassee. On August 12, 1776, a Revolutionary War battle
known as the "Ring Fight" was fought here between the
Cherokee and the South Carolina Militia under Captain Andrew
Pickens. The Cherokee were defeated and many years later
Gen. Pickens built his house here when he retired. The
Cherokee became his neighbors and friends.

Further Reading

Adair, James, *History of the American Indian*. Nashville, Tennessee: Blue and Gray Press, 1971.

Ansel, William H., Jr., *Frontier Forts Along the Potomac and its Tributaries*. Parsons, West Virginia: McClain Publishing Company, 1984.

Bass, Robert D., *Ninety-Six: The Struggle for the South Carolina Backcountry*. Lexington, South Carolina: The Sandlapper Store, Inc., 1978.

Brown, John P., *Old Frontiers: The Story of the Cherokee Indians from Earliest Times to the Date of Their Removal to the West, 1838*. Kingsport, Tennessee: Southern Publishers, Inc., 1938.

Evans, E. Raymond, "Notable Persons in Cherokee History: Ostenaco." *Journal of Cherokee Studies*, Volume 1, Number 1, Summer 1976, pages 41–54.

French, Christopher, "Journal of an Expedition to South Carolina." *Journal of Cherokee Studies*, Volume 3, Number 2, Summer 1977, pages 275–302.

Hamer, Philip M., *Tennessee: A History, 1673–1932*. New York, New York: American History Association, 1933.

Hatley, Thomas, *The Dividing Paths: Cherokees and South Carolinians through the Era of Revolution*. New York, New York: Oxford University Press, 1993.

Haywood, W. H., *The Civil and Political History of the State of Tennessee from its Earliest Settlement up to the Year 1796*. Nashville, Tennessee: Methodist Episcopal Publishing House, 1891.

Heard, J. Norman, *Handbook of the American Frontier, The Southeastern Woodlands: Four Centuries of Indian-White Relationships*. Metuchen, New Jersey: Scarecrow Press, 2nd Edition, 1993.

Henderson, Archibald. *The Conquest of the Old Southwest: The Romantic Story of the Early Pioneers into Virginia, the Carolinas, Tennessee and Kentucky 1740 to 1790*. Spartanburg, South Carolina: The Reprint Company, 1920, Reprinted 2010.

Kelly, James C., "Notable Persons in Cherokee History: Attakullakulla." *Journal of Cherokee Studies*, Volume 3, Number 1, Winter 1978, pages 2–34.

_____, "Oconostota." *Journal of Cherokee Studies*, Volume 3, Number 4, Fall 1978, pages 221–238.

King, Duane H., *The Cherokee Indian Nation: A Troubled History*. Knoxville, Tennessee: University of Tennessee Press, 1979.

_____, Editor, *The Memoirs of Lt. Henry Timberlake: The Story of a Soldier, Adventurer, and Emissary to the Cherokees, 1756-1765*. Cherokee, North Carolina: Museum of the Cherokee Indian Press, Distributed by University of North Carolina Press, 2007.

Koontz, Louis K., *The Virginia Frontier, 1754-1763*. Bowie, Maryland: Heritage Books, 1925, Reprinted 2006.

Maass, John R., *The French and Indian War in North Carolina: The Spreading Flames of War*. Charleston, South Carolina: The History Press, 2013.

Mooney, James, *Myths of the Cherokee and Sacred Formulas of the Cherokee*. Nashville, Tennessee: Charles and Randy Elder-Booksellers, 1982.

Oliphant, John, *Peace and War on the Anglo-Cherokee Frontier, 1756–63*. Baton Rouge, Louisiana: Louisiana State University Press, 2001.

Ramsey, Robert W., *Carolina Cradle: Settlement of the Northwest Carolina Frontier, 1747-1762*. Chapel Hill, North Carolina: University of North Carolina Press, 1964.

Tortora, Daniel J., *Carolina in Crisis: Cherokees, Colonists, and Slaves in the American Southeast, 1756–1763*. Chapel Hill, North Carolina: University of North Carolina Press, 2015.

Pontiac's War, 1763

Background

Strictly speaking, Pontiac's War, sometimes called Pontiac's Conspiracy or Pontiac's Rebellion, was not a southern Indian war. Chief Pontiac led a confederation of tribes from the Illinois and Ohio Country against the British forts and settlements west of the Allegheny Mountains, with most of the conflict taking place in western New York and Pennsylvania, as well as the Old Northwest Territory. However, one of the often-overlooked campaigns of Pontiac's War took place on the Virginia frontier.

Starting circa 1760, with the French and Indian War substantially over and Virginians believing that their border with the Indians would be moved westward to the Ohio River, pioneers quickly began to establish new settlements along the Greenbrier River Valley. By 1763, numerous cabins stood among fields of wheat and corn. After a couple of tranquil years, the settlers soon developed a false sense of security, considering the Shawnee hunting parties they saw as merely harmless nuisances. The Muddy Creek Settlement was situated on the north side of the Greenbrier River, west of Muddy Creek Mountain. About twenty miles away, the Clendenin Settlement was situated on the Big Levels, near modern Lewisburg, West Virginia. Together, the two settlements counted more than one hundred souls.

While Pontiac directed his allies to attack Detroit and Fort Pitt, as well as many other forts in the Old Northwest, Shawnee Chief Cornstalk planned his attack on the Virginia frontier.

Campaigns

Early in July 1763, Cornstalk led about sixty Shawnee warriors from their village on the Scioto River, in the Ohio Country, about sixty miles from the Virginia border. They crossed the Ohio River by canoe and secreted their canoes at the mouth of the Kanawha River, before traveling overland about 160 miles to Muddy Creek. On July 14, 1763, the Shawnee divided into small groups, each approaching a scattered homestead feigning peaceful intentions, before attacking the unsuspecting settlers, tomahawking and scalping everyone, except a few women and children who they kept as captives. No one escaped death or capture. The Shawnee then feasted on captured livestock and rested, before continuing their journey.

Leaving a few warriors behind to guard their captives, they proceeded the next day up the Greenbrier River to the Big Levels. When they arrived, they found all the settlers assembled at the homestead of Archibald Clendenin, who had just returned from a hunt with three fat elk. The Shawnee again approached feigning peace. After being entertained and fed, the Shawnee attacked the settlers, killing and scalping every man, except Conrad Yolkum -- who was some distance away at the time -- and capturing the women and children. The Shawnee sent their captives back to Muddy Creek under guard, before continuing their raid.

Yolkum heard the commotion, returned to his cabin, but stopped short upon seeing the Shawnee in the midst of their slaughter. He quickly fled east to the settlements on Jackson River and raised the alarm. At first, the settlers did not believe him; but, changed their minds when they saw the approach of the Shawnee for themselves and fled before any attack could be mounted. The Shawnee continued east, reaching the Timber Ridge Presbyterian Church, on Kerr's Creek, in modern Rockbridge County, on Sunday, July 17, 1763. The Shawnee attacked, killing most of the men and many of the women and children who were assembled there, and capturing more women and children. Cornstalk had his men round up their captives and proceed back across the Ohio River to their villages on the Scioto River. The long trek back was difficult for the prisoners, the Shawnee killing several along the way, even impaling an infant on a spear embedded in the ground along the trail, as a warning to deter any pursuers.

Other small Shawnee war parties also attacked the scattered settlements on the Virginia frontier, killing, scalping, pillaging, burning, and taking prisoners. That summer Cornstalk's village swelled with new captives, many of whom were returned later.

Aftermath

The Cornstalk raid desolated and depopulated the Greenbrier settlements, with nearly every man killed and not a drop of Shawnee blood spilled. The Greenbrier River Valley was not resettled for another six or seven years. From this and other raids, Virginian frontiersmen hated the Shawnee and looked forward to the opportunity to seek revenge for the atrocities. Their opportunity came a decade later, in 1774, when many who helped defeat Cornstalk and his hated Shawnee at the Battle of Point Pleasant, were simply exacting justice. When Cornstalk and his son were killed in 1777 at Fort Randolph, most settlers believed the infant-killing old chief deserved his ignominious death.

Points of Interest

Pontiac's War/Welsh Cemetery Historical Marker
Houfnaggle Road,
1.8 miles south of Lewisburg, in
Greenbrier County, West Virginia

Massacre of white families of Muddy Creek and of the
Clendenins near here by a band of Shawnee Indians led by
Chief Cornstalk, in 1763, completed the destruction of the
early settlements in the Greenbrier Valley.

On reverse side: In this cemetery are buried pioneer settlers,
including Ann (McSwain) Clendenin Rogers, the heroine of
the Clendenin massacre by Shawnee Indians, July 13, 1763, and the siege of Fort Donnally in
1778, by over 200 Indians.

Timber Ridge Church Historical Marker
Timber Ridge Road and
North Lee Highway
South River, Virginia

This Presbyterian Church was built in 1756, nineteen years
after the first settlement in Rockbridge County.

Fort Breckenridge Historical Marker
near Falling Spring, Virginia, in
Alleghany County, on U. S. Route 220
2.7 miles south of County Route 606

Three miles west at the mouth of Falling Spring Creek was a
post garrisoned by militia under Capt. Robert Breckenridge.
Washington inspected it in 1756. It survived an attack by
Shawnees under Cornstalk during Pontiac's war in 1763.

Last Indian Clash Historical Marker
near Churchville, Virginia
in Augusta County, on
Churchville Road, just west of
Eagle Rock Lane County Route 721

Near this spot in 1764, Shawnee Indians killed John Tremble (Trimble) in the last such event in Augusta County. During the preceding decade, a series of conflicts between Native Americans and European settlers occurred along the western frontier of the colonies. They included the French and Indian War (1754–1763), Cherokee War (1759–1761), and Pontiac's War (1763–1764). Although Chief Pontiac conducted most of his warfare between Detroit and Pittsburgh, the effects of that conflict rippled up and down the frontier.

Further Reading

Auth, Stephen F., *The Ten Years' War: Indian-White Relations in Pennsylvania, 1755–1765*. New York, New York: Garland, 1989.

Barr, Daniel, Editor, *The Boundaries Between Us: Natives and Newcomers along the Frontiers of the Old Northwest Territory, 1750–1850*. Kent, Ohio: Kent State University Press, 2006.

Crytzer, Brady and Alan Gutchess, *Fort Pitt: A Frontier History*. Charleston, South Carolina: History Press, 2012.

Eckert, Allan W., *The Conquerors: A Narrative*. Ashland, Kentucky: Jesse Stuart Foundation, 2002.

Farmer, Silas. (1884) (Jul 1969) *The History of Detroit and Michigan, or, The Metropolis Illustrated: a Chronological Cyclopaedia of the Past and Present: Including a Full Record of Territorial Days in Michigan, and the Annuals of Wayne County*. Charleston, South Carolina: BiblioLife/BiblioBazaar, 2002.

McConnell, Michael N., *Army and Empire: British Soldiers on the American Frontier, 1758–1775*. Lincoln, Nebraska: University of Nebraska Press, 2004.

Ward, Matthew C., *Breaking the Backcountry: The Seven Years' War in Virginia and Pennsylvania, 1754–1765*. Pittsburgh, Pennsylvania: University of Pittsburgh Press, 2003.

Lord Dunmore's War, 1774

Background

After the First Cherokee War, colonists began to explore and settle the territory recently ceded by the Cherokee, south and east of the Ohio River, in what is now southwestern Pennsylvania, West Virginia, southwestern Virginia, and eastern Kentucky. The Iroquois, as well as other tribes, claimed the territory and regularly hunted there. In 1768, the British acquired the territory from the Iroquois by the Treaty of Fort Stanwix. However, the Shawnee and their allied tribes who hunted there rejected the treaty, vowing to protect their hunting grounds. As the tide of settlement grew, the prospects for open warfare grew substantially.

In 1773, a band of Cherokee, Delaware, and Shawnee warriors attacked a small group of men and boys from the recently established settlement in Kentucky led by Daniel Boone. They captured James Boone, Daniel's 16-year-old son and another teenaged boy. The boys' capture, gruesome torture, and murder frightened the settlers, who abandoned their fledgling settlement. The Shawnee and the other tribes opposed to the treaty continued their attacks on the scattered frontier settlements, brutally torturing and killing the men and capturing and enslaving the women and children.

As the attacks continued, stories from the survivors shocked the entire frontier and many fled to Zanesburg, now Wheeling, West Virginia, seeking safety. In 1774, Captain Michael Cresap, who owned a trading post at Redstone Old Fort, now Brownsville, Pennsylvania, led a group of men to settle his land claims at the mouth of Middle Island Creek, now Sistersville, West Virginia. Ebenezer Zane led another party of men to settle his land at the mouth of Sandy Creek, now Ravenswood, West Virginia. George Rogers Clark, assembling a larger group at the mouth of the Little Kanawha River, intended to settle on land in Kentucky.

On April 26th, Cresap's large party of men declared war on the offending Indians. The next day, the group chased some Indians down the river to Pipe Creek, where they attacked them, killing and wounding a few. To avoid retaliation, Clark's and Cresap's parties removed to Redstone Old Fort. Soon thereafter, Daniel Greathouse, at the head of some 30 frontiersmen, murdered several relatives of the Mingo Chief Logan at John Baker's cabin on Yellow Creek, about 30 miles above Zanesburg. Many settlers, fearing even more attacks, sought safety behind fortifications or by leaving the frontier. In revenge for the Yellow Creek Massacre, Chief Logan started a series of attacks against the settlers. Other small parties of Shawnee and Mingo joined Logan in seeking revenge.

John Murray, the 4th Earl of Dunmore and Governor of Virginia, learning that open warfare had broken out, asked the House of Burgesses to declare war against the raiding Indians. The burgesses agreed and authorized the governor to raise an army to prosecute the war.

Campaigns

In July 1774, Dunmore ordered Colonel Andrew Lewis, of Botetourt County, to raise 1,100 men from Augusta, Botetourt, and Fincastle counties and immediately proceed to the Ohio River and wait for him there. Dunmore raised the northern wing of his army of about 1,700 volunteers from Berkeley, Dunmore (now Shenandoah), Frederick, and Hampshire counties, with which he intended to link up with Lewis, then proceed to defeating the Ohio Indians.

On October 6th, Lewis and his men reached the mouth of the Great Kanawha River, where they established Camp Pleasant, on a peninsula of land bounded on the west by the Ohio River, on the south by the Kanawha River, and on the east by Crooked Creek. On the night of October 9th, a party of Shawnee crossed the Ohio River, to surprise and attack the militia at sunrise the next morning. The Shawnee posted warriors on the north bank of the Ohio River to kill any soldiers attempting escape.

Chief Cornstalk led his warriors in the surprise attack. The fighting was fierce, close, and frequently hand-to-hand, lasting most of the day. By midafternoon, the Shawnee grew increasingly dispirited and began carrying off their dead and wounded, sometimes turning around and shooting to discourage any pursuit. Within an hour of nightfall, the Shawnee were gone. Lewis lost about 46 killed and 80 wounded, while Cornstalk lost about 40 warriors.

After burying their dead and leaving behind Captain Slaughter, with the Culpeper militia, to strengthen the defenses and tend to the wounded, Lewis led his men across the Ohio River to meet Dunmore. The two advanced into Ohio toward Cornstalk's town at Pickaway Plains, on the Scioto River. Dunmore established Camp Charlotte nearby and began peace negotiations with Cornstalk, the infamous Simon Girty acting as principal interpreter. A fragile peace was reached with the signing of the Treaty of Camp Charlotte on October 19, 1774. Chief Logan and his Mingo, who did not attend the negotiations, agreed to stop fighting but did not accept the terms of the treaty. In retaliation for continued raids by Chief Logan, Major William Crawford and 240 militia attacked Salt Lick Town, near today's Steubenville, Ohio, destroying two Mingo villages.

Aftermath

The victory at Point Pleasant, the submission of the Shawnee at Camp Charlotte, and Crawford's destruction of the Mingo villages, virtually closed the war. Governor Dunmore began his return, proceeding by way of the Youghiogheny River to Fort Cumberland, and then to the Virginia capital. The peace, however, did not last long. On March 24, 1775, a band of Shawnee crossed the Ohio River and attacked Boonesborough in Kentucky on the Wilderness Road. In May 1776, as the Revolutionary War began in earnest, the Shawnee joined renegade Cherokee Chief Dragging Canoe in declaring war on the Virginia colonists.

Hinderacker and Mancall summarized the significance of Dunmore's War as follows:

> *If Dunmore's War serves as the epilogue to one story, it is the prologue to another: the story of American independence. The events of the preceding decade amounted to nothing short of a revolution in backcountry affairs, and the military campaign led by Lord Dunmore against the Ohio Indians constituted the opening chapter of a new epoch in American affairs. From the perspective of the backcountry, the shots fired on the Ohio late in 1774, not those at Concord six months later, constituted the beginning of the American Revolution. Though the Ohio campaign was led by a royal governor, its muscle was provided by two thousand men who had waited a decade in mounting frustration and anger while the king neglected their needs. This was their declaration of independence.*

Places of Interest

Tu-Endie-Wei State Park
1 Main Street
Point Pleasant, West Virginia 25550

(304) 675-0869

The park, located at the confluence of the Ohio and Kanawha rivers in the heart of the town of Point Pleasant, is the home of the Point Pleasant Battle Monument, erected in 1909. The Colonel Charles Lewis Chapter, National Society Daughters of the American Revolution maintain the Mansion House Museum.

Camp Charlotte Historical Marker
On Ohio Route 56, one half mile north
of Ohio Route 159, in Pickaway County

Near this spot the famous treaty was made between Lord Dunmore, Governor of Virginia and Chief Cornstalk of the Shawnees and Allied Tribes in October 1774. This camp was named "Charlotte" after the Queen of England. Erected by Pickaway Plains Chapter, Daughters of the American Revolution, 1774-1928.

Indian-Settler Conflicts Historical Marker
on Crab Orchard Road, east of
B. F. Buchanan Highway, near
Frog Level, Virginia

During Dunmore's War (1774) and the Revolutionary War (1775–1783) conflicts between Indians and colonists often intensified as European powers encouraged Indians from the Ohio region to attack frontier settlers. Tensions also sometimes increased when settlers moved into lands that were once Indian territory. Nearby to the south, an early conflict occurred in the upper Clinch River Valley, when Indians attacked and killed John Henry, his wife and their children on 8 Sept. 1774. Additional conflicts took place during this period, including a March 1782 Indian attack on the house of James Maxwell that killed two of his daughters.

Simon Girty Memorial Stone and Plaque
1173 Front Road South
Ontario Route 20, on the Detroit Riverfront,
Malden Townshi
Essex County, Ontario, Canada

Simon Girty (1741-181), born near Harrisburg, Pennsylvania, was captured and adopted by the Seneca in 1756. By 1764, Girty was a gifted interpreter, fluent in eleven native tongues. In 1774, he was a scout in Lord Dunmore's War. During the Revolution, he operated from Fort Pitt. In 1778, disgusted by an atrocity committed by the rebels, he went to Detroit to join the British cause. From there, he led numerous raids against the American settlements in Kentucky, earning a bounty of $800 for his capture or death. After the Second Cherokee War, Girty settled in Canada on land granted to him by the crown for his loyal service.

Michael Cresap House
19015 Opessa Street SE
Oldtown, Maryland

The Michael Cresap House is significant for its age, as well as its association with Michael Cresap (1742-1775), the famous Ohio frontiersman. The town of Oldtown had been established by Cresap's father, Thomas, who built a fortified trading post and home. Until the establishment of Cumberland, Oldtown was the only settlement in Maryland west of the Conococheague Creek in Washington County.

Mathew Arbuckle Historical Marker
U. S. Route 219, at Lee Street, in
Lewisburg, West Virginia

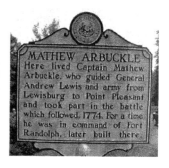

Here lived Captain Mathew Arbuckle, who guided General Andrew Lewis and army from Lewisburg to Point Pleasant and took part in battle which followed, 1774. For a time, he was in command of Fort Randolph, later built there.

Colonial Army Rendezvous Historical Marker
Jefferson Street and Randolph Street, in
Lewisburg, West Virginia

Here at Fort Union, built in 1770, a frontier army of
1100 men assembled in 1774 under command of
Gen. Andrew Lewis. On Sept. 12, the army began a
march through 160 miles of trackless wilderness to
the mouth of the Kanawha River and defeated
Cornstalk, gallant Shawnee Chief, and his warriors
in the bloody Battle of Point Pleasant Oct. 10, 1774. The cabin home of Matthew Arbuckle,
famous pioneer scout who led the army, stood nearby.

Andrew H. Lewis Grave
East Hill Cemetery
114 North Broad Street
Salem, Virginia

Andrew H. Lewis (1716-1781) was a Virginia
pioneer and militia officer. He served in George
Washington's Virginia Regiment. He was captured
and held prisoner by the French in the French and
Indian War. As a colonel, he led the Virginia
militia who fought and defeated Shawnee Chief
Cornstalk and his warriors at the Battle of Point
Pleasant.

Logan Massacre Historical Marker
State Route 2 north of Dry Run Road, near
Newell, in Hancock County, West Virginia

In April 1774, one of the events which led up to
Dunmore's War was the killing at this point of the
family of Chief Logan, eloquent leader of the Mingo
Indians, April, 1774, opposite their village at the
mouth of Yellow Creek in Ohio.

Further Reading

Dowd, Gregory Evans, *A Spirited Resistance: The North American Indian Struggle for Unity, 1745–1815*. Baltimore, Maryland: Johns Hopkins University Press, 1992.

Downes, Randolph C., *Council Fires on the Upper Ohio: A Narrative of Indian Affairs in the Upper Ohio Valley until 1795*. Pittsburgh, Pennsylvania: University of Pittsburgh Press, 1940, reprinted 1989.

Hinderaker, Eric and Peter C. Mancall, *At the Edge of Empire: The Backcountry in British North America*. Baltimore, Maryland: Johns Hopkins University Press, 2003.

Hintzen, William, *The Border Wars of the Upper Ohio Valley (1769–1794)*. Manchester, Connecticut: Precision Shooting, Inc., 2001.

Kegley, Mary B., *Soldiers of Fincastle County, Virginia, 1774*. Dublin, Virginia: Kegley Books, 1974.

Lewis, Virgil A., *History of the Battle of Point Pleasant*. Charleston, West Virginia, The Tribune Publishing Company, 1909, Reprinted, Bowie, Maryland: Heritage Books, Inc., 2000.)

Rice, Otis K., *The Allegheny Frontier: West Virginia Beginnings, 1730-1830*. Lexington, Kentucky: University Press of Kentucky, 1970.

Skidmore, Warren with Donna Kamisky, *Lord Dunmore's Little War of 1774: His Captains and their Men Who Opened up Kentucky & the West to American Settlement*. Bowie, Maryland: Heritage Books, Inc., 2002.

Thwaites, Reuben Gold and Louise Phelps Kellogg, *Documentary History of Dunmore's War 1774*. Madison, Wisconsin: State Historical Society of Wisconsin, 1905, Reprinted Baltimore, Maryland: The Clearfield Company, 2002.

Revolutionary War, 1775-1783

Background

Because most of the American Revolution took place in the eastern portions of the thirteen colonies, with little or no involvement with the Indians, those aspects of the war are beyond the scope of this guide. However, the area that would become the Northwest Territory, as well as western Pennsylvania, western Virginia, West Virginia, Kentucky, Tennessee, and Missouri experienced significant fighting between native tribes, allied with the British, and American settlers on the long frontier. Moreover, participants in these engagements included men from the southern colonies.

Many colonists resented the King's Proclamation of 1763, banning any settlement west of a line along the crest of the Allegheny mountains. Some already had settled west of the line and many others wanted to leave the older settlements east of the mountains and make their homes in the new territory. In 1768, the Treaty of Fort Stanwix and the Treaty of Hard Labour officially opened the land south of the Ohio River for new settlement, easing tensions between the colonists and the crown. However, no one consulted or included the tribes who actually lived and hunted in the region, the Delaware, Mingo, Shawnee, and Wyandot, in the treaty negotiations. While Lord Dunmore's victory forced the Shawnee to relinquish their claims south of the Ohio River, many Shawnee and Mingo chiefs refused to accept those terms.

In 1775, Mingo Chief Pluggy and Shawnee Chief Blackfish led attacks against the settlers in Kentucky. Patrick Henry, the Governor of Virginia, refused to retaliate, concerned that the militia, unwilling or unable to tell the friendly or neutral tribes from the hostile ones, would only foment more hostility and violence from the natives. As the attacks against the isolated settlements increased across the frontier, many settlers fled to safety back over the mountains to the east.

By 1777, less than 200 settlers were behind the fortified walls of Boonesborough, Harrodsburg, and Logan's Station, the only inhabited settlements remaining in Kentucky. While working for Richard Henderson and Nathaniel Hart of the Transylvania Company, in 1775, Daniel Boone established Boone's Station, later called Boonesborough. Founded by James Harrod in 1774, the town was abandoned during Dunmore's War, but then resettled the following year. Harrodsburg was the first seat of Virginia's Kentucky County. In 1776, Benjamin McKinley Logan constructed Logan's Station, eventually growing into the town of Stanford.

Starting in 1777, from their base in Detroit, the British incited the Ohio tribes to wage war against the Americans, arming war parties to attack the settlements along the frontiers of modern Pennsylvania, West Virginia, Virginia, and Kentucky. The summary execution of Chief Cornstalk, who favored neutrality, at Fort Randolph, in Point Pleasant, in November 1777, further fanned the flames of war.

Campaigns

Virginia defended its western border with three large forts on the Ohio River, Fort Pitt at Pittsburgh, Fort Henry at Wheeling, and Fort Randolph at Point Pleasant, manned by militia. On September 27, 1777, Captain William Foreman at the head of a small company of 45 militia from Fort Henry were ambushed at McMechen Narrows on the Ohio River. They beat off the attack, but not before losing 21 killed, including Captain Foreman.

In 1778, the settlers went on offense. In February, 500 Pennsylvania militia, led by Brigadier General Edward Hand, set out to attack the Mingo towns along the Cuyahoga River, but severe winter weather forced them to turn back. On their return, they attacked and killed several peaceful Delaware, including Chief Captain Pipe's mother, brother, and a few of his children.

In 1779, about 30 militia were stationed at Holiday's Cove Fort, located where downtown Weirton, West Virginia is today. Because the defensive forts were not effective in protecting the frontier, the Americans wanted to build a fort in Ohio, from which they could mount offensive operations. The Treaty of Fort Pitt, negotiated with the Delaware, authorized the erection of Fort Laurens near the Delaware towns on the Tuscarawas River. However, when militia murdered Chief White Eyes, his successor, Captain Pipe, renounced the treaty, moved his people to the Sandusky River, and formed an alliance with the British. Because the Continental Congress had its hands full with the war in the east, it did not support offensive operations against Detroit, forcing the abandonment of Fort Laurens.

Virginia Governor Patrick Henry authorized George Rogers Clark to raise seven companies, of fifty men each, and commissioned Clark a lieutenant colonel. The men were to serve three months after they reached Kentucky. Henry also ordered Clarke to capture Kaskaskia, on the east bank of the Mississippi River and then proceed as he saw fit to silence the other British outposts in present-day Illinois and Indiana. Clark made his way to Redstone Old Fort, where he authorized Joseph Bowman, Leonard Helm, and William Harrod to begin recruiting. Clark also promoted Captain William Bailey Smith to major and instructed him to raise four companies in the Holston River settlements, then rendezvous in Kentucky.

Clark was unable to recruit 350 volunteers, because many Pennsylvanians were unwilling to defend what they considered Virginia territory, while others thought Kentucky was too sparsely settled to warrant the effort and should be abandoned. Moreover, Virginians along the Holston and Clinch rivers were more concerned about the Cherokee to their south than they were about the tribes from north of the Ohio River. On May 12, 1778, Clark set out with about 150 volunteers, formed into three companies commanded by Captains Bowman, Helm, and Harrod. Clark made his way down the Ohio River to the Falls of the Ohio, where he established a camp on Corn Island. When his last recruits arrived from the Holston and Kentucky, Clark formed them into a fourth company of 20 men under Captain John Montgomery, sending the remainder to bolster the defenses of the Kentucky settlements.

On June 24th, Clark and his Illinois Regiment, composed of 170 volunteers, began their audacious expedition to secure the Illinois County. Along the way, they were met by a party of 20 hunters, who agreed to join the expedition. Clark approached the outskirts of the French village of Kaskaskia late on July 4th. At midnight, Clark quickly secured the town and took the adjacent Fort Gates, capturing Philippe-François de Rastel de Rocheblave, the Frenchman hired by the British to command the fort, all without a fight. Most residents willingly signed an oath of allegiance to Virginia and the United States. Believing that a few of his captives were hostile, including Rocheblave, Clark kept them in custody, eventually sending them back to Virginia under guard.

Within weeks Clark had taken Prairie du Rocher, St. Phillippe, Cahokia, and Vincennes, again without firing a shot. Henry Hamilton, Lieutenant Governor of the Province of Quebec and British Superintendent of Indian Affairs at Detroit, led about 30 British soldiers, 145 local Canadian militia, and 60 Ottawa warriors under Chief Egushawa, to retake Fort Sackville at Vincennes. Along his 300-mile journey, Hamilton recruited friendly Indians to join him, his force growing to about 500 by the time he reached Vincennes on December 17th. Such an imposing force left the few Americans holding the fort with no choice but to surrender immediately. Soon after, most of the Indians and the militia returned home, Hamilton staying at Fort Sackville with about 90 soldiers to retake the other Illinois towns in the spring.

On February 6, 1779, Clark led about 170 soldiers, about half of the local militia from Kaskaskia, 180 miles across the Illinois plains to retake Fort Sackville. The going was difficult, as the frequent rains flooded much of the flat land, forcing the men to wade through the cold water, sometimes as deep as their shoulders. Clark and his men reached Vincennes at sunset on February 23rd, immediately securing the town and laying siege to Fort Sackville. After protracted negotiations, Hamilton surrendered the fort on February 25th. Clark paroled the Canadian militia, after they signed oaths of neutrality, and sent Hamilton, seven of his officers, and eighteen other prisoners to Williamsburg. After news of Clark's success reached Virginia, settlers again began to flock into Kentucky, swelling the settlements there. Clark and his men were never paid, but received grants for land across the river from Louisville, the so-called Clark's Grant.

In 1780, the British launched a comprehensive campaign to rid the entire territory west of the Mountains, all the way to the Mississippi, of the Spanish and all colonial resistance. The 5th Duke of Argyll, General John Campbell, was ordered to capture New Orleans, proceed up the Mississippi River to Natchez, and then capture St. Louis. Captain Charles de Langlade was ordered to lead his troops down the Illinois, retake Vincennes, then link up with Campbell for the assault on St. Louis. Captain Henry Bird, from Detroit, was ordered to face George Rogers Clarke and prevent him from interfering with the overall plan.

Bird led his army, composed of 1,000 warriors and 150 men from the 8th (The King's) and 47th (Lancashire) Regiments of Foot, Royal Regiment of Artillery, and militia from Detroit, proceeding down the Miami River to the Ohio. Instead of turning toward Clark, they moved up the Licking River, arriving at the settlement of Ruddle's Station on June 21, 1780. When their cannon blew a large hole in the wooden stockade, the Indians rushed through the breech to loot the station, killing and wounding many, and taking the survivors prisoner. Bird then proceeded a few miles to Martin's Station, capturing the settlers there. In all, about 20 settlers were killed and another 400 or so were taken prisoner.

In the early morning hours of June 27th, a war party attacked a caravan of wagons, carrying 41 settlers from ten families to Harrod's Station, led by Jacobus Westervelt, and camped for the night along Floyd's Fork and Broad Run. Most of the men were killed, several of the wives and children were killed, and the rest were captured. At least three managed to escape. Later, the war party was paid £5 for each scalp that they presented to British authorities.

Bird then declared his mission accomplished and headed his men back to Detroit. In retaliation, Clark led his militia into Ohio, destroying two Shawnee towns on the Mad River.

Meanwhile, General Campbell abandoned his plans to take New Orleans, after the Governor of Spanish Louisiana, Bernardo de Gálvez, captured Mobile in March. Emanuel Hesse led a British force, composed of two dozen fur traders and about 1,000 Indians, Chippewa, Fox, Menominee, Sac, Sioux, and Winnebago, down the Mississippi River to attack Fort Don Carlos at St. Louis. Lieutenant Governor Fernando de Leyba, commanding at St. Louis, guided the fortification and defense of the town. In May, Hesse attacked both St. Louis and the former British post of Cahokia across the river. Both attacks failed and the British forces returned upriver. In retaliation, American militia from Cahokia raided Fort St. Joseph, on the St. Joseph River in Michigan. On their return, laden with their plunder, they were attacked at Petit Fort in northwestern Indiana, by British Lieutenant Dagreaux du Quindre, leading a party of fur traders and Potawatomi.

In 1781, Virginia Governor Thomas Jefferson authorized George Rogers Clark to raise 2,000 volunteers for an attack against the British at Detroit. In April, while Clark recruited at Fort Pitt, Colonel Daniel Brodhead, with 150 regulars, 134 militia, and a few friendly Delaware, with Lewis Wetzel as scout, destroyed the Moravian Mission at Indaochaic and the Delaware capital at Coshocton. Clark left Fort Pitt with only about 400 volunteers in August. Colonel Archibald Lochry, commander of the Westmoreland County militia, raised more than 100 volunteers, and set off to join Clark down the Ohio River. On August 24th, Mohawk Chief Joseph Brant attacked Lochry near the mouth of the Miami River, killing and scalping 37 and capturing 64, before returning up the Miami River, where they divided the prisoners among the tribes. Some of the prisoners were killed, some were sold to the British and transferred to prison in Montreal, some were adopted into the tribes, and a few escaped. After the war, most of the prisoners were released. In all, only about half of Lochry's men ever made it home. The Lochry Massacre dealt a death blow to Clark's plans to attack Detroit.

The British surrender at Yorktown, on October 19, 1781, ended the Revolutionary War in the east, but did not bring peace to the western frontier. In March 1782, Lieutenant Colonel David Williamson, seeking revenge for the continual attacks and murders, led 160 Pennsylvania militia in capturing 96 Christian Delaware at Gnadenhutten, accusing them of aiding the raiders, and killing all of them, men, women, and children.

Colonel William Crawford led 480 volunteers, mostly from Pennsylvania, into Ohio to attack the Indians on the upper Sandusky River. However, the British, with their Indian allies from Detroit, about 440 in all, arrived on the Sandusky River in time to attack Crawford. The fighting lasted most of the day and ended with the Pennsylvanians being routed from the field. Most of the militia made it home, but about 70 were killed. The British captured Crawford and a few of his men, brutally torturing Crawford, before burning him at the stake.

Settlers along the frontier came to call 1782 the Bloody Year, as the deadly Indian attacks increased. In July, the 8th (The King's) Regiment of Foot, out of Niagara, accompanied by Mingo Chief Guyasuta and about 100 of his warriors, attacked Hannastown, Pennsylvania, sacking and burning the town, killing nine, and capturing twelve.

In Kentucky, the situation was worse for the settlers. In March, a band of Wyandot attacked Fort Estill in Richmond County, killing and scalping young Jennie Glass, capturing a slave named

Monk, and killing all the cattle. The raiders decided to break off their attack, after the captured Monk exaggerated the fort's defenses. Captain James Estill led his militia in pursuit, catching up with the Wyandot near Little Mountain. The fierce battle lasted for two hours, before the militia were forced to retreat, after suffering seven killed and six wounded.

On August 15, 1782, Captain William Caldwell, of Butler's Rangers, with about 50 Loyalist militia and 300 native warriors, and Simon Girty as a guide and interpreter, laid siege to Bryan's Station, at present-day Lexington, Kentucky. Two days later, after killing the livestock and destroying the crops, Caldwell lifted the siege and withdrew. The next day, 182 militia from Fayette and Lincoln counties arrived at Bryan's Station, then took off in pursuit of Caldwell. The militia caught up with the raiders at Little Blue Licks, on the Licking River, on the morning of August 19th. In the ensuing battle, Caldwell's men slaughtered his pursuers, killing 72 and capturing 11.

In retaliation, George Rogers Clark led 1,000 of his Virginia militia across the Ohio to the Great Miami River, where they destroyed five unoccupied Shawnee villages in the last military operation of the war. With peace negotiations well underway, the British instructed Caldwell to cease further offensive operations.

Aftermath

In 1783, the Treaty of Paris formally recognized the independence and sovereignty of the thirteen American states and extended their boundaries westward to the Mississippi River. In a separate treaty, Britain ceded its provinces of East and West Florida to Spain. However, the treaties did not clearly define the border between Georgia and Spanish Florida, providing the kindling for future fires. None of the tribes were included, or even considered, during the negotiations, forcing them to at least tacitly accept the new boundary lines, but providing the sparks to light the kindling.

The Americans had defended their settlements, which continued to grow, while the tribes had retreated to the north and west. Both sides were capable of landing devastating blows, but neither side was yet capable of delivering nor had delivered that fatal knockout punch. The tribes lost their valuable hunting grounds south of the Ohio River. Fearing Indian attacks, Americans declined to settle north of the Ohio River, those fertile lands remaining unoccupied for the time being. For much of the northern frontier, matters remained unsettled, but in a state of relative calm. From western Virginia southward, however, the war with the Cherokee continued in earnest.

Places of Interest

George Rogers Clark National Historical Park
401 South 2nd Street
Vincennes, Indiana 47591

(812) 882-1776 x1210

https://www.nps.gov/gero/index.htm

The park features a visitor center, bookstore, museum, as well as the Clark Memorial. The museum has exhibits exploring Fort Sackville, the various cultures involved in the Clark story, and other facets of the conquest of the Northwest Territory. A 30-minute movie, *Long Knives*, tells the story of Clark's campaign and is offered every half hour.

Fort Boonesborough State Park
4375 Boonesboro Road
Richmond, Kentucky 40475

(859) 527-3131

http://parks.ky.gov/parks/recreationparks/fort-boonesborough/

Fort Boonesborough has been reconstructed as a working fort complete with cabins, blockhouses and furnishings. Resident artisans perform craft demonstrations and give modern-day visitors a true sense of what life was like for pioneers in Kentucky. Most of the historic, craft, and educational programs at the park are supported by the Fort Boonesborough Foundation.

Blue Licks Battlefield State Resort Park
10299 Maysville Road
Carlisle, Kentucky 40311

(859) 289-5507

http://parks.ky.gov/parks/resortparks/blue_licks/

The 148-acre park, encompassing much of the original battlefield, has a visitor center, bookstore, and museum. The park also has camp sites, a lodge, restaurant, and hospitality center. In August, the park hosts an annual reenactment of the battle.

Logans's Station
500 Water Street
Stanford, Kentucky 40484

(606) 365-4547

http://www.kentuckytourism.com/logans-station/394446/

Today the battlefield is preserved and a partial reconstruction of the fort sits adjacent to the site. An ice house, built in the early 20th century, is currently being adapted for use as a visitor center. The site and fort are open daily, and visitors can lead their own self-guided exploration.

Fort Harrod Historical Marker
South College Street and West Lexington Street
Harrodsburg, Kentucky

Begun in 1774 by James Harrod and Company, the Fort was crucial to the settlement of Harrodsburg and Kentucky. The present replica was erected in 1927 on Old Fort Hill, also known as Seminary Hill. President Franklin D. Roosevelt visited the Fort in 1934 to dedicate the granite monument commemorating the first permanent settlement west of the Allegheny Mountains.

Chief Cornstalk Grave
Tu-Endie-Wei State Park
1 Main Street
Point Pleasant, West Virginia 25550

(304) 675-0869

http://www.tu-endie-weistatepark.com/

Chief Cornstalk (1720-1777), probably born in western Pennsylvania, migrated into the Ohio Country in face of ever-expanding American settlement. He fought with the French against the British in the French and Indian War. In 1763, allied with Chief Pontiac, he led an expedition against the settlements along the Greenbrier River, in what is now West Virginia. In the early 1770s, Cornstalk became the leader of a confederation of Ohio tribes. Cornstalk led a large party of Shawnee and Mingo warriors to defeat against the Virginians at the Battle of Point Pleasant. During the Revolution, he kept many Shawnee neutral. He was executed at Fort Randolph in 1777.

Fort Henry Historical Marker
on Main Street, south of Tenth Street,
Wheeling, West Virginia

Attacked, 1777, by Wyandot, Mingo, and Shawnee Indians who
were repulsed by garrison under David Shepherd after white
scouting parties had lost heavily. Maj. Samuel McCullough made
famous ride over cliff during attack.

Last battle of the American Revolution fought here, Sept. 11–13,
1782. Ebenezer and Silas Zane led force which defeated British and Indians under British
officers, carrying a British flag. Scene of Betty Zane's heroic act.

Carter's Fort Historical Marker
on U. R. Route 58, 6.2 miles north of
Natural Tunnel Parkway, near
Glenita, Virginia

Near here stood a fort first known as Crissman's Fort, and later as
Carter's or Rye Cove Fort, and by militia officers as Fort Lee. Built
by Isaac Crissman, Sr. in 1774, it was acquired by Thomas Carter
(1731 1803) after Crissman's death at the hands of Indians in 1776.
The fort was rebuilt in 1777 by Col. Joseph Martin and his militia
troops who occupied it until at least 1794. The fort was under the
command of Captain Andrew Lewis, Jr. from 1792 to 1794.

Ruddle's Station Historical Marker
Paris Pike and New Lair Road, in
Cynthiana, Kentucky

Settled by John Hinkston 1775. Abandoned 1776. Rebuilt
by Isaac Ruddle 1779. Destroyed by British and Indians
under Captain Henry Bird 1780. Hinkston later settled
opposite this site.

Broadhead Massacre Historical Marker
1629-1635 Chestnut Street
Coshocton, Ohio

Around the spring nearby, was perpetrated, on April 20, 1781, the massacre of 20 Indians by Col. Daniel Broadhead's army of 300. This slaying was committed following destruction, the same day, of the two villages, Goschachgunk, (Coshocton) and Indaochaic, formerly Lichtenau, the Moravian mission. The first act of this incident was the stealthful slaying, by tomahawk, of a chief who came across the river as a peace emissary, by the Indian fighter, Lewis Wetzel. The night before, 16 warrior captives had been taken south of Coshocton, bound, slain by tomahawk and scalped.

Delaware Nation Council House Historical Marker
Main Street at Second Street
Coshocton, Ohio

Goschachgunk (Blackbear Town), now Coshocton, was the capital city of the Delaware Nation. On this parkway stood their Council House. In this House on March 9, 1777, a Great Council of the Delawares, under the leadership of Chief White Eyes, met and decided to refuse the Hatchet from the British and to remain neutral. This decision was a great aid to the colonists in winning the Revolutionary War. Later, hostilities by the Indians caused Col. Broadhead of Virginia to lead an expedition of 800 men against them, destroying the town and burning the Council House in April, 1781.

Lochry's Defeat Historical Marker
State Route 56, at bridge crossing Laughery Creek
in Dearborn County, Indiana

On Aug. 24, 1781, Col. Archibald Lochry and 107 recruits for Gen. Clark were ambushed at Lochry Creek by Joseph Brant's raiders. One-third were killed, the rest captured. Lochry and the wounded were later murdered.

Fort Estill Historical Marker
Berea Road and Pace Ramsey Road
near Richmond, Kentucky

Established about four miles Southeast of Richmond and
east of this place in 1779-1780, by Col. Samuel and
Captain James Estill. It was noted for land locators,
surveyors, horse hunters, travelers, and scouts. It
commanded the hunting grounds on Silver Creek, Muddy
Creek and Station Camp. Some prominent inhabitants
were James Estill and his slave Monk, Samuel Estill, George Robertson, Joseph and Nicholas
Proctor, William Cradlebaugh, David Gass, Peter Hackett, John and Archibald Woods, David
Lynch, Adam Caperton, John and Thomas Miller, and Green Clay. A little later Col. Estill
established Estill's Station about 2 miles east of the Fort.

Attacked by Wyandottes, March 20, 1781, Mrs. Cathright and James Estill's slave, Monk, were
captured and Jenned Gass, daughter of David Gass, was killed. Monk's exaggeration of the
number of men in the Fort caused the Indians to depart. Captain Estill organized a company of 25
men, followed the Indians, and suffered what is known as Estill's Defeat, in the Battle of Little
Mountain March 22, 1782 in Montgomery Co. Captain Estill and nine of his men were killed.
Both Indians and Whites withdrew, the Indians suffering greater losses. Nicholas Proctor married
Estill's widow. Captain Estill's mother, Monk (freed later by the Estills), and Cradlebaugh were
buried at Estill's Station.

Twitty's, or Little Fort Historical Marker
Berea Road and Pace Ramsey Road
near Richmond, Kentucky

Site of the first fort in Kentucky. Built March 1775 by Daniel
Boone and party. Named for William Twitty killed by Indians and
buried by his slave Sam, near the fort.

Daniel Boone's Trace Historical Marker
Berea Road and Pace Ramsey Road
near Richmond, Kentucky

Two miles east is location of the trail blazed in 1775 by Daniel
Boone, who was then agent for the Transylvania Co. This famous
road was used by thousands of settlers traveling to Kentucky.
Boone's Trace entered Kentucky at Cumberland Gap, crossed the
Cumberland River at Pineville, ran northwest past London, and ended at the fort at
Boonesborough on the Kentucky River.

Bryan's Station Historical Marker
Bryan Station Road
Lexington, Kentucky

Camping place in 1775-76 of the brothers Morgan, James, William
and Joseph Bryan. In 1779 was fortified as a station which in Aug.
1782 repelled a siege of Indians and Canadians under Capt. William
Caldwell and Simon Girty.

Simon Kenton Grave
Oak Dale Cemetery
Urbana, Ohio

The noted frontiersman served as a scout during Lord Dunmore's War
in 1774. By 1775, he moved to Boonesborough, Kentucky where he
worked as a scout for the settlement. During the Revolution, he
participated in a number of battles against the British and Indians. In
1778, he joined George Rogers Clark on a successful expedition into
the Illinois Country. That same year he accompanied Daniel Boone
in an attack on the Shawnee settlement of Chillicothe near Oldtown,
Ohio. In 1779, he served with George Rogers Clark as a scout. He
settled near Maysville, Kentucky in 1794 and served in the militia
under General Anthony Wayne at the Battle of Fallen Timbers. In 1798, he moved to Ohio,
became a Brigadier General in the Ohio Militia in 1805, and participated in the Battle of the
Thames, Canada, during the War of 1812.

Ebenezer Zane Grave
Walnut Grove Cemetery
Martins Ferry, Ohio

Colonel Ebenezer Zane (1747-1811) founded the
town that would become Wheeling, West
Virginia. In 1777, he commanded the Virginia
militia in the defense of Fort Henry against a
large force of Indians, the first significant British
attempt against the frontier settlements. In 1782,
he again led the defense when British Captain
Pratt led a large party of Indians in attacking Fort Henry. In 1788, Zane served in the Virginia
House of Burgesses that ratified the U. S. Constitution.

Lewis Wetzel Grave
McCreary Cemetery
Limestone, West Virginia

Lewis Wetzel (1763-1808) was a noted frontiersman and scout.
He participated in the first defense of Fort Henry in 1777 and
numerous other skirmishes in Kentucky, Ohio, and Virginia.

Benjamin McKinley Logan Grave
Logan Family Cemetery
Shelbyville, Kentucky

Benjamin Logan (1743-1802) was a noted pioneer, soldier, and
politician. As Colonel of the Kentucky County militia, he was
second in command of all the militia in Kentucky.

Site of Pluggy's Town Historical Marker
East Lincoln Avenue,
east of Blymer Street, in
Delaware, Ohio

Near this location was a large Mingo town of significance during
the Revolutionary period of the 1770's. The chief was Te-caugh-
ye-te-righ-to, known to the settlers as Pluggy. The village
consisted of perhaps 300 inhabitants. Among them were
Delaware, Mohawk, Shawnee, Wyandot, and Mingo. Individuals
known to have lived here were Mohawk Soloman, the Big Apple
Tree, the Stone, Conesseway, Black Wolf, and the Snake. Here, too, lived Chief Logan for
several years. The village was made up of some twenty dwellings including long houses and
wigwams. There was one cabin belonging to a blacksmith of French origin. The British
Commander at Fort Detroit, Henry Hamilton, had won the support of Pluggy and his warriors and
convinced them to attack settlers living east and south of the Ohio River. Chief Pluggy was killed
on January 1, 1777, while leading such an attack on McClellan's Station, Kentucky. This village
moved further north in 1778.

Further Reading

Abernethy, Thomas Perkins. *Western Lands and the American Revolution.* New York, New York: Russell & Russell, 1937.

Bakeless, John, *Background to Glory: The Life of George Rogers Clark.* Lincoln, Nebraska: University of Nebraska Press, 1957.

Barnhart, John D., *Henry Hamilton and George Rogers Clark in the American Revolution, with the Unpublished Journal of Lieut. Governor Henry Hamilton.* Crawfordville, Indiana: Banta, 1951.

Belue, Ted Franklin, "Crawford's Sandusky Expedition." *The American Revolution, 1775–1783: An Encyclopedia,* Volume 1, pages 416–420, Richard L. Blanco, Editor. New York, New York: Garland Publishers, 1993.

Blackmon, Richard D., *Dark and Bloody Ground: The American Revolution Along the Southern Frontier.* Yardley, Pennsylvania: Westholme Publishing, 2012.

Brackenridge, H. H., Editor, *Indian Atrocities: Narratives of the Perils and Sufferings of Dr. Knight and John Slover Among the Indians During the Revolutionary War.* Fairfield, Washington: Ye Galleon Press, 1867, Reprinted 1983.

Butterfield, Consul Willshire, *History of George Rogers Clark's Conquest of the Illinois and the Wabash Towns 1778–1779.* Columbus, Ohio: F. J. Heer, 1903.

Calloway, Colin G., *The American Revolution in Indian Country: Crisis and Diversity in Native American Communities.* Cambridge, England and New York, New York: Cambridge University Press, 1995.

Cayton, Andrew R. L., *Frontier Indiana.* Bloomington, Indiana: Indiana University Press, 1999.

Commager, Henry Steele and Richard B. Morris, Editors, *The Spirit of 'Seventy-Six: The Story of the American Revolution as Told by Participants.* New York, New York: Harper & Row, Publishers, 1958, 2nd Printing, 1967.

Dowd, Gregory Evans, *A Spirited Resistance: The North American Indian Struggle for Unity, 1745–1815.* Baltimore, Maryland: Johns Hopkins University Press, 1992.

Downes, Randolph C., *Council Fires on the Upper Ohio: A Narrative of Indian Affairs in the Upper Ohio Valley until 1795.* Pittsburgh, Pennsylvania: University of Pittsburgh Press, 1940.

English, William Hayden, *Conquest of the Country Northwest of the River Ohio, 1778–1783, and Life of Gen. George Rogers Clark.* Indianapolis, Indiana: Bowen-Merrill, 1896.

Evans, William A., Editor, *Detroit to Fort Sackville, 1778-1779: The Journal of Normand MacLeod.* Detroit, Michigan: Published by Wayne State University Press for the Friends of the Detroit Public Library, 1978.

Garraty, John A. and Mark C. Carnes, Editors, *American National Biography*. New York, New York: Oxford University Press, 1999.

Grenier, John, *The First Way of War: American War Making on the Frontier, 1607–1814*. Cambridge, England and New York, New York: Cambridge University Press, 2005.

Harrison, Lowell H., *George Rogers Clark and the War in the West*. Lexington, Kentucky: University Press of Kentucky, 1976.

Hurt, R. Douglas. *The Ohio Frontier: Crucible of the Old Northwest, 1720–1830*. Bloomington, Indiana: Indiana University Press, 1996.

James, James Alton, *George Rogers Clark Papers*. Springfield, Illinois: Trustees of the Illinois State Historical Library, 1912.

_____, *The Life of George Rogers Clark*. Chicago, Illinois: University of Chicago Press, 1928.

_____, "The Northwest: Gift or Conquest?" *Indiana Magazine of History*, Volume 30, March 1934, pages 1–15.

Kegley, Mary B., *Militia of Montgomery County, Virginia, 1777-1790*. Dublin, Virginia: Kegley Books, 1975.

Kellogg, Louise Phelps, Editor, *Frontier Advance on the Upper Ohio, 1778–1779*. Madison, Wisconsin: State Historical Society of Wisconsin, 1916.

_____, *Frontier Retreat on the Upper Ohio, 1779–1781*. Originally published Madison, Wisconsin: State Historical Society of Wisconsin, 1917, Reprinted Baltimore, Maryland: Clearfield Company, 2003.

Kenton, Edna, *Simon Kenton: His Life and Period, 1755–1836*. Garden City, New York: Doubleday, Doran & Company, 1930.

Lobdell, Jared C., *Indian Warfare in Western Pennsylvania and North West Virginia at the Time of the American Revolution*. Bowie, Maryland: Heritage Books, Inc., 1992

Marshall, Frances Jane, *Influence of the Southern Indians on the Revolutionary War*. MA dissertation, Chicago, Illinois: University of Chicago, 1925.

Nelson, Larry L., *A Man of Distinction Among Them: Alexander McKee and the Ohio Country Frontier, 1754–1799*. Kent, Ohio: Kent State University Press, 1999.

Nester, William. *The Frontier War for American Independence*. Mechanicsburg, Pennsylvania: Stackpole Books, 2004.

Nogay, Michael Edward, *Every Home a Fort, Every Man a Warrior: Stories of the Forts and Men in the Upper Ohio Valley During the American Revolutionary War*. Weirton, West Virginia: M. E. Nogay, 2009.

Quaife, Milo Milton, "The Ohio Campaigns of 1782." *Mississippi Valley Historical Review*, Volume 17, Number 4, March 1931, pages 515–529.

_____, Editor, *Col. George Rogers Clark's Sketch of his Campaign in the Illinois in 1778-9.* New York, New York: Arno, 1971.

Scaggs, David Curtis, Editor, *The Old Northwest in the American Revolution: An Anthology.* Madison, Wisconsin: The State Historical Society of Wisconsin, 1977.

Schaaf, Gregory, *Wampum Belts & Peace Trees: George Morgan, Native Americans, and Revolutionary Diplomacy.* Golden, Colorado: Fulcrum Publishing, 1990.

Schanchez-Saavedra, E. M., *A Guide to Virginia Military Organizations in the American Revolution, 1774-1787.* Richmond, Virginia: Virginia State Library, 1978.

Schmidt, Ethan A., *Native Americans in the American Revolution: How the War Divided, Devastated, and Transformed the Early American Indian World.* Santa Barbara, California: Praeger, 2014.

Sheehan, Bernard W., "The Famous Hair Buyer General: Henry Hamilton, George Rogers Clark, and the American Indian." *Indiana Magazine of History*, Volume 69, March 1983, pages 1-28.

Smith, Dwight L., *The French, the Indians, and George Rogers Clark in the Illinois Country.* Indianapolis, Indiana: Indiana Historical Society, 1977.

Smith, Thomas H., Editor, *Ohio in the American Revolution: A Conference to Commemorate the 200th Anniversary of the Ft. Gower Resolves.* Columbus, Ohio: Ohio Historical Society, 1976.

Sosin, Jack M., *The Revolutionary Frontier, 1763–1783.* New York, New York: Holt, Rinehart & Winston 1967.

Thwaites, Reuben Gold and Louise Phelps Kellogg, Editors, *Frontier Defense on the Upper Ohio 1777–1778.* Madison, Wisconsin: State Historical Society of Wisconsin, 1912, Reprinted Millwood, New York, Kraus, 1977.

_____. *The Revolution on the Upper Ohio, 1775–1777.* Madison, Wisconsin: State Historical Society of Wisconsin, 1908.

Van Every, Dale, *A Company of Heroes: The American Frontier, 1775–1783.* New York, New York: Morrow, 1962.

Waller, George M., *The American Revolution in the West.* Chicago, Illinois: Nelson-Hall, 1976.

White, Richard, *The Middle Ground: Indians, Empires, and Republics in the Great Lakes Region, 1650–1815.* Cambridge, England and New York, New York: Cambridge University Press, 1991.

Second Cherokee War, 1776-1795

Background

The Second Cherokee War, sometimes called the Chickamauga War, consisted of a series of ambushes, battles, raids, and skirmishes, beginning at the start of the American Revolution and continuing until 1795, between the Cherokee and the settlers on the frontiers of Georgia, South Carolina, North Carolina, and Virginia, later spreading to the frontier settlements in Kentucky and Tennessee. The Cherokee often fought alongside their Creek allies in the Old Southwest and with their Shawnee allies in the Old Northwest. Other smaller tribes sometimes joined with the Cherokee. The Second Cherokee War may be considered in two successive phases, the first, from 1776-1783, occurred during the Revolution, when the Cherokee fought against the encroachment of the settlements in the Overmountain and Cumberland River regions, as allies of the British against the Americans. In the second phase, from 1783 to 1795, the Cherokee fought as allies of Spain, who controlled the Mississippi River and the Gulf Coast. While the war lasted nearly two decades, the fighting was episodic, lulls in the action sometimes lasting for months.

The different bands of Cherokee generally were identified by the name of their towns. In 1775, there were six groupings of Cherokee towns. The Overhill Towns were situated on the Tellico and lower Little Tennessee rivers, in Tennessee. The Valley Towns occupied the upper Hiwassee and Valley rivers, in southwestern North Carolina. The Middle Towns sat on the upper Little Tennessee River and its headwaters in western North Carolina. The Out Towns, also known as the Hill Towns, were on the Tuckasegee River and the Oconaluftee River, in North Carolina. The original Lower Towns were situated along the Chatooga, Keowee, and Tugaloo rivers, and the headwaters of the Chattahoochee River in western South Carolina and northern Georgia. The Hiwassee Towns were on the lower Hiwassee and Ocoee rivers, in East Tennessee, sometimes considered part of the Overhill Towns.

The Chickamauga Towns, occupied after 1776, were in modern Hamilton and Bradley counties, Tennessee, with one town in modern Catoosa County, Georgia. After 1782, the Lower Towns were in present Marion County, Tennessee, Dade County, Georgia, and Jackson County, Alabama. The Upper Towns were in Georgia, north of the Chattahoochee River, settled by those from the original Lower Towns.

On June 1, 1773, the Cherokee and Creek signed the Treaty of Augusta, ceding all claim to about one and a half million acres of land to Georgia, in return for the cancellation of their debts to Georgian traders. In 1777, the Ceded Lands, sometimes called the New Purchase, became old Wilkes County, now encompassing at least part of the modern counties of Clarke, Elbert, Glascock, Hancock, Hart, Lincoln, Madison, Oglethorpe, Taliaferro, Warren, and Wilkes. Almost immediately settlers began to pour into the Ceded Lands, by 1790, old Wilkes County holding one third of the total population of Georgia.

By the start of the war, the pioneer settlements in Tennessee primarily were situated in Washington District, along the Watauga and Nolichucky rivers, in Pendleton District, north of the Holston River, and in Carter's Valley, in present Hawkins County. In 1771, Evan Shelby established the first fort, trading post, and settlement along the border between Virginia and Tennessee, on the waters of the Holston River, that grew to become the town of Bristol. The same year, Jacob Brown established another settlement on the Nolichucky River and John Carter began a third settlement in Carter's Valley, just west of modern Kingsport. After the Battle of Alamance, in the War of the Regulation, James Robertson led a party of twelve or thirteen families of North Carolina Regulators to settle along the Watauga River. All four settlements believed they were in Virginia. Alexander Cameron, Deputy Superintendent of Indian Affairs, ordered the settlers to abandon their settlements, after a survey revealed they were not in Virginia. Principal Cherokee Chief Attakullakulla prevailed upon Cameron to allow the settlers to remain, provided no additional settlers were allowed. On May 8, 1772, the settlers on the Watauga and Nolichucky rivers established the Watauga Association. The Washington District comprised the Watauga and Nolichucky settlements, and Shelby's settlement, North-of-Holston, comprised the Pendleton District. The Carter's Valley settlements were in modern Hawkins County.

In 1774, Lord Dunmore ordered the construction of a series of seven forts to defend the settlements along the Clinch River in Virginia, four situated on the lower Clinch River under the command of Captain William Russell and three on the upper Clinch River under the command of Captain Daniel Smith. Fort Preston, named by Captain Russell, but called Russell's Fort, as it was his headquarters, was erected on the land of David Cowan, at modern Castlewood, in Russell County. Fort Christian, usually called the Glade Hollow Fort, was on Cedar Creek, between modern Dickensonville and Lebanon, in Russell County. It was sometimes called Smith's Fort, after James Smith, who is thought to have owned the land. Captain Russell named Fort Byrd, but most commonly it was called Moore's Fort, after William Moore on whose land it stood, near Castlewood, on the road from Dungannon. Moore's fort was the largest of the forts, with a capacity to hold as many as 200 people. Daniel Boone and his family sheltered here after returning from Kentucky in 1773. Built on the lands of Captain William Blackmore, on the Clinch River, near the mouth of Stony Creek, between modern Gate City and Dungannon, in Scott County, Fort Blackmore was one of the smaller forts. All four of the forts on the lower Clinch River were attacked multiple times, but none was ever captured.

The three forts on the upper Clinch River included Elk Garden Fort, Big Crab Orchard Fort, and Maiden Spring Fort. The Elk Garden Fort was built just south of U. S. Route 19, between modern Lebanon and Rosedale, in Russell County. William Whitten built Big Crab Orchard Fort on a hillside overlooking the Clinch River just outside of modern Tazewell. The Maiden Spring Fort was built on the land of Rees Bowen on the Maiden Spring Branch of the Clinch River.

Fort Chiswell, built in 1758, was strategically important during the Revolutionary War and the Second Cherokee War, located where the Richmond Road met the Great Trading Path, in modern Wythe County. It guarded a lead deposit, mined to make bullets. There were scores of other fortified houses, blockhouses, and stockades defending the scattered settlements along the Clinch, Holston, and Powell rivers in southwestern Virginia.

Campaigns

At the beginning of the Revolutionary War, British operations were concentrated in the north and New England, leaving the Cherokee to fend for themselves, except for British supplies, mostly from their Gulf Coast ports. After withdrawing from their failed attempts to capture Charleston, in June 1776, the British abandoned the South for the next two-and-a-half years. However, British officials did not halt plans already in motion for supporting attacks by the Cherokee and Loyalists. The Cherokee planned a four-pronged campaign. One band of warriors, led by Alexander Cameron, the British Indian agent, would lead the attacks on the frontier settlements of Georgia; another band from the Middle, Out, and Valley Towns would attack the settlements in South Carolina; a third band from the lower Little Tennessee and Hiawassee rivers would attack in North Carolina and Virginia; and, the fourth band from the Overhill Towns would attack the settlements in Tennessee. Dragging Canoe would lead a party against the Pendleton District, Chief Abraham would lead a second party against the Washington District, and Chief Savanukah would lead a third party against Carter's Valley.

In 1776, to prepare themselves for the upcoming campaign, the Overhill Cherokee began raiding into Kentucky, often accompanied by Shawnee. Dragging Canoe led a small war party into Kentucky, returning with four scalps. On July 14th, Chief Hanging Maw led another war party, capturing three teenage girls, Jemima Boone and Elizabeth and Frances Callaway. A rescue effort, led by Daniel Boone, Jemima's father and Richard Callaway, Elizabeth and Frances' father, successfully recovered the girls three days later.

In June, Cherokee from the Lower Towns attacked the settlements on the South Carolina frontier. The following month, warriors from the Middle, Out, and Valley Towns hit settlements east of the Blue Ridge Mountains in North Carolina. On July 3rd, warriors attacked and laid siege to McDowell's Station, at Quaker Meadows, on the Catawba River, in North Carolina, after killing 37 settlers along the river. Lieutenant Colonel Charles McDowell, with ten militia, defended the station, filled with about 120 settlers, mostly women and children. Brigadier General Griffith Rutherford, at the head of a militia army of 2,400, marched to their rescue and forced the Cherokee to withdraw.

As the Cherokee attacks began in South Carolina, many settlers fled to the closest frontier fortification, seeking shelter and safety. One of those was Lindley's Fort, in present Laurens County. On July 14th, Major Jonathan Downs arrived with reinforcements, increasing the militia defenders to about 150. On the next day, about 190 Cherokee and Loyalists attacked, but their small weapons were insufficient to breach the stout walls of the stockade. As the attackers slipped away, Major Downs led a sortie in pursuit and, in the ensuing battle, captured ten Loyalists.

Cherokee from the Overhill Towns burned the vacant Fort Lee, on the Nolichucky River, depriving the settlers of a place of refuge. The warriors divided into three groups. Chief Dragging Canoe led the first up the Great Indian War Path, sometimes called the Great Indian War and Trading Path, a series of interwoven trails linking the tribes from the woods of Maine, southward through the Appalachian Mountains, deep into Alabama, proceeding toward his target, the fort at Long Island on the Holston River. Along the way, Dragging Canoe encountered about 20 militia and chased them some distance. Captain John Thompson led a company of militia from Eaton's Station to intercept the raiders and punish them. The adversaries met about six miles from Long Island and fought the Battle of Island Flats. After Dragging Canoe was wounded, the Cherokee withdrew, but continued their raids on isolated settlements in southwestern Virginia, along the Clinch and Holston rivers.

Old Abraham of Chilhowee led the second war party from the Overhill Towns against the settlers on the Watauga River. Up to 200 settlers fled to the safety of Fort Caswell, at the Sycamore Shoals on the Watauga River, defended by 75 men commanded by John Carter. Old Abraham laid siege to the fort. After two weeks of ineffective attacks and inflicting little damage, the Cherokee withdrew. The third war party from the Overhill Towns, led by Chief Savanukah, raided through the settlements in Carter's Valley in Tennessee and continued deep into the Clinch River Valley in Virginia, plundering and taking scalps along the way.

Georgia, South Carolina, North Carolina, and Virginia agreed that a coordinated and overwhelming response was needed to put down the Cherokee and end the uprising. South Carolina raised 1,800 militia to punish the Cherokee along the Savannah River. Georgia sent 200 militia against the villages along the Chattahoochee and Tugaloo rivers. North Carolina directed Rutherford, with his militia army of 2,400 men, against the Cherokee along the Little Tennessee, Hiwasee, Oconaluftee, and Tuckasegee rivers.

On July 23rd, Cherokee warriors ambushed Rutherford's column at Cowee Gap, in southwestern North Carolina, but were repulsed with few casualties. On August 1st, Cherokee attacked the South Carolina militia, under Andrew Williamson, at Isunigu, also called Seneca, a Lower Town on the Keowee River, near modern Clemson. The warriors prevailed at the Battle of Twelve Mile Creek, Williamson withdrawing and joining the militia led by Andrew Pickens. On August 10th, the combined force defeated the Cherokee at Tugaloo, then destroyed the town and burned the crops. On August 12th, Pickens completed his destruction of the Lower Towns, with the burning of Tamassee. Pickens then led his men to link up with Rutherford in North Carolina.

The South Carolina militia were attacked on September 19th, but repulsed the Cherokee at the Battle of Black Hole, near present-day Franklin. Williamson and Pickens, as well as a smaller unit of Georgia militia, managed to join forces with Rutherford for a campaign to punish the Out, Valley, and Middle Towns, in western North Carolina. Together, they destroyed more than 50 towns and villages, burning the houses and crops, slaughtering livestock, destroying orchards, and killing and capturing hundreds. Many of the captives were sold into slavery in the British colonies in the Caribbean.

As part of the overall plan to punish the Cherokee, Virginia sent Colonel William Christian, with a battalion of Continentals, 500 militia from Virginia, 300 militia from North Carolina, and 300 rangers to attack the Overhill Towns on the lower Little Tennessee River. Before they could reach their destination, Dragging Canoe sent the elderly, women, and children to safety down the Hiwassee River, burned their towns, and headed to the French Broad River, where he intended to ambush Christian and his army.

In late October, Christian arrived on the Little Tennessee only to find the towns of Chilhowee, Citico, Great Tellico, Toqua, and Tuskegee already destroyed. Christian's expedition saw little military action, but helped convince at least some of the chiefs to negotiate peace. Negotiations began in April 1777 and culminated in the Treaty of Fort Patrick Henry on July 20th between the Cherokee and North Carolina and Virginia. On May 20th, the Cherokee made peace with Georgia and South Carolina by signing the Treaty of Dewitt's Corner, ceding almost all their land in South Carolina.

Most of the other tribes in the south remained allied with the British and continued to attack scattered settlements. Upper Creek Chief Emistisigua joined forces with Dragging Canoe and his followers. Alexander McGillivray, a mixed blood and former British army colonel, became chief of the Coushatta and British Indian agent. Thomas Brown commanded a mounted Loyalist company, the King's Carolina Rangers, and often accompanied the Seminole from East Florida, led by Chief Cowkeeper. The majority of Lower Creeks remained neutral during the war. To prevent further American encroachment, the Choctaw patrolled the Mississippi River and western Tennessee rivers. The Chickasaw helped protect Pensacola and Mobile from Spanish incursion. Unlike their other native brethren, the Catawba in western South Carolina and North Carolina joined the Patriot cause, supplying hundreds of warriors in support.

Dragging Canoe, who refused to accept the terms of the peace, led many Overhill Cherokee south to establish eleven new towns in the vicinity of modern Chattanooga, where the Chickamauga River crosses the Great Indian Warpath. Dissenting Cherokee from other towns also joined Dragging Canoe and his Chickamauga Cherokee. The British maintained a trading post on the Chickamauga River, opposite Dragging Canoe.

The Chickamauga Cherokee, along with their allied tribes, principally Upper Creeks, launched raids against frontier settlements in Georgia, South Carolina, North Carolina, Virginia, and Kentucky, sometimes venturing into the Ohio country. Dragging Canoe led a war party through Carter's Valley, plundering and killing along the way, taking twelve scalps. A large war party of Cherokee and Upper Creek attacked settlements on the frontiers of Georgia, South Carolina, and North Carolina during the summer of 1777. At the same time, bands of Shawnee attacked settlements in Kentucky. Early in 1778, the Cherokee also established an encampment at the Mouth of the Tennessee River.

In August 1778, Dragging Canoe resumed his raids. In December, Hamilton seized Vincennes. From there, he planned to recruit 500 warriors from the Cherokee, Chickasaw, Shawnee, and other tribes, to defeat Clark in Illinois, then sweep into Kentucky to expel the American settlements there. At the end of December, Savannah fell to the British and their allies, the Chickamauga and other Cherokee, McGillivray's Upper Creek, and McIntosh's Hitichiti warriors. At the end of January, 1779, they attacked and captured Augusta. Soon thereafter, the previously neutral Lower Creeks joined the British cause.

Dragging Canoe sent numerous small raiding parties against the Holston River settlements. In April, a party of 300 Cherokee and fifty Loyalists left the Chickamauga Towns to raid the frontier in Georgia and South Carolina. John Montgomery, commanding a Continental regiment, and Evan Shelby, commanding 1,000 Overmountain Men, set out in mid-April to attack the Chickamauga Towns, arriving about ten days later, immediately starting their campaign of destruction. Because most of the warriors were far away on their raids, they faced no resistance while they burned the eleven towns and everything in them, as well as the British trading post. Dragging Canoe responded to the devastation of their homes by rebuilding the towns, conducting continued raids along the entire frontier from Georgia to Virginia, and sending 100 of his warriors north to join their Shawnee allies in the fight there.

In the summer of 1779, 300 Chickamauga Cherokee joined a company of Loyalists to ravage the South Carolina and Georgia backcountry. South Carolina reacted by dispatching Andrew Williamson and his militia, who successfully attacked several Cherokee towns.

In 1780, George Rogers Clark, leading a company of 500, with allied Kaskaskia, established Fort Jefferson and the adjacent Clarksville, in Illinois near the mouth of the Ohio River. In June, a large Chickasaw war party, destroyed the town, besieged the fort, and sent war parties against the settlements in Kentucky, continuing those attacks into the next year. That summer, Elijah Clarke and his Georgia militia attacked the British at Augusta, defended only by the King's Carolina Rangers and fifty Creek warriors. Clarke was forced to retreat, when a large war party arrived from the Chickamauga and Overhill Towns. The Cherokee pursued Clarke, but Clarke slipped away, as his pursuers turned their attention to plundering Patriot settlements.

The British urged Dragging Canoe and other Cherokee chiefs to attack the frontier settlements left undefended as their militias were on their way to battle Major Patrick Ferguson at King's Mountain. Virginia Governor Thomas Jefferson learned of the Cherokee plans and sent Colonel John Sevier and 700 Virginia and North Carolina militia, fresh from their recent victory at King's Mountain, against the Cherokee. Advancing down the French Broad River, Sevier met a large Cherokee war party on December 16th, routing it at the Battle of Boyd's Creek. Sevier's force then swelled with reinforcements from Colonel Arthur Campbell, commanding militia from Washington County, Virginia, and Major Joseph Martin, leading other Virginia militia. Sevier then promptly proceeded against the Overhill Towns along the Little Tennessee and Hiwassee rivers, destroying seventeen.

Throughout 1780, the Cherokee, Chickasaw, Creek, Delaware, Shawnee, and Wyandot all mounted repeated raids into the Cumberland settlements in Tennessee, at a cost of about forty settlers. In March, to thwart the Cherokee of the Middle Towns from avenging the destruction of their towns, Sevier led another militia force in burning fifteen towns, killing 29, and capturing nine. On April 2, 1780, Dragging Canoe, at the head of a large war party, attacked Fort Nashborough, at present-day Nashville. The attackers withdrew the following day, when the defenders began firing their deadly cannon. Because of the extensive carnage, many settlers abandoned their new homes and returned to safer territory back east.

Parallel to the attacks on the Cumberland settlements, the Shawnee began a deadly series of raids against the settlements along the Clinch and Holston rivers, in southwestern Virginia and adjoining Tennessee, that continued until the end of the war.

In mid-1781, a party of Cherokee traveled west over the mountains to attack the French Broad River settlements. Sevier with 150 militia found and attacked them in camp on Indian Creek, driving them away. In July, the Overhill Towns made peace with the Overmountain settlements by signing the second Treaty of Long Island on the Holston. Warriors from the Middle Towns, however, continued their attacks. In November 1781, Loyalist Captain William Bates, with Dragging Canoe, led a war party of Chickamauga Cherokee and Loyalists disguised as Indians in attacking the settlements around modern Landrum, South Carolina. Upon hearing of the approaching war party, the settlers ran to the safety of Gowen's Fort, near Williams' Mill, on the waters of South Pacolet River. The settlers waged a good defense; but, running out of ammunition, the defenders agreed to surrender, provided they would be protected from the Indians. Bates agreed, yet ordered his men to attack as soon as the gates were opened. Ten men, women, and children were killed and scalped. Bates took a few prisoners, to be burned at the stake later, and the slaves. Only Mrs. Abner Thompson survived, after being scalped and left for dead.

In June 1782, the Patriots defeated the British and Creek defenders, placing Savannah back in Patriot hands. Starting in the spring that year, Chickamauga Cherokee began raiding the Holston settlements in Virginia and Tennessee. In September, John Sevier and his militia destroyed many of the Chickamauga Towns, as well as the Cherokee towns in north Georgia. Instead of rebuilding, Dragging Canoe moved his people further west, to the Five Lower Towns, situated downstream from the Tennessee River Gorge. Other Cherokee bands, mostly from Georgia, joined Dragging Canoe and his people, now called the Lower Cherokee. Dragging Canoe also welcomed many others into his coalition, including, numbers of Loyalists, runaway slaves, Chickasaw, Creek, Natchez, Shawnee, and Yuchi. He also welcomed a few Spanish, French, Irish, and Germans. Late in 1782, Dragging Canoe sent seventy of his warriors north to fight with his northern allies, the Ojibwa, Ottawa, Potawatomi, and Wyandot.

In the fall of 1782, Lieutenant Colonel Thomas Waters, with his Loyalist Rangers, accompanied by Cherokee and Creek warriors, began attacking frontier settlements in Georgia and South Carolina. A joint expedition, commanded by Andrew Pickens and Elijah Clarke, set out to end the depredations. They invaded Cherokee territory and destroyed thirteen towns and captured many prisoners. The Loyalists managed to escape, but the Cherokee asked for peace.

In 1783, Dragging Canoe attempted to forge a formal alliance among all the Southern tribes to fight the Americans in a coordinated way in a series of meetings and councils at St. Augustine and Tuckabatchee. Their plans, however, were thwarted by the signing of the Treaty of Paris ending the American Revolution.

The Treaty of Long Swamp Creek, signed on May 30, 1783, established the northern boundary of Georgia, the Cherokee ceding all the territory between the Savannah and Chattahoochee rivers. Despite the treaty, war parties continued to attack the frontier settlements, especially those along the Holston River. After the British withdrew their trading posts and Indian agents, Dragging Canoe sought assistance from the Spanish, while still maintaining his ties to the British at Detroit.

The end of the war brought a new wave of people into the Overmountain settlements, instigating retaliatory strikes by the Cherokee from the Middle Towns. Following those attacks, Major Peter Fine led his militia east, over the mountains, and burned Cowee Town.

On November 6, 1783, the Treaty of French Lick established permanent peace with the Chickasaw. The Lower Creeks agreed to cease attacking the Cumberland settlements. On November 1st, the friendly Lower Creeks signed the Treaty of Augusta, ceding all their lands between the Oconee and Ogeechee rivers. McGillivray was so incensed that he burned the homes of the friendly chiefs and ordered more attacks against the Georgia settlements.

After taking possession of East and West Florida, the Spanish began to arm and supply the southern tribes, encouraging them to continue their attacks on the Americans. The French trading post at Coldwater, near modern Tuscumbia, Alabama, also supplied arms to the Lower Cherokee and Upper Creek and encouraged them to fight. On May 30, 1784, the Treaty of Pensacola formalized the alliance between the Spanish and the Lower Cherokee and Upper Creek. On June 22, 1784, the Treaty of Mobile established a similar alliance with the Choctaw and Alabama. That summer, the Lower Town Cherokee again began raiding the Overmountain settlements. In May 1785, with Spanish support, McGillivray began raiding the new settlements on the Oconee River, continuing his deadly attacks well into 1794, the campaign of Creek raids and militia reprisals often called the Oconee War.

By 1784, the Cherokee had established three large groups in the Old Northwest. One group lived among Delaware, the second among the Mingo and Wyandot on the Upper Mad River, and the third among the Shawnee at Chillicothe. In 1785, the northern tribes began raiding the new settlements north of the Ohio River and the settlements in Kentucky, gradually increasing the raids in both size and frequency. From the onset in 1784, until 1790, almost 1,500 American settlers were killed. As allies of the northern tribes, the Cherokee participated enthusiastically in virtually every raid.

On November 12, 1785, some friendly Lower Creek chiefs signed the Treaty of Galphinton, ceding all the land between the Altamaha and St. Mary's rivers, further angering McGillivray and his followers. On November 28th, the Overhill, Hill, and Valley Cherokee signed the Treaty of Hopewell, at Andrew Pickens' plantation, on the Seneca River, in modern Pickens County, South Carolina. On January 3, 1786, the Choctaw signed a similar Treaty of Hopewell and, on January 10, the Chickasaw signed a third Treaty of Hopewell. The four treaties, especially the Hopewell Treaties, so angered Dragging Canoe and the chiefs allied with him, that they renewed their attacks. Warriors from the Lower Towns mostly raided the Cumberland settlements, while those from the Overhill and Valley Towns raided the settlements in eastern Tennessee.

At first, the Lower Towns sent only small war parties, whose raids necessarily were small and infrequent through the spring of 1786. All summer, assisted by the Creek, Dragging Canoe led his warriors against the Cumberland settlements, sometimes raiding far into Kentucky. At the urging of their Creek allies, the Overhill and Valley Towns mobilized as many as a thousand warriors. On July 20th, they attacked a lone homestead on Baker's Creek, near the newly constructed White's Fort, where Knoxville is today, then fanning out into smaller groups, attacking the settlements in eastern Tennessee, principally along the upper Holton River.

Militia under the command of William Cocke and Alexander Outlaw, repelled the raiders on the Holston River, then proceeded to attack Coyatee Town, near the mouth of the Little Tennessee River, where they destroyed the crops and the council house, but spared the rest of the town. John Sevier led a second expedition against the Valley Towns on the upper Hiwassee River. Their defeats caused most of the Overhill chiefs, on August 3, 1786, to sign the Treaty of Coyatee, ceding more of their land to the Americans.

In late November, representatives from the Cherokee already in Ohio, as well as from their brothers from the southern towns, joined a large council of the northern tribes, including the Delaware, Ojibwa, Ottawa, Potawatomie, Six Nations Iroquois, Wabash, and Wyandot, at Upper Sandusky, a Wyandot town. For three weeks, with British agents from Detroit in attendance and led by the Mohawk Chief Joseph Brant, the chiefs established the Western Confederation, to coordinate their attacks and defense against the American settlers, with Dragging Canoe and his Cherokee full-fledged members. Tribal anger against the Americans increased significantly with the passage of the Northwest Ordinance, in 1787, establishing the Northwest Territory and seizing the tribal lands where they lived. However, despite the seemingly ever present attacks, settlers continued to move onto the frontier.

Beginning circa 1785, under the leadership of the French traders, from their clandestine base at Coldwater Town, a small band of Cherokee and Creek warriors launched sporadic attacks against the Cumberland settlements. In 1787, after receiving intelligence on its location, Colonel James Robertson led 150 volunteers to stop the attacks emanating from Coldwater Town. The Americans attacked, killing about half of the raiders, wounding many more, and dispersing the rest. Robertson shipped the trade goods back to Nashville, then burned the town. In retaliation, Creek warriors raided the Cumberland settlements for the next two years.

The next wave of Cherokee attacks began in the spring of 1788, when a war party attacked the home of John Kirk, on the south side of Little River, about twelve miles south of Knoxville, killing and scalping eleven members of the household. The massacre of the Kirk family started a series of attacks by both sides, each attack in retaliation for the previous one, lasting well into the next year.

In June, John Sevier, at the head of 100 volunteers, attacked the Overhill Towns, burning one on the Hiwassee River and a second on the Little Tennessee River. Sevier dispatched Major James Hubbard to punish those responsible for the Kirk massacre. Under a flag of truce, Hubbard summoned Chief Old Tassel and Chief Abraham to Chillhowee, then placed them and four others in a cabin under guard. John Kirk, Jr. entered the cabin and tomahawked the six Indians inside, including the two peaceful chiefs, in revenge for the murder of his family.

The blatant murder of the chiefs greatly angered the Cherokee, even those who had remained neutral in the earlier conflicts. As a result, the Overhill Towns, Lower Towns, and Creek joined forces in mounting a new round of raids. Expecting the Cherokee to attack, Captain Fain led a reconnaissance from Houston's Station to determine the situation. He found Citico Town deserted. The patrol was ambushed by a larger war party, while picking apples from the Cherokee orchard and lost 16 men killed. The weakened garrison desperately defended Houston's Station against a large party of Cherokee, until Sevier arrived with reinforcements and drove the attackers away. Sevier then proceeded to burn Chilhowie on the Little Tennessee River.

Dragging Canoe assembled 3,000 warriors and organized them into smaller, more manageable war parties. John Watts, called Little Tassel, led a war party of 300 up the Holston River, attacking Gillespie's Station, below the mouth of Little River, on October 17th. The defenders put up a valiant effort, but were overwhelmed, after running out of ammunition, as the attackers climbed over the roofs of the cabins forming part of the fortification, killing the men, and taking 28 women and children captive. Watts subsequently attacked White's Fort and Houston's Station, but was repulsed both times.

A second war party attacked Sherrill's Station, on the Nolichucky River, but also was repulsed. In retaliation for those and other attacks, Sevier led his militia against the Middle and Valley Towns in North Carolina. At Ustalli Town, on the Hiwassee River, the Cherokee evacuated before Sevier and his men arrived. Sevier burned the town, then pursued the evacuees, before getting ambushed at the mouth of the Valley River. Sevier then destroyed the corn crop at another town. Before Sevier could inflict more damage, Watts with 400 warriors attacked, forcing his withdrawal. Watts harassed their return all the way back to the settlements.

In January, 1789, Sevier, leading a mounted force with cannon, managed to find and surround Watts and his band. The firing was furious from both sides, ending only after a cavalry charge and severe hand-to-hand combat killed half of Watts' warriors. The Cherokee continued their war against the settlements in eastern Tennessee, then still part of the State of North Carolina. The settlers continuously appealed to North Carolina for protection and other support. In order to relieve itself of the burden, North Carolina simply ceded its western territory to the federal government. In May 1790, the government created the Southwest Territory and appointed William Blount Governor and Superintendent for Southern Indian Affairs. The counties encompassing the Cumberland settlements were assigned to the Mero District and the counties comprising the Overmountain settlements assigned to the Washington District.

About 40 warriors, led by Doublehead, with their families, established a new town above Muscle Shoals, in 1790. Soon, the town grew from an influx of Cherokee, Chickasaw, Creek, and Shawnee. For the next few years, Doublehead directed numerous raids against the settlements in the Mero District and Kentucky.

On August 7, 1790, McGillivray, at the head of a delegation of Creek chiefs, signed the Treaty of New York, on behalf of the entire Creek Nation, requiring the Creek to return all white prisoners, respect the borders established by previous treaties, and return runaway slaves. The treaty also required the settlers to respect the same boundaries. Many Creek were angry that they could not keep the Oconee Country and many settlers were angry that they had to abandon their settlements there, making further warfare inevitable.

Chief Bob Benge, an Overhill Cherokee, in alliance with Doublehead, began to strike the settlements in eastern Kentucky, southwestern Virginia, and Kentucky, in 1791. At the same time, Creek war parties renewed their attacks on the Cumberland settlements in the Mero District. The settlers defended themselves, suffered no significant defeats, but mounted no major offensive operations. The government was unable to prevent new settlements on Indian lands, much less remove the settlers already there. On July 2, 1791, the Treaty of Holston, negotiated at Knoxville, mandated the Upper Towns to cede more land, in return for peace.

In the Old Northwest, Major General Arthur St. Clair commanded an army consisting of the 1st Infantry Regiment, under Major Jean François Hamtramck, 2nd Infantry Regiment, under Major Jonathan Hart, the Artillery Battalion, under Major William Ferguson, 1st Levy Regiment, under Lieutenant Colonel William Clarke, 2nd Levy Regiment, under Lieutenant Colonel George Gibson, and Kentucky militia, under Lieutenant Colonel William Oldham. The two levy regiments, serving as infantry, were composed of men conscripted for six months. At its peak, the army consisted of 600 regulars, 800 conscripts, and 600 militia; but, primarily due to desertion and illness, the army had shrunk to about 1,100 by November 1791.

On the morning of November 4th, an Indian force of about 1,000, led by Blue Jacket and Little Turtle, with the participation of numerous Cherokee, attacked St. Clair at the Battle of the Wabash, near modern Fort Recovery, Ohio. After three hours of fierce fighting and suffering heavy casualties, St. Clair ordered a retreat, which quickly turned into a rout. The army suffered 632 killed or captured and 264 wounded, not including civilian workers, women, and children.

By March, 1792, when Dragging Canoe died, after the long and savage warfare, the Cherokee gained a grudging and reluctant respect from the American settlers. John Watts assumed leadership over the Lower Cherokee. Starting in April, Bob Benge led his Cherokee warriors, accompanied by their Shawnee allies, on raids against the settlements along the Holston River, although the frequency of the raids gradually diminished through the summer. Other Cherokee war parties also raided throughout the Washington District. On June 26, a large party of Cherokee, Creek, and Shawnee attacked and burned Zeigler's Station on Bledsoe Creek, in modern Sumter County.

In September, John Watts assembled about 1,000 warriors, with whom he invaded the Mero District. Watts sent one group of warriors along the Walton Road, another group under

Doublehead against the Cumberland Road, and a third group under Bob Benge against the Kentucky Road. Watts lead the rest of his army, about 300 strong, against Buchanan's Station, on Mill Creek, about four miles south of Nashville. The twenty defenders led by Captain John Buchanan, successfully foiled the attack, with no one hurt, but inflicted many casualties, including wounding Watts.

Bob Benge's group continued raiding into October, attacking Black's Station, on Crooked Creek, in modern Blount County, inflicting casualties, then withdrawing to raid other targets. In November, the group scouting the Walton Road ambushed a large armed force, completely routing them, with no loss of their own. Doublehead's group attacked a party of six settlers, took one scalp, then headed for Nashville to rendezvous with Watts. A contingent of militia followed and attacked them, inflicting thirteen casualties. Hearing of Watt's defeat, Doublehead led his group home, hitting isolated settlements along the way.

In early 1793, another war party struck deep into Kentucky, cooking and eating their victims. They celebrated with scalp dances at friendly villages on their way home. Partly in an effort to cement their alliance, the Shawnee sent warriors south to fight with the Cherokee and Creek, while Cherokee and Creek warriors traveled north. Throughout the year and into the next, the Cherokee concentrated their offensive action primarily in the Northwest Territory, save for a series of coordinated attacks along the Holston River. The Shawnee encouraged the Cherokee to join them in attacking the Chickasaw, in revenge for fighting with the Americans at the Battle of the Wabash. The Cherokee agreed and open warfare erupted between the tribes.

Through much of 1793 and continuing through the summer of 1794, Chief Lesley led his Creek warriors on raid after raid against the Washington District. Other Creek war parties, as well as war parties from the Overhill, Valley, and Upper Towns, conducted numerous raids in eastern Tennessee. In April 1793, other war parties attacked Bledsoe's Station and Greenfield Station, in the Mero District, now in Sumner County. In June, still another war party attacked Hay's Station. In addition to their direct attacks on the fortified locations, the various war parties sought scalps by raiding small outlying settlements. A Coushatta war party raided the settlements around modern Clarksville and a Tuskeegee war party took numerous scalps. Overall, 1793 was a difficult and bloody year for the settlements in the Mero District.

In August, Colonel George Doherty led 180 volunteers from the Washington District in retaliation, destroying Tynoita Town, on the Hiwassee River, then pressed on to destroy several small villages and Big Valley Town. Doherty continued to attack any Cherokee they encountered, killing, wounding, and capturing dozens, before returning home.

Growing tired of war, Chief Watts requested a meeting with Governor Blount, who referred him to President Washington. A meeting was arranged for June in Philadelphia to discuss peace. Delegations of chiefs assembled at Coyatee, an Overhill Town, on the Little Tennessee River, before heading to Philadelphia for the peace conference. Unknown to the gathering chiefs, a Lower Cherokee war party, arrived on their way home after raiding, with militia following in hot pursuit. The militia crossed the river and attacked the entire town. Eleven chiefs and other leading men were killed in the melee. In retaliation, John Watts assembled more than 1,000 Cherokee and Creek warriors for an assault against Knoxville.

Watts divided his army into four war parties, each to travel different routes, then meet near Knoxville for the assault, after attacking settlements along the way. The four columns met on the

Tennessee River a few miles southwest of their target. On September 25th, they approached and surrounded Cavett's Station, just west of modern downtown Knoxville. After they surrendered, Doublehead and his men murdered the twelve inhabitants, including men, women, and children. Watts then divided his army once again, sending some to Kentucky, some to North Carolina, but most to raid the settlements in Georgia.

John Sevier, at the head of 800 mounted volunteers from Tennessee, caught up with Watts at Etowah Town, overlooking modern Rome, Georgia. On October 17th, in the ensuing Battle of Hightower, Sevier soundly defeated Watts. When the Indians fled, he burned the town and crops. Unopposed, Sevier moved his troops down the Coosa River, destroying both Creek and Cherokee towns, before returning to Knoxville.

By September 1794, the Mero District that year suffered at least forty raids, many led by Doublehead. Bob Benge led numerous attacks against the Washington District and southwestern Virginia. Doublehead and Benge were not alone, as there were many other attacks that year conducted by Cherokee, Creek, and Shawnee. In retaliation, Captain John Beard led 150 volunteers from the Washington District in attacking and destroying two Hiwassee Towns, burning their crops, and killing several Cherokee. Doherty again assembled his men, attacking and burning Great Tellico Town and two Valley Towns.

On June 26, 1794, the Cherokee and the federal government consummated the Treaty of Philadelphia, ratifying the provisions of the Treaty of Hopewell and Treaty of Holston. The following month, Chief Hanging Maw directed his men, accompanied by militia from the Washington District, to find and stop the Creek war party led by Chief Lesley. The Cherokee found them, killed two, and gave many of them to the militia to stand trial. Hanging Maw also sent his warriors to stop another Creek war party, eventually catching up with them and defeating them near Craig's Station. Other Creek war parties managed to evade pursuit to continue attacking the Holston settlements for several weeks.

More than one hundred Cherokee and Creek warriors joined their Shawnee allies under Chief Bluejacket to face the American army commanded by Major General Anthony Wayne at the Battle of Fallen Timbers, on the Maumee River, in modern Lucas County, Ohio. On August 20, 1794, Wayne earned a decisive victory, effectively ending armed conflict with the Indians in the Northwest.

In August and September of that year, three small war parties, composed of both Cherokee and Creek, raided throughout the Mero District. Seeking to end the war, General Robertson ordered a small army to assemble at Brown's Blockhouse, near Nashville. Under the overall command of Colonel John Montgomery, the army consisted of Montgomery's Mero District militia, a company of regulars commanded by Major James Orr, and a contingent of Kentucky militia from Lincoln County, commanded by Colonel William Whitley, amounting to about 500 in all. On September 13th, Montgomery reached Nickajack Town, on the Tennessee River, near where the states of Alabama, Georgia, and Tennessee meet, finding the inhabitants fleeing toward nearby Running Water Town. Warriors from Running Water advanced to meet their fleeing brethren. The pursuing Montgomery met the combined foe and soundly defeated them at the Narrows on the Tennessee River, then destroyed both towns and the crops.

After the crushing defeat and destruction of the towns, as well as the death of Bob Benge, John Watts sued for peace. On November 7, 1794, Upper Cherokee Chief Hanging Maw, Lower Creek

Chief John Watts, and Governor Blount agreed to terms and signed the Treaty of Tellico Blockhouse, at modern Vonore in Montgomery County, Tennessee. The treaty effectively ended the war with the Cherokee; however, the Creek continued fighting.

In October, the Creek attacked Bledsoe's Station and, in the following month, attacked Sevier's Station, at modern Clarksville, Tennessee, killing more than a dozen. In December, the Cherokee stopped another Creek war party headed toward the Georgia frontier. For a time, Creek military efforts were directed against the Chickasaw, until a peace was formalized by the Treaty of Greenville in August 1795.

At the trading post of Colerain, at St. Mary's Georgia, the Creek finally made peace by signing the Treaty of Colerain on June 29, 1796. The treaty affirmed the boundaries established by previous treaties and required they give up their prisoners and return "*all citizens, white inhabitants, negroes, and property*" taken by the Creek.

Aftermath

On October 27, 1795, the Treaty of San Lorenzo, also called Pinckney's Treaty, established the 31st parallel as the boundary between Spanish Florida and the United States, granted the Americans unfettered access to the Mississippi River, called for the removal of Fort San Fernando de las Barrancas, on the Fourth Chickasaw Bluff, the site of modern Memphis, and stipulated that both sides would stop stirring up the various tribes.

The Second Cherokee War, one of the longest in American History, had a profound impact during the conflict and continued to influence events well into the next century. Three Lower Cherokee disciples of Dragging Canoe, Little Turkey, Black Fox, and Pathkiller, served as Principal Chief of the Cherokee Nation from 1788 to 1827. Other Lower Cherokee chiefs filled influential roles in the Cherokee national councils for many years.

The government established two permanent military posts, Fort Southwest Point, at the junction of the Clinch and Tennessee rivers, and Fort Pitt, at Pittsburgh. With peace now established, the formerly sporadic stream of settlers turned into a tsunami, with new settlers pouring into the backcountry of Georgia, South Carolina, North Carolina, southwestern Virginia, West Virginia, Kentucky, and Tennessee. In 1792, the former Kentucky County, Virginia, became its own state. In 1796, the State of Tennessee was admitted to the Union.

Places of Interest

Sycamore Shoals State Historic Area
1651 West Elk Avenue
Elizabethton, Tennessee 37643

(423) 543-5808

The visitor center houses a number of displays interpreting the history of the area, a theater screening a documentary about the Revolutionary War at Sycamore Shoals and the Overmountain Men, bookstore, and gift shop. The park includes a reconstructed version of Fort Carswell, later named Fort Watauga, and the original Carter Mansion built during the Revolution.

Wheatlands Plantation
2507 Boyd's Creek Highway
Sevierville, Tennessee 37876

(865) 365-1052

The Battle of Boyd's Creek was fought on land that later became an antebellum plantation named Wheatlands. The Mansion House is on the National Register of Historic Places and is home to a monument commemorating the battle. Visitors may take their History Tour around the plantation grounds, walk on the battlefield, see the burial mound for the fallen Indians, and view the slave grave yard.

Cavett's Station Historical Marker
Intersection of Kingston Pike (U. S. Route 11) and Gallaher View Road, in Knoxville, Tennessee

About ½ mile north was this early fortified settlement. Here, on September 25, 1793, Alexander Cavett and 12 other settlers were massacred by a Cherokee war party under Doublehead, one of the more savage chiefs of the tribe.

122

Running Water Town Historical Marker
U. S. Route 41, 100 feet from Memorial Bridge over
Tennessee River, near Jasper, Tennessee

700 yards southeast, troops under Major Ore defeated the
Chickamauga Cherokee under the half-breed John Watts and
destroyed their town, Tuskgigagee, on Sept. 13, 1794. The town
was in the pass in the distance. Dragging Canoe, the great chief,
is buried near there.

David Crockett Monument
11th Street, between Avenues D and E
Ozona, Texas

David Crocket (1786-1836) was a famous frontiersman, soldier,
and politician. During the First Creek War, he first served as a
scout in Captain Francis Jones's Company of Mounted Rifleman,
in the Second Regiment of Volunteer Mounted Riflemen, under
Colonel John Alcorn. He then served as a scout in Captain John
Cowan's Company, in the East Tennessee Volunteer Mounted
Gunmen under Major John Chiles. Both regiments served under
Brigadier General John Coffee. Crockett was killed at the Alamo during the Texas Revolution.

Captain James White's Fort
205 East Hill Avenue
Knoxville, Tennessee 37915

(865) 525-6514

The fort was restored and opened to the public in 1970 by the
City Association of Women's Clubs. Today, visitors may
experience the frontier lifestyle through hands-on interpretation,
including open hearth cooking, blacksmithing, and spinning.
Special events are held throughout the year including: Cherokee
Heritage Day.

Tellico Blockhouse
Fort Loudon State Historic Area
338 Fort Loudoun Road
Vonore, Tennessee 37885

(423) 884-6217

Tellico Blockhouse is in a state of stabilized ruin, on the site of the
Fort Loudon State Historical Area, a day use area. Visitors can
walk the ground once walked by the Cherokee, soldiers, and
agents of government. The visitor center offers information on the
history of the area, displays artifacts from the site, and has a gift shop and book store. A living
history program is offered throughout the year.

Davidson's Fort Historic Park, Inc.
P. O. Box 1636
Old Fort, North Carolina 28762

http://www.davidsonsfort.com/

The nonprofit presents colonial living history
events on the third Saturday of every month at
the reconstructed stockade fort. Major events
are presented quarterly. The site is open daily for viewing and photography.

Griffith Rutherford Monument
Rutherford County Courthouse
Murfreesboro, Tennessee

Griffith Rutherford, 1721-1805, led Rowan County militia in the
French and Indian War and the Second Cherokee War. In 1776,
Rutherford led his militia first against the Middle Towns and then
against the Valley Towns, destroying three dozen towns and villages
and burning crops and storehouses, leaving the Cherokee to face
starvation in the coming winter.

Oconee Station State Historic Site
500 Oconee Station Road
Walhalla, South Carolina 29691

(864) 638-0079

oconeestation@scprt.com

http://southcarolinaparks.com/oconeestation/introduction.aspx

The stone blockhouse, then on the South Carolina frontier, was used by the militia in the 1790s to defend against attack by the Cherokee and Creek.

Fort Southwest Point
Southwest Point Park
South Kentucky Street
Kingston, Kentucky

(865) 376- 3641

http://www.southwestpoint.com/

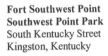

Fort Southwest Point is the only fort in Tennessee being reconstructed on its original foundation. The completed sections of the fort include a barracks, a blockhouse and 250 feet of palisade walls. The fort is owned, operated, and maintained by the City of Kingston. The park also features a reconstructed blacksmith shop, Cherokee cabin, and visitor center.

Historic Crab Orchard Museum & Pioneer Park
3663 Crab Orchard Road
Tazewell, Virginia 24651

(276) 988-6755

info@craborchardmuseum.com

https://craborchardmuseum.wordpress.com/

The national historic landmark is the site of the Big Crab Orchard Fort, sometimes called Whitten's Fort. The Museum Center houses the permanent collection as well as a series of rotating special exhibitions. The Pioneer Park consists of 15 historic log and stone structures and the Red Barn, an exhibition building also used for community events.

William Moore Historical Marker
Sand Hill Road, in
Enka Village, in
Buncombe County, North Carolina

Moore was a captain of a militia force which marched against
the Cherokee in Nov., 1776. A fort which he built stood near
here. His home was 200 yards East.

Thomas Sumter Memorial Park
Action Road, off Meeting House Road
Stateburg, in
Sumter County, South Carolina

During the First Cherokee War, Sumter served in
the Virginia militia. In 1760, he moved to Eutaw
Springs, South Carolina. In the Revolution, he was
a colonel in the North Carolina Continental Line. In
1780, he was commissioned brigadier general in the
militia and won the Battle at Fish Dam Ford. After
the war, he founded the town of Statesburg, and served in the State Assembly, the U. S.
Congresses, and the U. S. Senate.

Benge's Gap Historical Marker
Orby Cantrell Highway, at the
James Walker Robinson Memorial Scenic Overlook,
just south of Norton, in
Wise County, Virginia

Beginning in 1774, Chief Benge led a part of the Shawnee
from the Ohio River on raids along the frontier. Benge, who
was part white and part Cherokee. frequently captured slaves
and then resold them; he also seized white women and
children who were then adopted by various Indian groups. On
6 Apr. 1794, Benge attacked the Henry and Peter Livingston farm on the Holston River, took
several residents prisoner, and marched them northeast. Three days later, when they entered the
Powell Mountain gap just south, Lt. Vincent Hobbs and eleven Lee County militiamen ambushed
them, killed Benge with the first volley, and freed the captives.

Flowerdew Hundred Historical Marker
James River Drive and
Flowerdew Hundred Road, near
Hopewell, in
Prince George County, Virginia

Four miles north of here, Governor Sir George Yeardley
established Flowerdew Hundred settlement by 1619. In 1621
a windmill was built there, the first one recorded in English
North America.   In response to English expansion in
Powhatan lands, such as occurred at Flowerdew and
elsewhere, paramount chief Opechancanough planned a
coordinated assault on English settlements. The settlement survived the attack on 22 March 1622,
and was inhabited through the 18th century. On 14-16 June 1864, U. S. General Ulysses S. Grant
and Major General George G. Meade's Army of the Potomac landed there and marched toward
Petersburg to attack it.

Further Reading

Adair, James, *History of the American Indian*. Nashville, Tennessee: Blue and Gray Press, 1971.

Alderman, Pat, *Dragging Canoe: Cherokee-Chickamauga War Chief*. Johnson City, Tennessee: Overmountain Press, 1978.

Allen, Penelope, *The Fields Settlement*. Penelope Allen Manuscript, Archive Section, Chattanooga-Hamilton County Bicentennial Library.

Anderson, William and James A. Lewis, *A Guide to Cherokee Documents in Foreign Archives*. Metuchen, New Jersey: Scarecrow Press, 1995.

Bays, Bill, *James Robertson: Father of Tennessee and Founder of Nashville*. Bloomington, Indiana: WestBow Press, 2013.

Brown, John P., "Eastern Cherokee Chiefs." *Chronicles of Oklahoma*, Volume 16, Number 1, 1938, pages, 3–35, Oklahoma City, Oklahoma: Oklahoma Historical Society.

_____, *Old Frontiers: The Story of the Cherokee Indians from Earliest Times to the Date of Their Removal to the West, 1838*. Kingsport, Tennessee: Southern Publishers, 1938.

Calloway, Colin G., *The American Revolution in Indian Country: Crisis and Diversity in Native American Communities*. Cambridge, England: Cambridge University Press, 1995.

Dean, Nadia, *A Demand of Blood: The Cherokee War of 1776*. Cherokee, North Carolina: Valley River Press, 2012

Doddridge, Joseph, *Notes on the Settlement and Indian Wars of the Western Parts of Virginia and Pennsylvania from 1763 to 1783*. Baltimore, Maryland: Genealogical Publishing Company, 1912, Reprinted 2005.

Drake, Benjamin, *Life of Tecumseh and of His Brother, The Prophet: With a Historical Sketch of the Shawanoe Indians*. Cincinnati, Ohio: E. Morgan, 1841.

Durham, Walter T., *Before Tennessee: The Southwest Territory, 1790–1796: A Narrative History of the Territory of the United States South of the River Ohio*. Rocky Mount, North Carolina: Rocky Mount Historical Association, 1990.

Eckert, Allan W., *A Sorrow in Our Heart: The Life of Tecumseh*. New York, New York: Bantam, 1992.

Evans, E. Raymond, Editor, "The Battle of Lookout Mountain: An Eyewitness Account by George Christian." *Journal of Cherokee Studies*, Volume III, Number 1, 1978, Cherokee, North Carolina: Museum of the Cherokee Indian.

_____, "Notable Persons in Cherokee History: Ostenaco." *Journal of Cherokee Studies*, Volume 1, Number 1, 1976, pages 41–54, Cherokee, North Carolina, Museum of the Cherokee Indian, 1976.

_____, "Notable Persons in Cherokee History: Bob Benge." *Journal of Cherokee Studies*, Volume 1, Number 2, 1976, pages 98–106, Cherokee, North Carolina, Museum of the Cherokee Indian.

_____, "Notable Persons in Cherokee History: Dragging Canoe." *Journal of Cherokee Studies,* Volume 2, Number 2, 1977, pages 176–189, Cherokee, North Carolina, Museum of the Cherokee Indian.

_____, "Was the Last Battle of the American Revolution Fought on Lookout Mountain?" *Journal of Cherokee Studies,* Volume V, Number 1, 1980, pages 30–40, Cherokee, North Carolina, Museum of the Cherokee Indian.

Evans, E. Raymond and Vicky Karhu, "Williams Island: A Source of Significant Material in the Collections of the Museum of the Cherokee." *Journal of Cherokee Studies,* Volume 9, Number 1, 1984, pages 10–34, Cherokee, North Carolina, Museum of the Cherokee Indian.

Evarts, Jeremiah, *Essays on the Present Crisis on the Condition of the American Indians.* Boston, Massachusetts: Perkins & Martin, 1829.

Faulkner, Charles H., *Massacre at Cavett's Station: Frontier Tennessee during the Cherokee Wars.* Knoxville, Tennessee: University of Tennessee Press, 2013.

Flint, Timothy, *Indian Wars of the West.* Cincinnati, Ohio: E. H. Flint, 1833.

Flora, Joseph, Lucinda Hardwick MacKethan, and Todd Taylor, "Old Southwest". *The Companion to Southern Literature: Themes, Genres, Places, People, Movements, and Motifs.* Baton Rouge, Louisiana: Louisiana State University Press, 2001.

Gilmore, James R., "Alexander McGillivray," *Appleton's Cyclopaedia of American Biography.* Volume 4, James Grant Wilson and John Fiske, Editors, New York, New York: Appleton and Company, 1888.

_____, *John Sevier as a Commonwealth Builder.* New York, New York: D. Appleton and Company, 1887.

Goodpasture, Albert V., "Indian Wars and Warriors of the Old Southwest, 1720–1807." *Tennessee Historical Magazine,* Volume 4, 1918, pages 3–49, 106–145, 161–210, and 252–289.

Green, Thomas Marshall, *The Spanish Conspiracy: A Review of Early Spanish Movements in the South-West, Containing Proofs of the Intrigues of James Wilkinson and John Brown; of the Complicity therewith of Judges Sebastian, Wallace, and Innes; the Early Struggles of Kentucky for Autonomy; the Intrigues of Sebastian in 1795–7; and the Legislative Investigation of His Corruption.* Cincinnati, Ohio: Robert Clarke & Company, 1891.

Hamer, Philip M., *Tennessee: A History, 1673–1932.* New York, New York: American History Association, 1933.

Hays, J. E., Editor, *Indian Treaties Cessions of Land in Georgia 1705–1837.* Atlanta, Georgia: Georgia Department of Archives and History, 1941.

Haywood, John, *The Civil and Political History of the State of Tennessee from its Earliest Settlement up to the Year 1796*. Nashville, Tennessee: W. H. Haywood, 1823.

Heard, J. Norman, *Handbook of the American Frontier, The Southeastern Woodlands: Four Centuries of Indian-White Relationships*. Metuchen, New Jersey: Scarecrow Press, 1993.

Henderson, Archibald, *The Conquest of the Old Southwest: The Romantic Story of the Early Pioneers into Virginia, the Carolinas, Tennessee and Kentucky 1740 To 1790*. New York, New York: The Century Company, 1920.

_____, *The Spanish Conspiracy in Tennessee*. Tennessee Historical Magazine, Volume 3, Nashville, Tennessee: Tennessee Historical Society, 1917.

Hoig, Stanley, *The Cherokees and Their Chiefs: In the Wake of Empire*. Fayetteville, Arkansas: University of Arkansas Press, 1998.

Hunter, C. L., *Sketches of Western North Carolina: Historical and Biographical*. Raleigh, North Carolina: Raleigh News Steam Job Print, 1877.

King, Duane H., *The Cherokee Indian Nation: A Troubled History*. Knoxville, Tennessee: University of Tennessee Press, 1979.

Klink, Karl and James Talman, Editors, *The Journal of Major John Norton*. Toronto, Ontario: Champlain Society, 1970.

Kneberg, Madeline and Thomas M. N. Lewis, *Tribes That Slumber*. Knoxville, Tennessee: University of Tennessee Press, 1958.

Lavender, Billy, *A Pioneer Church in the Oconee Territory: A Historical Synopsis of Antioch Christian Church*. New York, New York: iUniverse, Inc., 2005.

Lowrie, Walter and Matthew St. Clair Clarke, Editors, *American State Papers: Foreign Relations*. Volume I, Washington, DC: Giles and Seaton, 1832.

McLoughlin, William G., *Cherokee Renascence in the New Republic*. Princeton, New Jersey: Princeton University Press, 1992.

Mastromarino, Mark A., Editor, *The Papers of George Washington*, Presidential Series, Volume 6, 1 July 1790 – 30 November 1790, Charlottesville, Virginia: University Press of Virginia, 1996.

Mays, Terry, "Cherokee Campaign of 1776." *Historical Dictionary of the American Revolution*, Metuchen, New Jersey: Scarecrow Press, 1999.

Miles, Tiya, *The House on Diamond Hill: A Cherokee Plantation Story*. Chapel Hill, North Carolina: University of North Carolina Press, 2010.

Milling, Chapman, *Red Carolinians*. Chapel Hill, North Carolina: University of North Carolina Press, 1940.

Mooney, James, *Myths of the Cherokee and Sacred Formulas of the Cherokee*. Washington, DC: Smithsonian Institution, Nashville, Tennessee: Charles and Randy Elder-Booksellers, 1891 and 1900, Reprinted 1982.

Moore, John Trotwood and Austin P. Foster, "Indian Wars and Warriors of Tennessee." *Tennessee, The Volunteer State, 1769–1923*. Volume 1, Chapter IX, 1923, pages 157–250, Chicago, Illinois: S. J. Clarke Publishing Company.

Murphy, Justin D., "Grand Council on Muscle Shoals." *The Encyclopedia of North American Indian Wars, 1607–1890: A Political, Social, and Military History*. Spencer C. Tucker, Editor, Santa Barbara, California, ABC-CLIO, 2011.

O'Brien, Greg, Editor. *Pre-Removal Choctaw History: Exploring New Paths*. Norman, Oklahoma: University of Oklahoma Press, 2008.

O'Donnell, James, *Southern Indians in the American Revolution*. Knoxville, Tennessee: University of Tennessee Press, 1973.

Phelan, James, *History of Tennessee: The Making of a State*. Boston, Massachusetts and New York, New York: Houghton, Mifflin & Company, 1888.

Ramsey, James Gettys McGregor, *The Annals of Tennessee to the End of the Eighteenth Century*. Knoxville, Tennessee: East Tennessee Historical Society, 1967.

Reynolds, William R., Jr., *Andrew Pickens: South Carolina Patriot in the Revolutionary War*. Jefferson, North Carolina: McFarland & Company, Inc., 2012.

Roosevelt, Theodore. *The Winning of the West, Part IV: The Indian Wars, 1784–1787*. New York, New York: Current Literature Publishing Company, 1905.

Royce, C.C., *The Cherokee Nation of Indians: A Narrative of their Official Relations with the Colonial and Federal Governments*. Fifth Annual Report, Bureau of American Ethnology, 1883–1884. Washington, DC: Government Printing Office, 1889.

Starr, Emmet, *History of the Cherokee Indians, and their Legends and Folklore*. Oklahoma City, Oklahoma: The Warden Company, 1992.

Summers, Lewis Preston, *History of Southwest Virginia, 1746–1786, Washington County, 1777–1870*. Richmond, Virginia: J. L. Printing Company, 1903.

Tanner, Helen Hornbeck, "Cherokees in the Ohio Country." *Journal of Cherokee Studies*, Volume III, Number 2, 1978, pages 95–103, Cherokee, North Carolina, Museum of the Cherokee Indian.

Toulmin, Llewellyn M., "Backcountry Warrior: Brig. Gen. Andrew Williamson." *Journal of Backcountry Studies*, Volume 7 Number 1, 2010, Greensboro, North Carolina.

Whitaker, Arthur Preston and Samuel Eliot Morrison, *The Spanish American Frontier: 1783-1795, The Westward Movement and the Spanish Retreat in the Mississippi Valley*. Gloucester, Massachusetts: Peter Smith, 1962.

Wilkins, Thurman, *Cherokee Tragedy: The Ridge Family and the Decimation of a People.* New York, New York: MacMillan Company, 1970.

Williams, Samuel Cole, *Early Travels in the Tennessee Country, 1540–1800.* Johnson City, Tennessee: Watauga Press, 1928.

_____, *History of the Lost State of Franklin.* New York, New York: Press of the Pioneers, 1933.

Wilson, Frazer Ells, *The Peace of Mad Anthony.* Greenville, Ohio: Chas. B. Kemble Book and Job Printer, 1907.

First Creek War, 1813-14

Background

After the turn of the 19th century, more and more Creek abandoned their hunting and trading economy, adopting the more modern economy of raising crops and livestock. With no industry of their own, the Creek had to rely on outside traders for arms, clothing, tools, and other essentials. As the cost of the trade goods increased, many Creek became indebted to the traders. The Creek National Council reluctantly agreed to use their annual annuity payments from the government to settle debts, infuriating many Creek who had no debt and believed that those funds should be used for the benefit of all, not just the major debtors.

The ever-increasing encroachment of white settlement, primarily along the new Federal Road, linking Athens, Georgia to Fort Stoddert on the Mobile River, and in the Cumberland River Valley in Tennessee, further increased Creek resentment. In 1812, Creek and Shawnee leaders met to discuss their frustrations. One Creek war party killed two travelers on the Federal Road and massacred two families on the Duck River, in Tennessee. Benjamin Hawkins, General Superintendent of Indian Affairs for all tribes in the Old Southwest, demanded the execution of the murderers. The National Council acquiesced and ordered eight executions.

Early the next year, Hawkins demanded that the National Council punish another group of warriors who had murdered several whites. The council sent William McIntosh, leading warriors called Law Menders, mostly from the Upper Towns, to locate and bring the murderers to justice. Because such law enforcement matters traditionally were handled at the clan or town level, such actions by the National Council were considered a usurpation of power and infringement of traditional clan authority. At the same time, a spiritual awakening was occurring among many Creek, advocating a return to a traditional way of life and armed resistance to recover their lost hunting grounds. Influenced by Shawnee Chief Tecumseh and his brother The Prophet, Creek spiritual leaders encouraged discontent with the National Council. Tecumseh and The Prophet traveled throughout the southeast, encouraging the Chickasaw, Choctaw, and Creek to resist American settlement and return to a traditional way of life. Principally due to the efforts of Choctaw chief Pushmataha, the Chickasaw and Choctaw did not heed Tecumseh's exhortations.

As more dissidents spoke against the National Council and their centers of power at Coweta and Tuckabatchee, Hawkins demanded that the Creek denounce the dissidents and their prophets, asserting that those who did not were enemies of the United States. Serious resistance to the National Council and increasing encroachment of new settlements became clear as new prophecies of war were heard and new war songs and dances were performed. For many Creek, the sudden appearance of a comet at Tecumseh's arrival and his prediction of the New Madrid earthquake confirmed his calls to return to the traditional Creek way of life and fight against the American settlers.

Dissidence grew into rebellion when the dissident Red Stick warriors attacked Tuckabatchee and the homes of other chiefs in the Upper Towns who supported the National Council and accommodation with the federal government. The Red Sticks killed their domestic livestock, believing that the Great Spirit intended animals to roam free for the benefit of all. For the rest of 1813, hunger became a problem for many Creek families due to the loss of livestock, the sharply decreased deer population, scarcity of ammunition for hunting, and disrupted trade.

Thus, the First Creek War started as an internal Creek civil war, while America was fighting the British in the War of 1812. To maintain Creek neutrality and keep the Red Sticks and other tribes from joining the British in the war, the government was eager to put down the Red Stick rebellion.

Campaigns

Peter McQueen, a mixed-blood Red Stick chief and prophet, led 350 warriors to Pensacola to get arms and ammunition from the Spanish, greatly alarming the Tensaw settlements in the Mississippi Territory, but now in Alabama. Colonel James Caller, commander of the local militia, determined to intercept the Red Sticks before they could deliver their war supplies. Caller led three mounted companies and another company under Captain Samuel Dale, in all about 180 militia and friendly Creek. On the morning of July 27, 1813, Caller surprised the Red Sticks at their camp in a horseshoe bend of Burnt Corn Creek, near modern Brewton, in Escambia County, Alabama, forcing them to flee and abandon the gunpowder and lead. After realizing there was no pursuit, McQueen organized a counterattack, forcing the militia to withdraw in disarray. Caller became lost as he fled and was not found until two weeks later. Their victory instilled the Red Sticks with pride and confidence in their ability to defeat the Americans.

In retaliation, the Red Sticks began attacking the scattered settlements in the Tensaw District, compelling the terrified settlers to flee to the relative safety of one of the numerous makeshift stockade forts erected for their defense. Brigadier General Ferdinand L. Claiborne led a large force of Mississippi Territory militia to bolster the local defense, dividing his militia into smaller detachments that reinforced the garrisons at the various stockades. Major Daniel Beasley, with 175 militia, reinforced Fort Mims, one of the largest stockades, about forty miles north of Mobile. At noon, on August 30th, William Weatherford, Paddy Walsh, and Peter McQueen led about seven hundred Red Stick warriors against Fort Mims. After a few hours, the defense collapsed. The Red Sticks swarmed into and sacked the stockade, leaving it in flames. Nearly all the inhabitants were killed, many were scalped, less than three dozen managing to escape. A relief party later found the dead bodies of 247 defenders and 100 Red Sticks.

On September 1st, Prophet Francis led his Red Stick war party in attacking the cabins of Ransom Kimbell and Abner James. Most of the men escaped to nearby Fort Sinquefield, near modern Grove Hill in Clarke County, but twelve women and children were murdered and scalped. Not long after the massacre, 100 Red Sticks attacked the fort, killing several before withdrawing. The Red Sticks also attacked several settlements along the Chattahoochee River, significantly increasing their support in the Upper Towns. Recognizing that they faced an invasion, the Red Sticks gathered their scattered followers into three fortified towns. The Alabama gathered at Econochaca, known as the Holy Ground, located on the bluffs above the Alabama River about 30 miles west of Montgomery. The Red Sticks erected a second fortification at Tohopeka, a horseshoe bend in the Tallapoosa River. The Tallapoosa Red Sticks congregated at Autossee, near modern Shorter, in Macon County, Alabama.

Secretary of War John Armstrong and Major General Thomas Pinckney, commander of the Sixth Military District planned a three-pronged response to the outrages at Fort Mims, Fort Sinquefield, and along the Chattahoochee: the first by Georgia militia against Autossee, the second by militia from the Mississippi Territory against Econochaca, and the third by Tennessee militia against Tohopeka. The invasion of the Red Stick territory began in earnest by October 1813.

The first prong of the overall offensive was led by Brigadier General John Floyd, who assembled 3,600 Georgia militia at Fort Hawkins, located on a hill by the Ocmulgee River, at modern Macon, Georgia. Using Fort Hawkins as his base, Floyd ordered the construction of a line of blockhouses and forts extending westward to the Alabama River. In November, Floyd led his army across the Chattahoochee River, where he built Fort Mitchell, about 10 miles south of modern Phenix City, Alabama, in Russell County. Leaving the main body of his army at Fort Mitchell, Floyd led 950 men about 60 miles west through the wilderness. On November 29th, Floyd attacked the fortified towns of Autossee, on the east bank of the Tallapoosa, at the mouth of Calabee Creek, and Tallassee, near the modern town of the same name. The fighting was fierce, but Floyd's men prevailed, killing more than 200 warriors and allowing his Creek allies to plunder before burning the towns. Floyd then returned to Georgia to tend to his wounded and replenish his supplies. While Floyd and his militia were recuperating, Major General David Adams led 500 Georgia militia westward to keep the Red Sticks on the defensive. On December 17th, Adams found Nuyaka town deserted, the Red Sticks and their families having fled before their arrival. Adams burned the town and destroyed the crops, before returning to Georgia.

In January 1814, Floyd led 1,100 militia and 600 friendly Indians across the Chattahoochee River, erected Fort Hull, about 40 miles west of Fort Mitchell, and the fortified Camp Defiance on Calabee Creek. On January 27th, Chief Paddy Walsh led 1,300 Red Stick warriors in a surprise attack, called the Battle of Calabee Creek. Paddy Walsh almost prevailed, but the Georgians eventually won the battle, killing 50 Red Sticks, severely wounding Paddy Walsh, while losing 17 killed and 132 wounded. Because many of the militia enlistments were about to expire, Floyd took his army back to Georgia.

The second prong was led by Brigadier General Ferdinand Claiborne, in command of a brigade of Louisiana and Mississippi volunteers, consisting of about 250 men under Colonel Joseph Carson, 150 men under Major Benjamin Smoot, 150 mounted militia under Major Cassels, and 150 Choctaw warriors led by Pushmataha. In July 1813, Claiborne marched his troops to Fort Stoddert, on the Mobile River. From there, his men began to scour the lower Tombigbee and Alabama river area to flush out bands of Red Stick Creek. In November, Captain Sam Dale and two privates, rowed by a free man of color named Caesar, fought more than twice their number of Red Sticks from their canoe. Using bayonets, knives, gun butts, and oars, in a brief hand-to-hand battle, Dale and his men defeated the Red Sticks. The sensational affair, dubbed the great Canoe Fight, greatly boosted American morale and made Dale a national hero.

In November, Claiborne moved about 80 miles north of Fort Stephens, where he constructed Fort Claiborne as a base of operations for his campaign. In December, Claiborne's army, bolstered by the 3rd Infantry Regiment commanded by Colonel Gilbert C. Russell, set out to attack and destroy the Red Sticks. Claiborne attacked the Holy Ground, a fortified town of two hundred buildings situated on a bluff overlooking the Alabama River, on December 23rd, but most of the Red Sticks fled after a brief fight. One of the last to retreat was William Weatherford, who made his escape by leaping his horse Arrow over the fifteen-foot bluff into the river and disappearing in a hail of bullets into the dense forest on the other side. Claiborne lost only one casualty in the one-hour engagement and inflicted about thirty Red Sticks killed and many more wounded. In the town, they discovered a pole from which hundreds of scalps were hung, probably at least some grisly trophies from the massacre at Fort Mims. Claiborne's men then plundered for corn and other supplies before putting the town to the torch.

William Blount, Governor of Tennessee, issued a call for 3,500 volunteers to be organized into two armies, one led by Andrew Jackson and the other led by John Cocke. In this third prong of the offensive, Major General Andrew Jackson, led his 1,000 West Tennessee militia, a 1,300-man strong cavalry brigade, and a large band of Cherokee warriors. The infantry brigade commanded by Colonel William Hall consisted of Colonel Edward Bradley's 1st Regiment of Tennessee Volunteer Infantry and Colonel William Pillow's Regiment of Tennessee Volunteer Infantry. The cavalry, commanded by Brigadier General John Coffee, consisted of Colonel John Alcorn's 2nd Regiment of Volunteer Mounted Riflemen and Colonel Robert Dyer's 1st Regiment of Volunteer Mounted Gunmen.

In November, Jackson established Fort Strother, on a bluff overlooking the Coosa River, near Ohatchee, to serve as his headquarters and base of operations. There Jackson waited for Cocke to join him. On November 3rd, Coffee led about 900 troopers against the Red Sticks at Tallusahatchee, about 15 miles away, in just half an hour killing 186 warriors and many women and children and destroying the village. Tennessee volunteer David Crockett remarked afterward that "we shot them like dogs." Thrilled with the victory, Jackson wrote Governor Blount, "We have retaliated for the destruction of Fort Mims."

After Coffee returned to Fort Strother, Jackson learned that Red Stick Chief William Weatherford with 1,000 warriors was attacking the friendly Creek town of Talladega. On November 9th, Jackson led his army against Weatherford's force, killing 300, wounding 110, driving the rest away, and rescuing the friendly Creek. By December, due to casualties, illness, expiration of enlistments, and desertion, Jackson's army was reduced to 500 effectives. In mid-January, Jackson led 175 militia, 30 artillerymen, and 200 Cherokee warriors towards the Red Stick town of Emuckfaw, a few miles northwest of Tohopeka. On January 22nd, the Red Sticks struck first by attacking Jackson's camp. After several assaults, the Red Sticks were forced to withdraw, but Jackson needed to return to Fort Strother, to tend his wounded and resupply his troops. As Jackson re-crossed Emuckfaw Creek, on January 24th, the Red Sticks attacked again, but were driven off.

Meanwhile, Major General John Cocke, commander of the East Tennessee militia, was ordered to join Jackson at Fort Strother. But Cocke halted his march and, on November 11, 1813, ordered Brigadier General James White, with his Hamilton District militia, to attack and destroy the Creek towns at Hillabee. Over several days, White attacked town after town, destroying them all, killing nearly 100, and capturing several hundred.

Upon his return from Emuckfaw, Jackson erected Fort Williams, on a bluff above the Coosa River, near modern Talladega, as a base for regrouping and rebuilding his army. By March, Jackson received new volunteers, his army growing to more than 2,600 effectives, including the 39th U. S. Infantry, commanded by Colonel John Williams, and the East and West Tennessee militias, supplemented by about 500 Cherokee and 100 Lower Creek warriors led by William McIntosh. On the morning of March 27th, Jackson began his assault on Chief Menawa's fortifications at Tohopeka, defended by 1,000 warriors, with an artillery bombardment against the fortified breastworks. Jackson ordered a party of Cocke's Cherokee to assault the village from the rear. They crossed the river and pressed on into the village, setting it on fire as they went. After seeing the smoke from the fires, Jackson ordered a frontal assault, with the 39th Regiment in the forefront, supported by a brigade of Tennessee militia. Within minutes, the soldiers scaled the breastworks and the fighting turned into a bloodbath for the Red Sticks. By nightfall, as many as 900 defenders lay dead on the field, more Indians dying that day than in any other battle fought in United States history. Jackson lost 49 dead and 154 wounded and later wrote his wife, "The carnage was dreadful."

After this famous Battle of Horseshoe Bend, Jackson moved his troops to the site of the old French Fort Toulouse, at the fork of the Tallapoosa and Coosa rivers, where he constructed Fort Jackson, near present-day Wetumpka, Alabama. Along the way, Jackson burned four dozen Red

Stick towns, nearly every one of the Upper Towns. Total Creek war deaths were very high, estimates ranging from 2,000 to as many as 3,000. Remnants of the all but defeated Red Sticks hunkered down, licked their wounds, and hoped they could continue fighting. Over the next year, many more died of starvation and exposure. Total surrender came on August 9, 1814, with the signing of the Treaty of Fort Jackson.

Aftermath

The Treaty of Fort Jackson forced the Creek people to cede more than 23 million acres, including all their land in Georgia and much of central Alabama, to the federal government as reparations for the cost of prosecuting the war. Andrew Jackson became a celebrated national hero after his victories over the Creek at the Battle of Horseshoe Bend and over the British at the Battle of New Orleans the following January. His celebrity and his pledge to remove the Indians to the Indian Territory propelled him to the White House in 1828.

The end of hostilities encouraged a renewed wave of settlement into what would become Alabama of settlers from Georgia and the Carolinas from the east and Tennesseans and Virginians from the north. In the decade from 1810 to 1820, the population of Alabama exploded from about 9,000 to 150,000.

The Creek rebuilt their towns and their economy and recognized the National Council as their rightful leaders. The Creek people accepted the justice dealt by the Law Menders, led by Chief Menawa, a former Red Stick, even the execution of the popular Chief William McIntosh, for illegally ceding more Creek land in 1825. In addition, several thousand Creek left their homes and moved south into Spanish Florida, settling among the Seminole.

Places of Interest

Horseshoe Bend National Military Park
11288 Horseshoe Bend Road
Daviston, Alabama 36256

The park hosts the annual Muster on the Tallapoosa, where reenactors meet to provide insight into the everyday life of the American Indians as well as the militiamen, including musket and cannon firing demonstrations, usually on a weekend in August near the anniversary of the battle. The event is free and open to the public.

Fort Mims Historical Marker
Fort Mims Road and Boatyard Road
North of Stockton, Alabama

Here in Creek Indian War 1813-14 took place the most brutal massacre in American history. Indians took the fort with heavy loss, then killed all but about 36 of some 550 in the fort. Creeks had been armed by British at Pensacola in this phase of War of 1812.

Fort Mims Massacre Monument
Fort Mims Historical Site
Fort Mims Road, 0.3 miles from Boatyard Road

In honor of the men, woman and children massacred by Creek Indians in brave defense of Fort Mims Aug. 30, 1813. Erected by U. S. D. of 1812 in Ala.

The Fort Mims Restoration Association hosts an annual reenactment on the anniversary of the massacre at the five-acre site. Another monument at the site lists the names of many of those who perished.

141

The Hermitage
4580 Rachel's Lane
Nashville, Tennessee 37076

(615) 889-2941

info@thehermitage.com

http://thehermitage.com/

The Hermitage was the home of President Andrew Jackson from 1804 until his death in 1845. Located just ten miles east of Nashville, the old plantation house is a museum. Jackson and his wife Rachel are buried there.

John Coffee Grave
Coffee Family Cemetery
Florence, Alabama

John Coffee (1772-1833) raised the 2nd Regiment of Volunteer Mounted Riflemen, composed mostly of men from Bedford, Rutherford, Smith, Dickson, Franklin, Lincoln, Sumner, Williamson, and Wilson counties, Tennessee. Andrew Jackson promoted him to Brigadier General during the First Creek War.

Creek Agency Old Agency Historical Monument
Intersection of Georgia Route 128 and Benjamin Hawkins Road about ¼ mile north of Taylor County line.

Here on the Flint River was the headquarters of the Agent for Indian Affairs South of Ohio until the area was acquired by Georgia in the Creek cession of Jan. 24, 1826. Here Benjamin Hawkins and David B. Mitchell, Agents, resided and in 1804 and 1818 negotiated treaties with the Indians. Hawkins, Agent from 1796 to 1816, here entertained hundreds of Indians and many white notables. He established an immense model farm and taught the Indians how to spin and weave and grow cotton, corn, grain and cattle.

Fort Sinquefield Historic Site

Located on Fort Sinquefield Fort Road,
west of U. S. Route 84, about 3 miles
southeast from Grove Hill, Alabama.

https://fortsinquefield.org/

Managed by the Clarke County Historical Society, interpretive signs on
site tell the story of the battle and place it in the context of the larger
Creek War of 1813-1814 and the War of 1812. A replica of the corner
of the old fort wall marks the place thought to be the original fort
location. Visitors are welcome to take a self-guided tour at any time of
year and can walk from the fort site to the spring that was part of the
events that unfolded at the battle. The full story of the battle is summarized in a slide presentation
on the website. In addition to self-guided tours, the Historical Society also hosts events at the fort
site periodically. The grounds include a stone monument dedicated to the victims of the Kimbell-
James Massacre.

Fort Strother Monument

Near Ohatchee, Alabama,
in Saint Clair County,
at the intersection of
State Highway 144 and Valley Drive.

http://www.hmdb.org/marker.asp?MarkerID=28144

Fort Strother Creek Indian War Headquarters of Gen. Andrew Jackson
1813 – 1814. Erected By St. Clair County.

Fort Mitchell National Historic Landmark Site

561 Highway 165
Fort Mitchell, Alabama 36856

(334) 855-1406

http://visitfortmitchell.org/

The fort was an important base of operations for the
army during the First Creek War, a trading post and
home of the Indian Agency between wars, and army base during the Second Creek War and
Creek removal. The visitor center inside the reconstructed fort houses the museum, theater, and
displays depicting historical scenes and events of this area and time period. There are artifacts
including arrowheads, tools, guns, pottery, and household items. In the theater, a film shows the
events and history that happened in the periods between 1813 and 1860.

Holy Ground Battlefield Park
300 Battlefield Road
Lowndesboro, Alabama 36752

(334) 875-6247

About two miles north of the town of White Hall, in Lowndes County, is the site of the 1813 battle between William Weatherford's Creek band and General Claiborne's forces accompanied by Chief Pushmataha's Choctaw warriors. The Americans killed 21 Creek and forced the survivors to retreat. Weatherford escaped by leaping his gray horse, Arrow, from the bluff into the Alabama River and swimming to the opposite shore with his rifle over his head and bullets whizzing around him.

William Weatherford Memorial Park
Red Eagle Road, Off T. J. Earle Road
Little River, Alabama 36550

One of the most notable Creek figures of the early 19th century lies buried beneath a stone cairn in Baldwin County, Alabama. William Weatherford, also known as Red Eagle, was one of the leaders of the attack on Fort Mims. He also fought at the Battle of Holy Ground. He surrendered to Andrew Jackson at Fort Jackson, afterwards guiding American forces against a number of Creek holdouts.

McIntosh Reserve Park
1046 West McIntosh Circle
Whitesburg, Georgia 30185

(770) 830-5879

http://carrollcountyga.com/293/McIntosh-Reserve-Park

The Reserve is named for William McIntosh, a prominent Creek Indian leader and planter. The plantation, in English, was called Acorn Bluff. McIntosh lived in a two-story log house, that served as an inn for travelers. A reconstructed house is open to park visitors. In 1825, McIntosh signed the second Treaty of Indian Springs, ceding Creek lands in Georgia and Alabama to the federal government. In exchange for signing the treaty, McIntosh was allowed to keep his plantation. The Creek National Council opposed the treaty and ordered his execution. A band of warriors killed McIntosh at his home. His grave is located across the road from the reconstructed house.

Butler Massacre / Fort Bibb Historical Marker
Pineapple Highway, 0.8 miles west of Bibb Road
Forest Home, Alabama

On March 20, 1818, Capt. William Butler, Capt. James
Saffold, William Gardener, Daniel Shaw and John Hinson
left Fort Bibb to meet Col. Sam Dale. They were attacked
near Pine Barren Creek by Savannah Jack and his warriors.
Gardener and Shaw were shot dead; Butler and Hinson
wounded. Saffold and Hinson escaped on horseback to Fort
Bibb, but Capt. Butler, thrown from his horse and left on foot, was killed by the Indians. Butler
County was named in his honor.

Named for Alabama Territorial Governor William Wyatt Bibb, Fort Bibb was built in winter
1817-1818 to protect settlers from Creek Indian attacks. It was said to be a stockade enclosing
Capt. James Saffold's home at the Flats (Pine Flats). Col. Sam Dale helped strengthen Fort Bibb
in spring 1818 before he and his militia built Fort Dale 13-14 miles northeast on the Federal
Road. These forts were Butler County's first election sites in 1820.

Major Samuel Dale Grave
Samuel Dale Memorial Park Cemetery
Daleville, Mississippi

Samuel Dale (1772-1841), known as the Daniel Boone of Alabama, was
a frontiersman, trader, scout, Army officer, and politician. In 1796, he
started a business hauling settlers to the Mississippi Territory and trading
with the Indians there. During the First Creek War, he organized the
defenses in southern Alabama. After the war, he was elected to the first
General Assembly of the Alabama Territory. In 1836, he was elected
Lauderdale County's first representative to the Mississippi Legislature.

Tallasahatchie Battle Field Historical Marker
McCullars Lane west of County Road 73,
near Alexandria, Alabama

This Stone Marks The Site Of The Tallasahatchie Battle Field. On this
spot Lieut. Gen. John Coffee with Gen. Andrew Jackson's men won a
victory over the Creek Indians, Nov. 3, 1813. Erected by the Frederick
Wm. Gray Chapt. Daughters of the American Revolution. Nov. 3, 1913.
Anniston Ala.

Lincoyer and The Battle of Tallasehatchee Historical Marker
McCullars Lane west of County Road 73,
near Alexandria, Alabama

At this site, on Nov. 3, 1813, after the Battle of Tallasehatchee, known then as Talluschatches, during the Creek Indian War, Gen. Andrew Jackson found a dead Creek Indian woman embracing her living infant son. Gen. Jackson, upon hearing that the other Creek Indian women were planning to kill the infant, as was their custom when all relations were dead, became himself the protector and guardian of the child. Gen. Jackson took the infant to Fort Strother, in present day Ohatchee, where he nursed him back to health. Gen. Jackson then took the baby to his family home, the Hermitage, in Nashville, Tenn., where he and his wife Rachel named the child Lincoyer and adopted, raised, loved and educated him as their son. Lincoyer fell ill and died of tuberculosis at home with his family, when he was 16 years old. The General and his wife mourned the loss of their son for the rest of their lives.

Canoe Fight Historical Marker
Madison Road and Tennessee Road, near
Gainestown, Alabama

On November 12, 1813, the Canoe Fight, one of the key assaults of the Creek War, took place nearby at the mouth of Randon's Creek where it flows into the Alabama River. Following the Fort Mims Massacre in August, small bands of Creek warriors persisted in attacks on settlements in the region. Capt. Sam Dale, stationed at Ft. Madison in Clarke County, volunteered to lead a mission to drive the Creeks from the area. The American militiamen, led by Dale, had launched their canoe the day before at Brazier's Landing (now French's Landing) and moved upriver where they encountered a canoe containing nine Indian warriors. The American militiamen were: Dale, Jeremiah Austill, and James Smith. A ferryman named Caesar paddled the canoe and as the battle ensued, he held the two canoes together. One Indian was thrown into the water and the other eight were killed. As a result of this battle, the inroad of the Creek warriors on the west side of the Alabama River was checked and the settlers of Clarke County were able to return to their plantations and gather their crops and enlarge their improvements.

Fort Madison-Creek War 1812-13 Historical Marker
Bird Jackson Road, 5.9 miles south
of Simmons Creek Road, near
Suggsville, Alabama

This marks the site of pioneer stockade commanded by
Captains Sam Dale and Evan Austill. Choctaw Chieftain
Pushmattaha was often here. Expedition terminating in
noted Canoe Fight on Alabama River immediately east of
this site, was launched here.

**Battle of Enitachopko Creek Indian War 1813-14
Historical Marker**
Shady Grove Road and Alabama Route 63, Near
Goodwater, Alabama

Hostile Creeks attacked Andrew Jackson here,
withdrawing to Ft. Strother, Jan. 24, 1814. His troops
broke through lines, kept on to Ft. Strothe, and Creeks
boasted that they defeated 'Capt. Jack', and drove him to
the Coosa.

Pioneer Massey Cemetery Historical Marker
Trussville, Jefferson County, Alabama

Samuel Massey and his brother-in-law, Duke William
Glenn, first came to this Territory in February 1814, with
Lt. Col Reuben Nash's Regt. South Carolina Volunteer
Militia, to help defeat the Creek Indians in the War of
1812. Samuel Massey returned to settle this land months
before Alabama became a state on December 14, 1819.
Samuel's son, William Duke Massey, married Ruth Reed,
daughter of William 'Silver Billy' Reed. Born October 28,
1817, she was the first white girl born in Jefferson County.

Battle of Talladega Nov. 9, 1813 Historical Marker
East Battle Street and Court Street North
Talladega, Alabama

Here Andrew Jackson led Tennessee Volunteers and friendly
Indians to victory over hostile "Red Sticks." This action
rescued friendly Creeks besieged in Fort Leslie. Creek Indian
War 1813 - 1814.

Major General David Adams Grave
Adams Family Cemetery
Gladesville, in Jasper County,
Georgia

David Adams (1766-1831) led an expedition here against the
Creek in the First Creek War.

John Floyd Grave
Floyd Family Cemetery
Fairfield Plantation on
Floyd Neck
Camden County, Georgia

John Floyd (1769-1839) began his military career on May 2, 1804 as a captain in the Camden
County militia. As a brigadier general, he commanded Georgia militia in the First Creek War.
From 1820 to 1826, Floyd represented Camden County in the Georgia House of Representatives
and, from 1827 to 1829, he represented his district in the U. S. House of Representatives.

Pushmataha's Grave
Congressional Cemetery
1801 E Street SE
Washington, DC 20003

Pushmataha (ca1760s-1824), the "Indian General", was one of three regional chiefs of the Choctaw. He was highly regarded among Native Americans, Europeans, and white Americans, for his skill and cunning in both war and diplomacy. Pushmataha rejected the urging of Tecumseh to fight the Americans and instead joined the American side in the War of 1812 and First Creek War. In 1824, he traveled to Washington to petition the government against further cessions of Choctaw land. He died there from croup and was buried with full military honors.

John Williams Grave
First Presbyterian Church Cemetery
620 State Street
Knoxville, Tennessee

John Williams (1778-1837) studied law at Salisbury, North Carolina and served as captain in the 6th U. S. Infantry Regiment in 1799 and 1800, before moving to Knoxville, Tennessee, where he practiced law. He was appointed state attorney general in 1807. In late 1812, Williams raised more than 200 volunteers from Tennessee and Georgia, with whom he invaded Florida, destroying several Seminole villages, burning more than 300 houses, and confiscating a large number of horses and livestock. In 1813, he was commissioned a colonel in the U. S. Army and recruited 600 men and organized the 39th Infantry Regiment. He and his men were instrumental in Andrew Jackson's victory at the Battle of Horseshoe Bend.

Further Reading

Bassett, John Spencer, Editor, *Correspondence of Andrew Jackson*. Washington, DC: Carnegie Institution, 1926.

Black, Jason Edward, "Memories of the Alabama Creek War, 1813-1814: U. S. Governmental and Native Identities at the Horseshoe Bend National Military Park." *American Indian Quarterly*, Volume 33, Number 2, 2009, pages 200-229.

Braund, Kathryn E. Holland, *Tohopeka: Rethinking the Creek War and the War of 1812*. Tuscaloosa, Alabama: University of Alabama Press, 2012.

Brewer, Willis, *Alabama: Her History, Resources, War Record, and Public Men*. Baltimore, Maryland: Genealogical Publishing Company, 1872, Reprinted 2000.

Bunn, Mike and Clay Williams, *Battle for the Southern Frontier: The Creek War and the War of 1812*. Charleston, South Carolina: History Press, 2008.

Claiborne, John Francis Hamtramck, *Life and Times of Gen. Sam Dale, the Mississippi Partisan*. New York, New York: Harper and Brothers, 1860.

Claiborne, John Francis Hamtramck, *Mississippi: as a Province, Territory, and State, with Biographical Notices of Eminent Citizens*. Jackson, Mississippi: Power and Barksdale, 1880.

Collins, Gilbert, *Guidebook to the Historic Sites of the War of 1812*. Toronto, Ontario: Dundurn Press, 1998.

Drake, Samuel G., *Indian Captives: or, Life in the Wigwam, Being True Narratives of Captives Who Have Been Carried Away by the Indians, from the Frontier Settlements of the U. S., from the Earliest Period to the Present Time*. Auburn, New York: Derby, Miller & Company, Bowie, Maryland: Heritage Books, 1850, Reprinted 1995.

Eaton, John Henry and John Reid, *The Life of Andrew Jackson, Major General in the Service of the United States: Comprising a History of the War in the South, from the Commencement of the Creek Campaign to the Termination of Hostilities Before New Orleans*. Philadelphia, Pennsylvania: McCarty and Davis, 3rd Edition, 1828.

Ethridge, Robbie Franklyn, *Creek Country: The Creek Indians and Their World*. Chapel Hill, North Carolina: University of North Carolina Press, 2003.

Foster, Thomas, *The Collected Works of Benjamin Hawkins*, 1796-1810. Tuscaloosa, Alabama: University of Alabama Press, 2003.

Frank, Andrew K., *Creeks and Southerners: Biculturalism on the Early American Frontier*. Lincoln, Nebraska: University of Nebraska Press, 2005.

Fretwell, Mark E., *This So Remote Frontier: The Chattahoochee Country of Alabama and Georgia*. Eufaula, Alabama: Historic Chattahoochee Commission, 1980.

Gayarré, Charles, *History of Louisiana*. New York, New York: William D. Widdon Publishers, 1866.

Grant, C. L., *Journals and Writings of Benjamin Hawkins*. Savannah, Georgia: Beehive Press, 1980.

Griffith, Benjamin. W., Jr., *McIntosh and Weatherford: Creek Indian Leaders*. Tuscaloosa, Alabama: University of Alabama Press, 1988.

Halbert, H. S. and T. H. Ball. *The Creek War of 1813 and 1814*. Chicago, Illinois: Donohue & Henneberry, Tuscaloosa, Alabama: University of Alabama Press, 1895, Reprinted 1995.

Haynes, Robert V., *The Mississippi Territory and the Southwest Frontier, 1795–1817*. Lexington, Kentucky: University Press of Kentucky, 2010.

Heidler, David S. and Jeanne T. Heidler, Editors, *Encyclopedia of the War of 1812*. Santa Barbara, California: ABC-CLIO, 1997.

Henri, Florette, *The Southern Indians and Benjamin Hawkins, 1796–1816*. Norman, Oklahoma: University of Oklahoma Press, 1986.

Holland, James W., *Andrew Jackson and the Creek War: Victory at Horseshoe Bend*. Tuscaloosa, Alabama: University of Alabama Press, 1990.

Hood, Charlotte, *Jackson's White Plumes: An Historical and Genealogical Account of Selected Cherokee Families Who Supported Andrew Jackson during the Creek Indian War of 1813–1814*. Bay Minette, Alabama: Lavender Publishing, 1995.

Hudson, Angela Pulley, *Creek Paths and American Roads: Indians, Settlers, and Slaves and the Making of the American South*. Chapel Hill, North Carolina: University of North Carolina Press, 2010.

Kanon, Thomas. "A Slow, Laborious Slaughter: The Battle of Horseshoe Bend." *Tennessee Historical* Quarterly, Volume 58, Number 1, 1999, pages 2-15.

Lackey, Richard S., *Frontier Claims in the Lower South, Records of Claims Filed by Citizens of the Alabama and Tombigbee River Settlements in the Mississippi Territory for Depredations by the Creek Indians During the War of 1812*. New Orleans, Louisiana: Polyanthos, 1977.

Latour, Arséne Lacarriére, *Historical Memoir of the War in West Florida and Louisiana in 1814-1815, with an Atlas*. Gene A. Smith, Editor, Expanded Edition, Gainesville, Florida: University Press of Florida, for the Historic New Orleans Collection, 1999.

Lossing, Benson, *The Pictorial Field-Book of the War of 1812*. New York, New York: Harper & Brothers, Publishers, 1868.

Martin, Joel W., *Sacred Revolt: The Muskogees' Struggle for a New World*. Boston, Massachusetts: Beacon Press, 1991.

Mason, David and James H. Faulkner, *Five Dollars a Scalp: The Last Mighty War Whoop of the Creek Indians.* Huntsville, Alabama: Strode Publishers, 1975.

Owsley, Frank L., Jr., *Struggle for the Gulf Borderlands: The Creek War and the Battle of New Orleans, 1812-1815.* Gainesville, Florida: University Press of Florida, 1981.

Patrick, Rembert W., *Florida Fiasco: Rampant Rebels on the Georgia-Florida Border, 1810-1815.* Athens, Georgia: University of Georgia Press, 1954.

Pickett, Albert James, *History of Alabama, and Incidentally of Georgia and Mississippi, from the Earliest Period.* Charleston, South Carolina: Walker and James, 1851, Reprinted, Birmingham, Alabama: Birmingham Book and Magazine Company, 1962.

Pound, Merritt B., *Benjamin Hawkins, Indian Agent.* Athens, Georgia: University of Georgia Press, 1957.

Saunt, Claudio, *A New Order of Things: Property, Power, and the Transformation of the Creek Indians, 1733–1816.* Cambridge, England: Cambridge University Press, 1999.

Southerland, Henry DeLeon, Jr. and Jerry Elijah Brown, *The Federal Road through Georgia, the Creek Nation, and Alabama, 1806-1848.* Tuscaloosa, Alabama: University of Alabama Press, 1989.

Stephen, Walter W., "Andrew Jackson's Forgotten Army." *The Alabama Review*, Volume 12, April 1959, pages 126-131.

Thomason, Hugh M., "Governor Peter Early and the Creek Indian Frontier, 1813–1815." *Georgia Historical Quarterly,* Volume 45, Fall 1961, pages 223–37.

_____, "Notes and Documents: Letters of John Floyd, 1813–1838." *Georgia Historical Quarterly,* Volume 33, September 1949, pages 228–41.

Weir, Howard T., III, *A Paradise of Blood: The Creek War of 1813-1814.* Yardley, Pennsylvania: Westholme Publishing, 2016.

Waselkov, Gregory A., *A Conquering Spirit: Fort Mims and the Redstick War of 1813-1814.* Tuscaloosa, Alabama: University of Alabama Press, 2006.

Wright, Amos J., Jr., *McGillivray and McIntosh: Traders on the Old Southwest Frontier 1716–1815.* Montgomery, Alabama: New South Books, 2001.

First Seminole War, 1817-1818

Background

When the Spanish first arrived, hundreds of thousands of Native Americans, comprised of many different tribes, inhabited what today is Florida. After two centuries of colonial rule, these tribes nearly were extinct, due to a combination of war, forced labor, and various diseases brought from Europe. In the 18th century, numerous groups from Georgia and Alabama, including bands of Alabama, Choctaw, Creek, Yamasee, and Yuchi, migrated to Florida, seeking new hunting grounds, escaping white encroachment, or fleeing conflicts with their own or neighboring tribes. These groups settled at different places at different times, sometimes intermingling with the remnants of the indigenous people. One large group settled around Lake Mickosukee near Tallahassee, while another large group settled the Alachua Prairie. Gradually, Europeans who encountered these groups began to call them Seminole, which meant runaway or outsider, although most considered themselves members of different tribes. Other native groups in Florida included the so-called "Spanish Indians," thought to be descendants of the Calusa, "rancho Indians," probably of Calusa and Creek origin, and those of mixed native and Spanish origin living in fishing camps along the coast and in the Keys. Eventually, whites applied the term Seminole to all the natives in Florida, regardless of their origin, where they lived, or what language they spoke.

Almost from the beginning, raising cattle gradually became a significant source of food and an important part of Seminole culture. Many white settlers coveted the Seminole cattle and the land where it grazed, resulting in frequent skirmishes between the whites and Seminole over rustled cattle. Thus, the Seminole, especially the black Seminole, were openly hostile toward white Americans and feared their incursions.

For more than forty years, the Seminole fought the United States for their freedom and the right to stay in Florida unmolested. Unlike other conflicts between Indians and settlers, slavery was an important contributing factor in the Seminole wars, sometimes called the Florida wars. Over more than a century, hundreds of escaped slaves, mostly from Georgia and the Carolinas, fled to Florida. The ruling Spanish gave them freedom and land, provided they swore allegiance to the King of Spain and became Roman Catholic. Many settled around Pensacola and St. Augustine. Gracia Real de Santa Teresa de Mose, commonly called Fort Mose, just north of St. Augustine and the first free community of ex-slaves, was an important part of the capital city's defenses. In 1763, many of the blacks at Fort Mose accompanied the departing Spanish to Cuba. Many fleeing slaves settled among the Seminole, integrating into the tribes, intermarrying, learning the languages, and adopting the culture. Some Black Seminole rose to become significant tribal leaders.

In 1763, the new British rulers divided what had been Spanish Florida into East and West Florida. West Florida extended from the Apalachicola River westward to the Mississippi River and East Florida comprised the rest of the peninsula. During the Revolution, the British enticed American slaves to escape by guaranteeing their freedom. The British recruited and armed the Seminole to attack the settlements in the Georgia backcountry, making the Seminole an enemy of the United States.

In 1783, the Treaty of Paris gave Spain control of the Louisiana Territory and both East and West Florida, surrounding and blocking the United States on the south and west. In 1803, the Louisiana Purchase gave the United States control of the Mississippi River, but much of Georgia, Alabama, and Mississippi were drained by rivers that flowed through Spanish-held Florida on their way to the Gulf of Mexico.

In 1810, American settlers in the far western portion of West Florida rebelled, occupied the fort at Baton Rouge, expelled the Spanish officials, and established the Republic of West Florida, from the Mississippi River to the Pearl River. President James Madison proclaimed the new republic U. S. territory, claiming the Florida Parishes were part of the Louisiana Purchase. Under presidential orders, the Governor of the Territory of Orleans, William C. C. Claiborne, seized control of the republic and annexed the Florida Parishes to Louisiana. Madison then sent former Georgia Governor, General George Matthews, to Pensacola to negotiate the status of what was left of West Florida. When his negotiations proved fruitless, Matthews turned his attention to fomenting another rebellion in East Florida, but discovered the residents there generally had no interest in joining the United States. Mathews raised a body of "Patriots" from Georgia and, with the assistance of the American navy, seized the town of Fernandina on Amelia Island in March 1812. In June, the United States declared war on Great Britain. The greatest fear for many settlers in Georgia came to pass when the Seminole allied themselves with the Spanish and attacked Patriot homes and settlements in Florida and Georgia.

Campaigns

In 1814, the British erected a fort on Prospect Bluff, overlooking the Apalachicola River, about 15 miles from its mouth and 60 miles from the Georgia border, from which they armed and supplied their Seminole allies. The fort, commanded by Lieutenant Colonel Edward Nicolls, was manned by a company of Royal Marines and a Corps of Colonial Marines, composed of several hundred black African-Americans, many ex-slaves. After the war, the British left the fort in the hands of the mustered-out Negroes. Prospect Bluff, protected by the Negro Fort, became a safe haven and magnet for escaped slaves. Andrew Jackson determined that supplying Fort Scott, built near the mouth of the Flint River to protect the settlements in southwest Georgia, would require navigating the Apalachicola River, through Spanish Florida, past the fort, without approval from the Spanish. At various time, the fort was known as Nicolls Fort, Prospect Bluff Fort, Blount's Fort, Fort Apalachicola, and African Fort, but most commonly as the Negro Fort.

In November 1814, Major Uriah Blue led 1,000 Mississippi militia and allied Chickasaw and Choctaw warriors into Florida to quell the Red Sticks there. Most of the militia, David Crockett among them, were veterans of the First Creek War. After searching through the unfamiliar territory and running low on supplies, Blue returned to Fort Montgomery, about two miles from Fort Mims, on January 9, 1815, without having found the fort. In 1816, men from one of the resupply boats heading to Fort Scott went ashore near the Negro Fort to refill their canteens. A body of men from the fort, attacked the interlopers, killing all save one. Andrew Jackson was furious and ordered the destruction of the Negro Fort. Brigadier General Edmund Pendleton Gaines led more than 100 troops overland to the fort, while two gunboats commanded by Master Jarius Loomis moved up the river. On the morning of July 27, 1816, the gunboats opened fire and the cannons in the fort returned fire. The firing was intense, but short-lived, as a hot round hit the fort's powder magazine, causing a huge explosion, killing 270 of the 320 inhabitants, wounding many others, and destroying the fort. The American troops immediately attacked through the ruins and captured the survivors. Garson, the fort's commander was executed by firing squad. The prisoners were taken back to Fort Scott, where they were returned to their owners or sold as slaves.

Because he had not signed the 1814 Treaty of Fort Jackson, by which the Creek Nation ceded most of southwest Georgia to the United States, Neamathla, chief of the Lower Creek village of Fowltown, refused to be bound by the treaty. Fowltown, in modern Decatur County, Georgia was located about 15 miles east of Fort Scott, which was situated on a bluff overlooking the Flint River a few miles north of the Florida border. A war of words soon erupted between the U. S. Army and Neamathla, over the chief's loud complaints about white encroachment on his lands. The land was his, he said, and he was "directed by the Powers above to defend it."

Anticipating violence, Gaines marched the 4th and 7th Infantry Regiments from Alabama to Fort Scott. On November 21, 1817, Major David E. Twiggs, commanding 250 troops from Fort Scott, marched on Fowltown with orders to bring the chief back with them. As the troops were surrounding the village, the Indians opened fire. The soldiers responded with a single volley, killing four warriors and one woman, Neamathla then escaping with his people into the surrounding swamps. Lieutenant Colonel Matthew Arbuckle, leading 300 troops in a second attempt to capture the chief, occupied the abandoned village on the morning of November 23rd. Neamathla led about 60 warriors in a surprise attack on the soldiers, fighting furiously before evaporating again back into the swamps.

Outraged by the army raid on Fowltown, Red Stick Creek, Seminole, and Black Seminole warriors from across the region determined to block the movement of supplies for Fort Scott from moving up the Apalachicola River. Aware that one small boat loaded with supplies, commanded by Lieutenant Richard Scott, was slowly making its way up the river, a force of several hundred warriors prepared an ambush for him at present-day Chattahoochee. On November 30th, Homathlemico, a Red Stick Creek leader, hid his warriors in the adjacent foliage where the river's current would force the vessel toward the riverbank. When Scott's boat drew close, the warriors rose from their concealment and opened fire, killing most of the men on board, then rushed aboard to kill the rest. The massacre resulted in the death of 33 men, 6 women, and 4 children.

On December 13, 1817, a different force of warriors attacked Blunt's Town, a friendly allied Creek village at present-day Blountstown. The chief, John Blunt, had sided with the whites in the conflict and barely escaped with his life. With the war quickly turning in their direction, the alliance of Creek, Seminole, and Black Seminole warriors continued to focus on ending even the possibility of resupplying the American forts in southern Georgia via the Apalachicola River. Led by the Creek Prophet Josiah Francis, they attacked three supply vessels commanded by Major Peter Muhlenburg of the 4th U. S. Infantry at Ocheesee Bluff, firing from both banks of the river. The battle lasted for more than two weeks, from December 15th to the 31st, before the vessels managed their escape.

In retaliation, President James Monroe ordered Major General Andrew Jackson to invade Florida and drive the Seminole from northern Florida. Jackson gathered his forces at Fort Scott in March 1818, including 800 army regulars, 1,000 Tennessee volunteers, 1,000 Georgia militia, and about 1,400 friendly Lower Creek warriors, commanded by Brigadier General William McIntosh, a Creek chief. On March 15, Jackson's army entered Florida, marching down the Apalachicola River. Upon reaching the ruins of the Negro Fort, Jackson erected Fort Gadsden. After destroying the Indian town of Tallahassee on March 31st, Jackson took the town of Miccosukee the next day, destroying more than 300 Seminole homes. Jackson then turned south, capturing the Spanish Fort San Marcos on April 6th.

On April 12th, advanced elements of Jackson's army fought a battle with Red Stick Creeks led by Peter McQueen at Econfina Creek, killing about 40 warriors and capturing 100 others. There they recovered Elizabeth Stewart, who had been captured the previous November at a friendly Chehaw village. On April 18th, the army defeated a body of Seminoles and Black Seminoles at the Battle of Old Town on the Suwannee River. Jackson found the other villages along the Suwannee River empty, many of the Black Seminole having escaped to the Tampa Bay area. After destroying the major Seminole and black villages, Jackson declared victory and sent the Georgia militia and the Lower Creek home. The remaining army then returned to Fort San Marcos.

Jackson's foray into Florida left the frontier settlements defenseless against attacks from the few remaining bands of Red Sticks. Georgia Governor William Rabun ordered Captain Obed Wright to attack and subdue two hostile bands along the Flint River. Instead, on April 22, 1818, Wright led 270 men against a friendly Chehaw village at modern Leesburg, Georgia, killing 40 to 50 and burning the village.

Claiming that the Spanish were supplying and providing sanctuary to the Seminole and Red Sticks, General Jackson led a force of 1,000 men on May 7th, heading for Pensacola. The governor of West Florida protested that most of the Indians there were women and children and that the men were unarmed, but Jackson kept coming. When he reached Pensacola on May 23rd, the governor and the 175-man Spanish garrison retreated to Fort Barrancas, leaving the city of Pensacola to Jackson. The two sides traded cannon fire for a couple of days, before the Spanish surrendered Fort Barrancas on May 28th. Jackson appointed Colonel William King as military governor of West Florida and went home.

Aftermath

When Jackson captured Fort San Marcos, he found Alexander Arbuthnot, an elderly Bahamian trader, who had written letters in support of the Seminole. During Jackson's advance to the Suwannee River, he captured Robert Armbrister, a Bahamian soldier of fortune and former Royal Marine officer. After returning to Fort San Marcos, Jackson placed both men on trial for aiding the enemy and inciting the Indians to war against the Americans. Both men were found guilty, sentenced to death, and executed.

Both Britain and Spain were furious with the United States; Britain for the arrest and execution of two of its citizens and Spain by the invasion of Florida and the capture of San Marcos and Pensacola. Because Spain did not have the means to retaliate or regain West Florida by force; President Monroe let the Spanish officials protest, then issued a letter blaming the war on the British, Spanish, and Indians, apologizing for the seizure of West Florida, and offering to give San Marcos and Pensacola back to Spain.

Spain accepted, eventually resuming negotiations for the sale of Florida. After lengthy negotiations, not including the Seminole, Spain agreed to cede Florida to the United States. In 1821, when the territory formally changed hands, Andrew Jackson became the first Governor of the Florida Territory.

Places of Interest

Fort Mose State Park
15 Fort Mose Trail
St. Augustine, Florida 32084

(904) 823-2232

https://www.fortmose.org/

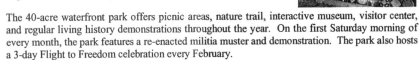

The 40-acre waterfront park offers picnic areas, nature trail, interactive museum, visitor center, and regular living history demonstrations throughout the year. On the first Saturday morning of every month, the park features a re-enacted militia muster and demonstration. The park also hosts a 3-day Flight to Freedom celebration every February.

San Marcos de Apalache Historic State Park
148 Old Fort Road
St. Marks, Florida *32355*

(850) 925-6216

https://www.floridastateparks.org/park/San-Marcos

The many different flags flying over San Marcos de Apalache Historic State Park welcome visitors to the park and demonstrate the colorful history of the site, from the Spanish explorers to the present day. The museum at the park displays pottery and tools unearthed near the original fort and highlights the history of the site. Interpretive displays explain the history of the San Marcos site. An 18-minute video recounts the days of the Spanish, English, American, and Confederates.

Fort Scott Historical Marker
Georgia Route 310, south of Lake Seminole,
about 3.5 miles north of Georgia Routes 310 and 97

In June 1816 Lt. Col. D. L. Clinch and a detachment of the 4th U. S. Infantry set up camp one mile west of here, calling it Camp Crawford. They began construction of a fort on the site in September 1816, naming it Fort Scott. Need for a fort was prompted by the presence of restless Indians who had emigrated to nearby areas – refugees largely composed of Seminoles and "Red Sticks" (a hostile faction of the Creeks). Prematurely evacuated December 1816 and almost immediately pillaged by hostile Indians, Capt. S. Donoho and his artillery company reoccupied Fort Scott in the Spring of 1817, reinforced later that year by additional troops of the 4th and 7th Regiments. March 9, 1818, Gen. Andrew Jackson arrived here with his staff and troops of the Georgia Militia. He was joined by Kentucky and Tennessee militiamen, who had marched through Alabama. At Fort Scott, Jackson concentrated troops for his march into Spanish Florida against Indians who had been raiding U. S. territory. He took with him the force at Fort Scott, excepting 60 men left as garrison. Following Jackson's campaign the garrison largely consisted of companies of the 7th Regiment. Frontier peace and increase of malaria probably account for the abandonment of Fort Scott in September 1821.

Village of Fowltown Historical Marker
Georgia Route 97, 0.6 miles north of Green Shade Road
in Decatur County

In this vicinity stood the Seminole village of Fowltown,
scene of battle, Nov. 21, 1817, which marked the beginning
of the First Seminole Indian War. The engagement resulted
when Major Twiggs with 250 soldiers from Fort Scott
attempted to arrest its warriors for depredations against the
white frontier. A second conflict occurred at the village and
nearby swamp Nov. 23rd, 1817, U. S. Soldiers being led by
Lt. Col. Arbuckle. On Jan. 4, 1818, the village was found deserted and destroyed.

Oldtown Historical Marker
On the Suwanee River, near
U. S. Route 19 and Florida Route 349, in
Dixie County, Florida

Inhabited by the Upper Creeks, Oldtown, often called
Suwanee Oldtown, was one of the largest Indian villages in
northern Florida. In Andrew Jackson's punitive expedition
into Florida in April, 1818, Oldtown was captured. Most of
the renegade Indians escaped, but Jackson caught Robert
Armbister, a British subject, who was tried and executed for aiding the Creeks in border raids into
Georgia. This produced tension between the United States and Great Britain.

Scott Massacre
Near the dock at River Landing Park in
Chattahoochee, Florida.

On November 30, 1817, the bloodiest battle of the First
Seminole War was fought on the Apalachicola River at
today's Chattahoochee, Florida. The warriors took up a
position along the east bank of the river, at a point where
they knew the strong current of the river would force
Lieutenant Richard W. Scott's boat to within striking
distance. They were led by Homathlemico, a Red Stick Creek leader who had fled to Florida after
Andrew Jackson's victory at the Battle of Horseshoe Bend. The Scott Massacre resulted in the
deaths of 33 men, six women, and four children. Another five men were wounded, but escaped.

Fort Gadsden Historic Site
Prospect Bluff Interpretive Area
Apalachicola National Forest
Ranger District
11152 NW Florida Route 20
Bristol, Florida 32321

(850) 643-2282

https://www.fs.usda.gov/recarea/apalachicola/recare
a/?recid=75221

The site of two successive forts, the first built during the War of 1812 by the British, and of the tragic massacre of more than 300 African-Americans who held the fort under the British flag in 1816, Prospect Bluff played an important role in Florida history. Located along the Apalachicola River, this interpretive area offers detailed information about the site and its history along with trails, river access, and a picnic area.

Fort Barrancas
1801 Gulf Breeze Parkway
Gulf Breeze, FL 32563

(850) 934-2600

Fort Barrancas overlooks the entrance to Pensacola Bay. It is on the Pensacola Naval Air Station and part of the Gulf Islands National Seashore. Maintained and administered by the National Park Service, the area includes the fort, hiking trails, picnic areas, and a visitor center.

Mathew Arbuckle (1778-1851) Grave
Arbuckle Cemetery
Lavaca, Arkansas

As a lieutenant colonel, Arbuckle led the second expedition against Fowltown at the start of the First Seminole War. Later, as a brigadier general, he commanded at Fort Gibson in the Indian Territory, and was responsible for constructing roads and maintaining peaceful relations between the tribes indigenous to the region and those then forced to migrate to the Indian Territory.

Edmund Pendleton Gaines Grave
Church Street Cemetery
Mobile, Alabama

Edmund Pendleton Gaines (1777-1849) was a distinguished military officer, eventually rising to the rank of major general. He is best known for arresting Aaron Burr for treason, gallant service at Fort Erie in 1814, conducting surveys for the post road from Nashville to Natchez, serving with Andrew Jackson in the First Creek War and First Seminole War, commanding the Western Military Department during the Black Hawk War, and leading an expedition in the Second Seminole War.

Peter Muhlenberg Grave
Charles Evans Cemetery
1119 Centre Avenue
Reading, Pennsylvania

Major Peter Muhlenberg (1787-1844) served with distinction in the First Seminole War. He died at his post at Grand Ecore, Natchitoches Parish, Louisiana.

Further Reading

Covington, James, *The Seminoles of Florida*. Gainesville, Florida: University Press of Florida, 1993.

Cusick, James G., *The Other War of 1812: The Patriot War and the American Invasion of Spanish East Florida*. Athens, Georgia: University of Georgia Press, 2007.

Giddings, Joshua R., *The Exiles of Florida, or, Crimes Committed by our Government Against Maroons, who Fled from South Carolina and other Slave States, Seeking Protection under Spanish Laws*. Columbus, Ohio: Follet, 1858.

Goggin, John M., "The Seminole Negroes of Andros Island, Bahamas." *Florida Historical Quarterly*, Volume 24, July 1946, pages 201-206.

Heidler, David S. and Jeanne T. Heidler, *Old Hickory's War: Andrew Jackson and the Quest for Empire*. Mechanicsburg, Pennsylvania: Stackpole Books, 1996.

Knetsch, Joe, *Florida's Seminole Wars:1817-1858*. Charleston, South Carolina: Arcadia Publishing Company, 2003.

Littlefield, Daniel F. Jr., *Africans and Seminoles: From Removal to Emancipation*, Oxford, Mississippi: University of Mississippi Press, 1977.

Porter, Kenneth W., *The Black Seminoles: History of a Freedom-Seeking People*, by Kenneth W. Porter. Gainesville, Florida: University Press of Florida, 1996.

Wright, J. Leitch, Jr., "A Note on the First Seminole War as Seen by the Indians, Negroes, and Their British Advisers." *The Journal of Southern History*, Volume 34, November 1968, pages 565-575.

Second Seminole War, 1835-1842

Background

In 1819, Spain ceded Florida to the United States, but the territorial government was slow to organize and take effective control. In 1822, the temporary Indian agent, estimated that some 22,000 Indians, who owned 5,000 slaves, resided in Florida. As many as 15,000 of them were refugees from the First Creek War and held no rightful claim to any land in Florida. The Indian settlements primarily were situated along the Apalachicola River, Suwanee River, Alachua Prairie, and in an arc extending from there southwestwardly to the vicinity of Tampa Bay.

In 1823, the Treaty of Moultrie Creek established a reservation for the Seminole, about 4 million acres in size, extending from just above modern Ocala southward to near modern Avon Park, but set well back from the coasts, to prevent contact with traders from Cuba and the Bahamas. Six chiefs were allowed to keep their villages along the Apalachicola River. The treaty also required the government to protect the Seminole, provide them with farm implements, cattle, and hogs, and pay the tribe $5,000 per year for twenty years.

In 1824, the government built Fort Brooke, garrisoned by four infantry companies, at Tampa Bay. Because the Seminole largely were reluctant to relocate, William Pope Duval, the second territorial governor, ordered the Seminole to move to the reservation by October 1st. The Seminole gradually relocated. In 1826, Fort King was built near the reservation agency, on the site of the future city of Ocala. The following year, the army reported that the Seminole were on their new reservation. However, many white settlers continued to call for the removal of the Indians. In 1828, Andrew Jackson was elected President. At his urging, Congress passed the Indian Removal Act, in 1830, requiring the relocation of all Native Americans to reservations west of the Mississippi River.

In 1832, negotiators coerced the Seminole into signing the Treaty of Payne's Landing, on the Oklawaha River, requiring them to relinquish their rights to their homes in Florida in exchange for land in the Indian Territory. Over the next few years, most of the Seminole quietly resisted any attempts to assemble the tribe for deportation. Because they suffered most from American encroachment, the Seminole living along the Apalachicola River agreed to relocate and went west in 1834. That same year, Seminole Agent Wiley Thompson called the chiefs to Fort King to discuss relocation. Since the chiefs did not feel bound by the treaty, because they had been forced to sign it, they told Thompson that they had no intention of leaving their homes. Fearing the worst, Thompson called for reinforcements and forbade the sale of arms and ammunition. In March 1835, President Jackson wrote to the chiefs that if they did not move voluntarily, he would remove them by force. After much wrangling and argument between Thompson and the Seminole leaders, eight chiefs agreed to move by the end of the year. Five chiefs, Micanopy among them, refused to leave.

Campaigns

Relations between the whites and Seminole deteriorated, hostile feelings rose and erupted into open warfare on December 28, 1835, when a party of 1,800 warriors ambushed Major Francis Langhorne Dade leading a column of 100 men from Fort Brooke to Fort King. After the first volley, Dade and nearly half of his men lay dead. The fighting continued until all but three of Dade's men were killed. On the same day, Osceola killed Agent Thompson at Fort King.

Brigadier General Duncan Lamont Clinch commanded federal troops in Florida. He led 750 soldiers, including 500 volunteers, to start gathering the Seminole living south of the Withlacoochee River. On December 31st, Osceola and war chief Alligator, with 350 warriors, attacked Clinch while his troops were crossing the river, inflicting heavy casualties. In order to deal with the growing number of wounded, Clinch ordered a withdrawal. In all, Clinch lost four killed and 59 wounded. By the middle of January, the Seminole had destroyed nearly every sugar plantation, murdering many of the inhabitants, wrecking the Territory's economy, and freeing hundreds of slaves, many of whom joined the Seminole.

In February 1836, Major General Gaines brought 1,100 troops from New Orleans and proceeded to the Withlacoochee settlements. Confronted by the Seminole, Gaines erected a makeshift enclosure and remained under siege for more than a week, before being rescued and withdrawn. Another force of 5,000 troops attempted to surround the Seminole, then close in and capture them. However, the attempt ended in failure and was viewed as an embarrassment. Events continued badly for the army in April, with the Seminole attacking Fort Alabama, on the Hillsborough River, Fort Barnwell near Volusia, and Fort Drane on Colonel Clinch's sugar plantation.

Due to the heavy rains and widespread disease, the army halted offensive operations for the summer, abandoned their interior forts, and moved to healthier posts on the coasts. In July, the Seminole attacked the Cape Florida Lighthouse on the south end of Key Biscayne, wounding the keeper, killing his assistant, and burning the lighthouse. In September, Governor Richard K. Call led a large force of volunteers, supported by regulars, back to the Withlacoochee country, but met with little success. In November, Call made another attempt, managing to cross the river, but finding the Seminole stronghold abandoned. Call then led his troops upstream, routing the Seminoles from their camp on November 17th. Four days later, Call's men entered Wahoo Swamp, but the Seminole resisted his advance. Unable to cross a deep stream of unknown depth while under fire, and running low on supplies, Call disengaged and headed for Volusia.

The year 1837 proved pivotal. Major General Thomas Jesup was appointed overall commander in Florida. He immediately began a methodical campaign to force the Seminole to surrender, building a large force of 9,000 men, erecting forts throughout the Seminole lands, keeping the forts well supplied, and continually sending out patrols to scour the countryside and harass the natives. Jesup's force consisted mostly of regular army and volunteer militia, but also included significant contingents from the Marines, Navy, and Revenue Marines, the precursor of today's Coast Guard. At the start of the war, the Seminole had no more than about 1,400 warriors to face Jesup's overwhelming force.

The constant patrols were effective in killing or capturing a number of Seminole and blacks in January. On January 27, Colonel Archibald Henderson with his Marine regiment supported by Alabama militia and allied Indians, attacked a Seminole village on Hatchee Lustee Creek, now

169

Reedy Creek in Orange County, capturing about three dozen mostly women and children, 100 horses loaded with supplies, and 1,400 cattle. Fighting continued into March. Many Seminole chiefs, including Micanopy, succumbed to the relentless pressure and, in March, signed the Articles of Capitulation at Fort Dade. The Articles permitted the Seminole to bring their allies and their Negros with them to the Indian Territory. The Seminole began to gather at Fort Brooke for emigration. Early in June, Osceola went to Fort Brooke, talked to the chiefs, and led away 700 Seminole who had surrendered, breathing new life into the war, one that Jesup thought he had won.

Faced with fighting the Seminole in a watery wilderness interlaced by innumerable lakes, rivers, and swamps, Jesup called on the Navy and Revenue Marines for assistance. Warships guarded the long coastline to prevent Cuban and Bahamian traders from supplying the Seminole. Both sailors and marines garrisoned forts, guarded wagon trains, and fought alongside the army and militia. The navy developed small watercraft capable of navigating the Everglades to attack villages and destroy crops. This new type of warfare, combined army-navy operations utilizing the innovative small craft, dubbed the Mosquito Fleet, constantly pressed the Seminole.

The constant patrols continued to bear fruit, in September capturing two important chiefs, King Phillip and Uchee Billy. Under the ruse of negotiating under a flag of truce, Jesup arrested many other Seminole chiefs, including Osceola, who soon died in confinement. While Jesup was successful in capturing many chiefs, his deceitful tactics also strengthened Seminole resolve to resist. By promising freedom, Jesup enticed many Black Seminole to surrender and join their Seminole brethren already moved to the west.

In November 1837, Jesup mounted a huge campaign, with more than 9,000 troops, about half volunteers. Several large columns swept across Florida, engaging Seminole wherever they could be found. On Christmas Day, Colonel Zachary Taylor, with 850 troops, 120 Missouri volunteers and the 1st, 4th, and 6th Infantry Regiments, attacked about 400 hundred Seminole, under Coacoochee, Sam Jones, and others perched upon a heavily wooded hammock at the edge of Lake Okeechobee. Taylor ordered the Missouri volunteers to attack, but they fell back after suffering heavy casualties. The 6th Infantry Regiment mounted the second attack, but also were repulsed with heavy casualties. The 4th Infantry Regiment then rushed the hammock with fixed bayonets, driving the Seminole from the field. Taylor then sent his remaining troops to sweep up the retreating foe. Americans considered the Battle of Okeechobee a great victory, establishing Taylor a national hero and prompting his promotion to brigadier general. However, the Seminole also considered the engagement a victory, because they suffered few casualties and gained sufficient time to escape with their families safely into the Everglades.

Navy Lieutenant Levin Powell led a joint amphibious operation with 75 soldiers and sailors up the Southwest Fork of the Loxahatchee River, where they disembarked and marched inland to locate a Seminole village. On January 15, 1838, in what has been called alternately the First Battle of Loxahatchee, Battle of Jupiter Inlet, and Powell's Battle, Powell stumbled upon a large number of Seminole warriors who immediately engaged. With casualties mounting, Powell ordered his men back to their boats. After learning of Powell's defeat, Jesup ordered his 1,600 men forward to locate and engage the Seminole who had defeated Powell. On January 24th, Seminole scouts met Jesup's column and fired on the lead dragoons, who chased them into a cypress swamp, where they found and attacked the main group of Seminole. The fighting continued back and forth, until the Seminole once again simply melted away into the swamp, bringing an end to the Battle of Loxahatchee River.

In May 1838, Zachary Taylor assumed command of the forces in Florida, as the war entered a new phase, a war of attrition, that lasted another four years, but accomplished very little, apart from the loss of hundreds of Seminole, black, and white lives. With a reduced force of about 2,300 men, Taylor concentrated on defending the settled areas of the Florida Territory and building forts, roads, and bridges. The Seminole continued to raid the northern settlements, in July murdering a family on the Santa Fe River, a second family near Tallahassee, and two more in southern Georgia. In October 1838, Taylor managed to relocate the remaining Seminole from the Apalachicola River villages to the Indian Territory.

On July 23, 1839, a party of 150 warriors attacked the trading post on the Caloosahatchee River, defended by Colonel William S. Harney and 23 soldiers. Harney and a few soldiers escaped by boat, but most of the soldiers and civilians were killed. Seminole raids continued into 1840; in February a mail stage was ambushed, in May six travelers were killed near St. Augustine, and four soldiers in Alachua County were killed.

In 1840, Brigadier General Walker K. Armistead assumed command in Florida, but did not pursue an aggressive offense, emboldening the Seminole to raid the settlements in northern Florida. His total force consisted of ten companies of the 2nd Dragoons, nine companies of the 3rd Artillery, and the 1st, 2nd, 3rd, 6th, 7th, and 8th Infantry Regiments. Throughout the summer months, the army assumed the offensive, destroying Seminole villages, burning their crops, and taking captives. In August, Chief Chakaika led a war party in attacking Indian Key, the first seat of Dade County, killing nearly a dozen inhabitants, looting the stores, and burning the town.

By the Spring of 1841, Armistead had resettled another 450 Seminole in the Indian Territory and had another 236 at Fort Brooke waiting for transportation west. He estimated there were no more than 300 warriors remaining to be subdued.

In May 1841, Colonel William Jenkins Worth was given command of the army in Florida. That summer, Worth began a campaign of conducting search and destroy missions, driving most of the remaining Seminole from their strongholds.

The following is a partial list of the numerous volunteer units who served in Florida.

Alabama: A total of 2,357 men served in Florida between 1835 and 1840.

      Colonel William Chisolm's Regiment of Alabama Volunteers, 1836.

      Major Caulfield's Battalion of Alabama Mounted Volunteers, 1836-1837.

District of Columbia: A total of 139 men served in Florida between 1836 and 1838.

      Captain Irvin's Company of District of Columbia Volunteers, 1836-1837.

Florida: A total of 6, 854 men served from 1835 to 1839.

      General Richard K. Call's Brigade of Florida Mounted Volunteers, 1835.

      Major Leigh Read's Battalion of Florida Volunteers, 1836.

      Warren's 1st Regiment of Florida Mounted Volunteers, 1836-1837.

Georgia: A total of 2, 574 men served in Florida between 1836 and 1838.

Major Mark A. Cooper's 1st Battalion of Georgia Foot, 1836.

Major Robertson's Augusta Battalion, 1836.

Major Nelson's Battalion of Mounted Volunteers, 1836-1837.

Louisiana: A total of 1,179 men served in Florida between 1836 and 1838.

Colonel P.F. Smith's Regiment of Louisiana Volunteers, 1836.

Captain H. Marks' Company of Louisiana Volunteers, 1836.

Missouri: A total of 474 men served in Florida from 1837 to 1838.

Colonel Richard Gentry's 1st Regiment of Missouri Volunteers, 1837-1838.

Major Morgan's Spy Battalion, Missouri Volunteers, 1837-1838.

New York: A total of 90 men served in Florida between 1837 and 1838.

New York Volunteer Company, 1837-1838.

Pennsylvania: A total of 510 men served in Florida between 1837 and 1838.

Pennsylvania Battalion of Infantry Volunteers, 1837-1838.

South Carolina: A total of 2,265 men served in Florida between 1836 and 1838.

Colonel Goodwyn's Regiment of South Carolina Mounted Volunteers, 1836.

Colonel William Brisbane's Regiment of South Carolina Volunteers, 1836.

Captain Elmore's Corps of Columbia and Richland Riflemen, 1836.

Tennessee: A total of 1,651 men served in Florida from 1836 to 1838.

General Armstrong's Brigade of Tennessee Mounted Volunteers, 1836-1837, consisting of the 1st and 2nd Regiments of Tennessee Mounted Volunteers.

Major Lauderdale's Battalion of Tennessee Volunteers, 1837-1838.

Creek Indian: A total of 748 Creek warriors served in Florida from 1836 to 1837.

Colonel Lane's Regiment of Creek Indian Volunteers, 1836-1837.

Delaware and Shawnee: A total of 178 Delaware and Shawnee served in Florida from 1837 to 1838.

Captain Park's Delaware & Shawnee Volunteers, 1837-1838.

Choctaw: A total of 485 Choctaw were mustered into service for Florida, but did not see active service.

Aftermath

Worth continued to round up small bands of Seminole for resettlement and accepted the surrender of others. He also offered inducements, including money and provisions, to either resettle in the Indian Territory or move to a reservation in southern Florida. In August 1842, Worth declared the war over, thinking that the remaining Seminole would settle on the reservation, but their sporadic raids continued. Worth continued his patrols into the next year. In November 1843, Worth reported that only 42 Seminole, 33 Mikasuki, ten Creek, and ten Tallahassee warriors, with their women and children, remained in Florida, bringing the total to about 300, all living peacefully on their reservation.

In 1842, Congress passed the Armed Occupation Act, providing free land to settlers who improved the land and were prepared to defend themselves from Indians. With the coming of relative peace, white settlement increased. Under the Armed Occupation Act, the government issued 1,317 grants for 210,720 acres of land in 1842 and 1843. For the most part, the remaining Seminole stayed on their reservation, purposefully limiting their contact with the white settlers, but occasional incidents occurred. To put an end to the violent clashes, Floridians resumed their demand for removal. Gradually, individual clashes between the Seminole and white settlers increased in frequency and severity. At the urging of Florida, the federal government determined to relocate the Seminole, sowing the seeds for the Third Seminole War.

Places of Interest

Dade Battlefield Historic State Park
7200 County Road 603
Bushnell, Florida 33513

(352) 793-4781

https://www.floridastateparks.org/park/Dade-
Battlefield

The 80-acre park features a walking trail across the
battlefield and a visitor center, with interpretive
exhibits and artifacts from the battle and other items
that shed light on what life was like in Florida during the Seminole War period. The park also
hosts periodic living history demonstrations, including an annual reenactment of the battle.

Okeechobee Battlefield Historic State Park
3500 SE 38th Avenue
Okeechobee, Florida 34974

(863) 462-5360

https://www.floridastateparks.org/park/okeechobee-battlefield

The park is located on a portion of the historical battlefield and features the original battlefield
monument erected in 1939 by descendants of Colonel Richard Gentry, who commanded the
Missouri volunteers. The park hosts an annual reenactment of the battle.

Missouri Volunteer Graves
Jefferson Barracks National Cemetery
2900 Sheridan Road
St. Louis, Missouri 63125

In 1837, President Martin Van Buren authorized Colonel Richard
Gentry to raise 600 men for service in the Second Seminole War. In
October, he and his men left Columbia, headed for Florida. Under the
command of future president Zachary Taylor, Gentry led his men into
battle at Lake Okeechobee on Christmas Day 1837, where he was
killed. Several years later Gentry's remains as well as those of several
others were brought back to Missouri and reburied in Jefferson Barracks
National Cemetery.

Loxahatchee River Battlefield Park
9060 Indiantown Road
Jupiter, Florida 33478

(561) 741-1359

http://discover.pbcgov.org/parks/Riverbend/LoxahatcheePark.aspx

Operated by the Palm Beach County Department of Parks and
Recreation, the park offers battlefield tours on Saturdays and an annual reenactment of the battle
featuring reenactors, weapons demonstrations, exhibitors, and speakers.

St. Francis Barracks and Cemetery
82 Marine Street
St. Augustine, Florida 32084

(904) 823-0696

The old Franciscan monastery was converted to a
barracks and military headquarters for the war.
Just to the south of the barracks is a small National
Military Cemetery, where a number of soldiers
were buried. At the south end of the cemetery are
three stone pyramids that sit atop the last remains of hundreds of fatalities, an obelisk
commemorating the war dead, and a marker commemorating West Point graduates who died in
the war.

Fort Foster State Historic Site
15402 U. S. Route 301 North
Thonotosassa, Florida 33592

(813) 987-6771

https://www.floridastateparks.org/park/Fort-Foster

The fully reconstructed fort is on the Hillsborough
River State Park. Park Rangers and reenactors
provide tours, explain the fort operations and living
conditions, and interpret the history of the
Seminole Wars in Florida. The park hosts two annual, historic reenactments: The Candlelight
Experience in December and the Fort Foster Rendezvous in January.

176

Fort Cooper State Park
3100 South Old Floral City Road
Inverness, Florida 34450

(352) 726-0315

https://www.floridastateparks.org/park/Fort-Cooper

The park features a Seminole Heritage Trail, with kiosks providing the history of the fort, local Indians, and the Seminole War. The park hosts the annual Fort Cooper Days, with reenactments depicting the events that took place in 1836.

Town of Micanopy and
Micanopy Historical Society Museum
607 NE Cholokka Boulevard
Micanopy, Florida 32667

(352) 466-3200

http://micanopyhistoricalsociety.com/

The town of Micanopy was the site of Forts Micanopy and Defiance. The museum features several exhibits on the wars and the Seminole people. A small park east of the town was the site of a battle between Osceola, leading 250 warriors, against soldiers from Fort Defiance.

Burnsed Blockhouse
Heritage Park Village
102 South Lowder Street
Macclenny, Florida 32063

(904) 259-7275

http://heritagepark.cityofmacclenny.com/home

The preserved blockhouse, built in 1833, is the last surviving example of the architecture employed by settlers for protection against raiding Indians. The village has several small museums, each highlighting different aspects of pioneer life.

Fort Christmas Historical Park
1300 North Forth Christmas Road
Christmas, Florida 32709

(407) 254-9310

http://www.nbbd.com/godo/FortChristmas/

The park features a reconstructed fort, museum with
a large Seminole War exhibit, and seven pioneer
homes, with exhibits explaining the Florida Cracker
culture.

William Pope Duvall Grave
Congressional Cemetery
Washington, DC

During the War of 1812, William Pope Duvall (1784-1854) commanded a
company of Kentucky volunteer militia. After representing his Kentucky
district in Congress, he was appointed to succeed Andrew Jackson as
governor of the Florida Territory, serving from 1822 to 1834, under
presidents Monroe, Adams, and Jackson.

Richard Keith Call Grave
Call Family Cemetery
The Grove Plantation
Tallahassee, Florida

As a lieutenant, Richard Keith Call (1792-1862) served as
an aide to Andrew Jackson during the War of 1812 and
First Seminole War. He accompanied Jackson to Florida
to assist in the formation of the first territorial
government. During his first gubernatorial term, as
brigadier general of the territorial militia, Call led forces
in fighting the Seminole, winning victories at the second
and third battles of Wahoo Swamp in the Second Seminole War. In 1839, following a dispute
over government support in the war, President Van Buren replaced him as governor.

Thomas Sidney Jesup Grave
Oak Hill Cemetery
Washington, DC

During the War of 1812, Thomas Sidney Jesup (1788-1860) was a major in the 19th Infantry Regiment. In 1836, President Jackson directed Jesup to quell the Creek uprising in Alabama and Georgia, then to assume overall command of military forces in Florida during the Second Seminole War.

Osceola Grave
Fort Moultrie National Monument
1214 Middle Street
Sullivan's Island, South Carolina 29482

(843) 883-3123

https://www.nps.gov/fosu/learn/historyculture/fort_moultrie.htm

Osceola (1804-1838), probably the best-known Seminole leader, was born in a Creek town near Tallassee (modern Tuskegee) Alabama, the son of William Powell, a trader, and Polly Copinger, a Creek woman. After the First Creek War, his Red Stick band moved further south to northern Florida, between the St. Marks and Suwannee rivers. During the Second Seminole War, Osceola was a leading war chief. Under a flag of truce, he was taken prisoner and transported to Fort Moultrie, in Charleston Harbor. Osceola died there on January 30, 1838, of a severe throat ailment, and was buried outside the front entrance of the fort, albeit without his head which had been removed as a medical curiosity.

Zachary Taylor Grave
Zachary Taylor National Cemetery
Louisville, Kentucky

In recognition of his success at the Battle of Lake Okeechobee, Zachary Taylor (1784-1850) was promoted to of brigadier general and placed in command of all federal troops in Florida, a position he held for the next two years. He gained a national reputation as a military leader as well as the sobriquet "Old Rough and Ready." His fame continued to grow, eventually culminating in his election to the presidency.

179

Duncan Lamont Clinch Grave
Bonaventure Cemetery
330 Bonaventure Road
Savannah, Georgia

Duncan Lamont Clinch (1787-1849) was a professional soldier and politician. He began his military career as a lieutenant in the 3rd Infantry Regiment in 1808. He was promoted to brigadier general in 1829 and commanded the U. S. forces at the Battle of Ouithlacoochee against the Seminole, in December 1835. He resigned his commission the next year and settled on his plantation near St. Marys, Georgia. In 1844, he was elected to Congress, serving until 1845. Clinch died at the age of 61 in Macon, Georgia.

Further Reading

Belko, W. Stephen, *America's Hundred Years' War: U. S. Expansion to the Gulf Coast and the Fate of the Seminole, 1763-1858.* Gainesville, Florida: University Press of Florida, 2011.

Bittle, George Cassel, *In Defense of Florida: The Organized Florida Militia From 1821 to 1920.* PhD dissertation, Florida State University, 1965.

Buker, George E., *Swamp Sailors: Riverine Warfare in the Everglades, 1835-1842.* Gainesville, Florida: University Press of Florida, 1975.

Covington, James W., *The Seminoles of Florida.* Gainesville, Florida: University Press of Florida, 1993.

Florida Board of State Institutions, *Soldiers of Florida in the Seminole Indian, Civil and Spanish-American Wars.* Macclenney, Florida: R. J. Ferry, 1903, Reprinted 1983.

Foreman, Grant, *A Traveler in Indian Territory: The Journal of Ethan Allen Hitchcock, Late Major-General in the United States Army.* Norman, Oklahoma: University of Oklahoma Press, 1996.

Howe, Daniel Walker, *What Hath God Wrought: The Transformation of America, 1815–1848.* Oxford, England: Oxford University Press, 2009.

Knetsch, Joe, *Florida's Seminole Wars: 1817-1858.* Charleston, South Carolina: Arcadia Publishing, 2003.

Lancaster, Jane F., *Removal Aftershock: The Seminoles' Struggles to Survive in the West, 1836-1866.* Knoxville, Tennessee: University of Tennessee Press, 1994.

Mahon, John K., *History of the Second Seminole War, 1835-1842.* Gainesville, Florida: University Press of Florida, 1967.

Martin, Sidney Walter, *Florida During the Territorial Days.* Philadelphia, Pennsylvania: Porcupine Press, 1944, Reprinted 1974.

Motte, Jacob Rhett, *Journey into Wilderness: An Army Surgeon's Account of Life in Camp and Field During the Creek and Seminole Wars, 1836-1838.* Gainesville, Florida: University Press of Florida, 1953.

Meltzer, Milton, *Hunted Like a Wolf.* Sarasota, Florida: Pineapple Press, 1972.

Milanich, Jerald T., *Florida Indians and the Invasion from Europe.* Gainesville, Florida: University Press of Florida, 1995.

Missall, John and Mary Lou Missall, *The Seminole Wars: America's Longest Indian Conflict.* Gainesville, Florida: University Press of Florida, 2004.

Thrapp, Dan L., *Encyclopedia of Frontier Biography.* Glendale, California: A. H. Clark Company, 1988-1994.

Viele, John, *The Florida Keys: A History of the Pioneers*. Sarasota, Florida: Pineapple Press, Inc., 1996.

Weisman, Brent Richards, *Unconquered People*. Gainesville, Florida: University Press of Florida, 1999.

Wickman, Patricia R., *Osceola's Legacy*. Tuscaloosa, Alabama: University of Alabama Press, 1991.

Second Creek War, 1836-1837

Background

In 1814, the Treaty of Fort Jackson forced the Creek to cede half of their ancestral hunting grounds to the federal government. In 1821, William McIntosh and other Lower Creek chiefs signed the first Treaty of Indian Springs, relinquishing all the Creek lands east of the Flint River. In 1825, McIntosh and six other chiefs signed the second Treaty of Indian Springs, this time giving away the last of the Lower Creek lands in Georgia. In retribution, the Creek National Council sent Chief Menawa and 200 Law Menders to punish McIntosh, brutally executing him and burning his plantation. The council then sent a delegation to negotiate with President John Quincy Adams, successfully convincing him that the treaty was invalid. In 1826, they signed the Treaty of Washington, ceding all the Creek lands in Georgia for a payment of $200,000. The new treaty confined the Creek to a large portion of east central Alabama.

White settlers poured into the ceded territory, often cheating or stealing land from the resident Creek, sometimes even forcibly removing the Creek families and seizing their lands. In the early 1830s, the federal government tried to remove the settlers in Alabama, but violence erupted. Alabama Governor Clement Clay claimed all the Creek land as part of the state, and said that the settlers should be free to move in, declaring that the federal government and President Jackson were violating Alabama's rights by establishing a Creek Reservation without Alabama's permission. President Jackson maintained that the federal government had the sole right and authority to negotiate and deal with the Indians. Settlers on Creek land refused to move, while crooked land dealers stole individual land allotments from the unsuspecting Creek owners. By 1835, the once powerful Creek Confederation had lost most of its land through various treaties and crooked land deals. The dispossessed Creek who stayed were of many different categories; some almost totally assimilated to the white American culture, working simple labor jobs, remaining quiet, a threat to no one, but accepted or trusted by no one. Others, who had supported the United States during previous conflicts, had everything taken away from them despite their friendship. Red Stick Creek, who maintained their traditional way of life, were chagrined to discover that McIntosh and other Lower Creek chiefs had given away their land without their permission. Adding insult to injury, all three Creek factions watched as settlers moved onto their former lands, developed farms, built towns, and grew prosperous.

The Creek appealed to the President for help, but the government was unable to stop the outrages, the situation soon spinning out of control. Many Creek also felt that armed resistance was their only viable recourse to the forced removal of their families to the Indian Territory west of the Mississippi River, in accordance with the Indian Removal Act. In February 1836, Colonel John H. Watson, leading 22 local militia from Columbus, went to investigate the rumors that Creek warriors were crossing the river near Bryant's Ferry, on the Chattahoochee River, in Stewart County, Georgia. At the mouth of Hitchity Creek, Watson discovered 40 warriors returning to the ferry, who immediately took cover and opened fire. After several volleys with no clear result, the militia withdrew, with two killed and two wounded. This brief encounter, styled the Battle of Hitchity, marked the first shots of the Second Creek War.

Campaigns

In the Spring of 1836, Hitchiti, Yuchi, and other bands of Creek warriors determined to drive out the settlers and retake their lands. Everyone knew that the Seminole were on the warpath in Florida and many believed that the Seminole were winning, or even had won. Chiefs Jim Henry and Neamathla led their Hitchiti war parties on numerous raids, killing settlers, destroying their homes, and burning their crops. On May 14, 1836, a Yuchi war party attacked and burned the town of Roanoke, on the Chattahoochee River in Stewart County, Georgia, igniting the full fury of the Second Creek War.

Roanoke's visibility on the east bank of the Chattahoochee River was a thorn in the side of the Creek, who resented the town growing on their ancestral hunting grounds. The residents anticipated an attack and, when they saw Creek warriors in their neighborhood, evacuated the women and children to Lumpkin. Militia Colonel Felix Gibson and his men prepared to defend their town from the blockhouse they had built, standing guard continuously. When no attack came, many men became complacent and some went to Lumpkin to visit their families. On May 14th, only twenty men were left. At 2 a. m., Jim Henry led at least 200 warriors across the river and attacked. The sleeping defenders attempted to resist but were overwhelmed by the attackers. As resistance became futile, six of the defenders managed to escape under cover of darkness. The rest were killed and scalped or burned to death. Jim Henry then torched the town, completely destroying it, carrying away numerous horses, slaves, and other plunder.

Word of the Roanoke Massacre spread panic across the frontier. Settlers abandoned their farms and fled to safety in Columbus and other frontier forts. Small bands of warriors continued raiding the scattered settlements in southwestern Georgia, growing ever bolder as their campaign of destruction escalated. The Creek attacked steamers on the Chattahoochee River, sinking one, and killing and wounding the crew and passengers on another. Soon, as many as 2,400 refugees flooded into Columbus. Georgia Governor William Schley authorized the affected counties to mobilize their militia to defend themselves. General Winfield Scott, commander of the federal army, with his hands full prosecuting the war against the Seminole in Florida, could provide little help and Alabama militia refused to cross the river to fight in Georgia. The people of southwestern Georgia were on their own.

On May 16, 1836, Brigadier General William Otho Beall led 500 militiamen into Chambers and Macon counties, Alabama and located an armed party of hostiles at Liehatoca Town. In the ensuing skirmish, Beall killed two or three Creek and managed to capture the local chief, prophet, and a half dozen others. The captives were placed in the Chambers County Jail. On June 3rd, Captain Carr marched his company of Crawford County militia from Fort Twiggs to the Boykin Plantation, on the Chattahoochee River in Troup County, where he was informed that hostiles were just across the river. In response to a request for reinforcements, Captain McCrary joined him that evening with a contingent from Fort McCrary. The next morning a party of a dozen Creek appeared on the opposite bank, the militia opened fire, and the two sides exchanged volleys for more than an hour. The Creek lost six killed and at least two wounded, while the militia lost one killed and none wounded.

In early June, the Columbus *Enquirer*, a local newspaper, noted that 700 militia had assembled in preparation for an expedition against the Creek uprising, listing the individual companies as Captain McCall's Bibb Cavalry, Captain Fluelenn's Monroe Cavalry, Captain Bush's Pike Cavalry, Captain Dennard's Houston Cavalry, Captain Lynch's ___ Cavalry, Captain Miller's

Southern Rifles (Infantry), Captain Vardeman's Company of drafts from Harris County, three companies of drafts under Captains Russell and Stewart, Captain Simson's Fayette Cavalry, and Captain Hardeman's Infantry Company from Jones County.

Captain Hammond Garmany's militia company from Gwinnet County was mustered into federal service and then proceeded down the river to Shepherd's plantation, about 40 miles south of Columbus. He sent 25 of his troops to guard a nearby fort. On June 9th, hearing shots not far away, Garmany led a detachment to investigate. About a half mile away, he discovered a band of Creek warriors and a sharp fight resulted in which Garmany was wounded. To avoid being completely overwhelmed by the larger force, the small detachment began to retreat. The Creek pursued them closely, firing continuously. A detachment of local militia from Fort Jones, commanded by Major H. W. Jernigan, arrived just in time to attack the Creek, drive them away, and save the rest of Garmany's men.

Late in June, some 300 Creek, many of whom had burned Roanoke, began a long journey to Florida to join the Seminole in fighting the Americans. While traveling through modern Baker County, Georgia, they discovered that local militia were following them. The warriors made defensive preparations on an island in the Chickasawhachee Swamp. Colonel Thomas Beall, at the head of 500 militia, surrounded the island and attacked. After a sharp fight, the Creek were routed, broken, and scattered into the surrounding swamp, leaving behind most of their horses and supplies.

On July 10th, Major Michael Young, at the head of a battalion of Georgia militia, pursued a large party of Creek retreating into Florida, meeting them at the confluence of Little River and Big Warrior Creek. The militia attacked, driving the Creek through the swamp, killing 23, wounding many more, and capturing 18, while losing two killed and nine wounded. On July 24th, a company of Georgia militia was surprised and bested in a skirmish near Wesley Chapel, in Stewart County. The following day, Major Jernigan with a company of militia continued pursuing the retreating Creek, engaging them in a fierce fight in the swamp on Nochoway Creek. Outnumbered, Jernigan was forced to withdraw, but kept the Creek in his sites. When reinforcements arrived, the militia again pressed their attack, pushed the Creek onto a hummock, which they assaulted from two sides, decisively defeating the Creek and driving them from the area.

On August 27th, two companies of Georgia militia led by Colonel Henry Blair pursued a band of Creek entering the Okefenokee Swamp and overtook them in a cypress swamp along Cow Creek, routing them, killing two, and capturing several more. Rather than be forced to relocate to the Indian Territory west of the Mississippi River, many small bands decided to join the Seminole in Florida, while others continued to hide in the swamps and other remote areas and mount sporadic raids against the settlers. In turn, units of Alabama and Georgia militia scoured the countryside searching for both groups, preferring to kill them rather than taking them prisoner and transporting them west. On February 3, 1837, Alabama militia skirmished with a Creek band near Cowikee Creek, about six miles above Eufala, in Barbour County, Alabama.

A large body of refugee Creek, including men, women, and children, sought shelter in the floodplain swamps along the Pea River, in modern Barbour County, Alabama. In February 1837, small militia units conducted several brutal attacks against the Creek hiding in the swamp. In response, the Creek began to fortify their position in the swamp. To help feed their families and to take some revenge for the February attacks, warriors began to strike the isolated farms and cabins close to the swamp.

Brigadier General William Wellborn, at the head of a large force of militia and volunteers, was quick to mount a response, reaching Hobdy's Bridge, over the Pea River, about seven miles west of the town of Louisville, on March 24th. There, Wellborn split his force, sending Captain Harrell up the east side of the river and the main force up the west side, to attack the Creek encampment located about one mile upriver from the bridge. When Wellborn approached his destination, he heard firing off to the east and realized Captain Harrell had engaged the Creek. Wellborn ordered his men immediately to attack through the swamp. The ensuing battle raged for nearly four hours, as the militia attempted to overrun the heavily fortified camp. Some women and children attempted to escape, while others joined their men in defending the camp, fighting with muskets, bows, and knives. Wellborn ordered a direct frontal assault on the camp, breeching the fortifications, and scattering the Creek, who fled with their families, many escaping south down the Pea River, into Florida, where they joined the Seminole in fighting the Americans. The militia lost two killed and seven wounded, but counted 23 dead warriors on the field, in the last battle of the war.

In June 1840, a band of hostile Creek made one last futile attack on the steamboat Irwinton, on the Chattahoochee River, not far downriver from Eufaula. John Gill, the cabin boy was killed, but the others escaped the gunfire by lying prone on the deck. Three warriors managed to board the steamboat, but were assaulted by the crew and thrown onto the turning paddlewheel, tearing them apart.

Aftermath

No treaty ended the Second Creek War of 1836. Instead, the war simply wound down gradually, as the Creek were killed, captured, and transported west, or fled to Florida to join the Seminole and continue fighting there.

Places of Interest

The Columbus Museum
1251 Wynnton Road
Columbus, Georgia 31906

(706) 748-2562

http://www.columbusmuseum.com/

The museum features a series of galleries from their History Collection, including those dedicated to early settlement, the founding of Columbus, Creek War of 1836, and the Trail of Tears. The museum also offers short films on the history and culture of the Chattahoochee River Valley, with local historians, reenactors, and original images.

Battle of Hitchity Historical Marker
On US Route 27, and 3 miles south of
Cusseta, at Hitichty Creek

In February, 1836, after rumors of unrest among the Creek Indians and a report of 500 having crossed the Chattahoochee River at Bryants Ferry, 22 members of the Georgia Militia under Col. John H. Watson were sent out from Columbus to investigate the rumor. At the mouth of Upatoi Creek they found 40 armed Indians returning to the ferry. The Indians took cover immediately and commenced firing. After some firing on both sides two of the white men were killed and two wounded. The Militia left the field, returning to Columbus, and the Indians continued to their homes in Alabama. This fight became known as the Battle of Hitchity.

Fort Jones Historical Marker
Georgia Route 39, about 3 miles south of Florence

Fort Jones, a stockade fort built during the Creek uprising of 1836, stood on this site. After the burning of Roanoke, the frightened settlers sought refuge in its blockhouse, built of upright skinned logs with high windows for gun holes. The fort was built under command of Major H. W. Jernigan and garrisoned by a company of Stewart County citizen soldiers. Among them were Thos. J. Still, Capt. Robert Billups, David Delk, Col. A. P. Rood, and James Fitzgerald who rode to Fort McCreary for aid for the Battle of Shepherd's Plantation.

Shepherd's Plantation Monument
On County Road 39, north of Florence, Georgia.

A concrete monolith monument honors those who died in the Battle of Shepherd's Plantation, by the side of the road, built by the Works Progress Administration, and placed and dedicated by the Daughters of the American Revolution. There is a convenient place to park 50 yards north of the monument with an easy walk back to it. There are several steps that lead up to the level of the monument.

Battle of Chickasawachee Swamp Historical Marker
Intersection of Georgia Route 37 and Clear Lake Road

Near here in Chickasawachee Swamp a decisive battle of the Southern Indian Wars was fought July 3, 1836. About 300 warriors were entrenched on an island in the swamp, after a raid in which they killed several settlers. A force of militia under command of Col. Thomas Beall followed them into the swamp and a fierce battle was fought. A number of Indians were killed, and 13 soldiers wounded, 1 mortally. A large amount of plunder taken on the raid on Roanoke was recovered here. This battle broke the Indians' march into Florida, and scattered their main force into small parties.

Battle of Brushy Creek Historical Marker
At Rest Area Number 5, on northbound I-75,
in Cook County, Georgia

Near here in July, 1836, a battalion of Georgia Militia under command of Major Michael Young, defeated a band of Indians in the Battle of Brushy Creek. In pursuit of the Indians, who had been raiding the frontier as they fled into Florida, the soldiers came upon them in the forks of the Big Warrior Creek and Little River and drove them into the swamp. A general engagement followed, fought over a distance of 3 miles, through cypress ponds and dense canebrakes. The result was victory for the militia, with 2 killed, 9 wounded. Of the enemy, 23 were killed, many wounded, and 18 prisoners captured.

Skirmish at Cow Creek Historical Marker
At intersection of U. S. Route 129,
at Mile Post 17, and
Wayfare Road, near Statenville,
Echols County, Georgia.

Near here, on August 27, 1836, Georgia Militia companies commanded by Col. Henry Blair, Captain Lindsay and Capt. Levi J. Knight, fought a skirmish with Creek Indians and routed them, killing two and taking several prisoners. During this summer the Indians had committed many raids and massacres as they traversed the border counties on their way to Florida to join the Seminoles. Georgia troops had been following them for weeks, and overtook this band in the cypress swamp on the edge of Cow Creek.

Hobdy's Bridge: last Indian Battles in Alabama Historic Marker
On Alabama Highway 130, on the Pike County
end of the modern bridge over the Pea River

The Second Creek War of 1836 broke out when many Creek Indians resisted forced removal after an 1832 treaty ceded the last of their tribal lands in Alabama. As hostility increased between white settlers pouring into the area and Creeks who were reluctant to move to the West, the Pea River became a favored route for those Indians traveling south to seek sanctuary in a new homeland in Florida. State militia forces attacked and routed Creek Indians camped near here at Hobdy's Bridge in February, and again in March of 1836

The 1836 date on the marker is incorrect, the correct date is 1837. Also incorrect is the claim that it was the last battle in Alabama, as two later skirmishes took place in modern Dale and Geneva counties.

Fort Browder Historical Marker
U. S. Route 82 and County Route 79
Batesville, Alabama

Approximately one mile south-southwest of here stood Fort Browder, a small wooden fortification built in 1836 for protection in the last war with the Creek Indians and named for Isham Browder, a prominent local planter. In 1861, the fort witnessed the formation of a Confederate infantry company known as the Fort Browder Roughs initially commanded by Captain Moses Worthington. The Roughs were subsequently enrolled as Company D, 15th Alabama Infantry. Of the 106 officers and men of Company D, 21 were killed

190

in battle (including 1 captain and 2 lieutenants), 46 were wounded but survived, and 26 died of disease.

Memorial to the Fallen of 1836
Gwinnett Historical Courthouse
North Perry Street and
West Pike Street
Lawrenceville, Georgia

In memory of Gwinnett Company of Mounted Volunteers, under the command of Capt. Hammond Garmany who were slain by Creek Indians 9 June 1836 in a Battle at Shepherd's Plantation in Stewart County: Ens. Isaac Lacy, Sgt. James E. Martin, Pvt. William M. Sims, Pvt. John A. V. Tate, Pvt. Robert T. Holland, Pvt. James H. Holland, Pvt. Henry W. Paden, Pvt. James Allen. Their remains rest beneath this monument.

William Otho Beall Grave
Beall Cemetery
Carrollton, in
Carroll County, Georgia

William Otho Beall (1795-1851), soldier and politician, was born in Franklin County, Georgia. He represented Carroll County in the state senate intermittently from 1831 to 1846. A brigadier general in the state militia, he served as Assistant Adjutant General from 1836 to 1840, and led troops in the Second Creek War.

Levi J. Knight Grave
Union Primitive Baptist Church Cemetery
Lakeland, in
Lanier County, Georgia

Levi J. Knight (1803-1870) was a captain in the Lowndes County, Georgia militia and led a company of volunteers at the Battle of Brushy Creek in 1836. He later raised two companies for the Confederate cause and served as the major in the 29th Regiment of Georgia Infantry.

Further Reading

Cherry, F. L., *History of Opelika and Her Agricultural Tributary Territory*. Opelika, Alabama: Genealogical Society of East Alabama, 1996.

Ellisor, John T., *The Second Creek War: Interethnic Conflict and Collusion on a Collapsing Frontier*. Lincoln, Nebraska: University of Nebraska Press, 2010.

Foreman, Grant, *Indian Removal: The Emigration of the Five Civilized Tribes of Indians*. Norman, Oklahoma: University of Oklahoma Press, 1932.

Green, Michael D., *The Politics of Indian Removal: Creek Government and Society in Crisis*. Lincoln, Nebraska: University of Nebraska Press, 1982.

Haveman, Christopher D., "With Great Difficulty and Labour: The Emigration of the McIntosh Party of Creek Indians, 1827-1828." *Chronicles of Oklahoma*, Volume 85, Winter 2007-08, pages 468-490.

_____, "Final Resistance: Creek Removal from the Alabama Homeland." *Alabama Heritage*, Volume 89, Summer 2008.

Kane, Sharyn and Richard Keeton, *Fort Benning: Its Land and the People*. U. S. Army Infantry Center, Directorate of Public Works, Environmental Management Division, not dated.

Leitch Wright, James, *Creeks and Seminoles: The Destruction and Regeneration of the Muscogulge People*. Lincoln, Nebraska: University of Nebraska Press, 1986.

Third Seminole War, 1855-1858

Background

In 1845, the Territory of Florida became a state. While white settlers continued to move into northern Florida, fear of the ferocious Seminole curtailed the desire to settle further south. Governor Thomas Brown encouraged cattlemen and farmers to settle the rich lands around Lake Okeechobee, under the protection of the state militia. To remove the threat of Seminole attack, the federal government once again began to pressure the Seminole to relocate to the Indian Territory. The principal chief, Billy Bowlegs, refused, making armed resistance inevitable.

White bounty hunters were offered rewards for capturing the Seminole, $500 for braves, $250 for women, and $100 for children. The government offered the same amounts to the Seminole, if they would surrender peacefully and relocate. Even a delegation of Seminole leaders from the Indian Territory could not convince them to surrender and relocate, Billy Bowlegs refusing all offers. In 1855, Billy Bowlegs was principal chief of only a few hundred Seminole who then remained in Florida. In late 1855, when army surveyors destroyed part of the chief's banana crop, Billy Bowlegs began to direct attacks against isolated settlements, causing the settlers to flee to nearby forts and blockhouses or larger cities on the coast, and touching off the Third Seminole War, sometimes called the Billy Bowlegs War.

Campaigns

In the early part of the war, the Seminole raided near Bradenton, Brooksville, Sarasota, and Tampa. In February, a war party attacked Braden Castle, a plantation owned by Dr. Joseph Addison Braden, near modern Bradenton, in Manatee County. On March 2, 1856, Seminole warriors attacked the Hamlin Snell Cabin on Sarasota Bayou, where one man was killed and the house burned to the ground. On April 17, 1856, a Seminole war party attacked, killed, and scalped John Carney, a private in Captain Lesley's Company, Florida Mounted Volunteer Regiment, while he was plowing his field, near Alafia, in modern Hillsborough County. Lesley led a body of volunteers in pursuit, chased the murderers down, and killed most of the war party. On May 16th, a train of three wagons, accompanied by a guard of militia, halted at a creek about 12 miles from Tampa, was attacked by a Seminole war party. Private Levi Starling, a private in Captain Francis M. Durrance's Company, led the guard. Several whites were killed. A body of militia chased the attackers, but were not successful in catching them.

On the morning of June 14, 1856, a Seminole war party attacked the Willoughby Tillis homestead, near Fort Meade, in modern Polk County. Tillis and his family took refuge in their cabin and returned fire, while the warriors slaughtered his livestock and attempted to burn the cabin. Hearing the distant gunfire, Lieutenant Alderman Carton, led seven mounted volunteers from Fort Meade to rescue the family. After a brisk but short fight, the Seminole withdrew, with three killed on each side. More volunteers joined in the pursuit, catching up with the Seminole on the banks of the Peace River, near Zolfo Springs. At the head of nineteen volunteers, Lieutenant Streaty Parker surprised the war party, killing several and wounding more in fierce hand-to-hand combat, Chief Oscen Tustennuggee among the fallen. With the loss of the chief and so many warriors, Seminole raiding stopped north of Lake Okeechobee.

The fighting continued for another two years, but consisted only of numerous small skirmishes. In 1857, the federal government withdrew most of its troops for deployment elsewhere, leaving the fight to Florida militia and volunteers. As the army had in the Second Seminole War, the militia formed boat companies, who scoured the Everglades and the rivers and streams around it, finding and destroying the Seminole villages and crops. As small bands of Seminole were captured, they were transported to the Indian Territory.

The federal government brought delegations of Seminole leaders from the Indian Territory to convince their Florida brethren to surrender and relocate. Most of the remaining Seminole refused to negotiate. Eventually, however, the war of attrition took its toll. In early 1858, Chief Wild Cat was brought back to Florida to convince Billy Bowlegs to relocate. The government offered Bowlegs $10,000 and his chiefs $1,000 each. At first Bowlegs refused, but on May 4th the chief surrendered at Fort Myers with his band of 123 and submitted to relocation, effectively ending the Third Seminole War.

Aftermath

At the end of the war, no more than about 300 Seminole refused to surrender and remained in Florida.

Places of Interest

Collier County Museum
3301 East Tamiami Trail
Naples, Florida 34112

(800) 224-5937

http://www.colliermuseums.com/

The museum features a large display on the Seminole Wars. On the grounds is a replica of a small fort typical of the type used during the war, and a native village.

Paynes Creek Historic State Park
888 Lake Branch Park
Bowling Green, Florida 33834

(863) 375-4717

https://www.floridastateparks.org/park/Paynes-Creek

On the National Register of Historic Places, the park offers viewing of the Fort Chokonikla site, the Captain George S. Payne and Dempsey Whiddon Monument, and the Kennedy-Darling Trading Store site, where Captain Payne and Dempsey Whiddon were both killed by Seminole.

Willoughby Tillis Battle Monument
Monument Park
Second Street
Fort Meade, Florida 33841

A group of United States Army soldiers led by Lt. Carlton engaged the Seminole Indians in what is known as the Willoughby Tillis Battle in this vicinity on June 14-16, 1856. The five men who lost their lives in this engagement are buried here.

In memory of Lt. Alderman Carlton, Lott Whidden, William Parker killed June 14, 1856, and Robert F. Prine, George Howell killed June 16, 1856, and others who were wounded.

This monument erected by descendants of Alderman Carlton.

Cracker Trail Museum & Village
2822 Museum Drive
Zolfo Springs, Florida 33890

(863) 735□0119

http://www.hardeecounty.net/crackertrailmuseum/index.html

The park was the site of the decisive battle fought on June 16, 1856, following the attack on the Willoughby Tillis homestead. The museum has an exhibit on the Seminole Wars as well as a good collection of genealogical materials and publications.

Ah-Tah-Thi-Ki Seminole Museum
Big Cypress Seminole Indian Reservation
34725 West Boundary Road
Clewiston, Florida 33440

(877) 902-1113

http://www.ahtahthiki.com/

The official museum of the Seminole Tribe of Florida, the museum features exhibits, artifacts, and an archives and library.
The collections include historical newspapers, manuscripts, militaria, and other artifacts.

Fort Denaud Historical Marker
On State Route 78-A at
Caloosahatchee River bridge, in
Hendry County, Florida

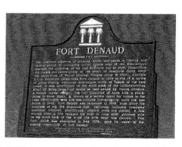

The combined pressure of growing white settlement in Florida and federal policy of relocating Indian tribes west of the Mississippi sparked the outbreak of the 2nd Seminole War in 1835. Controlling the coasts and campaigning in the heart of Seminole lands were the objectives of Major General Thomas Jesup in 1837. Captain B. L. E. Bonneville established Fort Denaud in 1838 as one of a series of posts linking American operations south of Tampa to the east coast. It was constructed on the south bank of the Caloosahatchee River 27 miles from Fort Myers on land owned by Pierre Denaud, a French Indian trader. The fort consisted of tents with a blockhouse in their midst. It served as a supply depot for troops in the Lake Okeechobee area and was utilized intermittently until the war ended in 1842. Fort Denaud was reopened in 1855, soon after the outbreak of the 3rd Seminole War. Additions included company quarters, a hospital guardhouse, sutler's store, and stables. A few months after a fire ravaged the post in June 1856, another site on the north bank of the river two miles west was chosen. The fort, which was abandoned in May 1858, gave its name to the nearby town of Ft. Denaud.

Chief Billy Bowlegs Historical Marker
2800 Palm Beach Boulevard at Billy's Creek
Fort Myers, Florida

Billy Bowlegs was a Seminole Indian Chief during the second (1835-1842) and third (1855-1858) Seminole wars. He and his followers resisted their removal to the Indian Territory in Oklahoma until 1858. That year, Bowlegs and about 125 other Seminoles were placed aboard the steamer Gray Cloud for transport across the Gulf to New Orleans and from there up the Mississippi and Arkansas rivers to Fort Gibson, then overland to Wewoka, Oklahoma.

The war later termed the "Billy Bowlegs War" began in 1855 when Bowlegs's gardens of squash and bananas were destroyed by the troops of First Lieutenant George Hartsuff. After his removal to Oklahoma, Bowlegs continued his own war by serving on the Confederate side during the Civil War. He died during the fall or winter of 1863-64 but his name is preserved by his descendents, a town named Bowlegs in Oklahoma, and in the name of Billy's Creek.

Fort Myers Historical Marker
First and Jackson Streets
Fort Myers, Florida

Army post Fort Myers was established 14 February 1850 with 116 men and officers. Winfield Scott Hancock, Q.M. Captain was assigned in 1856. During the last years of the Seminole War there were 835 personnel in residence. The fort was deactivated in 1858, then reactivated in 1863 during the War Between the States. The long pier was near present day Hendry Street; the hospital was west of Fowler. The riverfront officers quarters were where Bay Street is now.

Fort Myers Military Cemetery Historical Marker
Second and Fowler Streets
Fort, Myers, Florida

During the Seminole Wars, this was the site of a military cemetery for soldiers of Fort Harvie, 1841-42, and Fort Myers, 1850-58. The cemetery was located outside the breastworks of the respective forts which were in the vicinity of the present Federal Building in downtown Fort Myers. When Fowler Street was cut through, the graves were moved to the civilian cemetery on Michigan Avenue.

Southwest Florida Museum of History
2031 Jackson Street
Fort Myers, Florida 33901

info@museumofhistory.org

http://www.museumofhistory.org/

The museum has extensive exhibits of the history of Fort Myers and the Seminole Wars, with a strong emphasis on the Third Seminole War.

Capt. John Parkhill of Leon Volunteers Monument
Monroe Street and Apalachee Freeway
Tallahassee, Florida

This monument is erected by Captain Parkhill's fellow citizens of Leon County, Florida, as a testimonial of their high esteem for his character and public services. The memory of the hero is the treasure of his country. He was born July 10, 1823 and was killed at Palm Hammock in South Florida while leading his company in a charge against the Seminole Indians, November 28 A.D. 1857.

Further Reading

Covington, James W., *The Billy Bowlegs War, 1855-1858: The Final Stand of the Seminoles Against the Whites*. Cluluota, Florida: Mickler House Publishers, 1982.

Gifford John C., *Billy Bowlegs and the Seminole War*. Coconut Grove, Florida: Triangle Company, 1925

Knetsch, Joe, *Florida's Seminole Wars: 1817-1858*. Charleston, South Carolina: Arcadia Publishing Company, 2003.

_____, *Fear and Anxiety on the Florida Frontier*. Dade City, Florida: Seminole Wars Foundation Press, 2008.

Procyk, Richard J., *Guns Across the Loxahatchee: Remembering the Seminole Wars*. Cocoa, Florida: Florida Historical Society Press, 2011.

West, Patsy, *The Enduring Seminoles*. Gainesville, Florida: University Press of Florida, 1998.

Williams, John Lee, *The Territory of Florida*. Gainesville, Florida: University Press of Florida, 1962.

Removal to the Indian Territory, 1830-1838

The Trail of Tears generally refers to the removal, either voluntarily, reluctantly, or forcibly, of the Five Civilized Tribes from their lands in Alabama, Florida, Georgia, Mississippi, North Carolina, South Carolina, and Tennessee. Starting with President Washington, the federal government adopted an official policy of acculturation, that is, the Indians could remain on their ancestral homelands, provided they stayed on reservations with clearly defined boundaries, converted to Christianity, learned English, adopted the white economic system, and respected the rights of individuals owning land, slaves, and other property. President Jefferson encouraged the tribes to adopt an agrarian system and abandon their hunting and trading culture. At least to some degree, the acculturation policy worked, as more and more individual bands turned to agriculture, remained friendly, and began to adopt American ways. However, many others did not accept the policy and wanted to maintain their traditional culture and way of life. Their refusal to accept acculturation was one of the principal causes of the various wars.

Andrew Jackson believed that, as things stood, the tribes were doomed. As settlement increased in the northeast, towns and farms sprang up on former hunting grounds, state laws governed everyone and everything within state boundaries, and individual tribes gradually disappeared. Jackson asserted that, if the southern tribes wanted to survive and maintain their culture, they could be successful only on federal reservations in the west, because the push for settling the southern states was inevitable and unstoppable. In short, Jackson believed that Indian removal was a wise, humane, and generous act of mercy. In 1828, Jackson campaigned for President on a platform advocating the removal of the southern Indians to reservations west of the Mississippi River, in exchange for their ancestral lands, calling for immediate removal in his inaugural address. Two years later, on May 28, 1830, Congress passed and Jackson signed the Indian Removal Act.

The Act authorized the president to negotiate treaties with individual tribes, in which the tribes would cede all rights to their lands east of the Mississippi River in exchange for reservations on federal land in the Indian Territory, where their own laws and customs would not be subject to any state government. The Act did not authorize the forced removal of any tribes; however, Jackson pursued an aggressive policy, pressuring the tribes to negotiate new treaties.

By far, most members of the Five Civilized Tribes relocated to the Indian Territory. However, some members refused to leave their ancestral lands, with those staying behind eventually organized into formal tribal groups: the Mississippi Band of Choctaw Indians, Eastern Band of Cherokee, Poarch Band of Creek Indians, and Seminole Tribe of Florida.

Cherokee Removal

In late 1828, Georgia passed a series of laws, abolishing Cherokee independent sovereignty and extending the jurisdiction of state law over the Cherokee. In 1829, the discovery of gold further increased Georgians' desire to remove the Cherokee and take their land. In 1832, President Jackson appointed Major General Winfield Scott commander of the army in the Cherokee country. Scott made his headquarters at Fort Butler, situated on a hill overlooking the Hiwassee River, at modern Murphy, North Carolina. According to a census taken in 1835, 16,542 Cherokee, 201 whites who had intermarried, and 1,592 slaves lived on Cherokee land in northwestern Georgia, northeastern Alabama, eastern Tennessee, and western North Carolina.

On December 29, 1835, a small group of Cherokee leaders, including John Ross, negotiated the Treaty of New Echota, named for the Cherokee capitol town, situated at the confluence of the Coosawattee and Conasauga rivers, exchanging their ancestral lands for new land in the Indian Territory. The treaty was not accepted by the rest of the Cherokee leadership, who sent a delegation to present their grievances to Congress. The Congress ratified a modified version of the treaty on May 23, 1836, providing for the Cherokee to remove themselves voluntarily by May 23, 1838. Only several hundred Cherokee voluntarily relocated under the treaty. As the deadline approached, newly-elected President Martin Van Buren gave Winfield Scott overall responsibility for enforcing the treaty. Because the Cherokee people were reluctant to relocate, Scott determined to begin the process of rounding up and removing the Cherokee. He divided the Cherokee into three districts: The Eastern Military District, commanded by Brigadier General Abram Eustice, headquartered at Fort Butler, to collect the Cherokee in North Carolina; the Middle Military District, led by Brigadier General Charles R. Floyd, commanding mostly Georgia militia, to collect the Cherokee in most of Georgia; and, the Western Military District, commanded by Colonel William C. Lindsay, to collect the Cherokee in Alabama, Tennessee, and northwestern Georgia. Scott's overall command consisted of 2,200 regular army troops and about 5,000 state militia and volunteers from Alabama, Georgia, North Carolina, and Tennessee.

Scott ordered the construction of 33 forts and encampments to support the removal, five in Alabama, fourteen in Georgia, six in North Carolina, and eight in Tennessee. The largest deportation depot was located at Fort Cass, on the Hiwassee River, at modern Charleston, Tennessee. Other major deportation depots were located at Ross' Landing, at Chattanooga, Fort Payne, Alabama, and Gunter's Landing, now Guntersville, Alabama.

On May 17, 1838, Scott arrived at New Echota and told the chiefs that removal would begin immediately. Admonishing his troops to treat the Cherokee with kindness and humanity, Scott ordered Floyd to begin collecting the Cherokee in Georgia and take them to deportation encampments, or depots, in Tennessee. Within a month, Floyd's men had delivered more than 3,000 Cherokee to the encampments. On June 10th, Scott ordered the removal to begin in Alabama, North Carolina, and Tennessee. Within weeks, most Cherokee had been removed from their homes at gunpoint and taken to deportation depots, often with few, if any, of their possessions. About 1,000 Cherokee managed to evade capture by secreting themselves in the mountains of western North Carolina. Others, mostly property owners, also managed to avoid deportation.

By August 1838, the militia had collected and transported about 3,000 Cherokee, in four groups. On June 6th, Lieutenant Edward Deas led the first group of 800, who traveled by boat. A Lieutenant Monroe led the second group of 164, departing on June 12th. The third group of 800, led by Lieutenant R. H. K. Whitely, departed by boat on June 12th. Captain Gustavus S. Drane departed with the last group of 1,072, by boat on June 17th.

Because of the difficulties encountered by the first four groups, including frequent loading and unloading due to low water, lack of food and medicine, disease, and desertions, Scott suspended the deportations with as many as 13,000 remaining in encampments waiting for transportation. Because of the pleas from Chief Ross, Scott allowed those remaining to travel on their own, unarmed, and without any army or militia guards, later in the year when the weather would be cooler. Conditions in the encampments were bad; thus, the Cherokee suffered and many died from overcrowding, lack of food, unsanitary conditions, rampant disease, and lack of adequate medical care. Chief Ross organized the Cherokee into twelve wagon trains, each to be accompanied by hired wagon masters, teamsters, medical doctors, commissaries, and interpreters. He also provided a steamboat to transport the tribal leaders and their families. About 12,000 Cherokee relocated to the Indian Territory and about 1,500 remained, most in North Carolina, and others in Alabama, Georgia, South Carolina, and Tennessee. Those remaining eventually became the Eastern Band of the Cherokee Nation.

Another group of Cherokee avoided forced removal. In 1809, in order to continue living their traditional ways of life, a party from the Lower Towns was sent to search for new land along the Arkansas and White rivers, in what is now northwestern Arkansas and northeastern Oklahoma. Archeological evidence suggests that Cherokee began migrating to the area as early as the last decade of the 18th century. In 1817, the Treaty with the Cherokee, signed by representatives from the federal government, the eastern Cherokee, and the Cherokee on the Arkansas River, exchanged Cherokee land in the east for a new reservation in Arkansas. Possibly as many as 4,000 migrated to Arkansas and were known as Western Cherokee, Old Settlers, or Keetoowah Cherokee. Another treaty, signed in 1828, provided for the Keetoowah to move to a new reservation further west, on seven million acres on the Arkansas, Canadian, and Grand rivers, in the Indian Territory. Also in 1828, the Keetoowah Cherokee formally adopted a written constitution. Cherokee continued to migrate to join the Keetoowah, usually in small groups, until 1838, when the Keetoowah were joined by 12,000 of their eastern brethren.

Chickasaw Removal

At first, the Chickasaw resisted the government's efforts to convince them to relocate; but, President Jackson told them that they had to move, or submit themselves to the laws of the State of Mississippi and be subsumed by white culture. On August 27, 1830, the Chickasaw chiefs signed the Treaty of Franklin, at Franklin, Tennessee, giving up their lands in Mississippi and agreeing to move west. Because the Chickasaw found the new lands unacceptable after visiting the proposed area and the Senate had not ratified the treaty, the Chickasaw refused to move. They continued to suffer from the continuing encroachment of white settlers and the effects of the supremacy of state law over their own tribal government. On October 20, 1832, the Chickasaw chiefs signed the Treaty of Pontotoc, at the Chickasaw capitol, again agreeing to relocate, provided that acceptable lands in the Indian Territory could be located and surveyed, where they would be free to govern themselves. The treaty further stipulated that the government would protect them from the white settlers, compensate them for the improvements they left behind, and give them the proceeds received from the sale of their lands, to fund the cost of their relocation.

After searching for new lands, under the Treaty of Doaksville in 1837, the Chickasaw purchased the right to settle on a portion of the Choctaw reservation for $530,000. President Jackson convinced the Senate to ratify the treaty between the two tribes. In 1837 and 1838, 4,914 Chickasaw with 1,156 slaves migrated to their new reservation. The Chickasaw migration was not as difficult as those of the Cherokee and Choctaw, because they controlled their departures and traveled only in favorable seasons.

As the Chickasaw settled on their new lands, they discovered that Plains tribes freely roamed across their land and often raided their settlements. In response to their cries for help, the government established Fort Washita, at modern Durant, Oklahoma, and then Fort Arbuckle on the Washita River, one mile north of modern Davis, Oklahoma. In 1856, the Chickasaw formally separated from the Choctaw, establishing their own government and constitution.

Choctaw Removal

On September 27, 1830, upon signing the Treaty of Dancing Rabbit, at their village on Dancing Rabbit Creek, in modern Noxubee County, Mississippi, the Choctaw became the first to agree to removal. When Congress ratified the treaty on November 24, 1831, the Choctaw officially ceded 11,000,000 acres of land, mostly in Mississippi, for 15,000,000 acres of land in the Indian Territory. The Choctaw relocated in three principal phases: the first in the autumn of 1831, the second in 1832, and the third the following year. At the time, about 20,000 Choctaw, plus a number of whites who lived among them and 1,000 slaves, lived east of the Mississippi River. Of those, about 15,000 relocated and five or six thousand remained in Mississippi.

The first group to arrive on their new reservation suffered more than those who followed, due to a major winter blizzard and cholera epidemic. The later arrivals planted their crops immediately and suffered less than most of the other relocated tribes. Both during and after their migration, as many as 4,000 died, many from cholera. After the first three waves, Choctaw continued to move to the new reservation, including about one thousand in 1846 alone. By 1930, only 1,665 still resided in Mississippi.

In 1831, Alexis de Tocqueville witnessed their migration in Memphis, later writing

> In the whole scene there was an air of ruin and destruction, something which betrayed a final and irrevocable adieu; one couldn't watch without feeling one's heart wrung. The Indians were tranquil, but sombre and taciturn. There was one who could speak English and of whom I asked why the Chactas were leaving their country. "To be free," he answered, could never get any other reason out of him. We watch the expulsion of one of the most celebrated and ancient American peoples.

Creek Removal

On February 12, 1825, William McIntosh, and other Lower Creek chiefs, signed the Treaty of Indian Springs, ceding all the lands in Georgia and a large tract in Alabama for $200,000 to acquire new land in the Indian Territory. Most Creek people objected to the treaty and sale of Creek land. The Creek National Council complained successfully to the federal government and signed the Treaty of Washington on January 24, 1826, voiding the previous treaty, restoring Creek lands in Alabama, and ceding their lands in Georgia.

In late 1827, 703 Lower Creek, with 86 slaves, began their journey to their new lands west of the Mississippi River. At Tuscumbia, a large group of the elderly, women, and children traveled by keelboat from there down the Tennessee River, eventually making their way to Memphis. There they rendezvoused with the rest of the party who traveled overland. From there both parties continued their journeys, the largest continuing overland to Fort Gibson on the Grand River, just upstream from its confluence with the Arkansas River. When they arrived in February 1828, the agents there noted that they were totally worn out from the difficult journey, having to abandon many of their wagons, owing to the rivers and streams flooded by recent heavy rains. The keelboats brought the other party up the Arkansas River to Fort Gibson.

In late 1828, a second party of about 400 Lower Creek, with their slaves, voluntarily migrated along the same route. In June, a party of about 1,200 Creek, mostly from their towns in Georgia, started their long journey, taking both land and water routes. Other parties continued the voluntary migration. In 1829, an epidemic of cholera swept through the new reservation, taking many lives and causing some Creek to return to Alabama.

On March 24, 1832, the Creek National Council signed the Treaty of Cusseta, ceding their tribal sovereignty for individual legal title to their Alabama lands that individual Creek could keep or sell. However, white encroachment continued unabated. While legitimate land sales did take place, many unscrupulous whites cheated the Creek owners or just stole the land outright. In 1834 and again in 1835, additional parties voluntarily chose to migrate. Among those Creek who resisted removal, resentment against the white settlers grew, eventually bringing the start of the Second Creek War in 1836. President Jackson used the war as an excuse, ordering Major General Winfield Scott, commander of all federal troops in the Cherokee territory, to force removal and relocation.

The army, with the assistance of Alabama and Georgia militia, captured Creek warriors, then shackled and marched them and their families to Montgomery, from there taking them by steamboat most of the way, finishing their journey to Fort Gibson by trekking overland, some still in shackles and all under armed guard. The Creek who took no part in the uprising were rounded up in August and September 1836, then sent west on an overland route in five successive groups. In October 1837, a sixth group of 600 Creek were taken by steamboat but lost half their number in a collision with another vessel. The government continued rounding up Creek families, including those who had sought safety among other tribes. Nearly 500 were taken from Cherokee land, marched to Gunter's Landing on the Tennessee River, and from there shipped west to Fort Gibson. About 300 Creek accompanied the Chickasaw on their migration.

In 1837, the government stopped the forced removal, but individuals, families, and other small groups continued to migrate well into the 1840s. In all, from 1827 through 1837, more than 23,000 Creek migrated voluntarily or were forcibly removed.

Seminole Removal

The Seminole hated the 1830 Indian Removal Act and resisted any efforts to enforce it. In 1832, the Treaty of Payne's Landing required the Seminole to relinquish their claims to land in Florida in exchange for new land on the Creek reservation in the Indian Territory. In accordance with the terms of the treaty, the Seminole sent a delegation to view the territory. Dissatisfaction with the quality of the new land, with having to live under Creek jurisdiction, and their reluctance to leave Florida, gradually erupted into the Second Seminole War. Over the next several years, the army destroyed Seminole towns and villages, driving the inhabitants further into the swamps, but capturing many and shipping them west to their new lands. In 1837, more than 250 Seminole and Black Seminole, as well as Seminole prisoners held at Fort Moultrie, South Carolina, were taken to New Orleans and held at Fort Pike to await transportation to the Indian Territory. The prisoners were loaded onto steamboats that arrived at Fort Gibson in June 1838.

Some Seminole, however, did accept relocation to the Indian Territory. In late 1835, one group of 407 went to Tampa to await removal. In April 1836, led by Lieutenant Joseph W. Harris, the group boarded a steamer bound for New Orleans, where they boarded another steamboat towing a keelboat, eventually reaching Fort Gibson in May. Only 320 of the group survived the arduous journey. Other small groups followed later that year and next, including a group of 90 Black Seminole who had been captured that winter and shipped to New Orleans in June 1837.

In 1838, the army captured numerous Seminole and transported them to Fort Pike, just east of New Orleans, to await transportation. By May, more than one thousand Seminole (about one third Black Seminole) were at Fort Pike. Later that month, Lieutenant John G. Reynolds arrived with 160 more. The army then shipped the Seminole up the Mississippi River, but kept the Black Seminole behind, intending to return them to their rightful owners or sell them into slavery. The Seminole protested, claiming they owned the Black Seminole, and eventually prevailed. Nathaniel Collins transported the Black Seminole by riverboat, arriving at Fort Gibson in June. Three more groups of Seminole were transported in May: one group of 453 on the steamboat *Renown*, a second group of 674 on the steamboat *South Alabama*, and a third group of 117 Seminole and two Black Seminole on the steamboat *Ozark*.

In June, Captain Pitcairn Morrison conducted a group of 335, including 30 Black Seminole, to Fort Gibson, via New Orleans and the Mississippi River. One group of 33 Black Seminole were held briefly at New Orleans, because some whites claimed them as slaves. The army did not give up custody and directed them by boat upriver, reaching Fort Gibson in July. That same month, Lieutenant John G. Reynolds conducted a group of 67, including one Black Seminole, upriver to Fort Gibson, arriving in August. In October, most of the last remnants of the Apalachicola Seminole, and a small number of Creek, were transported west to Fort Gibson. In November, another group of 31 Seminole and two slaves were transported by the same water route, arriving at Fort Gibson in February 1839. In late November, Major Daniel Boyd transported another group, consisting of a few Apalachicola Seminole and 34 Creek, to Fort Gibson.

In February 1839, General Taylor conducted a party of 96 captured Seminole to Tampa, where Captain Morrison took them by boat across the Gulf and up the Mississippi River, where a boiler explosion killed several of the passengers. Morrison and the survivors reached Fort Gibson in April. In November that year, Lieutenant Buckner Board conducted another group of 48 Seminole from St. Augustine, via New Orleans to Fort Gibson in December.

The army conducted several more removals in 1840. Major William B. Belknap departed with a group of 220 Tallahassee captives in March. Another group of 205, including several Black Seminole, departed in May. In October, the Seminole sent a delegation of 14 leaders back to Florida, to talk more of their brethren to relocate to the Indian Territory, but had limited if any success.

In March 1841, Major Belknap transported a group of 221 Tallahassee to Fort Gibson. Also in March, Legrande G. Capers with a group of 212, including seven Black Seminole, were removed. In May, Captain Henry McKavett conducted a party of 206, including 15 Black Seminole, to the Indian Territory. In June, Chief Wildcat and his band, were transported to New Orleans, then ordered to return to Florida to convince more Seminole to surrender and relocate. In October, a group of about 200, including Chief Wildcat and his followers, departed by water, heading for Fort Gibson. Also in October, a second group of 200, including 15 Black Seminole, were relocated. Late in 1841, the army collected another 300 Seminole and their slaves at Tampa; the following spring, Captain Thomas Ludwell Alexander transported the group to Fort Gibson.

The army continued to capture and transport groups of Seminole, their families, and slaves in 1842. In April, Second Lieutenant Edward R. S. Canby conducted another relocation party of 102. In November, Chief Pascofa and 350 of his mostly Creek band surrendered. Lieutenant McKavett conducted their relocation party in early 1843. For all practical purposes, forced relocation came to a halt in 1843. However, relocation began in earnest again during the Third Seminole War.

In May 1856, the first sizable group of 165 captured Seminole were transported from Fort Myers. Chief Billy Bowlegs and about 160 of his band surrendered and soon were transported. In December, the chief returned to Florida and convinced 75 more to surrender and relocate. Their departure in February 1859 was the last forced removal from Florida.

Places of Interest

New Echota Historic Site
1211 Chatsworth Highway NE
Calhoun, Georgia 30701

(706) 624-1321

http://gastateparks.org/info/echota/

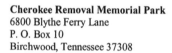

New Echota is one of the most significant Cherokee Indian
sites in the nation. In 1825, the Cherokee established their
capital at the headwaters of the Oostanaula River. It was the site of the first Indian language
newspaper office, a court case which carried to the U. S. Supreme Court, one of the earliest
experiments in national self-government by an Indian tribe, the signing of a treaty which
relinquished Cherokee claims to lands east of the Mississippi River, and the assembly of Indians
for removal to the Indian Territory. Visitors can see twelve original and reconstructed buildings,
including the Council House, Court House, Print Shop, home of Missionary Samuel Worcester,
and an 1805 store, as well as outbuildings such as smoke houses, corn cribs and barns.

Cherokee Removal Memorial Park
6800 Blythe Ferry Lane
P. O. Box 10
Birchwood, Tennessee 37308

(423) 339-2769

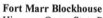

http://www.meigstn.com/cherokee-removal-memorial-park/

The park is a multipurpose facility dedicated to those who died during the forced removal of the
Cherokee. It is located at the confluence of the Hiwassee River and Tennessee River, overlooking
Blythe Ferry, where 9,000 Indians camped several weeks, waiting to start their journey. The area
has been a significant cross road for development of Indian culture for centuries.

Fort Marr Blockhouse
Hiwassee Ocoee State Park
Gee Creek Ranger Station
404 Spring Creek Road
Delano, Tennessee 37325

(423) 263-0050

http://tnstateparks.com/parks/about/hiwassee-ocoee

The original fort was built on the Old Federal Road, near the
Tennessee-Georgia state line. It was used in 1838 to detain Cherokee Indians prior to their forced
removal on the Trail of Tears. Time erased most of the fort, but the block house survived and was
moved to the grounds of the state park ranger station. A short walk from the fort will take you to
the Hiwassee River where a Native American fish weir is still visible.

210

Fort Butler Historical Marker
Hiwassee Street, ¼ mile north of U. S. Route 64
Murphy, North Carolina

One of forts in which Gen. Winfield Scott gathered the
Cherokee before moving them west in 1838. Stood 1/4 mile
southwest.

Cherokee Agency Historical Marker
U. S. Route 11, just south of Hiwassee River,
in Bradley County, Tennessee

One-fifth of a mile east was the site of the Cherokee Indian Agency, 1821-1838. Famous
agents were Col. Return John Meigs, 1801-23, and ex-Governor Joseph McMinn, 1823-
24. East of the agency was Fort Cass, headquarters for the removal westward of the
Cherokees in 1836-38. Lewis Ross, trader and brother of Chief John Ross, lived here.

Ross's Landing Historical Marker
Ross's Landing Riverfront Park
Chattanooga, Tennessee

Established about 1816 by John Ross some 370 yards from this
point. It consisted of a ferry, warehouse, and landing. With the
organization of Hamilton County in 1819 north of the river, it
served not only the Cherokee trade but also as a convenient
business center for the county. Cherokee parties left from the
landing for the West in 1838, the same year the growing
community took the name Chattanooga.

Fort Payne's Fort Historical Marker
Union Park, on Gault Avenue North,
east of Fourth Street, in
Fort Payne, Alabama

The fort, consisting of a log house and large stockade, was built
in 1838 by order of General Winfield Scott, commander of
military forces responsible for the removal of Cherokee
Indians. Soldiers occupying the fort were commanded by
Captain John C. Payne, for whom the fort was named. Indians
in the DeKalb County area who refused to move westward
voluntarily were gathered and held in the stockade pending their forceful removal to the Indian
territory. Chimney still stands on site of fort near the railroad at 4th Street SE.

211

Chickasaw Agency Historical Marker
Natchez Trace Parkway, Mile Post 241.4

The United States agents to the Chickasaws lived from 1802 to 1825 west of here on the Old Natchez Trace. That Americans could peacefully travel the road through Indian lands was due in large measure to the agents. Their efforts to preserve harmony included such thankless tasks as collecting debts, recovering stolen horses, removing trespassers and capturing fugitives. Winters were lonely, but spring and summer brought thousands of "Kaintucks" on the long journey from Natchez to their Ohio Valley homes. Many expected the agency to supply medicine or food or just a good night's rest.

Chickasaw Council House
Natchez Trace Parkway, Mile Post 251.1

Westerly on the Natchez Trace stood an Indian village "Pontatock" with its council house which, in the 1820's, became the "Capitol" of the Chickasaw Nation. The chiefs and headmen met there to sign treaties or to establish tribal laws and policies. Each summer two or three thousand Indians camped nearby to receive the annual payments for lands they had sold to our Federal Government. After the treaty of 1832, the last land was surrendered. The Council House disappeared, but its memory remains here in the names of a Mississippi County and town and went west with the Chickasaws as a county and village in Oklahoma.

Chickasaw Council House Museum
209 N. Fisher
Tishomingo, Oklahoma 73460

(580) 371-3351

https://chickasaw.net/Services/Chickasaw-Council-House-Museum.aspx

Located on the Capitol Square, the museum holds one of the largest collections of Chickasaw art, artifacts and archive materials. It is the first Chickasaw Council House built in Indian Territory. Exhibits trace the history and culture of the Chickasaw. The museum gift shop offers a variety of souvenirs, books, music, and Chickasaw language materials.

Chickasaw National Capitol
411 West 9th
Tishomingo, Oklahoma 73460

(580) 371-9835

Completed in late 1898 after seven months of construction
for a total cost of $15,000, the Victorian, gothic-style
building is over 8,000 square feet in area, and served as the
Chickasaw National Capitol until 1906. The building
serves as a museum highlighting the Chickasaw people and
their culture. Admission is free and guided tours are
available.

Chickasaw White House
6379 East Mansion Drive
Milburn, Oklahoma 73450

(580) 235-7343

https://chickasaw.net/Services/Chickasaw-White-
House.aspx

Once considered a mansion on the frontier, it was home to
Chickasaw Governor Douglas Henry Johnston and his family from 1898 to 1971.

Pontotoc Creek Treaty Historical Marker
South Main Street and West Marion Street
Confederate Park
Pontotoc, Mississippi

S.E. about 7 miles is site of council house where on October
20, 1832, a treaty was signed providing for cession of over
6 million acres to U. S. and removal of Chickasaws to
West.

213

Dancing Rabbit Creek Treaty Historical Marker
On Monument Road, southwest of
Macon, Mississippi in
Noxubee County

In this area on September 27, 1830, the Choctaw Nation of Indians surrendered their lands to the United States and moved west of the Mississippi River. This treaty was known as Dancing Rabbit Creek Treaty. U. S. Commissioners present: John William Coffee and John H. Eaton. Choctaw Chiefs present: Greenwood Lefleur, Mushulatubbee, and Little Leader. Interpretor: John Pitchlynn

Choctaw Agency Historical Marker
Natchez Trace Parkway, Mile Post 100.7

U. S. agents like Silas Dinsmoor lived among the Choctaw and represented their interests while implementing U. S. policy. The Agent's duties included surveying and preventing illegal settlement on Choctaw land. He also encouraged the Choctaw to be more reliant on modern farming practices. He was tasked to collect tribal debts owed to American companies and insure that the Choctaw were paid for land ceded to the U. S. The agency moved four times to stay within the shrinking boundaries of the Choctaw Nation. It was located here, along the Natchez Trace, from 1807 until just after the Treaty of Doak's Stand in 1820.

Choctaw Nation of Oklahoma Capital Museum
Council House Road
Tuskahoma, Oklahoma 74574

(918) 569-4465

https://www.choctawnation.com/tribal-services/cultural-services/museum

The museum, located in the old capital building, features exhibits on the Trail of Tears, as well as Choctaw history, culture, and family life.

214

Chahta Immi Cultural Center
Choctaw Shopping Center
Highway 16 West
Pearl River, Mississippi 39350

(606) 650-1687

http://www.choctaw.org/culture/cicc.html

The center features exhibits on Choctaw culture, history, and art. It houses the tribal archives collection.

Coweta Town Historical Marker
Brick Yard Road and State Docks Road, in
Phenix City, Alabama

Coweta Town, located east of this marker on the banks of the Chattahoochee River, is sometimes called New or Upper Coweta to distinguish it from its predecessor, Coweta Tallahassee, down river. Among other well-known Creek towns, Coweta was the birthplace of William McIntosh, the controversial half-blood who was executed by his own people for having signed the fraudulent 1825 Treaty of Indian Springs. Mary Musgrove, who was such a help to James Edward Oglethorpe and the Savannah colony in Georgia, claimed Coweta ancestry. Oglethorpe visited Coweta in 1739 and negotiated an important treaty here and across the river in Cusseta Town.

Creek Trail of Tears Historical Marker
Removal of the Creeks Historical Marker
Fort Mitchell, Russell County, Alabama

Approximately one mile due east of this marker, back down the Old Federal Road, called by frontiersmen and Indians the Three Notched Trail or the Three Chopped Way, stood Fort Mitchell, an early 19th century American fort that in 1836 was one of the principal gathering places for the forced removal of the Creek Indians from their homes on the Chattahoochee River to the West. Weakened by starvation, defrauded of their lands and swindled out of most of their possessions, thousands of Creeks, including some in chains and shackles, made the forced journey from Alabama to what is now Oklahoma, where many of their descendants now live. Alabama also remains the home of many Creek Indians today.

Chattahoochee Indian Heritage Center
Adjacent to Fort Mitchell Historic Site
Enter through Fort Mitchell

http://www.chattahoocheetrace.com/index.php/cihc

The removal of the Creek Nation is memorialized today at the Chattahoochee Indian Heritage Center. Located adjacent to Fort Mitchell, a key post in both Creek wars, the center occupies land where thousands of Creeks camped and burned their last fires before starting west on the Trail of Tears. The center features interpretive signs and a beautiful monument designed to symbolize the sacred fire of the Creek Nation, which here last burned on original Creek lands.

Creek Heritage Trail

http://chattahoocheetrace.com/index.php/historic-markers/creek-heritage-trail-locations

The Creek Heritage Trail is a series of interpretive panel installations throughout the lower Chattahoochee Valley, relating to the history of the Creek people. Featured topics include the causes and consequences of the Creek and Seminole Wars, Creek-American diplomacy, and the Creek Removal. Panel installations are situated at or near town sites, battlefields, meeting grounds, and other significant locations.

Fort Cusseta Chambers County Historical Marker
Martin Luther King Drive and County Road 82 in
Cusseta, Alabama

Following the signing of the Creek Treaty in 1832, the early white settlers constructed a 16 by 30 foot hand hewn log fort for protection against a possible Indian uprising from Cussetaw Indian Village on Osanippa Creek just north of here. Walls of the fort were 4 and 6 feet high, with portholes at a height of 4 feet, still visible after 140 years. Last known fort of its kind in Southeast.

216

Fort Morgan Historic Site
110 State Highway 180
Gulf Shores, Alabama 36542

(251) 540-7127

http://fort-morgan.org/

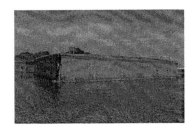

In 1836 and 1837, Fort Morgan became an important stop on the Trail of Tears as the Creek Indians of Alabama were forcibly removed to new lands west in what is now Oklahoma. Among the grieving people that camped briefly at the fort was Milly Francis, a woman remembered today as the Creek Pocahontas.

Fort Pike State Historic Site
27100 Chef Menteur Highway
New Orleans, Louisiana 70129

(225) 342-8111

http://www.crt.state.la.us/louisiana-state-parks/historic-sites/fort-pike-state-historic-site/index

During the Seminole Wars in the 1830s, Fort Pike served as a staging area for many troops on their way to Florida, and as a collection point for hundreds of Seminole prisoners and their black slaves who were being transported to Oklahoma. Cannons were removed from some of the casemates to convert them to cells. At one point, only 66 soldiers guarded 253 Indian and black prisoners.

Fort Gibson Historic Site
907 North Garrison Avenue
Fort Gibson, Oklahoma 74434

(918) 478-4088

http://www.okhistory.org/sites/fortgibson.php

The first military installation in the Indian Territory, this modern 80-acre historic site is home to 29 historic buildings and several archeological sites. Exhibits and living history events depict the role of the fort as the terminal end of the Trail of Tears and the settlement of the Indian Territory. The site features a visitor center, significant museum, book shop, and historic period structures.

Winfield Scott Grave
U. S. Military Academy Post Cemetery
West Point, New York

Winfield Scott (1786-1866) was the foremost
American military figure of the first half of the
19th century. He served as a brigadier general in
the War of 1812. In 1832, Scott took command
of federal troops in the Cherokee Nation and was
in overall command of federal troops in the
Second Creek War, Second Seminole War, and the removal of the Cherokee to the Indian
Territory.

Charles Rinaldo Floyd Grave
at Fairfield Plantation, near the
Floyd Family Cemetery, on Floyd's Neck
Camden County, Georgia

http://www.glynngen.com/~thecrypt/history/floyds.htm

Charles Rinaldo Floyd (1797-1845) began his military career, at the
age of sixteen, as an aide to his father, Brigadier General John Floyd,
in the First Creek War. Brigadier General Charles Floyd commanded
Georgia militia responsible for removing the Cherokee from most of
Georgia and flushing the Seminole from the Okefenokee Swamp.
Upon his death, his loyal soldiers wrapped him in an American flag,
buried him on his beloved Fairfield Plantation, and erected a marble
obelisk in his honor.

Chief John Ross Grave
Ross Cemetery
Parkhill in
Cherokee County, Oklahoma

John Ross (1790-1866) was the principal chief of the Cherokee Nation
from 1828 until his death. As a militia lieutenant, he fought with
Samuel Houston at the Battle of Horseshoe Bend in the First Creek
War. He led his people during their removal to the Indian Territory.

219

Fort Washita
3348 State Road 199
Durant, Oklahoma 74701

580-924-6502

ftwashita@okhistory.org

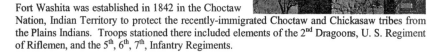

Fort Washita was established in 1842 in the Choctaw Nation, Indian Territory to protect the recently-immigrated Choctaw and Chickasaw tribes from the Plains Indians. Troops stationed there included elements of the 2nd Dragoons, U. S. Regiment of Riflemen, and the 5th, 6th, 7th, Infantry Regiments.

Further Reading

Agnew, Brad, *Fort Gibson: Terminal on the Trail of Tears*. Norman, Oklahoma: University of Oklahoma Press, 1980.

Anderson, William L., Editor, *Cherokee Removal: Before and After*. Athens, Georgia: University of Georgia Press, 1991.

Black, Jason Edward, *American Indians and the Rhetoric of Removal and Allotment*. Oxford, Mississippi: University Press of Mississippi, 2015.

_____, *U. S. Governmental and Native Voices in the Nineteenth Century: Rhetoric in the Removal and Allotment of American Indians*. PhD dissertation, College Park, Maryland: University of Maryland, 2006.

Brands, H. W., *Andrew Jackson: His Life and Times*. New York, New York: Anchor Books, 2009.

Carter, Samuel, *Cherokee Sunset: A Nation Betrayed*. New York, New York: Doubleday, 1976.

Covington, James W., *The Seminoles of Florida*. Gainesville, Florida: University Press of Florida, 1993.

Duncan, Barbara R. and Brett H. Riggs, *Cherokee Heritage Trails Guidebook*. Chapel Hill, North Carolina: University of North Carolina Press, 2003.

Ehle, John, *Trail of Tears: The Rise and Fall of the Cherokee Nation*. New York, New York: Doubleday, 1988.

Foreman, Grant, *Indian Removal: The Emigration of the Five Civilized Tribes of Indians*. Norman, Oklahoma: University of Oklahoma Press, 1932.

_____, *The Five Civilized Tribes: A Brief History and a Century of Progress*. Muskogee, Oklahoma: Hoffman Printing Company, 1948.

Garrison, Tim Alan, *The Legal Ideology of Removal: The Southern Judiciary and the Sovereignty of Native American Nations*. Athens, Georgia: University of Georgia Press, 2002.

Gibson, Arrell Morgan, Editor, *America's Exiles: Indian Colonization in Oklahoma*. Oklahoma City, Oklahoma: Oklahoma Historical Society, 1976.

Howe, Daniel Walker, *What Hath God Wrought: The Transformation of America, 1815-1848*. New York, New York: Oxford University Press, 2007.

Jahoda, Gloria, *The Trail of Tears: The Story of the American Indian Removals 1813-1855*. New York, New York: Holt, Rinehart and Winston, 1975.

Kappler, Charles Joseph, *Indian Affairs: Laws and Treaties*. Washington, DC: Government Printing Office, 1903.

221

King, Duane and David G. Fitzgerald, *The Cherokee Trail of Tears*, Portland, Oregon: Graphic Arts Center Publishing Company, 2007.

Latty, John W. and Ezekiel Lafayette Buffington, *Carrying Off the Cherokee: History of Buffington's Company, Georgia Mounted Militia*. Charleston, South Carolina: John W. Latty, 2011.

Littlefield, Daniel F., Jr., *Africans and Seminoles: From Removal to Emancipation*. Westport, Connecticut: Greenwood Press, 1977.

McLoughlin, William G., *Cherokee Renascence in the New Republic*. Princeton, New Jersey: Princeton University Press, 1986.

McReynolds, Edwin C., *The Seminoles*. Norman, Oklahoma: University of Oklahoma Press, 957.

Perdue, Theda and Michael D. Green, Editors, *The Cherokee Removal: A Brief History with Documents*. Boston, Massachusetts: Bedford Books of St. Martin's Press, 1995.

Prucha, Francis Paul, *The Great Father: The United States Government and the American Indians*. Lincoln, Nebraska: University of Nebraska Press, 1984.

_____, *American Indian Treaties: The History of a Political Anomaly*. Berkeley, California: University of California Press, 1994.

Remini, Robert V., *Andrew Jackson and his Indian Wars*. New York, New York: Viking, 2001.

Satz, Ronald N., *American Indian Policy in the Jacksonian Era*. Originally Published Lincoln, Nebraska: University of Nebraska Press, 1975, Republished, Norman, Oklahoma: University of Oklahoma Press, 2002.

Thornton, Russell, *American Indian Holocaust and Survival: A Population History Since 1492*. Norman, Oklahoma: University of Oklahoma Press, 1987.

Wallace, Anthony F.C., *The Long, Bitter Trail: Andrew Jackson and the Indians*. New York, New York: Hill and Wang, 1993.

Warren, Mary B. and Eve B. Weeks, Editors, *Whites Among the Cherokees, Georgia, 1828–1838*. Athens, Georgia: Heritage Papers, 1987.

Winn, William W., *The Triumph of the Ecunnau-Nuxulgee: Land Speculators, George M. Troup, State Rights, and the Removal of the Creek Indians from Alabama and Georgia, 1825–1838*. Macon, Georgia: Mercer University Press, 2015.

Zinn, Howard, *A People's History of the United States*. New York, New York: Harper Collins, 2005.

Part Two
Records of the Southern Indian Wars

Federal Repositories

National Archives and Records Administration
700 Pennsylvania Avenue, NW
Washington, DC 20408

(866) 272-6272

https://www.archives.gov/

Most of the original records cited herein are located at the main Archives building in Washington, DC, and may be viewed in person in the Archival Research Room. Many of the original records, but certainly not all, have been microfilmed and are available for viewing in the Microfilm Research Room. Virtually all the microfilmed records cited herein are widely available at the National Archives regional locations, as well as the Family History Library, most large genealogy libraries, and on a variety of free and subscription websites. Photocopies from the original records are available in person or may be requested online or by regular mail. Archives regional centers are located at Atlanta, Boston, Chicago, College Park, Maryland, Denver, Fort Worth, Kansas City, Missouri, New York, Philadelphia, Riverside, California, San Francisco, Seattle, and St. Louis. Many original records, especially those records concerning the Five Civilized Tribes, are located at the regional archives in Atlanta and Fort Worth.

Military Service Records

The archives holds federal military service records from the Revolutionary War to 1912 in the National Archives Building in Washington, D.C. They do not hold service records of state and local militia, unless those units were mustered into federal service. The military service records for the various branches of service cover different time periods, as shown in the following table.

Branch	Dates
Volunteers	Volunteers mustered into federal service, 1775 to 1902
Army	Enlisted, 1789 to October 31, 1912 Officers, 1789 to June 30, 1917
Navy	Enlisted, 1798 to 1885 Officers, 1798 to 1902
Marine Corps	Enlisted, 1798 to 1904 Officers, 1798 to 1895
Coast Guard	Persons who served in the Revenue Cutter Service (Revenue Marine), the Life-Saving Service, and the Lighthouse Service, 1791 to 1919

Compiled military service records consist of an envelope with card abstracts transcribed from extant muster rolls, unit returns, payrolls, and other similar records, for only those military units in federal service. Numerous state and local militia and other volunteer units were not mustered into federal service. Extant records for those units should be at the appropriate state archive, or possibly among the personal papers of the commanding officer in a collection of manuscripts held by a local historical society, research library, or other repository. Indexes to the compiled service records for the Revolutionary War, War of 1812, and early Indian wars are available on microfilm, as are the actual compiled service records for Revolutionary soldiers. More detailed information may be found in *Military Service Records: A Select Catalog of National Archives Microfilm Publications,* National Archives and Records Administration, 1985. Another useful guide is James C. Neagles' *U. S. Military Records: A Guide to Federal and State Resources, Colonial America to the Present* (Salt Lake City, Utah: Ancestry, Inc., 1994).

Microfilm M246, *Revolutionary War Rolls, 1775-1783,* contains muster rolls, payrolls, strength returns, and other miscellaneous personnel, pay, and supply records of individual army units. The records are arranged in numbered folders under three categories: state, Continental, and miscellaneous troops. State troops include those units raised by the states who were mustered into federal service. Continental troops include units created by the Continental Congress, infantry regiments organized under the Continental Congress resolutions of 1776, and units raised in more than one state. Miscellaneous troops include those units larger than a regiment and for special returns not easily classified under the previous categories.

The War Department compiled military service records from Record Group (RG) 93, War Department Collection of Revolutionary War Records, available on microfilm M881, *Compiled Service Records of Soldiers Who Served in the American Army During the Revolutionary War.* Microfilm M860, *General Index to Compiled Military Service Records of Revolutionary War Soldiers, Sailors, and Members of Army Staff Departments,* includes the names of the soldiers, sailors, members of army staff departments, and civilian employees of the army and navy, such as teamsters, carpenters, laundresses, and cooks. For each person, the index lists the name, rank, unit, and profession or office.

Other microfilm records that may be of interest include:

> M853, *Numbered Record Books Concerning Military Operations and Service, Pay and Settlement of Accounts, and Supplies in the War Department Collection of Revolutionary War Records*

> M859, *Miscellaneous Numbered Records (The Manuscript File) in the War Department Collection of Revolutionary War Records, 1775-1790's*

> M847, *Special Index to Numbered Records in the War Department Collection of Revolutionary War Records, 1775-1783*

From the end of the Revolutionary War to the beginning of the War of 1812, the military consisted of a small regular army, supplemented from time to time by units of state and territorial militia. These compiled service records were abstracted from RG 94, Records of the Adjutant General's Office, 1780s-1917, including correspondence, accounts, and other records concerning the mustering, paying, and providing for the volunteer forces, and are available on microfilm M905, *Compiled Service Records of Volunteer Soldiers Who Served from 1784 to 1811.* A name index of the compiled records is available on microfilm M694, *Index to Compiled Service Records 1784-1811*. Two transcriptions, with brief abstracts, are published in Virgil D. White's *Index to Volunteer Soldiers 1784–1811* (Waynesboro, Tennessee: National Historical Publishing, 1987) and Murtie June Clark's *American Militia in the Frontier Wars, 1790–1796* (Baltimore, Maryland: Genealogical Publishing Company, 1990).

Several numbered record volumes in RG 93, War Department Collection of Revolutionary War Records, including material from the period after the Revolutionary War, are available on microfilm M853, *Numbered Record Books Concerning Military Operations and Service, Pay and Settlement of Accounts, and Supplies in the War Department Collection of Revolutionary War Records.*

Most soldiers who served in the War of 1812 were volunteers, either in units raised directly by the federal government or in state and local militia units mustered into federal service. The War Department compiled military service records from the records in RG 94, but most of the original records have not been microfilmed. However, a name index to the records is available on microfilm M602, *Index to Compiled Service Records of Volunteer Soldiers Who Served During the War of 1812*. Other microfilm records of interest include:

> M250, *Index to Compiled Service Records of Volunteer Soldiers Who Served During the War of 1812 in Organizations from the State of North Carolina*

> M652, *Index to Compiled Service Records of Volunteer Soldiers Who Served During the War of 1812 in Organizations from the State of South Carolina*

> M678, *Compiled Service Records of Volunteer Soldiers Who Served During the War of 1812 in Organizations from the Territory of Mississippi, 1812*

> M1829, *Compiled Military Service Records of Maj. Uriah Blue's Detachment of Chickasaw Indians in the War of 1812*

The compiled service records generally contain all the information pertaining to the individual on the original record; however, the number of records for any individual generally are few, because most volunteers served very short enlistments, only weeks or a couple of months long.

Compiled military service records of volunteer soldiers who served in the First and Second Creek Wars, First, Second, and Third Seminole Wars, and in the Indian removals have not been microfilmed, except for those units from Florida. The compiled records of Florida units are on microfilm M1806, *Compiled Service Records of Volunteer Soldiers Who Served in Organizations from the State of Florida During the Florida Indian Wars, 1835-1858*. The records are arranged by unit, then alphabetically by surname. Microfilm M1277, *Original Florida Territorial Muster Rolls, 1826-1849*, includes muster rolls from the Second Seminole War. Microfilm M1281, *Seminole War Muster Rolls of Florida Militia, 1836-1841 and 1856-1858*, includes copies of muster rolls of Florida units in the Second and Third Seminole Wars. Indexes to the service records of veterans who served from other states are on the following microfilm.

M629, *Index to Compiled Service Records of Volunteer Soldiers Who Served During Indian Wars and Disturbances, 1815-1858*

M243, *Index to Compiled Service Records of Volunteer Soldiers Who Served During the Cherokee Removal in Organizations from The State of Alabama*

M244, *Index to Compiled Service Records of Volunteer Soldiers Who Served During the Creek War in Organizations from The State of Alabama*

M245, *Index to Compiled Service Records of Volunteer Soldiers Who Served During the Florida War in Organizations from the State of Alabama*

M246, *Index to Compiled Service Records of Volunteer Soldiers Who Served During the Cherokee Disturbances and Removal in Organizations from the State of North Carolina*

M907, *Index to Compiled Service Records of Volunteer Soldiers Who Served During the Cherokee Disturbances and Removal in Organizations from the State of Georgia*

M908, *Index to Compiled Service Records of Volunteer Soldiers Who Served During the Cherokee Disturbances and Removal in Organizations from the State of Tennessee and the Field and Staff of the Army of the Cherokee Nation*

Other records of interest relating to the Seminole Wars were created by military departments, including Headquarters, Troops in Florida (1854–56), and Headquarters, Department of Florida (1856–58). They may be found in RG 393, Records of U. S. Army Continental Commands, 1821–1920. The records consist of maps, summaries of reports, endorsements, letters sent and received, orders and special orders, monthly departmental returns, and post returns. Records of related divisions and departments, including the Western Division and Department, 1820–54; the Eastern Division and Department, 1817–61; the 5th Military Department, 1842–52; and records of the various posts, camps, and garrisons located in Florida, including those of Fort Brooke and Fort Myers, are available. Some of the records are available on microfilm, but most exist only in original form. In RG 391, Records of U. S. Regular Army Mobile Units, 1821–1942, are records of Regular Army units stationed in Florida, some of which cover 1854–58.

Additional records of interest on microfilm are:

M1084, *Letters Sent, Registers of Letters Received, and Letters Received by Headquarters, Troops in Florida, and Headquarters, Department of Florida, 1850–1858*

M1090, *Memoir of Reconnaissances With Maps During the Florida Campaign, Apr. 1854-Feb. 1858*

M1745, *Claims for Georgia Militia Campaigns Against Indians on the Frontier, 1792-1827*

Unlike the compiled military service records for the volunteers, the military service records for those who enlisted in the regular army have never been compiled. For enlisted men, records documenting their service may be found in RG 94, entry 91, Regular Army Enlistment Papers, 1798–1894. The records are arranged alphabetically by name of soldier and usually provide the soldier's name, place of enlistment, date, by whom enlisted, age, place of birth, occupation, personal description, regimental assignment, and certifications of the examining surgeon and recruiting officer. Soldiers who served more than one enlistment usually have multiple enlistment paper entries.

More information may be found on microfilm M233, *Register of Enlistments in the U. S. Army, 1798–1914.* The register of enlistments is arranged chronologically and thereunder alphabetically by the first letter of the surname. The register usually shows the individual's name, military organization, physical description, age at time of enlistment, place of birth, enlistment information, discharge information, and remarks. More detailed information concerning service may be found in the unit muster rolls, arranged by arm of service; then by regiment; then alphabetically by company, troop, or battery; arranged chronologically. The muster rolls are in RG 94, entry 53, Muster Rolls of Regular Army Organizations, 1784–October 31, 1912.

The soldier's carded medical records are in RG 94, entry 529, for the years 1821 to 1885. The records cover both enlisted soldiers and officers admitted to hospitals and may include the soldier's name, rank, organization, age, race, birthplace, date entered service, cause of admission, date of admission, hospital to which admitted, and disposition of their case. The records are arranged by regiment number and then alphabetically by the first letter of the surname. Artillery, cavalry, and infantry regiments are filed under the same regimental number.

Other records of interest include microfilm M1856, *Discharge Certificates and Miscellaneous Records Relating to the Discharge of Soldiers from the Regular Army, 1792-1815,* which reproduces discharge certificates and miscellaneous other records relating to the discharge of soldiers from the Regular Army, 1792-1815.

No military service records were kept or compiled for officers prior to the Civil War. Check Francis B. Heitman's *Historical Register and Dictionary of the United States Army, from its Organization, September 29, 1789, to March 2, 1903* (Baltimore, Maryland: Genealogical Publishing Company, 1903, Reprinted 1994). The first volume provides a brief history of each officer's service. The second volume lists the battles, skirmishes, and other actions in which the army was engaged. The original records are in multiple series in RG 94. Most of the records have been microfilmed as:

> M566, *Letters Received by the Office of the Adjutant General, 1805–1821*

> M567, *Letters Received by the Office of the Adjutant General (Main Series), 1822–1860*

> M619, *Letters Received by the Office of the Adjutant General (Main Series), 1861–1870*

> M711, *Registers of Letters Received, Office of the Adjutant General, 1812–1889*

Other possibly useful records include:

M688, *U. S. Military Academy Cadet Application Papers, 1805–1866*

M91, *Records Relating to the U. S. Military Academy, 1812–1867*

Army post and unit returns may provide additional information about individual soldier's service. Returns for many forts, posts, and other installations are on microfilm M617, *Returns from U. S. Military Posts, 1800–1916*. The returns usually include the units stationed at the post and their strength, the names and duties of officers, the number of officers present and absent, and a record of events. Monthly returns for individual army units are on the following microfilm:

M665, *Returns from Regular Army Infantry Regiments, June 1821– December 1916*

M744, *Returns from Regular Army Cavalry Regiments, 1833–1916*

M727, *Returns from Regular Army Artillery Regiments, June 1821– January 1901*

The regimental returns list the assigned stations of companies or batteries; names of company commanders; unit strength, including men present, absent, sick, on extra duty or daily duty, and in arrest or confinement; and other remarks.

Records of courts-martial may provide significant information on individual soldiers, as well as the conditions faced by the entire unit. Records of the proceedings of army courts-martial, courts of inquiry, and military commissions are in RG 153, Records of the Judge Advocate General. An index to the records is on microfilm M1105, *Registers of the Records of the Proceedings of the U. S. Army General Courts-martial, 1809–1890*. Individual case files are in RG 153, entry 15, which has not been microfilmed.

Again, no service records for naval enlisted men were kept or compiled, except for those who served during the Revolutionary War. The index to those compiled service records is on microfilm M879, *Index to Compiled Service Records of American Naval Personnel Who Served During the Revolutionary War*. The actual records are on microfilm M880, *Compiled Service Records of American Naval Personnel and Members of the Departments of the Quartermaster General and the Commissary General of Military Stores Who Served During the Revolutionary War*.

Records for enlisted sailors who served after the Revolution may be found in rendezvous reports and ship muster rolls and payrolls. A rendezvous was the recruiting station where the sailors enlisted. Rendezvous reports may include the sailor's name, date and term of enlistment, age, rating, previous service, residence, place of birth, occupation, and physical description. An index is on microfilm T1098, *Index to Rendezvous Reports, Before and After the Civil War, 1846–1861, 1865–1884*. More enlistment records are in RG 24, Records of the Bureau of Naval Personnel, entry 224, Keys to and Register of Enlistment Returns, 1846–1902. More records of enlisted men are in RG 24, entry 204, Records Relating to Enlisted Men Who Served in the Navy Between 1842 and 1885, 1885–1941. The records contain correspondence sent and received, endorsements, applications for honorable discharge certificates, and other records.

Specific information concerning the service of individual sailors may be found on the muster rolls and payrolls for ships, naval stations, and other installations. Muster rolls and payrolls usually include the sailor's name, rank, date of service, and sometimes the ship or station from which he was transferred. Usually, muster rolls and payrolls are arranged alphabetically by name of the ship or station, and then chronologically.

Researchers also should consult the Naval medical records in RG 52, Records of the Bureau of Medicine and Surgery (Navy):

> Entry 21, Medical Journals of Shore Stations, 1812–89,
> Entry 22, Medical Journals of Ships, 1813–1910,
> Entry 30, Reports of Diseases and Deaths, July 1828–December 1846,
>
> Entry 31, Certificates of Death, Disability, Pension and Medical Survey,
> June 1842–January 1896, and
> Entry 51, Registers of Patients, 1812–1929.

No official service records for naval officers were kept or compiled prior to the Civil War. Edward W. Callahan's *List of Officers of the Navy of the United States and of the Marine Corps from 1775 to 1900* (New York, New York: L. R. Hammersley, 1901) provides a place to begin. These abstracts of naval service records for officers are on microfilms:

> M330, *Abstracts of Service Records of Naval Officers ("Records of Officers"), 1798–1893*
>
> M1328, *Abstracts of Service Records of Naval Officers ("Records of Officers"), 1829–1924.* A name index is in the descriptive pamphlet for M1328.

Additional records of naval officers may be found in examining board and retiring board files in RG 125, Records of the Judge Advocate General (Navy), entry 58, Records of the Proceedings of Naval and Marine Examining Boards, 1861–1903, and entry 56, Records of Proceedings of Naval and Marine Retiring Boards, 1861–1909. The War Department compiled service records for naval officers who served during the Revolutionary War. An index is on microfilm M879, *Index to Compiled Service Records of American Naval Personnel Who Served During the Revolutionary War* and the compiled service records are on microfilm M880, *Compiled Service Records of American Naval Personnel and Members of the Departments of the Quartermaster General and the Commissary General of Military Stores Who Served During the Revolutionary War.* Navy records of courts-martial are in RG 125, Records of the Office of the Judge Advocate General (Navy). The records include an index. Early court records are on M273, *Records of General Courts-martial and Courts of Inquiry of the Navy Department, 1799–1867.*

National Archives Special List 44, *List of Logbooks of U. S. Navy Ships, Stations, and Miscellaneous Units, 1801–1947*, shows the deck logs that are available. Deck logs provide records on a ship's performance and location, weather conditions, names of officers, assignments, transfers, desertions, deaths, injuries, courts-martial, supplies received, and other miscellaneous information. James L. Mooney's *Dictionary of American Naval Fighting Ships* (Washington, DC: Government Printing Office, 1959-1981) provides detailed information on historical naval vessels, including their dates of service.

Service records, also called case files, for enlisted marines prior to 1905 are held by the archives in Washington, DC, in Record Group 127, Records of the U. S. Marine Corps, entry 76. The case files contain enlistment and reenlistment papers, descriptive lists, conduct records, discharge notice, service history, and issuance of campaign badges and awards. Case files for marines who enlisted before 1895 are arranged by date of enlistment. A card index is in RG 127, entry 75, Alphabetical Card List of Enlisted Men of the Marine Corps, 1798–1941. Muster rolls, 1798-1940, are arranged chronologically by year and month, and thereunder by post, station, ship detachment, or unit. Most volumes contain indexes to the names of ships, stations, and units. The Marine Corps muster rolls are on microfilm T1118, *Muster Rolls of the U. S. Marine Corps, 1798–1902.*

A single-volume register in RG 127 gives the name, rank, and state of birth of commissioned officers of the Marine Corps for each year from 1819 to 1848. The correspondence files in RG 127 contain letters received, reports, and general correspondence files covering the years 1799 to 1938, written by or about Marine Corps officers.

Records relating to the Coast Guard and its predecessor agencies, Lighthouse Service, Revenue Cutter Service, and the Lifesaving Service, are in Record Group 26, Records of the U. S. Coast Guard. Registers of Lighthouse Keepers, were compiled chronologically and are on microfilm M1373, *Registers of Lighthouse Keepers, 1845–1912.* Each volume has an index, arranged alphabetically by surname of the keeper or name of lighthouse. The registers include the names of keepers and assistant keepers; the district and the name of the light; dates of appointment, resignation, discharge, or death; and, sometimes other information. Correspondence Concerning Keepers and Assistant Keepers, 1821–1902, are arranged alphabetically by surname and may contain nominations of keepers and assistant keepers with testimonials, lists of examination questions, notifications of appointments, oaths of office, requests for transfer, recommendations for promotion, complaints, petitions, reports of inspectors, and letters of resignation.

Records relating to officers of the Revenue Cutter Service include records of officer personnel, 1791–1919, and are indexed alphabetically by name of officer. The records include dates of service, citations to pertinent correspondence, and copies of commissions.

The records relating to enlisted men of the Revenue Cutter Service include muster rolls and payrolls. Muster rolls, 1833–1932, provide for each crew member: name, rating, date and place of enlistment, place of birth, age, occupation, personal description, and number of days served during the reported month, along with notes if the crewman was detached, transferred, or discharged, or if he deserted or died during the report period, and are arranged alphabetically by the name of the vessel.

Military Pension Records

The archives has pension application files and records of pension payments for veterans, their widows, and their other heirs, based upon military service to the federal government between the years 1775 and 1916. Application files often contain supporting documents such as discharge papers, affidavits, depositions of witnesses, narratives of events during service, marriage certificates, birth and death records, pages from family bibles, and other supporting documents. The pension application files, divided into separate record series for the Revolutionary War, Old Wars, War of 1812, and Indian Wars, are arranged alphabetically by the name of the applicant. Each series has a separate name index.

Pension application files may provide clues that help facilitate research in the military service records. For example, an application may detail service in multiple units at different times or provide specific personal information that differentiates the applicant from another man with the same or similar name. For men who served in the navy or marines, the application may provide the names and dates of service on ships or at duty stations. Moreover, pension application files may include personal information or documents available in no other records. The pension application files for all the other veterans of the same unit should be reviewed to see if the subject of one's research is mentioned in their files. Similarly, the pension files of veterans who lived nearby or were related to the subject of one's research also should be reviewed.

There are about 80,000 individual pension and bounty-land-warrant application files, in RG 15, Records of the Veterans Administration, based upon military, naval, and marine service in the Revolutionary War. Three types of pensions were issued: invalid or disability pensions, for those veterans who were disabled in the line of duty; service pensions, for surviving veterans who served a minimum tour of duty; and, widow's pensions, for women whose husbands were killed during the war or who served the minimum tour of duty. Each file contains one or more applications, affidavits or other documents submitted as evidence of identity and service, and paperwork recording the actions taken on the application or applications. Specific eligibility requirements changed as Congress passed new laws, usually expanding eligibility each time. A useful guide to the various pension laws is Christine Rose's *Military Pension Laws from the Journals of the Continental Congress and the United States Statutes-at-Large* (San Jose, California: Rose Family Association, 2001). The original files are on microfilm M804, *Revolutionary War Pension and Bounty-Land Warrant Application Files*. The files are arranged alphabetically by the name of the applicant. Other records of interest include M910, *Virginia Half Pay and Other Related Revolutionary War Pension Application Files*. The files are in two sections, one each for soldiers and sailors, and thereunder arranged alphabetically by surname.

Congress required the Secretary of War to prepare and submit lists of pensioners in 1813, 1818, 1820, and 1835 to the Senate. All four lists have been published and are available online:

> U. S. War Department, *Revolutionary Pensioners: A Transcript of the Pension List of the United States for 1813.* Baltimore, Maryland: Genealogical Publishing Company, Reprinted 2002.

> U. S. War Department, *Revolutionary Pensioners of 1818.* Baltimore, Maryland: Genealogical Publishing Company, Reprinted 2008.

U. S. War Department, *Pension List of 1820, Letter from the Secretary of War Transmitting a Report of the Names, Rank and File of Every Person Placed on the Pension List in Pursuance of the Act of the 18th March, 1818, Etc. Washington, 1820.* Baltimore, Maryland: Genealogical Publishing Company, Reprinted 2000.

U. S. War Department, *The Pension Roll of 1835.* Baltimore, Maryland: Genealogical Publishing Company, Reprinted 2002.

Other published resources include:

Bockstruck, Lloyd de Witt, *Revolutionary War Pensions Awarded by State Governments 1775-1874, the General and Federal Governments Prior to 1814, and by Private Acts of Congress to 1905.* Baltimore, Maryland: Genealogical Publishing Company, Reprinted 2011.

Clark, Murtie June, *Index to U. S. Invalid Pension Records, 1801-1815.* Baltimore, Maryland: Genealogical Publishing Company, 1991, Reprinted 2000.

_____, *The Pension Lists of 1792-1795, With Other Revolutionary War Pension Records.* Baltimore, Maryland: Genealogical Publishing Company, 1991, Reprinted 1996.

U. S. Interior Department, *Rejected or Suspended Applications for Revolutionary War Pensions,* 1852. Batimore, Maryland: Genealogical Publishing Company, Reprinted 2003.

U. S. State Department, *A Census of Pensioners for Revolutionary or Military Services, 1840, [Published with] A General Index to a Census of Pensioners,* 1841. Baltimore, Maryland: Genealogical Publishing Company, Reprinted 2005.

U. S. War Department, *Pensioners of the Revolutionary War Struck Off the Roll,* 1836. Baltimore, Maryland: Genealogical Publishing Company, Reprinted 2008.

Pension application files for the War of 1812 also are in RG 15, Records of the Veterans Administration. A veteran's pension file can include his rank, place of residence, age or date of birth, and description of his service. A widow's application can also include her place of residence, her maiden name, the date and place of marriage, the date and place of her husband's death, and the names of children under 16 years of age. A child's or heir's file may contain information about both the veteran and the widow, as well as the child's place of residence, date of birth, and the date and place of the widow's death. The original records are not on microfilm. A name index is on microfilm M313, *Index to War of 1812 Pension Application Files.* Some widows remarried other pensioned veterans and later obtained a pension based upon the second husband's service. Usually, her applications are filed in her last husband's file. A name index is on microfilm M1784, *Index to Pension Application Files of Remarried Widows Based on Service in the War of 1812, Indian Wars, Mexican War, and Regular Army Before 1861.*

The information included in the pension application files for soldiers who fought in the various Indian wars is similar to those for previous wars. The files are part of RG 15, Records of the Veterans Administration. One index is on microfilm T316, *Old War Index to Pension Files, 1815-1926*. The files relate mainly to pensions granted due to death or disability, based upon service between 1783 and 1861. Also, the majority of the files pertain to regular army and navy service, although the index includes volunteer soldiers as well. A second index is on microfilm T318, *United States Index to Indian Wars Pension Files, 1892-1926*, and covers pensions for service in the Indian wars between 1817 and 1898.

Once a pension was granted, the government began to make the semi-annual payments, creating paperwork along the way. Each pensioner had to appear in person before a government agent to collect the payment, sometimes requiring arduous travel. Often, pensioners, especially those who were disabled, elderly, or otherwise infirm, arranged for a relative, friend, or paid agent to collect the money for them. The earliest pension and bounty-land warrants were granted by the Continental Congress, then the Confederation Congress. Thereafter, Congress enacted a series of laws regulating the entire pension process and delegating the responsibility of managing the process to a pension office whose name and place in the federal bureaucracy changed from time to time.

From the complete pension file, the researcher should note the specific acts of Congress under which the pension was granted, the names of the addressee and addressor of all correspondence in the file dated since the pension was granted, the dates of the correspondence, and the pension file and certificate numbers. The 2,404 original ledgers are designated Pension Agency Payment Books, 1805-1909 (RG 15, NM-21, Series 2). The records include the name of the pensioner, rank, payment amount, date of payment, name of the recipient, and other remarks, possibly the date of death of the pensioner. The Index to Pension Agency Payment Books, 1805-1909 (RG 15, NM-21, Series 1), is arranged by pension agency, then by Act of Congress, and type of pension, noting the dates covered by each pension payment ledger.

The records titled Lists of Veterans and Widows and Other Dependents of Veterans Pensioned Under Various Laws Enacted from 1818 to 1853 (RG 15, NM-21, Series 37) are arranged by pension agency, then by Congressional act, and include the pension certificate number, name, rank, monthly amount, date added to pension roll, effective date of pension, dates added or removed from the rolls of a pension agency, date of last payment, date of death, and act under which the widow or children were admitted.

Out of the numerous record series of correspondence, one important series is Letters Sent, 1800–1866 (RG 15, NM-22, Series 1). While much of the correspondence in the series is in the pension file, some of it is not. Some of the original volumes are indexed by the name of the addressee, not necessarily the pensioner, and all are arranged chronologically.

Treasury Department accountants also created records of pension payments in RG 217, Records of the Accounting Officers of the Treasury. The records are published in William F. Sherman's *Records of the Accounting Officers of the Department of the Treasury, Inventory 14, Revised*, (Lovettsville, Virginia: Willow Bend Books, 1997). The pension payment ledgers are on microfilm T718, *Ledgers of Payments, 1818–1872, to U. S. Pensioners Under Acts of 1818 Through 1858, from Records of the Office of the Third Auditor of the Treasury*. The ledgers, arranged by Congressional act, thereunder by pension agency, in alphabetical order by the first letter of the pensioner's surname, include the pensioner's name, rank, monthly amount, semi-annual payment, date payments began, month and year of each payment made, transfer to or from a different agency, and date of death.

Another series of pension payment ledgers is included in Registers of Pension Payments, ca. 1811–1868 (RG 217, Inventory 14, Series 206). The ledgers include the authorizing pension act, name and rank of veteran, or name of pensioner with their relationship to the veteran, amount of the pension, dates of payment, agency transfers, final payment date, and date of death.

The archives created a card index to the final pension payments in Index to Selected Final Payment Vouchers, 1818–64 (RG 217 Inventory 14, Series 722A). The index, arranged by state, then by name of the pensioner, includes the pension agency, Congressional act, payment date, and date of death. A hand-stamped star on the index card means that a final payment voucher is included in Selected Final Pension Payment Vouchers, 1818–64 (RG 217, Inventory 14, Series 722). The final pension payment vouchers include the records concerning the last payment made to the pensioner, widow, or other heirs, such as correspondence, affidavits, and powers of attorney. The records may prove the date of death, relationship to the deceased pensioner, and names and residences of children.

Vouchers for the pension agencies in Delaware and Georgia are on microfilm M2079, *Final Revolutionary War Pension Payment Vouchers: Delaware*, and M1746, *Final Revolutionary War Pension Payment Vouchers: Georgia*. Abstracted vouchers for these states have been published:

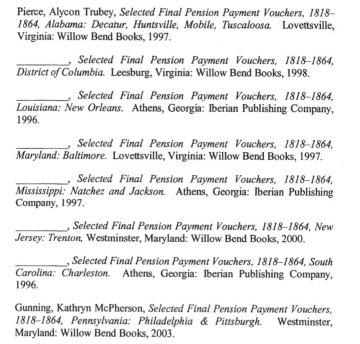

Pierce, Alycon Trubey, *Selected Final Pension Payment Vouchers, 1818–1864, Alabama: Decatur, Huntsville, Mobile, Tuscaloosa.* Lovettsville, Virginia: Willow Bend Books, 1997.

_____, *Selected Final Pension Payment Vouchers, 1818–1864, District of Columbia.* Leesburg, Virginia: Willow Bend Books, 1998.

_____, *Selected Final Pension Payment Vouchers, 1818–1864, Louisiana: New Orleans.* Athens, Georgia: Iberian Publishing Company, 1996.

_____, *Selected Final Pension Payment Vouchers, 1818–1864, Maryland: Baltimore.* Lovettsville, Virginia: Willow Bend Books, 1997.

_____, *Selected Final Pension Payment Vouchers, 1818–1864, Mississippi: Natchez and Jackson.* Athens, Georgia: Iberian Publishing Company, 1997.

_____, *Selected Final Pension Payment Vouchers, 1818–1864, New Jersey: Trenton,* Westminster, Maryland: Willow Bend Books, 2000.

_____, *Selected Final Pension Payment Vouchers, 1818–1864, South Carolina: Charleston.* Athens, Georgia: Iberian Publishing Company, 1996.

Gunning, Kathryn McPherson, *Selected Final Pension Payment Vouchers, 1818–1864, Pennsylvania: Philadelphia & Pittsburgh.* Westminster, Maryland: Willow Bend Books, 2003.

_____, *Selected Final Pension Payment Vouchers, 1818–1864, Rhode Island*. Westminster, Maryland: Willow Bend Books, 1999.

Military Bounty-Land Warrant Records

As an incentive to enlist and later as a reward for service, the government offered bounty-land for military service in the Revolutionary War, War of 1812, and the Indian wars between 1775 and 1855. The contents of the bounty-land warrant application files are similar to the contents in the pension files. Most, but not all, of the bounty-land application files for service in the Revolutionary War and the War of 1812 have been combined into the pension application files.

Unindexed bounty-land warrant application files and some rejected applications are in RG 15, Entry 26, Case Files of Bounty-Land Warrant Applications Based on Service Between 1812 and 1855 and Disapproved Applications Based on Revolutionary War Service. The files include applications from veterans of the War of 1812 and the Old Indian Wars and are arranged alphabetically.

Case files for veterans of the Revolutionary War are on microfilm M804, *Revolutionary War Pensions and Bounty-Land Warrant Applications*, listed alphabetically, and M829, *U. S. Revolutionary War Bounty-Land Warrants Used in the U. S. Military District of Ohio and Related Papers (Acts of 1788, 1803, and 1806), 1788–1806*, and are listed by warrant number, with a name index on the first roll. Early recipients had to exercise their warrants in specified districts in the Old Northwest Territory. Records of those warrants are on microfilm M829, *U. S. Revolutionary War Bounty-land Warrants Used in the U. S. Military District of Ohio and Relating Papers (Acts Of 1788, 1803, and 1806), 1788-1806.*

Case files for veterans of the War of 1812 and Indian wars between 1812 and 1815 are on microfilm M848, *War of 1812 Military Bounty-Land Warrants, 1815–1858*, arranged by warrant number, with a name index on the first roll; and M313, *Index to War of 1812 Pension Application Files*, arranged alphabetically.

Case files for veterans of all Indian wars who served from 1790 until 1861 are not indexed or microfilmed and, therefore, must be searched by hand. Most veterans who received bounty-land warrants sold their warrants to land speculators, rather than go through the process of obtaining legal title to the land. Land surrender warrants are in RG 49, Records of the General Land Office. To locate or request a copy of the surrender warrant, specify the war in which the veteran fought, warrant number, size of the warrant in acres, and Congressional act authorizing the original warrant, from the case file.

These indexes to the bounty-land warrant case files have been published:

> National Genealogical Society, *Index to Revolutionary War Pension [and Bounty-Land Warrant] Applications in the National Archives*. Washington, DC: National Genealogical Society, 1976.

> Smith, Clifford Neal, *Federal Bounty-Land Warrants of the American Revolution, 1799–1835*. Chicago, Illinois: American Library Association, 1973.

> White, Virgil D., *Index to War of 1812 Pension [and Bounty-Land Warrant] Files*. Waynesboro, Tennessee: National Historical Publishing Company, 1992.

Native American Records

The following is not intended as a primer on Native American genealogy research; instead, it is intended to be a guide for identifying those members of the Five Civilized Tribes who were removed, either voluntarily, reluctantly, or forcibly, from their homelands to the Indian Territory. Many of the original records prior to removal are at the regional archives in Atlanta and those after removal are at the regional archives in Fort Worth. Microfilmed copies of most of the records are available at many large libraries, and pertinent tribal and state archives. The following publications should be helpful in pursuing Native American genealogy research:

_____, *American Indians: A Select Catalog of National Archives Microfilm Publications.* Washington DC: National Archives Trust Fund Board, National Archives and Records Administration, 1998.

Byers, Paula K., *Native American Genealogical Sourcebook.* New York, New York: Gale Research Inc., 1995.

Chepesiuk, Ron and Arnold Shankman, *American Indian Archival Material: A Guide to Holdings in the Southeast.* Westport, Connecticut: Greenwood Press, 1982.

Hicks, Theresa M., *South Carolina Indians, Indian Traders, and Other Ethnic Connections Beginning in 1670, from the Papers of Theresa M. Hicks and Wes Takchiray.* Spartanburg, South Carolina: The Reprint Company, 1998.

Hill, Edward E., *Preliminary Inventory No. 163: Records of the Bureau of Indian Affairs.* Washington, DC: National Archives and Records Administration, 1965.

_____, *The Office of Indian Affairs, 1824-1880: Historical Sketches.* New York, New York: Clearwater Publishing Company, Inc., 1974.

_____, *Guide to Records in the National Archives of the United States Relating to American Indians.* Washington, DC: National Archives and Records Service, General Services Administration, 1981.

Hodge, Frederick Webb, *Handbook of American Indians North of Mexico.* Washington, DC: Smithsonian Institution, Bureau of American Ethnology, Bulletin Number 30, 1907.

Hudson, Charles, *The Southeastern Indians.* Knoxville, Tennessee: University of Tennessee Press, 1976.

Kavasch, E. Barre., *A Student's Guide to Native American Genealogy.* Phoenix, Arizona: Oryx Press, 1996.

Kirkham, E. Kay., *Our Native Americans and Their Records of Genealogical Value.* Logan, Utah: The Everton Publishers, Inc., 1980.

Lennon, Rachal M., "Southeastern Indians Prior to Removal: An Introduction to Research and Resources." *National Genealogical Society Quarterly*, Volume 85, 1997, pages 165-194.

Lennon, Rachal Mills, *Tracing Ancestors Among the Five Civilized Tribes: Southeastern Indians Prior to Removal.* Baltimore, Maryland: Genealogical Publishing Company, 2002.

Mooney, Thomas G., *Exploring Your Cherokee Ancestry.* Tahlequah, Oklahoma: Cherokee National Historical Society, Inc., 1992.

O'Donnell, James H., III, *Southeastern Frontiers: Europeans, Africans, and American Indians, 1513-1840.* Bloomington, Indiana: Indiana University Press, 1982.

Swanton, John R., *The Indian Tribes of North America.* Baltimore, Maryland: Genealogical Publishing Company, 1952, Reprinted 2007.

Tiller, Veronica E. Velarde, Editor, *American Indian Reservations and Trust Areas.* Washington, DC: Economic Development Administration, U. S. Department of Commerce, 1996.

Washburn, Wilcomb E., *The American Indian and the United States: A Documentary History.* New York, New York: Random House, 1973.

Wright, J. Leitch, Jr., *The Only Land They Knew: The Tragic Story of the American Indians in the Old South.* New York, New York: The Free Press, 1981.

Cherokee

The voluntary Cherokee migration westward to the Missouri Territory started about a decade after the Louisiana Purchase and continued until their forced removal began in 1838. In 1817 and again in 1819, treaties established an official emigration process. The 1828 Treaty created the Cherokee Reservation in the Indian Territory and abolished the earlier reservation in the Missouri Territory. In 1835, the Treaty of New Echota required the Cherokee to relocate to the Indian Territory.

Cherokee records from 1817 until 1838 were created pursuant to those treaties and fall into five primary categories: reservation rolls east of the Mississippi River, reservation surveys, emigration and muster rolls, the 1835 special census, and claims for compensation.

The 1817 reservation roll lists 330 individual Cherokee who wanted to stay in the east. Each applied for a life estate in individual 640-acre reservations that generally would revert to the state upon the death of the individual, provided the recipient remained on the reservation. The original record, *Register of Persons Who Wish Reservations Under Treaty, July 8, 1817, A21*, are not indexed. Bob Blankenship's *Cherokee Roots, Volume I: Eastern Cherokee Rolls*, 2nd Edition (Cherokee, North Carolina: Cherokee Roots, 1992) provides a more detailed description of the reservation rolls and provides an index.

One of the earliest records documenting large numbers of individual Cherokee is on microfilm A22, *Surveys of Reservations Under the Eighth Article of the Treaty of 1817 and Second Article of the Treaty of 1819*. The records are not indexed, but James L. Douthat's *Robert Armstrong's Survey Book of Cherokee Lands,* (Signal Mountain, Tennessee: Mountain Press, 1993) explains the records in more detail and serves as an effective index.

The Cherokee emigration rolls list the names of individuals who voluntarily moved west before the 1835 treaty, as follows:

Emigrants to Arkansas under the treaty of July 8, 1817.

List of widows who received one kettle and one blanket, 1818.

Emigrants to Arkansas under the treaty of May 6, 1828 (1828-1829).

Emigrants to Arkansas under the treaty of May 6, 1828 (1831-1832).

Chiefs and warriors who assent to a treaty proposed in 1832 who will settle west of the Mississippi, 1833-1834.

Muster Roll of Lieutenant Edward Deas, June 1838.

Emigrants to Arkansas, Fall 1817 to May 1819.

All the above are included in Bob Blankenship's *Cherokee Roots, Volume I: Eastern Cherokee Rolls*, 2nd Edition, (Cherokee, North Carolina: Cherokee Roots, 1992). The reservation, emigration, and muster rolls are on microfilm M208, *Register of Persons Who Wished Reservations Under the Treaty of July 8,* 1817 (A21) and *Cherokee Emigration and Six Muster Rolls, 1817-1838* (A23). Name indexes appear at the start of each section of the microfilm.

Additional helpful microfilm includes A42, *Muster Roll of Cherokee, 1838* and M1475, *Correspondence of The Eastern Division Pertaining to Cherokee Removal, April-December 1838.* The records, arranged chronologically, include correspondence, invoices, memoranda, orders, petitions, reports, and other miscellaneous records.

In 1835, a special census, often called the Henderson Roll, was taken, enumerating over 900 Cherokee heads of household, with data on each family, their slaves, and their farms. The census, indexed and arranged by state, then county, then river or creek, is on microfilm T496, *Census Roll of the Cherokee Indians East of the Mississippi and Index to the Roll, 1835.* The above is included in Bob Blankenship's *Cherokee Roots, Volume I: Eastern Cherokee Rolls*, 2nd Edition, (Cherokee, North Carolina: Cherokee Roots, 1992).

In 1851, a roll was created listing those Cherokee who had voluntarily migrated west before the forced removal began in 1838. The roll, arranged by tribal town and family group, is included on microfilm M685, *Records Relating to Enrollment Of Eastern Cherokee By Guion Miller, 1908-1910.* That and other later rolls are in Bob Blankenship's *Cherokee Roots, Volume II: Western Cherokee Rolls*, 2nd Edition, (Cherokee, North Carolina: Cherokee Roots, 1992).

The 1835 Treaty of New Echota permitted individual Cherokee to file damage claims for monetary compensation for abandoned lands and other injuries. Even though most claims were denied, the case files include the name of the claimant and descriptions of the residence or other damaged property, the claimed damage, and how the damage was inflicted. Some claims were filed by white men who had married Cherokee women. The indexed case files are on microfilm A17, *Decisions on Spoliation Claims, 1838.*

Other helpful microfilmed records include:

M15, *Letters Sent by the Secretary of War Relating to Indian Affairs, 1800-1824.*

M16, *Letters Sent by the Superintendent of Indian Trade, 1807-1823.*

M21, *Letters Sent by the Office of Indian Affairs, 1824-1881.*

T58, *Letters Received by the Superintendent of Indian Trade, 1806-1824.*

M208, *Records of the Cherokee Indian Agency in Tennessee, 1801-1835.*

M640, *Records of the Southern Superintendency of Indian Affairs, 1832-1870.*

M1062, *Correspondence of the War Department Relating to Indian Affairs, Military Pensions, And Fortifications, 1791-1797.*

T1105, *Historical Sketches for Jurisdictional and Subject Headings Used for the Letters Received by the Office of Indian Affairs, 1824-1880.*

Chickasaw

In 1832, the Treaty of Pontotoc Creek required the Chickasaw to relocate to the Indian Territory. Pursuant to the treaty, muster rolls identifying the names of the heads of household and the number of those in each household were prepared of the Chickasaw who were relocated from 1837 through 1839. Also, in 1847, a special census was taken of the Chickasaw then residing in the Indian Territory, listing the names of the heads of household as well as various statistics concerning each household. Both the muster rolls and the census schedules are on microfilm A36, *Chickasaw Census Roll, 1847, and Muster Rolls 1837 And 1839*. The latter two muster rolls are in Betty Wiltshire's *Choctaw and Chickasaw Early Census Records* (Carrollton, Mississippi: Pioneer Publishing Company, undated).

Other records that may be helpful in identifying individual Chickasaw include:

> Register of Letters Received, Chickasaw Cession of 1832. Indexed.
>
> Abstract of Reservations in the Chickasaw Cession. Not indexed.
>
> Abstract of Locations made by Colonel Benjamin Reynolds, Chickasaw Indian Agent, in Conjunction with Chiefs. Not indexed.
>
> Chickasaw Reservations under 5th Article of the Treaty of 1834 and 6th Article, and Reservations without Numbers. Not indexed.
>
> Chickasaw Reservations. Not indexed.
>
> Letters Sent Relating to the Chickasaw Session of 1832. Indexed.
>
> Abstracts of Accounts of the Secretary of War, Expenditures in Carrying into Effect the Chickasaw Treaty of October 22.
>
> Adjusted Accounts, Reports 1-140, Chickasaw Treaty of 1832. Indexed.
>
> Index to Chickasaw Reservation Lands in Mississippi in Patent Volumes 269-273, Reservation Volumes 1-5. No Dates.
>
> Abstract of Requisitions under the Chickasaw Treaty of October 1832, Volume A, War Department.
>
> Reservations under the 5th, 6th, and 8th Articles of the Chickasaw Treaty of May 24, 1834, 1 volume. Not indexed.
>
> Papers Relating to Indian Locations under the Chickasaw Treaty of 1834.

Choctaw

In 1830, the Treaty of Dancing Rabbit Creek required the Choctaw to relocate to the Indian Territory. The superintendent of the Choctaw removal, Francis Armstrong, compiled a list of the Choctaw to be removed. The list, naming the head of each household, number of persons in each family, the size and location of their farm, and other miscellaneous remarks, is on the unindexed microfilm A39, *Choctaw Armstrong Roll 1831*.

Pursuant to the treaty, individual Choctaw could elect to stay in Mississippi, become citizens and be subject to state law and jurisdiction, or relocate to the Indian Territory. Heads of households were allowed a reservation of land either in Mississippi or the Indian Territory. Lists of the individual land reservations, with the names of the heads of household, location of the land, and the article of the treaty authorizing the reservation, are on microfilms A37, *Alphabetical List of Choctaw Reserves*, and A38, *Alphabetical List of Choctaw Reserves*.

Muster rolls were compiled of the various groups of Choctaw who migrated, listing the names of the heads of household, number of persons in the household, and the date of arrival in the Indian Territory. Douglas Cooper, the government agent, conducted a census of the Choctaw who remained in Mississippi in 1856. The muster rolls and census are on microfilm A40, *Choctaw Removal Records: Choctaw Emigrants, 1838-1855; Register of Choctaw Indians and Eastern Choctaw Census, 1856*. The muster rolls are unindexed, but the census has an index.

Useful publications for further research include:

Kidwell, Clara Sue, *Choctaws and Missionaries in Mississippi, 1818-1918*. Norman, Oklahoma: University of Oklahoma Press, 1995.

Reeves, Carolyn Keller, *The Choctaw Before Removal*. Jackson, Mississippi: University Press of Mississippi, 1985.

Swanton, John R., *Source Material for the Social and Ceremonial Life of the Choctaw Indians*. Bureau of American Ethnology, Bulletin 103, Government Printing Office, Washington, DC, 1931.

Wells, Samuel J. and Roseanna Tubby, Editors, *After Removal, The Choctaw in Mississippi*. Jackson, Mississippi: University Press of Mississippi, 1986.

Wiltshire, Betty C., *Register of Choctaw Emigrants to the West, 1831 and 1832*. Carrollton, Mississippi: Pioneer Publishing Company, 1993.

Creek

In 1832, the Creek gave up their ancestral lands east of the Mississippi River under the terms of the Treaty of Cusseta. That same year, Benjamin S. Parsons prepared a census of the Upper Creek and Thomas J. Abbott did the same for the Lower Creek. Both schedules are on microfilm T275, *Census of Creek Indians Taken by Parsons and Abbott in 1832*. The schedules list the numbers of males, females, and slaves in each household, but are not indexed. A name index to the census is in Jeanne Robey Felldin and Charlotte Magee Tucker's *1832 Census of Creek Indians,* (Tomball, Texas: Genealogical Publications, 1978). For a published version of the census see James L. Douthat's *1832 Creek Census, Parsons – Abbott*. Signal Mountain, Tennessee: Mountain Press, 1995.

The treaty authorized individuals to get reservations in the ceded lands. The original three record volumes are arranged by Creek surname, with a cross reference to the Parsons and Abbott census number, in RG 49, Record of Creek Reservations in Alabama, 1834-1869.

Microfilm A41, *Roll of Creek Orphans and List of Payments Made, 1870 (Treaty of 1832)*, includes a list of orphans in 1832 and a related list of orphans and their heirs.

Other useful records include the following microfilm:

> M4, *Letter Book of the Creek Trading House, 1795-1816.*

> M1334, *Records of the Creek Factory of the Office of Indian Trade of the Bureau of Indian Affairs, 1795-1821.*

Publications that may be helpful include:

> Corkran, David H., *The Creek Frontier, 1540-1783.* Norman, Oklahoma: University of Oklahoma Press, 1967.

> Debo, Angie, *The Road to Disappearance: A History of the Creek Indians.* Civilization of the American Indian Series, Volume 22, Norman, Oklahoma: University of Oklahoma Press, 1941.

> Green, Michael D., *The Creeks: A Critical Bibliography.* Bloomington, Indiana: Indiana University Press, 1979.

> _____, *The Creeks.* New York, New York: Chelsea House Publishers, 1990.

> Hahn, Steven C., *The Invention of the Creek Nation, 1670-1763.* Lincoln, Nebraska: University of Nebraska Press, 2004.

> Kanen, Ronald, *A Bibliography of the Creeks and Other Native Americans of the Southeast.* Muscogee Words and Ways, III, Wakulla Springs, Florida: The Muscogee Press, 1983.

> Kersey, Harry A., Jr., *The Seminole and Miccosukee Tribes: A Critical Bibliography.* Bloomington, Indiana: Indiana University Press, 1987.

Peterson, Herman A., *The Trail of Tears: An Annotated Bibliography of Southeastern Indian Removal.* Lanham, Maryland: Scarecrow Press, 2010.

Saunt, Claudio, *A New Order of Things: Property, Power and the Transformation of the Creek Indians, 1733-1816.* New York, New York: Cambridge University Press, 1999.

Wright, J. Leitch, Jr. *Creeks and Seminoles: Destruction and Regeneration of the Muscogulge People.* Lincoln, Nebraska: University of Nebraska Press, 1986.

____, *The Only Land They Knew: The Tragic Story of the American Indians in the Old South.* New York, New York: Free Press, 1981.

Seminole

While some Seminole relocated to the Indian Territory voluntarily, most either reluctantly surrendered or were captured and forcibly removed during the Seminole Wars. The pertinent original records that have been microfilmed include:

M181, *1833 Removal muster rolls of Apalachicola towns (Seminoles) and slaves*, roll 1

M1831, *1836-37 Removal muster rolls of Seminoles and slaves,* roll 1

7RA20, *1868 Payment roll*, roll 1

7RA20, *1895 Payment rolls*, roll 1.

7RA70, *1896 Index and Dockets A-C of 1896 Citizenship Cases*, rolls 1-2.

7RA20, *1897 Census roll*, roll 1

7RA18, *1899-1905 Dawes Commission townsite plats*, roll 1.

7RA30, *1900-1907 Lease royalty records*, roll 2.

Publications that may be helpful include:

Campbell, J. B., *Campbell's Abstract of Seminole Indian Census Cards and Index*. Muscogee, Oklahoma: Oklahoma Printing Company, 1925. An abstract of the Dawes Rolls, with lists of Freedmen living with the Seminole.

Kersey, Harry A., Jr., *Pelts, Plumes, and Hides: White Traders Among the Seminole Indians, 1870-1930*. Gainesville, Florida: University Presses of Florida, 1975.

_____, *The Seminole and Miccosukee Tribes: A Critical Bibliography*. Bloomington, Indiana: Indiana University Press, 1987.

Lancaster, Jane F. *Removal Aftershock: The Seminoles' Struggles to Survive in the West, 1836-1866.* Knoxville, Tennessee: University of Tennessee Press, 1994.

Lantz, Raymond C., *Seminole Indians of Florida, 1850-1875.* Bowie, Maryland: Heritage Books, 1994. Lists of those in Oklahoma receiving annuity payments from the government.

Porter, Kenneth W., *The Black Seminoles: History of a Freedom-Seeking People.* Gainesville, Florida: University Presses of Florida, 1996.

Walton-Raji, Angela Y., *Black Indian Genealogy Research: African American Ancestors Among the Five Civilized Tribes*.

Wickman, Patricia R., *Osceola's Legacy*. Tuscaloosa, Alabama: University of Alabama Press, 1991.

Army Center of Military History
102 4th Avenue, Building 35
Fort McNair, DC 20319

http://www.history.army.mil/images/emailInquiries.jpg

http://www.history.army.mil/

The Center is responsible for incorporating the use of history throughout the United States Army. Traditionally, it has focused on recording the official history of the Army in both peace and war and advising the Army Staff on historical matters. Their art and document collections, library, and reference services are available to the general public. Official priorities permitting, its historians, curators, and archivists advise researchers on military history and stand ready to share their expertise concerning the location of sources.

The Center has produced more than 600 publications on military and army history, all of which are listed, described, and offered for sale on the Center's website. Some pertinent titles include:

> Blackmon, Richard D., *The Creek War, 1813-1814.* U. S. Army Campaigns of the War of 1812, CMH Publication 74-4, 2014.
>
> Coakley, Robert W., *Role of Federal Military Forces in Domestic Disorders, 1789-1878.* Army Historical Series, CMH Publication 30-13, Cloth, CMH Publication 30-13-1, Paper, 1988.
>
> Jessup, John E., Jr. and Robert W. Coakley, *Guide to the Study and Use of Military History.* Special Publications, CMH Publication 70-3, 1979, 2004.
>
> Maass, John R., *Defending a New Nation, 1783-1811.* U. S. Army Campaigns of the War of 1812, CMH Publication 74-1, 2013.
>
> Phillips, R. Cody, *The Guide to U. S. Army Museums*, Special Publications, CMH Publication 70-51, 1992, 2005.

The Center also maintains histories of the various units from all the branches of the army, brief summaries of which are available on the Center's website. The public should be aware that the Center is located within a secure military installation and should consult the Center's website for instructions and procedures before visiting.

Army Heritage and Education Center

Ridgeway Hall Research Room
950 Soldiers Drive
Carlisle, Pennsylvania 17013

(717) 245-3949

Army War College Library
Root Hall
122 Forbes Avenue
Carlisle, Pennsylvania 17013

(717) 245-3700

http://www.carlisle.army.mil/ahec/visit.cfm

The library and archives maintains a large collection of print, archival, audio-visual, and digital materials. They also administer, develop, and maintain a variety of databases to support their mission. The professional research team provides service in support of the Army War College curriculum and historical inquiries. The searchable catalog is available on the Center's website. The Center also houses the Army Heritage Museum.

Naval History and Heritage Command

805 Kidder Breese Street SE
Washington Navy Yard, DC 20374

(202) 433-7880

archives@navy.mil

https://www.history.navy.mil/

The Washington Navy Yard is home to the Naval History and Heritage Command, which oversees the National Museum of the U. S. Navy and an extensive archives of documents, artifacts, and art. The library emphasizes naval, maritime, and military history, with a manuscript collection of letters, journals, diaries, logbooks, and other original documents. They also research, write, and publish the *Dictionary of American Naval Fighting Ships*, now available on their webpage, which includes summary histories of the ships. Their webpage also features their searchable library catalog and number research guides.

Because the Washington Navy Yard is a secure naval facility, visitors should consult the webpage for the latest access and security procedures.

National Museum of the Marine Corps
18900 Jefferson Davis Highway
Triangle, Virginia 22172

(877) 635-1775

http://www.usmcmuseum.com/heritage-center.html

The National Museum of the Marine Corps is the centerpiece of a complex of facilities called the Marine Corps Heritage Center. This multi-use, 135-acre campus includes the Semper Fidelis Memorial Park and Chapel; a demonstration area with parade grounds; hiking trails and other outdoor recreational offerings. The museum records the significant contributions made by the Marine Corps to the American people and their history. Future plans could include a conference center and hotel; and an archive facility to restore and preserve Marine artifacts.

Coast Guard Museum
U. S. Coast Guard Academy
15 Mohegan Avenue
New London, Connecticut 06320

(860) 444-8511

http://www.uscg.mil/hq/cg092/museum/

The U. S. Coast Guard Museum, tucked away on the grounds of the picturesque Coast Guard Academy, contains artifacts that span the two hundred and twenty-plus-year history of the United States' premier maritime service. Featuring everything from models of a series of early steamships to the 270-foot cutter that plies the waters of today, the exquisite craftsmanship captures the changes in ship design over the last two hundred years. The museum immerses those who come to the Academy in the history of the Coast Guard and its predecessors: the Life Saving Service, the Steamboat Inspection Service, the Lighthouse Establishment, and the Revenue Cutter Service.

Library of Congress

Local History and Genealogy Reading Room
Manuscript Reading Room
Thomas Jefferson Building
101 Independence Ave, SE
Washington, DC 20540

(202) 707-5000

https://loc.gov/

The Library of Congress is the largest library in the world, housing more than 140 million books, recordings, photographs, newspapers, maps, manuscripts, and other items in its collections. Any serious discussion of such vast holdings is beyond the scope of this guide. All research should begin at the library website, first looking for guides and finding aids for specific topics, geographic locations, and collections. Onsite research should include a visit to the Local History and Genealogy Reading Room and the Manuscript Reading Room. Of particular interest are the online Research Guides to the collections of presidential papers, each providing links to digital materials related to the president from the library's collections as well as to relevant external websites.

The George Washington Papers: 65,000 items such as correspondence, diaries, account ledgers, military records, and other documents, amassed by Washington between 1745 and 1799, is organized into nine series. The online Series Notes provide a detailed description of the contents of each series, as follows:

> Series 1, *Exercise Books, Diaries, and Surveys, ca. 1745-1799.* The series includes 36 diaries kept by Washington from the age of 16 to his death in 1799.

> Series 2, *Letterbooks, 1754-1799.* The 41 letterbooks include both incoming and outgoing correspondence, dating from the beginning of the French and Indian War until his death

> Series 3, *Varick Transcripts, 1775-1785.* The 44 letterbooks include copies of the correspondence related to the Revolutionary War.

> Series 4, *General Correspondence, 1697-1799.* The 297 volumes contain original letters to and from Washington, family papers, speeches, military orders, and other papers.

> Series 5, *Financial Papers, 1750-1796.* The 34 volumes include ledgers, journals, account books, and other business records, some involving his military service in the French and Indian and Revolutionary Wars, as well as his presidency.

> Series 6, *Military Papers, 1755-1798.* The 26 volumes mostly include documents accumulated by Washington, except for an orderly book and a

Virginia militia memorandum book from the French and Indian War created by Washington.

Series 7, *Applications for Office, 1789-1796*. The 32 volumes contain letters from those seeking work when he was president.

Series 8, *Miscellaneous Papers, ca. 1775-1799*. The documents in Series 8 were filed separately only because they were received by the library after the other series were arranged.

Series 9, *Addenda, ca. 1732-1943*. The documents were acquired after 1970 or culled from previous series as extraneous.

The Thomas Jefferson Papers: 27,000 documents dated from the early 1760s up to his death in 1826, are divided into ten series, four of which are pertinent here:

Series 1, *General Correspondence, 1651-1827*. Original letters received and copies of letters sent, drafts of state papers and memoranda, and other papers.

Series 2, *Horatio Gates Letterbook, 1780-1781*. Copies of letters from General Gates related to Gates' southern campaign.

Series 8, *Virginia Records, 1606-1737*. The 21 volumes include Virginia colonial records collected and copied by Jefferson.

The James Madison Papers: 12,000 items, dating from 1723 to 1859, copied on 72,000 digital images, is divided into nine series. Pertinent series include:

Series 1, *General Correspondence, 1723-1859*. The 90 volumes include letters received, some draft letters sent, and related papers.

Series 2, *Additional General Correspondence, 1780-1837*. The eight volumes include letters received, some draft letters sent, and related papers.

Series 3, *Madison-Armstrong Correspondence, 1813-1836*. One volume of copies of letters Madison wrote to his Secretary of War John Armstrong.

The James Monroe Papers: 5,200 items dating from 1758 to 1839, include significant material from when Monroe was secretary of state, secretary of war, governor of Virginia, and president. The collection is divided into four series, the first three of which were microfilmed and all four digitized and available online. The researcher should consult *Index to the James Monroe Papers* (Washington, DC: Library of Congress, 1963) and the online *Guide to Using the James Monroe Papers*. Pertinent series include:

Series 1, *General Correspondence, 1758–1839*. The nine rolls contain letters written and received, memoranda, notes, and other documents, arranged chronologically.

Series 2, *Additional Correspondence, 1776–1838.* The two rolls contain photocopies of 381 documents from the James Monroe Museum and Memorial Library in Fredericksburg, Virginia.

Series 4, *Addenda, 1778–1831 and undated.* Miscellaneous correspondence and other documents.

The Andrew Jackson Papers: more than 26,000 items dating from 1767 to 1874, including. memoranda, journals, speeches, military records, deeds, and other documents. The collection is divided into twelve series and oversize. Series 1 through 9 and 11 were microfilmed in 1967. In addition to digitized images from the microfilm, Series 12 also is digitized, and all digitized images are available on line. Researchers should consult the online finding aids *Andrew Jackson Papers Finding Aid* and *Guide to Using the Series 5 Military Papers.*

Series 1, *General Correspondence and Related Items, 1775-1885* (119 volumes, reels 1-60). Letters received and drafts of letters sent, arranged chronologically.

Series 2, *Letterbook. 1829-31* (1 volume, reel 60). Copies of letters and related documents.

Series 3, *Letters and Orders. 1813-22.* (15 volumes, reels 61-63). Orders (1812-1816), journals of Indian treaty negotiations (1816, 1818), and documents relating to West Florida (1821).

Series 4, *Record Books. 1800-37* (10 volumes, reel 64). Various record books, including regimental orders (1800-1801), court martial records (1814), account of the Battle of New Orleans (1815), Creek War order book (1812-13), letters to William J. Duane (1833), Henry Lee's manuscript Life of Jackson, memoranda books (1829-32 and 1831-35), and Jackson's Farewell Address of 1837.

Series 5, *Military Papers. 1781-1832* (13 volumes. reels 65-70). Muster rolls, military returns, general and brigade orders, and other records.

Series 6, *Additional Correspondence. 1779-1855 and undated* (8 volumes. reels 71-74). Letters and related documents.

Series 7, *Miscellaneous Correspondence. 1789-1845 and undated* (3 boxes. reel 75) Some 600 items acquired by the Library in 1943.

Series 8, *Messages and Speeches, ca. 1829-36* (4 boxes. Reels 76-77). Reports and drafts of Jackson's annual messages and miscellaneous speeches.

Series 9, *Miscellaneous Manuscripts. 1795-1856* (1 box. Reel 78). Record books, financial and bank records, and copies of biographical work on Jackson.

Series 10, *Non-manuscript Material (Reproductions and Transcripts). 1788-1898* (Not filmed and not online). Correspondence and other miscellaneous materials.

Series 11, *Jackson-Kendall Letters. 1827-45* (1 box. Reel 78). 60 letters acquired in 1964.

Series 12, *Addenda. c. 1806-1874* (Not filmed, but available online). Materials acquired since 1966.

The Zachary Taylor Papers: approximately 650 items dating from 1814 to 1931, with the bulk from 1840 to 1861. The collection is made up primarily of general correspondence and family papers of Taylor (1784-1850), with some autobiographical material, business and military records, printed documents, engraved printed portraits, and other miscellany relating chiefly to his presidency (1849-1850); his service as a U. S. Army officer, especially in the Second Seminole War; management of his plantations; and, settlement of his estate.

The Index to the Zachary Taylor Papers, created by the Manuscript Division in 1960 when the bulk of the collection was microfilmed, provides a full list of the correspondents and notes the series number and dates of the items indexed. The information is helpful in finding an individual letter or document in the online version. Additional letters received by the library after 1960 and located in Series 6 are not in the Index. A current finding aid to the Zachary Taylor Papers is available online with links to the digital content on the website.

The collection is arranged into six series, the first five of which were reproduced in 1960 on two reels of microfilm, scans of which comprise the bulk of this online collection. Material added to the collection after the microfilm edition was completed forms Series 6, Additions.

Series 1, Autobiographical Account, circa 1826 (Reel 1). Fifteen-page holograph account of Taylor's life.

Series 2, General Correspondence, 1814-1850 (Reel 1). Letters and copies of letters by or to Taylor and other documents. Arranged chronologically.

Series 3, Family Papers, 1837-1887 (Reel 2). Letters, receipts, and other documents reflecting the settlement of Taylor's estate, the life of Richard Taylor (1826-1879), Taylor's son, and his management of a plantation in Louisiana. Arranged chronologically.

Series 4, Miscellany, 1820-1931 (Reel 2). Newspaper clippings, a map, pamphlets, and other miscellaneous material.

Series 5, Memorial Volume, 1850 (Reel 2). Volume in memory of Taylor.

Series 6, Additions, 1820-1863 (Not filmed; scanned from originals). Correspondence and photocopies of a lithograph, Taylor's will and testament, and an engraved portrait, acquired since the creation of the microfilm edition. Arranged by year of addition and therein alphabetically by type of material. The 1984 Addition includes, among other items, a typescript of Taylor's letter accepting the Whig Party's presidential nomination, January 23, 1848, as well as photocopies of a version of Taylor's will and testament. The 2014 Addition contains one original and one copy of letters written by Taylor to Thomas W. Ringgold, the overseer of Taylor's plantation "Cypress Grove" in Rodney, Mississippi. Also in the 2014 Addition is an 1863 engraved portrait of Taylor, depicting him in uniform as a military officer in the Mexican War.

The Shelby Family Papers, 1738-1916, are an important collection of 2,315 records, primarily concerning Evan Shelby and his son Isaac and their military careers on the Virginia frontier. The collection is arranged in nine boxes, as follows:

> Box 1, Accounts, receipts, bills, notes, surveys, deeds, military records, and occasional correspondence of Evan Shelby, 1738-1779
>
> Box 2, Accounts, receipts, bills, notes, surveys, deeds, military records, and occasional correspondence of Evan Shelby, 1780-1793
>
> Box 3, Letters sent and received by Isaac Shelby, supplemented by accounts, notes, receipts, bills, military records, deeds, and documents relating to land claims, 1794-1799
>
> Box 4, Letters sent and received by Isaac Shelby, supplemented by accounts, notes, receipts, bills, military records, deeds, and documents relating to land claims, 1800-1815
>
> Box 5, Letters sent and received by Isaac Shelby, supplemented by accounts, notes, receipts, bills, military records, deeds, and documents relating to land claims, 1816-1819
>
> Box 6, Letters sent and received by Isaac Shelby and Alfred Shelby, supplemented by accounts, notes, receipts, bills, military records, deeds, and documents relating to land claims, 1820-1829
>
> Box 7, Letters sent and received by Alfred Shelby, 1830-1862, and miscellaneous accounts, notes, receipts, bills, military records, deeds, and documents relating to land claims of Evan Shelby and Isaac Shelby, circa 1763-1862, undated
>
> Box 8, Miscellaneous correspondence, accounts, notes, receipts, bills and documents of Evan Shelby, Isaac Shelby, Alfred Shelby, and Susanna Preston Shelby Grigsby, circa 1741-1916
>
> Box 9, Miscellaneous correspondence, accounts, notes, receipts, bills and documents of Evan Shelby, Isaac Shelby, Alfred Shelby, and Susanna Preston Shelby Grigsby, Undated
>
> Box 9, Isaac Shelby memorandum book containing memoranda of official correspondence, orders, nominations, and appointments, 1792-1794

Selected other significant manuscript collections include the following.

Ebenezer Foote Family Papers, 1751-1871. Family and general correspondence, orders, petitions, and other papers of Foote and various members of his family, concerning the War of 1812 and the First Seminole War.

Gibson-Getty-McClure Families Papers, 1777-1926. Correspondence, diaries, financial papers, military papers, and other materials concerning various members of these allied families, relating to their military service in the Revolution and several Indian campaigns.

James Grant of Ballindalloch Papers, 1740-1819. He was a British army officer during the French and Indian War, First Cherokee War, and Revolutionary War, and the Royal Governor of East Florida, 1763-1773.

Nathaniel Greene Papers, 1775-1785. Major General Greene commanded the Continental Army in the South.

Samuel Peter Heintzelman Papers, 1822-1913. Correspondence, diaries, journals, and military papers detailing Heintzelman's service in the U. S. Army, including descriptions of activities in Indian wars in Florida.

Thomas Sidney Jesup Papers, 1780-1907. Correspondence, memoranda, diaries, reports, essays, family papers, financial records, journals, maps, photographs, printed matter, and miscellaneous items relating to various military campaigns and to Jesup's career as quartermaster general of the army.

F. W. Pickens and Milledge L. Bonham Papers, 1837-1920. Correspondence, reports, resolutions, military papers, applications for office, petitions, administrative papers, memoranda, and newspaper clippings relating to the two South Carolina governors.

State Archives

The following is intended to serve as a guide to the military and other related records for the Indian wars held by the various state archives. Many of the archives have microfilm copies of federal records, such as military service records, pension application files, bounty-land warrants, and miscellaneous Indian records. Because those records are discussed elsewhere, they are not included here. However, selected published guides, indexes, and abstracts of those federal records are included.

For the most part, the original military records held by the state archives consist of muster rolls, pay rolls, and similar records created under their colonial, territorial, and state governments. While the archives have most of the extant militia records, they may not have all of them. Other potential sources to consider include published state, regional, and county histories; county court records; the personal papers of governors and militia officers; and, official government records among the various manuscript collections. A published history of the county or region where one's research subject lived may contain muster rolls or other lists of militia and independent volunteer companies, as well as accounts of their exploits. Moreover, published state, regional, or county histories, from places where battles took place, forts were erected, or treaties were signed, may contain detailed accounts of those events with references to specific militia companies.

County court records often contain references to militia officers and occasionally, though rarely, include muster rolls or other militia lists. For example, Georgia militia districts, identified by the name of the commanding captain, were an important subdivision of county government. Justices of the peace, constables, and other local officials were appointed by militia district. Land and personal property taxes were assessed and collected by militia district; thus, the tax digest for a particular militia district provides a rough proxy for the muster roll for that captain's company. In other states, county court records may include the appointments of militia officers, affidavits attesting to the military service of veterans applying for pensions or bounty-land, and other references to the local militia.

The personal papers of colonial, territorial, and state governors often are rich with material concerning their militia and the various Indian wars. State archives usually hold the original or copies of the papers of their governors, but some of the papers may be held in other manuscript collections. State archives often do not hold the personal papers of their state's former militia officers. If such papers have survived, they may be held by state or local historical societies, university libraries, or other manuscript collections. One should also be aware that some manuscript collections hold official colonial, territorial, and state militia records. For example, the Southern Historical Collection, at the University of North Carolina Library, in Chapel Hill, holds two manuscripts with the accession number 536 NC and titled *North Carolina Militia Papers (Miscellaneous) 1810-1815.* The first is a 50-page manuscript of militia reports, orders, and muster rolls of the 5th Regiment when in active service in 1815. The second item is a list of artillery and cavalry officers in some eastern counties, dated 1810-1811.

Many state archives hold large collections of both original and microfilmed copies of newspapers which can be a rich source of information. Local newspapers may contain vivid accounts of battles, list those who marched off to fight, or name the heroes when they returned. Occasionally, later obituaries may list the names of other local surviving veterans.

Alabama

Alabama Department of Archives and History
624 Washington Street
Montgomery, Alabama 36130

(334) 242-4435

http://archives.state.al.us/

In 1702, the French established the first settlement in what would become Alabama at Old Mobile, at Twenty-Seven Mile Bluff on the Mobile River. Nine years later, they relocated the city to its present location. The territory encompassed by the modern counties of Baldwin and Mobile remained in French hands until the Treaty of Paris formally ended the French and Indian War and turned control over to the Britain. From 1763 to 1783, that part of Alabama officially was part of British West Florida. However, in 1780, the Spanish captured Mobile and retained control of West Florida after the Revolutionary War. In 1813, the United States annexed Spanish West Florida, from the Pearl River to the Perdido River, including Baldwin and Mobile counties.

Jurisdiction and control over the rest of Alabama, consisting of everything north of Baldwin and Mobile counties, was disputed. France claimed that French Louisiana extended from the Mississippi River eastward to the Chattahoochee River, the western boundary of modern Georgia. In 1717, they erected Fort Toulouse on the Coosa River to establish and enforce their jurisdiction. From its founding in 1732, the Province of Georgia claimed all the territory between the Carolinas and Florida, from the Atlantic Ocean westward to the Mississippi River. Gradually, British traders traveled extensively through the territory, establishing strong relations with many of the native tribes, who grew dependent on the trade. In 1763, France ceded all their territory east of the Mississippi to Britain. At the end of the Revolutionary War, Georgia claimed the territory. In 1798, the federal government organized the Mississippi Territory, composed roughly of the southern halves of the modern states of Alabama and Mississippi. In 1804, the northern halves were annexed to the Mississippi Territory. In 1817, the federal government created the Alabama Territory from the eastern portion of the Mississippi Territory. In 1819, Alabama was admitted to the Union as a state.

One important resource for researching military records at the archives is Alabamians at War - ADAH Public Information Subject Files, which are indexed on the archives website. The collection contains records that document the participation of Alabamians in the Revolutionary War, War of 1812, First Creek War, Second Creek War, and other conflicts. The material was compiled by Archives staff from clippings, brochures, reference correspondence, photocopies and typescripts of original documents, and various printed materials from the archives' collections. Most of the information is about people and events associated with the various wars.

Books and Private manuscript materials, as well as state and local government records, are described in the searchable online catalog, ADAHCAT. Some photographs and original documents have been scanned and are available in the online Digital Collections. One may browse each collection by topic or search for specific people, places, or events. In addition, microfilm reels of the military service surname cards are available in the research room. Each card, arranged alphabetically, contains the name of the soldier, rank, unit, dates of service, and the source of the information. The cards cover service in the Revolution, War of 1812, First Creek War, territorial service in 1818, the Indian disturbances in 1836, and other wars.

One helpful publication is *Roster of Revolutionary Soldiers and Patriots Alabama,* (Montgomery, Alabama: Alabama Society DAR, 1979), which lists those soldiers who lived and died in Alabama, as well as a few others. The information is a compilation from scattered published and unpublished sources and includes a brief biographical sketch, description of military service, and bibliographic citations to sources.

The archives holds one folder of Mississippi Territorial Militia records, 1806-1813, consisting primarily of payables to certain volunteers for their services, muster rolls, and lists of arms, ammunition, and other supplies in the possession of the 6th and 8th Regiments. Another folder of Mississippi Territorial Militia correspondence, 1806-1815, includes petitions to the Governor, letters from militiamen, lists of appointed and commissioned officers, correspondence concerning the Choctaw and Chickasaw Indians, drawings of the order in which troops marched, petitions by soldiers against the march towards Creek Indian towns, and other correspondence concerning the activities of the militia.

The Governor Clement Comer Clay militia files, 1835-1836, includes correspondence and reports relating to the militia and general military affairs. Records relating specifically to the Second Creek War are found in Governor Clay's administrative files. Included are several morning reports, an 1836 report of ordinance at Tuscaloosa, an 1835 abstract of the annual returns of the militia, and numerous muster rolls.

The Governor Arthur Bagby militia files, 1837-1841, include letters, petitions, reports, and military orders relating to the militia and general military affairs. Topics discussed include equipment and supplies, ordnance, formation of companies, election of officers, and troop movements. Of specific interest are letters pertaining to the Creek and Cherokee problems, and the call for men to report to assist with the removal of the Cherokee. The files also include correspondence regarding the Creek raids in south Alabama, a Creek uprising in Dale and Covington counties, other uprisings in Barbour County, and letters concerning numerous individual militia companies.

Florida

State Library and Archives of Florida
R.A. Gray Building, Second Floor
500 South Bronough Street
Tallahassee, Florida 32399

(850) 245-6600

http://dos.myflorida.com/library-archives/about-us/about-the-state-archives-of-florida/

During the Revolutionary War, East and West Florida were British colonies and remained loyal to the crown. Both colonies were havens for Southern Loyalists, especially from Georgia and South Carolina. Two publications that are helpful are:

> Fritot, Jessie Robinson, *Pension Records of Soldiers of the Revolution Who Removed to Florida.* Jacksonville, Florida: Jacksonville Chapter, Daughters of the American Revolution, 1946.

> Wright, J. Leitch, *Florida in the American Revolution.* Gainesville, Florida: University Presses of Florida, 1975.

During the War of 1812, East and West Florida were Spanish Colonies. The archives holds microfilm copies of the East Florida Papers, 1784-1821, the second Spanish period, the original manuscripts at the Library of Congress. Military matters are discussed in the correspondence of the Captain-General, the Departments of War and Navy, commandants of gunboats, colored militia, artillery, Council of War, and the militia at posts on the St. Johns River, St. Mary's River, and Amelia Island. A useful index to the papers is available at the University of Florida Library's webpage. The *Archives of the Spanish Government of West Florida, 1782-1816,* entirely in Spanish, is not in print, on microfilm, or online. However, an English translation is available at the National Archives on microfilm T1116, reel 3. An index to the records is Stanley C. Arthur's *Index to the Archives of Spanish West Florida* (New Orleans, Louisiana: Polyanthos, 1975). Another helpful source is *Assorted Garrison and Militia Muster Rolls, Spanish and British Florida*, Volume 127, of the Special Archives, Florida Department of Military Affairs (St. Augustine, Florida: State Arsenal, St. Francis Barracks, 1987).

Soon after the federal government obtained Florida from Spain in 1822, the Territorial militia was formed. The enrolled militia consisted of all able-bodied, free white males between the ages of 18 and 45. The men were assigned to a company, commanded by a captain, and required to drill at least four times a year. The Florida militia units who fought in the Second and Third Seminole Wars primarily were independent volunteer militia companies, raised locally, and not the regular militia. The archives holds the original Florida Territorial muster rolls, 1826-1849. The surviving rolls include a few from the 1820s, but most are from the Second Seminole War. For the most part, the rolls include the name and rank of the soldier, date and place of enlistment, and other remarks.

The archives holds a series of Florida militia records titled *Seminole War Muster Rolls of Florida Militia, 1836-1841, 1856-1858.* The Second Seminole War was fought by the federal army, supplemented by Florida militia and small militia contingents from Alabama, Georgia, South

Carolina, Tennessee, and other states. The Third Seminole War was fought by the federal army and the Florida militia. The record series consists of photocopies of muster rolls for the independent volunteer companies, most identified by the commander's name. The rolls generally list the soldier's name, rank, age, date and place of enlistment, and other remarks.

Georgia

Georgia Archives
5800 Jonesboro Road
Morrow, Georgia 30260

(678) 364-3710

http://www.georgiaarchives.org/

From its founding, Georgia was intended to be a buffer between the Carolinas and the Spanish to the south and the French to the west. During the colonial era, Georgia militia frequently were called into service, but few records of that service survive. An excellent publication of the few extant records is Murtie June Clark's *Colonial Soldiers of the South, 1732–1774* (Baltimore, Maryland: Genealogical Publishing Company, 1983).

At the start of the Revolutionary War, fewer than 20,000 people resided in Georgia, with about 3,500 of them white men of military age. Perhaps one-third fought as Patriots, a second third fought as Loyalists, and another third remained neutral. Georgia recruited numerous men from other colonies, especially the Carolinas, to fight for Georgia. Three helpful guides to Georgia's Revolutionary soldiers are:

> Candler, Allen D., *The Revolutionary Records of the State of Georgia*.
> Three Volumes, Atlanta, Georgia: State Printer, 1906.

> Davis, Robert Scott, Jr., *Georgia Citizens and Soldiers of the Revolution*.
> Easley, South Carolina: Southern Historical Press, 1979.

> Warren, Mary B., *Revolutionary Memoirs and Muster Rolls*. Athens,
> Georgia: Heritage Papers, 1994.

Georgia granted bounty-land to soldiers who served in Georgia military units, civilian residents of 1781 and 1782, and Georgians who went to other states to fight. After 1783, veterans could apply to the state for a warrant for land in Georgia. The state then issued certificates to approved applicants, that could be exchanged for warrants. The archives holds the original records. Published guides to those and other records pertaining to the Revolution are:

> Blair, Ruth, *Revolutionary Soldiers' Receipts for Georgia Bounty Grants*.
> Atlanta, Georgia: Department of Archives and History, 1928.

> Hemperley, Marion R., *Military Certificates of Georgia, 1776–1800*.
> Atlanta, Georgia: Georgia Surveyor General Department, 1983.

> Hitz, Alex M., *Authentic List of All Land Lottery Grants Made to Veterans of the Revolutionary War by the State of Georgia*. 2nd Edition, Atlanta, Georgia: Department of Archives and History, 1966.

> Warren, Mary B., *Georgia's Revolutionary War Bounty-land Records*.
> Athens, Georgia: Heritage Papers, 1992.

From the end of the Revolutionary War through the end of the Cherokee and Creek removal circa 1839, thousands of Georgians fought in the various Indian wars as well as the War of 1812. Surviving records indicate that one out of five adult Georgia men saw active military service between 1812 and 1815. Most of their military service and bounty-land records are at the National Archives. A helpful guide to those records is Judy Kratovil's *An Index to War of 1812 Service Records for Volunteer Soldiers of Georgia* (Atlanta, Georgia: the author, 1986). In 1940, Louise F. Hayes compiled the nine volume *Georgia Military Affairs, 1775–1842*, an indexed collection of unpublished typescripts of original records held by the archives, including, correspondence, muster rolls, and other materials.

Gordon Burns Smith's *History of the Georgia Militia 1783-1861*, Four Volumes (Milledgeville, Georgia: Boyd Publishing, 2000) is a comprehensive guide to the participation of the Georgia militia in the various Indian wars and the War of 1812, as well as other conflicts. Volume 1 provides detailed descriptions of the individual campaigns, with eye witness reports, lists of units in active service, and biographies of 205 militia generals. Also included are the significant militia acts. Volumes 2 and 3 include histories of the militia from forty counties, including muster rolls, pay rolls, and biographies of the county commanders. Volume 4 includes detailed histories of twenty-five independent volunteer companies. All four volumes are well documented and individually indexed.

Donna B. Thaxton, C. Stanton Thaxton, and Carlton J. Thaxton's *Georgia Indian Depredation Claims*, (Americus, Georgia: Thaxton Company, 1988) consists of abstracted claims compiled by the Works Progress Administration in 1938, from the original records at the archives. Also included is a federal document titled, *Indian Depredations in Georgia, 21st Congress, 1st Session, House of Representatives, War Department, Document No. 25*, dated 1830. The claims often include descriptions of the deaths of husbands, wives, and other family members, as well as the loss of homes, barns, horses, livestock, and other personal property. The claims usually are witnessed by survivors, neighbors, or local officials. The book includes abstracts of original documents, full copies of some documents, a name index, and a place name index.

Starting soon after the end of the Revolutionary War, the tide of settlers from the Carolinas, Virginia, and other states surged into the Georgia backcountry, many of them veterans of the late war. As the Cherokee and Creek ceded more and more of their lands, Georgia began to distribute the land in a series of land lotteries, starting in 1805. The statute authorizing the Third, or 1820, Land Lottery provided that veterans of the Indian wars, invalid or indigent veterans of the Revolution or War of 1812, and widows whose husbands were killed in the Revolution, War of 1812, or Indian wars, were entitled to extra draws, or chances to win land in the lottery. In the Fourth Land Lottery in 1821, extra draws were given to widows whose husbands were killed or died in the Revolution, War of 1812, or Indian wars; and orphans, whose fathers were killed or died in the Revolution, War of 1812, or Indian wars. The Fifth Land Lottery, in 1827, provided extra draws to widows whose husbands were killed or died in the Revolution, War of 1812, or Indian wars; orphans whose fathers were killed or died in the Revolution, War of 1812, or Indian Wars; wounded or disabled veterans of the War of 1812 or Indians wars who were unable to work; and, veterans of the Revolution, whether or not they had won land in previous lotteries. The Sixth Land Lottery, in 1832, provided extra draws for veterans, widows, and orphans, based upon the same criteria as the 1827 Land Lottery.

Complete lists of the fortunate drawers, those who won land, have been published, as follows:

> Lucas, Silas Emmett, *The Third or 1820 Land Lottery of Georgia*. Easley, South Carolina: Southern Historical Press, 1986.

> Lucas, Silas Emmett, *The Fourth or 1821 Land Lottery of Georgia*. Easley, South Carolina: Southern Historical Press, 1986.

> Houston, Martha Lou, *Reprint of Official Register of Land Lottery of Georgia, 1827*. Columbus, Georgia: Printed by Walton-Forbes Company, 1929. Reprinted 1967.

> Lucas, Silas Emmett, *The 1832 Gold Lottery of Georgia: Containing a List of the Fortunate Drawers in Said Lottery*. Easley, South Carolina: Southern Historical Press, 1976, Reprinted 1988.

> Smith, James F., *Cherokee Land Lottery of Georgia, 1832*. Easley, South Carolina, Southern Historical Press, 1838, Reprinted 1968 and 1969.

> Warren, Mary Bondurant, *Alphabetical Index to Georgia's 1832 Gold Lottery*. Danielsville, Georgia: Heritage Papers, 1981.

The archives holds the original ledgers for twenty counties listing those who qualified for draws and registered for the lotteries. The ledgers usually indicate the category under which the individual qualified. Because extant records documenting militia service are far from complete, land lottery ledgers may be the only surviving proof of a veteran's militia service. Published ledgers for two counties are:

> Ports, Michael A., *Baldwin County, Georgia Lottery Drawers for 1820 and 1821*. Baltimore, Maryland: Genealogical Publishing Company, 2016.

> Ports, Michael A., *Jefferson County, Georgia Lottery Drawers for 1827 and 1832*. Baltimore, Maryland: Genealogical Publishing Company, 2016.

Two additional helpful guides are:

> De Quesada, Alejandro M., *A History of Georgia Forts: Georgia's Lonely Outposts*. Charleston, South Carolina: The History Press, 2011.

> Rowland, Arthur Ray and James E. Dorsey, *A Bibliography of the Writings on Georgia History, 1900-1970*. Spartanburg, South Carolina: The Reprint Company, 1966, Reprinted 1978.

Kentucky

Kentucky Department for Libraries and Archives
300 Coffee Tree Road
Frankfort, Kentucky 40602

(502) 564-1770 or (800) 928-7000

http://kdla.ky.gov/researchers/Pages/default.aspx

During the Revolutionary War and most of the Second Cherokee War, Kentucky was part of Virginia, whose militia participated in both conflicts. Many Virginia veterans received grants for land in Kentucky. The names of many veterans who served in the early militia are in the records of the George Rogers Clark military expeditions. Selected records pertinent to military research that are held by the archives include:

> Militia books (rolls), Woodford County, 1792-1826 (bulk 1792-1795, 1807, 1815-1816, 1818, 1826).
>
> Commissioners' Tax Books, Tax Lists, and Militia Books, Meade County, 1826-1863.
>
> Governor's official correspondence file - military appointments, 1828-1832.
>
> Governor's official correspondence file - executive minute book, 1828-1832.
>
> Governor's official correspondence file - proposed regimental boundary line changes, 1828-1832?
>
> Governor's official correspondence file - messages to the General Assembly, 1804-1808 (bulk 1804, 1807-1808).
>
> Appointments by the governor - military appointments, 1836-1837.
>
> Governor's official correspondence file - executive journal, 1808-1812.
>
> Governor's official correspondence file - military appointments, 1808-1812.
>
> Governor's official correspondence file - military appointments, 1816-1820.
>
> Public Officials Settlements and Reports, 1795-1902.
>
> Governor's official correspondence file - military papers, 1796-1804.
>
> Governor's official correspondence file - military appointments, 1820-1824.
>
> Governor's official correspondence file - official papers, 1792-1796.
>
> House of Representatives, Journals, 1793-1798.

Quartermaster General invoice book, 1828-1838.

Governor's official correspondence file - executive journal, 1792-1796.

Governor's official correspondence file - military correspondence, 1812.

Quartermaster General journal, 1816-1838.

Governor's official correspondence file - executive minute book, 1808-1813.

Governor's official correspondence file - executive journal, 1804-1808.

A helpful guide to this and other archives in Kentucky is *The Guide to Archival and Manuscript Repositories* (Frankfort, Kentucky: Department for Libraries and Archives, 1986).

The following is a brief selected list of published works on pertinent Kentucky military records:

Burns, Annie Walker, *Abstracts of Pension Papers of Soldiers of the Revolutionary War, War of 1812, and Indian Wars Who Settled in Kentucky*. 20 Volumes, Washington, D.C.: the author, 1935-present.

Clift, G. Glenn., *The "Cornstalk" Militia of Kentucky, 1792–1811. 1957*. Baltimore, Maryland: Genealogical Publishing Company, 1982.

Harding, Margery Heberling, *George Rogers Clark and His Men: Military Records, 1778–84*. Frankfort, Kentucky: Kentucky Historical Society, not dated.

James, James Alton, *George Rogers Clark Papers*. Springfield, Illinois: Trustees of the Illinois State Historical Library, 1912.

Kentucky Adjutant General, *Kentucky Soldiers of the War of 1812*. Kentucky Adjutant General's Report, 1891, Nashville, Tennessee: Byron Sistler and Associates, Reprinted, 1992.

Kentucky Pension Roll of 1835: Report from the Secretary of War—in Relation to the Pension Establishment of the U. S. Baltimore, Maryland: Southern Book Company, 1959.

Quiseberry, Anderson C., *Revolutionary Soldiers in Kentucky*. Baltimore, Maryland: Genealogical Publishing Company, 1968.

Taylor, Philip F., *A Calendar of the Warrants for Land in Kentucky for Service in the French and Indian War*. Baltimore, Maryland: Genealogical Publishing Company, 1967.

Wilson, Samuel M., *Catalogue of Revolutionary Soldiers and Sailors to Whom Land Bounty Warrants Were Granted by Virginia*. Baltimore, Maryland: Genealogical Publishing Company, 1967.

Military Records and Research Branch
Kentucky Department of Military Affairs
1121 Louisville Road
Frankfort, Kentucky 40601

(502) 607-1713

pao@kentuckyguard.com

http://dma.ky.gov/Pages/index.aspx

The branch maintains historical records of all Kentucky militia since statehood. The collection includes:

> Documentation of the Kentucky Militia, Kentucky State Guard, Kentucky National Legion, and Volunteer regiments (1794 to 1912).
>
> Records from 1794-1860, including the Cornstalk Militia and War of 1812.

Louisiana

Louisiana State Archives
3851 Essen Lane
Baton Rouge, LA 70809

(225) 922-1000

http://www.sos.la.gov/HistoricalResources/Pages/default.aspx

For the Spanish colonial period, the most valuable collection is at the General Military Archives in Segovia, Spain, which holds military service records for all soldiers of the Spanish military from 1680 to 1920. The records usually include the soldier's name, rank, physical description, names of his parents, and other personal information.

Four useful finding aids for Louisiana soldiers serving in the American Revolution and War of 1812 are:

> Churchill, E. Robert, comp., *Soldiers of the American Revolution under Bernardo De Galvez.* Only five copies of the book were printed, one placed in the Sons of the American Revolution Library at the Howard-Tilton Library, Tulane University, one in the DAR Library in Washington, and one in the Library of Congress.

> Martinez, Leroy, *From Across the Spanish Empire: Spanish Soldiers Who Helped Win the American Revolutionary War, 1776-1783: Arizona, California, Louisiana, New Mexico, and Texas Military Rosters.* Baltimore: Maryland: Clearfield Company, 2015.

> Mills, Elizabeth Shown, *Natchitoches Colonials: Censuses, Military Rolls, and Tax Lists, 1722–1803.* Tuscaloosa, Alabama: Mills Historical Press, 1981.

> Pierson, Marion John Bennett, *Louisiana Soldiers in the War of 1812.* Baton Rouge, Louisiana: Louisiana Genealogical and Historical Society, 1963.

The majority of surviving records from the colonial period are in parish courthouses and in the Louisiana State Museum. Nearly all the state records from the antebellum period, 1812 to 1860, were destroyed during the Civil War and Reconstruction. Since 1977, the archives began collecting and microfilming colonial records from the parishes. A selected list of available records include:

> Avoyelles Parish, 1786-1803

> East Baton Rouge Parish (Spanish West Florida), 1782-1810

> Natchitoches Parish, 1732-1819

> Saint Charles Parish, 1740-1803

Saint James Parish, 1782-1787

Saint Landry Parish, 1764-1803

In the 18th century, the French Ministry of the Navy (Ministere de la Marine) was responsible for the French Navy and the troops in the French colonies in America. See Winston Deville's *Louisiana Recruits, 1752-1758* (Cottonport, Louisiana: Polyanthos, Inc., 1973) and *Louisiana Troops, 1720-1770* (Fort Worth, Texas: American Reference Publishers, 1965).

Helpful guides to Louisiana research include:

Beers, Henry Putney, *French and Spanish Records of Louisiana: A Bibliographical Guide to Archive and Manuscript Sources.* Baton Rouge, Louisiana: Louisiana State University Press, 1989.

Boling, Yvette Guillot, *A Guide to Printed Sources for Genealogical and Historical Research in the Louisiana Parishes.* Baton Rouge, Louisiana: Louisiana Genealogical and Historical Society, 1985.

_____, *A Guide to Printed Sources for Genealogical and Historical Research in the Louisiana Parishes, 1991 Supplement.* Baton Rouge, Louisiana: Land and Land, Inc. 1992.

Brasseaux, Carl A. and Glenn R. Conrad, *A Bibliography of Scholarly Literature on Colonial Louisiana and New France.* Lafayette, Louisiana: Center for Louisiana Studies, University of Southwestern Louisiana, 1992.

Cummins, Light Townsend and Glen Jeansome, Editors, *A Guide to the History of Louisiana.* Westport, Connecticut: Greenwood Press, 1982.

Hotard, Sandra and Troy Hayes, Editors, *Guide to the Non-Public Records of the Louisiana Archives.* Baton Rouge, Louisiana: Division of Archives, Records Management, and History, not dated.

Menier, Marie-Antoinette, Étienne Taillemite, and Gilberte de Forges, *Louisiana Letters, 1678-1803.* Baton Rouge, Louisiana: Calitor's Publishing Division, 2012.

Rowland, Dunbar, *General Correspondence of Louisiana: 1678-1763.* New Orleans, Louisiana: Polyanthos, Inc., 1907, Reprinted 1976.

Sanders, Mrs. Murrah A., *Genealogical Research Sources from Selected Libraries, Archives, and Societies, chiefly in Louisiana.* New Orleans, Louisiana: Vieux Carré Chapter DAR, 1974.

Mississippi

Mississippi Department of Archives and History
100 South State Street
Jackson, Mississippi 39201

(601) 576-6850

http://www.mdah.ms.gov/new/

The French claimed the territory that eventually would become the state of Mississippi as part of New France, establishing their first settlements along the Gulf Coast. In 1699, the French built Fort Maurepas at Old Biloxi, at modern Ocean Springs, Mississippi. In 1716, the French established Fort Rosalie, around which the city of Natchez gradually grew. In 1763, the British assumed control of British West Florida as well as the rest of modern Mississippi. After the Revolutionary War, in 1783, Spain took control of West Florida, while Georgia continued to claim its western boundary extended to the Mississippi River. In 1798, the Mississippi Territory was created, encompassing roughly the southern halves of modern Alabama and Mississippi above Spanish West Florida. In 1804, the northern halves were annexed to the Mississippi Territory. In 1812, that portion of Spanish West Florida between the Pearl and Perdido rivers was annexed to the Mississippi Territory. In 1817, the state of Mississippi was admitted to the Union. Helpful guides to the early records include:

> Rowland, Dunbar and Robert Farmar, Editors, *Mississippi Provincial Archives: English Dominion.* Nashville, Tennessee: Brandon Print Company, 1911.

> Rowland, Dunbar, A. G. Sanders, and Patricia Kay Galloway, Editors, *Mississippi Provincial Archives: French Dominion.* Baton Rouge, Louisiana: Louisiana State University Press, 1984.

At the start of the Revolution, Great Britain ruled the territory that would later be the state of Mississippi. The archives holds copies of British Provincial records and the Oliver Pollack Papers, from the records of the Continental Congress, both collections obtained from the British Public Records Office in London. An excellent source for that era is Robert V. Haynes' *The Natchez District and the American Revolution* (Jackson, Mississippi: University Press of Mississippi, 1976). After the Revolution, numerous veterans migrated into Mississippi, many of whom are included in Alice Tracy Welch's *Family Records: Mississippi Revolutionary Soldiers,* (Daughters of the American Revolution, Mississippi Society, Salt Lake City, Utah: Genealogical Society of Utah, 1956.) The archives has a card index to *Mississippi Cemetery and Bible Records,* an ongoing publication project of the Mississippi Genealogical Society, which includes references to many veterans.

Three helpful guides to the military records are:

> Henderson, Thomas W., *Guide to Official Records in the Mississippi Department of Archives and History.* Jackson, Mississippi: Mississippi Department of Archives and History, 1975.

Lipscomb, Anne S. and Kathleen S. Hutchison, *Tracing Your Mississippi Ancestors*. Jackson, Mississippi: University Press of Mississippi, 1994.

Rowland, Dunbar, Editor, *Publications of the Mississippi Historical Society*. Jackson, Mississippi: Mississippi Historical Society, 1921.

Rowland, Mrs. Dunbar, *Mississippi Territory in the War of 1812*. Baltimore, Maryland, Genealogical Publishing Company, 1996.

Selected important sets of records held by the archives include:

Mississippi Territory Administration Papers, 1769, 1798-1817: The papers consist of loose documents related to all aspects of the administration of the Mississippi Territory, pertaining to the workings of the territorial government, the governor, the legislature, the military, and the courts, as well as early county governments and the affairs of individuals. The collection has been digitized and is available on the archives webpage.

John Francis Hamtramack Claiborne Papers, 1707-1881: These papers include an important collection of letters, pamphlets, newspapers, and papers Claiborne assembled to document his *Mississippi as a Province, Territory, and State, with Biographical Notices of Eminent Citizens* (Jackson, Mississippi: Power & Barksdale, 1880). The extensive collection includes numerous letters by prominent figures of the Natchez area, manuscripts of Sir William Dunbar, a letter book related to the Natchez District, another concerning the Natchez Fencibles, and miscellaneous documents related to Natchez, Port Gibson, and Oakland College, Claiborne County. There are microfilm copies available for patron use. A published index to the Claiborne Collection is available in James M. White and Franklin L. Riley's "Libraries and Societies," *Publications of the Mississippi Historical Society*, Volume V (Oxford, Mississippi: Mississippi Historical Society, 1902), pages 203-227.

Adjutant General's Office Correspondence, 1817-1886 and 1926-1932: Incoming and outgoing correspondence of the Adjutant General's office. Material pertains to almost all aspects of the statewide militia operations, including letters of resignation, returns of elections of militia officers, company strength returns, and uniform descriptions, along with letters regarding courts martial, the procurement of arms and equipment, and receipts of commissions by militia officers. It also includes correspondence between the Adjutant General's office and the U. S. War Department's Militia Bureau regarding information necessary to update and correct the personnel records of militia officers.

Adjutant General's Office Militia Elections and Appointments, 1819-1840 and 1845: Official reports to the governor and adjutant general stating the results of elections of militia officers, notifications of appointments to fill vacancies caused by resignations and deaths, and requests for forwarding commissions of new officers. Arrangement is generally chronological.

Mississippi Territory Auditor, Accounts Ledgers, 1803-1819: Two accounts ledgers used throughout a range of years itemizing territorial accounts payable and paid, and often maintaining an ongoing balance carried over from one accounting period to the next. The ledgers are set up to show accounts classified by department or individual, with a breakdown of the accounts' debits and credits. Payee's name, warrant numbers and amounts, and certifying authorities are registered, although generally the column headings are not identified, and it is often difficult to determine exactly what information has been listed. Occasionally, there are folio citations whereby accounts can be tracked.

Mississippi Territory Auditor, Payment Certifications, Pay Warrants & Receipts, 1800-1817: Procedural paperwork required for the Auditor's authorization of payments drawn from the territorial treasury. Among the many services for which payment was certified were: fulfilling the offices of justice, juror, clerk, or witness during court sessions; serving as sheriff, constable, jailer, or militia officer; or, performing the duties of coroner, census-taker, or Choctaw interpreter. There are numerous certifications for members of the territorial Legislative Council and General Assembly, detailing the number of days attended at each legislative session as well as the number of miles traveled back and forth to the Assembly. Other Assembly expenses that were certified included the printing of the Acts passed at each Assembly session, and the furnishing of suitable housing, candles, firewood, and chairs.

Mississippi Territory Governor, Military Papers, 1807-1815: A collection of records pertaining to military affairs. These records can be classified as: correspondence, orders and receipts, muster rolls, lists and returns, unit and morning reports, and muster and payrolls for Choctaw troops under the command of Pushmataha in the service of the United States.

Mississippi Territory Governor, Executive Journals, 1798-1817: Executive Journals for each administration of territorial government, composed largely of copies of outgoing correspondence, also include addresses to the General Assembly; commissions and appointments of the governors ordinances and resolutions; pardons and remissions of sentences; proclamations and circulars; and, bills of exchange, elections directives, passports and certifications for travel and business, orders to the militia, transcripts and accounts of court martials, returns of military units, commissions, appointments and licensees. The documents cover the entire range of territorial affairs, with emphasis on military concerns, such as Indian unrest and the War of 1812.

Mississippi Territory Legislature, Bills, 1800-1816: Legislation introduced in the Territorial Legislature between the years 1800-1816. The nature of the bills varies greatly, with the bills originating for public and private reasons. Frequently recurring topics include the militia and other routine government matters.

Michael Woods Trimble Memoir: The collection consists of a typescript memoir of Michael Woods Trimble, who dictated the original narrative to the Reverend Henry McDonald in 1860. The recollections were later published in three installments in the Sunday edition of the *Commercial Appeal*, Memphis, Tennessee, during July of 1909. The typescript memoir ends with the beginning of the battle of New Orleans, while the newspaper version continues until the end of the battle. The memoir begins with Trimble's anecdotes of his father, John Trimble, who was an active member of the Presbyterian church in North Carolina. He also discusses his father's participation in the May 20, 1775, Mecklenburg Convention. Trimble also describes Cherokee uprisings in the Mecklenburg District of North Carolina. He relates significant events of his youth, including the Trimble family's journey to Bayou Pierre on flatboats in April of 1811. Of interest are Trimble's recollections of his service in Lieutenant Colonel Thomas Hinds's Mississippi Dragoons during the War of 1812, especially his participation in the capture of Pensacola, Florida, and the battle of New Orleans on January 8, 1815. Also included is genealogical information pertaining to Trimble's grandparents, parents, and siblings.

Levin Wailes Papers: A typescript of an account book and a surveyor's record book. The account book includes a list of expenses incurred while surveying the boundary between the United States and the Choctaw Nation in 1809. The surveyor's record book details Wailes' survey of the lines from Broken Bluff to Faluktabunnee and on the Fuketchepoonta Reserve, from May 23, 1809 to June 19, 1809. It contains an account of Wailes's survey of the boundary of the Indian reserve and describes his encounters with disgruntled Indians along the way. The record book also describes the assistance that Choctaw Chief Pushmataha rendered to the government during that period and describes the feelings of Pushmataha's fellow tribesmen regarding his relationship with the government, especially his involvement with the Treaty of Mount Dexter in 1805.

Albert G. Sanders Papers: Most of the correspondence pertains to translating and copying the *Journal of Travel of Sieur Regis du Roullet among the Choctaws and Chickasaws, 1729* and *Mississippi Provincial Archives: French Dominion, 1729-1740*.

Henry S. Halbert Manuscript: Halbert wrote several books and articles, many of them concerning the Choctaw Indians. The collection contains an 18-page manuscript titled "Tecumseh Among the Choctaws, " an account of Tecumseh's visit in 1811 to the Choctaw Nation to gain support for an Indian confederacy to join with the British in their war against the United States.

David W. Haley and Family Papers: Correspondence and business papers of David W. Haley, who came to Council Spring, Madison County, from Tennessee. He attained the rank of major under Andrew Jackson, carried mail on the Natchez Trace, was surveyor of Indian lands, held the contract to remove the Choctaw Indians after the Treaty of Dancing Rabbit Creek, and served as state senator from 1836 to 1840.

Choctaw Land-Claim List: The collection consists of an unsigned and undated list of nine land claimants from two Choctaw families. They had been determined by the Board of Choctaw Commissioners to be entitled to lands, referred to as reservations, under an August 23, 1842, act of Congress. The two heads of household listed in the document are "Mut. tubbe" and "Tobla Chubbee." Children in each family are also listed. The document ends with the statement that only five of the nine claimants could be located under the provisions of section three of the act. Townships and ranges are not specified.

Mississippi Territory Governor, Indian Affairs, Superintendent's Journal, 1803-1808: A letterbook in which copies of the territorial governor's correspondence concerning Indian affairs were entered. Correspondence is both incoming and outgoing. Almost all the territorial governors served during the period in which this journal was kept and are included. The correspondence pertains to peacekeeping and trade with the several tribes, safe passage through Indian territory, and salary discussions with the Indian agents and interpreters.

Mrs. Dunbar Rowland Papers: The volumes are as follows: "Correspondence and Papers Concerning the Mississippi Territory in the War of 1812, 1812-1827;" manuscript of Mrs. Dunbar Rowland's *Andrew Jackson's Campaign Against the British, or the Mississippi Territory in the War of 1812, Concerning the Military Operations of the Americans, Creek Indians, and Spanish, 1813-1815* (New York, New York: The MacMillan Company, 1926); and, manuscript of Mrs. Dunbar Rowland's *Life, Letters and Papers of William Dunbar of Elgin, Morayshire, Scotland, and Natchez, Mississippi: Pioneer Scientist of the Southern United States* (Jackson, Mississippi: Press of the Mississippi Historical Society, 1930).

North Carolina

North Carolina State Archives
109 East Jones Street
Raleigh, North Carolina 27601

(919) 807-7310

http://archives.ncdcr.gov/

North Carolina's war record begins with the Chowanoc Wars and continues with the Tuscarora War, but virtually no records survive for those conflicts. Men from North Carolina served in the French and Indian War, but again few records documenting their service survive. The few extant records, primarily lists of militia officers and muster rolls, are held by the archives and are published in Murtie June Clark's *Colonial Soldiers of the South*, 1732–1774 (Baltimore, Maryland: Genealogical Publishing Company, 1983, Reprinted 1999).

The Frontier Scouting and Indian Wars, 1754-1777, collection includes:

> 1754, Indian Attack on Buffalo Creek Settlement in Rowan County
>
> 1758, Dr. Andrew Scott for treating soldiers
>
> 1759, List of men at Fort More
>
> 1759, Rolls of scout companies, Accounts for scouting the frontier
>
> 1760, Expedition against the Cherokee Indians
>
> 1764, Claims for bounty on Indian scalps
>
> 1771, Expedition against the Cherokee Indians
>
> 1776, March against the hostile Indians
>
> 1777, Depositions on Indian attacks near Long Island, Holston River
>
> 1777, Payrolls of militia companies protecting Fincastle County, Virginia against the Cherokee Indians

While the War of the Regulation was not technically an Indian war, some of the militia were involved in defending the frontier from raiding tribes. The collection of records from that conflict, 1768-1779, include:

> 1768-1771, Undated anonymous statement of Colonel Edmund Fanning
>
> 1768, Governor Tryon's account of expenses of the Rowan Regiment
>
> 1768, Payrolls of the Granville militia keeping the peace at Hillsborough
>
> 1768, Robert Harris' account for the Granville Brigade

1768, Warrants for the Mecklenburg Battalion

1768, For guarding two prisoners

1770, Deposition in defense of Herman Husband

1770, Council of War at Lieutenant Colonel Bryan's house in Johnson County, regarding 100 Regulator prisoners

May 1770, Guilford County taxes paid Governor Tryon

1770, Petition against the Regulators

January – February 1771, For guarding prisoners

March 1771, Witnesses' receipts for testifying against the Insurgents

January 1771, Secretary's account of militia commissions

December 1770 – May 1771, Governor Tryon's accounts

1768 and June 1771, Riding expenses for Governor Tryon

February 1771, Expenses of Craven Regiment muster

April 1771, Thomas Sitgreaves' receipt of pay for taking Herman Husband the night he was expelled from the Assembly

1771, Payroll of the Orange Regiment

1771, Payrolls of the Dobbs militia

1771, Payroll of Captain Thompson's Company and payroll of Captain Thackston's Company

1771, Payrolls of the Rowan Regiment

March – April 1771, Enlistment certificates of Captain Moore's Artillery Company

April-May 1771, New Hanover Artillery accounts

July 1771, Colonel Moore, repair to artillery wagon

April-May 1771, Enlistment certificates for Cumberland and Pitt Counties

April 1771, Captain Robert Salter's accounts, Pitt County

April-July 1771, Colonel Shaw's accounts

April-June 1771, Captain Gideon Wright's accounts, Tryon and Surry Counties

1771, Accounts of and allowances to the Rowan Regiment, Colonel Lindsay

1771, Accounts of and allowances to Captain Moses Martin's Company

July 1771, General Waddell's account

April 1771, Mecklenburg Detachment's accounts

May 1771, Orange Detachment's accounts, Thomas Hart

April 1771, Colonel Caswell's account for colors

1771, Deputy Adjutant General Robert Campbell's pay and allowances

June-July 1771, Accounts of Richard Blackledge, Commissary

May 1768, Writ at large for the arrest of Regulators, writs for arrest and imprisonment of Herman Husband

1771, Pay to individuals serving in the expedition

April-July 1771, Accounts for carrying provisions and munitions up the Neuse

August 1771, Returned down the Neuse River

March-August 1771, Receipts for rations, provision returns, for wagons and teams, hauling provisions, for guns and swords impressed or lost, for horses, saddles, and bridles impressed or lost, flour invoices

May 1771, Claims for damage done by troops, John Husband's claim for destroyed estate

1771, For weapons and provisions taken by Fanning and his men

June 1771, For pasturing cattle

May-June 1771, Taking up a deserter, pursuing outlaws, and making hand cuffs and irons

May 1771, Accounts of horses and articles taken from the insurgents

July 1771, Sale of horses taken from the Regulators

June 1771, Expedition to Quaker Meadows and Silver Creek

June 1771, Expenses at Bethabara

June 1771, Ferriage of Craven and Carteret companies on their return

June 1771-May 1772, Medical expenses

1771, For guarding the jail and court at Salisbury, miscellaneous accounts and allowances

1771-1773, Depositions that John Husband, Samuel Paul, and Valentine Ray were not Regulators; Clerk of the Crown at trial of Regulators; James Green's services as armorer and swearing in of 3,000 Regulators

1771-1779 and 1785, Pensions for soldiers disabled at Alamance, extract from court minutes of Superior Court at Hillsborough, September 22, 1770, contemporary history of the Regulators, copies of letters and articles dealing with the War of the Regulation

1771, Order book of the Carteret Detachment, Orders Given by Governor Tryon to the Provincials of North Carolina Raised to March Against the Insurgents, unidentified payroll and account book, journal of the expedition against the insurgents in the western frontiers, Hugh Waddell's orderly book, May-June 1771

The War of the Revolution Collection is too voluminous to cite; however, a helpful finding aid is available on the archives' webpage. Starting in 1784, the state granted pensions to veterans who were disabled by wounds or otherwise were unable to support themselves, and to widows and orphans of veterans. Their pension files are in the Treasurer's and Comptroller's Papers, Military Papers. During the war, the state used pay vouchers, or certificates, to pay the militia and to pay for other goods and services that were purchased or impressed. The pay voucher, account book, and final settlement records also are in the Treasure's and Comptroller's Papers, Military Papers.

As an inducement to enlist and serve, the state offered land to soldiers in the Continental Line. North Carolinians who volunteered to serve at least two years were given bounty-land warrants that could be exchanged for land in what was to become Tennessee. From 1783 to 1797, the land grants were issued by North Carolina; but, from 1797 to 1841, the new State of Tennessee issued the grants. The Secretary of State's Military Land Warrant Book lists all of the bounty warrants issued by North Carolina.

The Military Collection includes a series of five boxes of original records labeled Troop Returns, 1747-1783. Records concerning the Continental Line are in Boxes 4 through 6 and records concerning the militia are in Boxes 3 and 7. The records generally consist of muster rolls, payrolls, field returns, and lists of prisoners. Draft and enlistment lists record the name of the soldier, and often his physical description, such as height, age, complexion, eye color, and hair color. The archives prepared two finding aids to the Troop Returns. The first is a descriptive catalog listing the records in each box, folder by folder. The second is a catalog card listing the contents of each folder, filed under the appropriate county.

Two helpful published sources include:

Hay, Gertrude May, North Carolina Society DAR, *Roster of Soldiers from North Carolina in the American Revolution.* Baltimore, Maryland: Genealogical Publishing Company, 1932, Reprinted 1977.

Clark, Murtie June, *Loyalists in the Southern Campaign of the Revolutionary War.* Baltimore, Maryland: Genealogical Publishing Company, 1980.

Records concerning General Griffith Rutherford and his militia army of more than 2,000 men during the Cherokee Expedition of 1776 may be found among the Treasurer's and Comptroller's Records in *Revolutionary Army Account Book 1-6, Revolutionary Army Account Book E-G,* and *Revolutionary Army Accounts Volume VIII.* Correspondence and other records are in the Secretary of State Records, *Provincial Council of Safety, 1775-1776* and *Provincial Conventions and Congresses, 1774-1776.* Records of Colonel William Christian's force of Virginia militia and their participation in the Cherokee Expedition are in the Treasurer's and Comptroller's Records in *Revolutionary Army Account Book 1-6* and *Revolutionary Army Account Book B.* In the archives are three payrolls of Fincastle County, Virginia militia for their service in modern Washington County, Tennessee. The rolls are in the Military Collection box named *Frontier Wars and Indian Scoutings, 1758-1777.* The rolls include the date the soldier joined the expedition, daily pay, days served, date of discharge, and total pay.

Records of payments to Colonels Evan Shelby's and John Montgomery's forces in the first Chickamauga Expedition in April 1779 are in the Treasurer's and Comptroller's Records in *Revolutionary Army Accounts Volume VIII.* Other than correspondence in Governor Alexander Martin's papers and letter books, there are no service records in the archives for Colonel John Sevier's expedition against the Chickamauga towns in the late summer of 1782. Payment records for the militia commanded by Colonel James Robertson, who participated in the third Chickamauga Expedition in June 1787, are in Treasurer's and Comptroller's Records, Military Papers. The pay vouchers are in *Vouchers for Services in Davidson and Sumner Counties and Against the Chickamauga Indians* and *Book No. 39: Certificates Issued by the Comptroller for Services Against the Chickamauga Indians and in Davidson County.* The actual payment records are in *Revolutionary Army Accounts, Volume VI.*

In 1785, North Carolina authorized (1) the construction of the Cumberland Road, from the Clinch River to Nashville, to facilitate settlers going into Tennessee, and (2) the 300-man Cumberland Battalion to defend it. The pay records of the battalion are nearly complete until 1790, when the federal government took responsibility for the men. The records of the Cumberland Battalion, 1786-1792, collection include:

1786, List of troops raised to defend Davidson County, Major Evans

1787, Resignations of James McDonald

1787-1789, Monthly returns

1787, Warrants to the commissary of troops raised to defend Davidson County against the Chickamauga Indians

1787, Provision returns and orders

1787, Account of rations delivered by John Markland

1767-1789, Payrolls of Captains Hunter's, Hadly's, and Martin's Companies

1787-1791, Account with John Markland, commissary

1788, Receipts for powder

1790-1791, Allowances for rations

1792, Receipt for payrolls and final settlements for Davidson County expedition

During the First Creek War, several companies of North Carolina militia accompanied Andrew Jackson on his campaign against the Creek in Alabama, but no specific records of their service are in the archives. Within the War of 1812 Military Collection are six books of muster rolls, Books 1 through 5, containing muster rolls of the detached militia, mostly enrolled in 1813 for coastal defense, and Book 6 containing muster rolls of the detached militia ordered to Wadesboro in 1815. The account books, pay vouchers, payrolls, and pay receipts held by the archives pertain chiefly to the militia called for coastal defense and the later Wadesboro rendezvous. The personal papers of Colonel Joseph Graham, in the Private Collections of Manuscripts, include descriptions of his participation in the First Creek War.

In 1851, the Adjutant General's office prepared *Muster Rolls of the Soldiers of the War of 1812: Detached from the Militia of North Carolina, in 1812 and 1814.* Sarah McCulloh Lemmon's *Frustrated Patriots: North Carolina and the War of 1812* (Raleigh, North Carolina: Department of Archives and History, 1971) is another useful guide.

South Carolina

South Carolina Department of Archives and History
8301 Parklane Road
Columbia, South Carolina 29223

(803) 896-6196

http://scdah.sc.gov/Pages/default.aspx

Unfortunately, few records survive documenting the military service of South Carolinians during the colonial period. The archives houses muster rolls and other records for the First Cherokee War, and a card index to the records is available in the search room. Most of the records have been published in the *South Carolina Historical and Genealogical Magazine* and the *South Carolina Magazine of Ancestral Research*. Other published resources include:

> Andrea, Leonardo, *South Carolina Colonial Soldiers and Patriots.* Columbia, South Carolina: Daughters of Colonial Wars in the State of South Carolina, 1952.

> Clark, Murtie June, *Colonial Soldiers of the South, 1732–1774.* Baltimore, Maryland: Genealogical Publishing, Company, 1986, Reprinted 1999.

Starting in 1776, the state paid wounded and disabled veterans, widows, and orphans. Those records, submitted by the State Treasurer to the House of Representatives, are under the heading House of Representatives: Annuities, Claims, and Pension Reports.

The primary records documenting Revolutionary War service are the Audited Accounts and the Stub Entries. After the capture of Charleston in 1780, the state government nearly ceased to function as it had before. Militia service went unpaid and those furnishing supplies and other services only received a written receipt in payment. After the war, unpaid veterans and those who had furnished goods or services presented their claims to the state for payment. Judith M. Brimelow's *Accounts Audited of Claims Growing Out of the Revolution in South Carolina* (Columbia, South Carolina: South Carolina Department of Archives and History, 1985) provides a detailed description of the records. The original records are transcribed in Alexander S. Salley, Jr.'s, *Accounts Audited of Revolutionary Claims Against South Carolina.* Columbia, South Carolina: The State Company, 1935-1943.

When the auditor approved the claim, he issued an Indent, which the claimant could present for payment. Some Indents were used to pay for state land grants, others were used to pay outstanding debts, and still others were sold for cash, such endorsements usually indicated on the reverse side of the Indent. Often the endorsements indicate the district of residence. The Stub Entries correspond with the Indents in the Audited Accounts much like a check stub relates to a check today and documents the actual payment of the claim. The records are held under Office of the Commissioners of the Treasury, *Stub Indents and Indexes, 1779–1791.* The records are published in Alexander S. Salley Jr.'s *Stub Entries to Indents Issued in Payment of Claims Against South Carolina Growing Out of the Revolution* (Columbia, South Carolina: University of South Carolina Press, 1910–27).

Additional references to both military and civilian service are in Auditor Generals Accounts, 1778-1780. Published resources for the Revolutionary War include

Burns, Annie W., *South Carolina Pension Abstracts of the Revolutionary War, War or 1812, and Indian Wars*. Washington, DC: the author, 193?

Clark, Murtie June *Loyalists in the Southern Campaign of the Revolutionary War*. Baltimore, Maryland: Genealogical Publishing Company, 1981, Reprinted 1999.

Ervin, Sarah Sullivan, *South Carolinians in the Revolution*. Baltimore, Maryland: Genealogical Publishing Company, 1949, Reprinted 1965.

Lesser, Charles H., *Sources for the American Revolution at the South Carolina Department of Archives and History*. Columbia, South Carolina: South Carolina Department of Archives and History, 2000.

Moss, Bobby Gilmer, *Roster of South Carolina Patriots in the American Revolution*. Baltimore, Maryland: Genealogical Publishing Company, 1983, Reprinted 1994.

Pruitt, Jayne C. C., *Revolutionary War Pension Applicants Who Served from South Carolina*. Fairfax, Virginia: Charlton Hall, 1946.

Revill, Janie, *Copy of the Original Book Showing the Revolutionary Claims Filed in South Carolina Between August 20, 1783 and August 31, 1786*. Baltimore, Maryland: Genealogical Publishing Company, 1941, Reprinted 1961.

Salley, Alexander S., Jr., *South Carolina Provincial Troops in Papers of the First Council of Safety, 1775*. Baltimore, Maryland: Genealogical Publishing Company, 1900-1902, Reprinted 1999.

Another source on microfilm is *South Carolina Royalist Troops, Muster Rolls, 1777–1783*, at the South Caroliniana Library. Extensive manuscript and microfilmed records of South Carolina units and soldiers for the War of 1812 are at the South Caroliniana Library in Columbia. The archives has a card index of *South Carolina Pay Lists*. Other pertinent records at the archives include:

S 126022 Comptroller General, Military pension accounts, 1812-1819

S 126039 Comptroller General, Letters received, 1800-1904

S 126040 Comptroller General, Letters sent, 1800-1891

S 192017 Military Department, Adjutant and Inspector General, Journal of the volunteer company from Columbia in the Second Seminole War, 1836

S 192070 Military Department, Adjutant and Inspector General, War of 1812 muster rolls and payrolls, 1812-1814

S 192071 Military Department, Adjutant and Inspector General, War of 1812 accounts, 1814-1815

S 192089 Military Department, Adjutant and Inspector General, annual returns and abstracts of returns from South Carolina in the records of the National Guard Bureau at the National Archives, 1814-1836

S 192138 Military Department, Adjutant and Inspector General, returns of the ordnance and laboratory stores of the regiment of artillery attached to the 7th Brigade, 1802

S 192135 Militia. 4th Brigade, Board of Field Officers, land title, construction, legal, and fiscal records, 1807-1879

S 192061 Military Department, Quartermaster General, accounts of the Quartermaster General, 1824-1827

A useful guide to the entire archives collection is Marion C. Chandler and Earl W. Wade's *The South Carolina Archives: A Temporary Summary Guide*, 2nd Edition (Columbia, South Carolina: South Carolina Department of Archives and History, 1976).

Other helpful publications include:

Bicentennial Project Editorial Board, *South Carolina's Blacks and Native Americans, 1776-1976.* Columbia, South Carolina: State Human Affairs Commission, 1976.

Draine, Tony and John Skinner, *South Carolina Soldiers and Indian Traders, 1725-1730.* Columbia, South Carolina: Congaree Publications, not dated.

Herd, E. Don, Jr., *The South Carolina Upcountry, 1540-1980: Historical and Biographical Sketches.* Greenwood, South Carolina: The Attic Press, 1981.

Ivers, Larry E., *Colonial Forts of South Carolina, 1670-1775.* Columbia, South Carolina: University of South Carolina Press.

Johnson, George Lloyd, Jr., *The Frontier in the Colonial South: South Carolina Backcountry, 1736-1800.* Westport, Connecticut: Greenwood Press, 1997.

Landrum, J. B. O., *Colonial and Revolutionary History of Upper South Carolina.* Spartanburg, South Carolina, The Reprint Company, 1897, Reprinted 1977.

Logan, John H., *A History of the Upper Country of South Carolina, From the Earliest Periods to the Close of the War of Independence.* Spartanburg, South Carolina: The Reprint Company, 1859, Reprinted 2009.

Tennessee

Tennessee State Library and Archives
403 7th Avenue North
Nashville, Tennessee 37243

(615) 741-2764

http://sos.tn.gov/tsla

From the beginning, Tennessee was part of the colony of North Carolina. The early counties of Greene, Sullivan, and Washington, in East Tennessee, comprised the Overmountain settlements and the early counties of Davidson, Sumner, and Tennessee, in Middle Tennessee, comprised the Cumberland settlements. In 1779, the Cumberland Association, erected Fort Nashborough, at the present site of Nashville, on the Cumberland River. The Cumberland and Overmountain settlements were separated by a large territory controlled by the Cherokee. In 1789, North Carolina ratified the Constitution and ceded its western lands to the new federal government, creating the Territory of the United States South of the Ohio River, commonly known as the Southwest Territory, or Old Southwest. The territory was divided into three districts, each with its own militia and courts. President Washington appointed William Blount as the first territorial governor. In addition to playing a substantial role in defending their own settlements against Indian attacks, the Tennessee militia contributed significant numbers of troops to the Creek Wars, Seminole Wars, and the various Indian removals.

A good general guide to Tennessee military records is John B. Lindsley's *The Military Annals of Tennessee.* (Spartanburg, South Carolina: The Reprint Company, 1886, Reprinted 1974.) By far, most records of Revolutionary War military service, pension, and bounty-land warrants are held by the National Archives. However, the following published guides should be helpful in locating Revolutionary veterans in Tennessee:

> Allen, Penelope Johnson, *Tennessee Soldiers in the Revolution: A Roster of Soldiers during the Revolutionary War in the Counties of Washington and Sullivan, Taken from the Revolutionary Army Accounts of North Carolina.* Baltimore, Maryland: Genealogical Publishing Company, 1935, Reprinted 1967.

> Armstrong, Zella, *Some Tennessee Heroes of the Revolution.* Chattanooga, Tennessee: Lookout Publishing Company, 1933–35, Reprinted, Baltimore, Maryland, Genealogical Publishing Company, Reprinted 1975.

> ———, *Twenty-Four Hundred Tennessee Pensioners—Revolution, War of 1812.* Chattanooga, Tenn.: Lookout Publishing Company, 1937.

When it ceded Tennessee to the federal government, North Carolina reserved the right to grant land to its Revolutionary War veterans. The archives holds both the original and microfilmed copies of the entry, survey, and grant books, in Record Group 50. Published guides to the land grant records include:

> Griffey, Irene M., *Earliest Tennessee Land Records & Earliest Tennessee Land History.* Baltimore, Maryland: The Clearfield Company, 2000.

Griffey, Irene M., *The Preemptors: Middle Tennessee's First Settlers.* Clarksville, Tennessee: I. M. Griffey, 1989.

Pruitt, A.B., *Glasgow Land Fraud Papers, 1783-1800: North Carolina Revolutionary War, Bounty Land in Tennessee.* A. B. Pruitt, 1988.

Sistler, Barbara, Byron Sistler, and Samuel Sistler, *Tennessee Land Grants*, Nashville, Tennessee: Byron Sistler & Associates, 1998.

Tennessee's Andrew Jackson was a key figure in the War of 1812, the First Creek War, the First Seminole War, and the Indian Removals. Jackson's personal papers are essential in understanding the conflicts and Tennessee's role in them. Two published guides to his personal papers are:

Bassett, John Spenser, Editor, *Correspondence of Andrew Jackson, Volumes 1 and 2.* Washington, DC: Smithsonian Institute of Washington, 1926. The guide is important for its inclusion of reports and accounts of Jackson 's military exploits.

Moser, Harold D., Editor, *The Papers of Andrew Jackson*, 2 Volumes. Knoxville, Tennessee: University of Tennessee, 1984. The guide improves upon Bassett's work with numerous, detailed footnotes.

The archives holds microfilm copies of many of the original Jackson papers, including a number of diaries, correspondence, and other personal records related to the War of 1812 and the First Creek War. Among the more important collections is the John Coffee Papers, in the Dyas Collection. Two helpful published guides include:

Armstrong, Zella, *Tennessee Soldiers in the War of 1812: Regiments of Col. Allcorn and Col. Allison.* Chattanooga, Tennessee: Tennessee Society U. S. Daughters of 1812, 1947.

McCown, Mary Hardin, and Inez E. Burns, *Soldiers of the War of 1812 Buried in Tennessee.* Johnson City, Tennessee: Tennessee Society U. S. Daughters of the War of 1812, Johnson City, Tennessee: Overmountain Press, 1959, Reprinted 1977.

The archives holds the original records of the state Adjutant General. The microfilm, titled *Officers and Soldiers, War of 1812, Tennessee*, is arranged alphabetically by surname and lists the soldier's rank, enlistment date, regiment, company, branch of service, and discharge date. The archives website has four important guides to military research of the War of 1812. The first is titled *Answering the Call: Tennesseans in the War of 1812*, an online exhibit showing the political and military actions of Tennesseans in the War of 1812. The second is a *Brief History of Tennessee in the War of 1812*, including a timeline of the significant battles and skirmishes. The third is *Materials Pertaining to the War of 1812 at the Tennessee State Library and Archives,* and the last is *Regimental Histories of Tennessee Units During the War of 1812*, listing the official unit designation, dates the unit was active, names of regimental officers, and the primary counties of residence from which the men served.

The archives houses the original militia muster rolls for the various Indian wars and removal, from 1818 to 1837. Microfilmed copies of the records include:

Index, Tennesseans in the Seminole War (Florida War), 1818 and 1836. The index includes the soldier's rank, date and place of enlistment, company, regiment, brigade, and place of residence.

Military Records, 1812-1836. The records include muster rolls and payrolls from the First Creek War and the First and Second Seminole Wars, arranged by the name of the captain.

Officers of the Cherokee War, 1836-1846, Muster Rolls and Index to Tennesseans, Cherokee Removal, 1836. The index lists the soldier's name, enlistment, rank, company, regiment, and brigade.

An old-fashioned index card file at the archives covers most of the aforementioned records.

Virginia

Library of Virginia
800 East Broad Street
Richmond, Virginia 23219

(804) 692-3500

http://www.lva.virginia.gov/

Virginia organized its colonial militia to defend itself against Indian attacks early in the 17th century. Military service records for soldiers in the colonial wars from 1622 to 1763 generally consist of muster rolls, payrolls, and others lists of soldiers, usually only providing the name of the militia unit, name of the soldier, rank, and date of the list. Most of the records have been published and are widely available. Five helpful guides to the records include:

> Bockstruck, Lloyd Dewitt, *Virginia's Colonial Soldiers.* Baltimore, Maryland: Genealogical Publishing Company, 1988, Reprinted 1998.

> Clark, Murtie June, *Colonial Soldiers of the South., 1732–1774.* Baltimore, Maryland: Genealogical Publishing Company, 1983, Reprinted 1999.

> Crozier, William A., *Virginia Colonial Militia, 1651–1776.* Baltimore, Maryland: Genealogical Publishing Company, 1905, Reprinted 2000.

> Eckenrode, Hamilton J., *List of the Colonial Soldiers of Virginia.* Baltimore, Maryland: Genealogical Publishing Company, 1917, Reprinted 2000.

> *Virginia Military Records: From the Virginia Magazine of History and Biography, the William and Mary Quarterly, and Tyler's Quarterly.* Baltimore, Maryland: Genealogical Publishing Company, 1983, Reprinted 2000.

During the Revolutionary War, Virginia troops fought across the continent from the Atlantic Ocean to the Mississippi River. Unfortunately, no single comprehensive or complete list of Revolutionary War veterans exists. However, several indexes have been compiled, including a card index at the National Archives that is not on microfilm. The indexes cite records held by the National Archives and the Library of Virginia. The cited records in the following publications mostly include muster rolls, payrolls, and bounty-land and pension records:

> Brumbaugh, Gaius Marcus, *Revolutionary War Records, Volume 1, Virginia.* Baltimore, Maryland: Genealogical Publishing Company, 1936, Reprinted 1995.

> Burgess, Louis A., *Virginia Soldiers of 1776.* Baltimore, Maryland: Genealogical Publishing Company, 1927-1929, Reprinted 1994.

> Eckenrode, Hamilton J., *Virginia Soldiers in the American Revolution.* Richmond, Virginia: Virginia State Library and Archives, 1989.

Gwathmey, John Hastings, *Historical Register of Virginians in the Revolution: Soldiers, Sailors, Marines, 1775 1783.* Richmond, Virginia.: Dietz Press, 1938.

Additional useful guides to Revolutionary War service include:

Harding, Margery, *George Rogers Clark and His Men, Military Records, 1778-1784.* Frankfort, Kentucky: Kentucky Historical Society, 1981.

McAllister, J. T., *Virginia Militia in the Revolutionary War.* Bowie, Maryland: Heritage Books, 1989.

Sanchez-Saavedra, E. M., *A Guide to Virginia Military Organizations in the American Revolution, 1776-1783.* Richmond, Virginia: Virginia State Library, 1978.

Van Schreeven, William J., Robert J. Scribner, and J. Brent Tarter, *Revolutionary Virginia and the Road to Revolution, 1763-1776.* Charlottesville, Virginia: University Press of Virginia, 1973-1983.

The library also holds a collection of the George Rogers Clark papers in its manuscript collection. The collection consists of the following materials:

Muster roll, November 1777, of Captain William Croghan's (1744-1822) company of the 8th Virginia Regiment commanded by Colonel John Bowman (1738-1784).

Articles of capitulation, 24 February 1779, of Fort Sackville at Vincennes (Indiana) by Henry Hamilton (d. 1796) to Clark.

Notice, 10 April 1779, by Clark permitting the Reverend Ichabod Camp (1726-1786) to occupy vacant land.

Bill of exchange, 25 June 1779, from William Shannon at Fort Clark (Illinois) to Fraincois Millehome.

Letter, 13 November 1782, from Clark to an unknown recipient discussing a battle with the Shawnee Indians in Ohio.

Survey, May 1785, for 1500 acres in Kentucky for Clark by William Roberts.

Bond, 5 May 1784, of Clark as principal surveyor for the Virginia State Line.

Bill of exchange, 21 April 1786, from Clark to Maurice Nagle.

Letter, 25 August 1786, from Richard Clough Anderson (1750-1826) of Louisville, Kentucky, to Edward Carrington (1748-1810), a Virginia representative to the Continental Congress concerning land distribution in

Kentucky and in particular, a land warrant of General Friedrich von Steuben (1730-1794).

Land grant, 5 December 1788, for 12,000 acres in Fayette County, Kentucky, from Governor Beverley Randolph (1754-1797) to John Crittenden (1750-1806).

Bill of exchange, 17 November 1808, from Clark.

Account, 30 May 1810, of Clark with Richard Ferguson of Louisville.

Virginia offered bounty-land to its veterans who served at least three years in the Continental Line, State Line, or State Navy, died while in service, or enlisted for the duration of the war. Direct heirs of deceased veterans also were entitled to apply. Prior to 1792, the bounty-land was located in Kentucky. After Kentucky became a state in 1792, warrants were issued for land in the Virginia Military District of Ohio. The bounty-land records are in Military Land Certificates, 1782-1876, available on microfilm. Records of the land surveys and grants are housed at the Kentucky Land Office Division and the Ohio Historical Society. Six essential guides to the bounty-land warrant records include:

> Bockstruck, Lloyd DeWitt, *Revolutionary War Bounty-land Grants Awarded by State Governments.* Baltimore, Maryland: Genealogical Publishing Company, 1996, Reprinted 1998.

> Brown, Margie G., *Genealogical Abstracts, Revolutionary War Veterans, Scrip Act of 1851.* Lovettsville, Virginia: Willow Bend Books, 1990, Reprinted 1997.

> Hopkins, William L., *Virginia Revolutionary War Land Grant Claims, 1783-1850 (Rejected).* Athens, Georgia: New Papyrus, 1988, Reprinted 2005.

> Jillson, Willard Rouse, *The Kentucky Land Grants: A Systematic Index to All of the Land Grants Recorded in the State Land Office at Frankfort, Kentucky, 1782–1924.* Baltimore, Maryland: Genealogical Publishing Company, 1925, Reprinted 1994.

> Smith, Clifford Neal, *Federal Land Series.* Five Volumes, Baltimore, Maryland: Clearfield Company, 1972-1982, Reprinted 2007.

> Wilson, Samuel M., *Virginia Land Bounty Warrants.* Baltimore, Maryland: Southern Book Company, 1953.

From the start of the Revolution, Virginia offered pensions to disabled veterans and widows of soldiers who died in service. The pension files contain proof of service, description of the disability, affidavits of disability from the county court, and pension payment and receipt records. The pension records are part of RG 48, Records of the Executive Branch, Auditor of Public Accounts, and are described in detail in Entry 230 of John S. Salmon and J. Christian Kolbe's *Auditor of Public Accounts Inventory.* The pension files, a few of which are for service in the

French and Indian War, are on microfilm. Abstracts of the pension files also have been published in:

> McGhee, Lucy Kate Walker, *Virginia Pension Abstracts of the Wars of the Revolution, 1812, and Indian Wars*. Washington, D.C.: L. K. McGhee, 1958-1966.

> Virginia Genealogical Society, *Virginia Revolutionary War Pensions*. Easley, South Carolina: Southern Historical Press, 1980, Reprinted 1982.

During the Revolution, the General Assembly authorized commissioners in each county to impress goods and services needed for the war. The library holds microfilm copies of the certificates receipting the impressed items that were issued to prove requests for reimbursement. In 1782, the legislature required that all claims be adjudicated by the county courts. The adjudicated claims are in booklets and lists survive for nearly all counties and are available on microfilm. The entries usually include the name of the claimant, description of goods or services provided, and the value of the claim. Janice L. Abercrombie and Richard L. Slatten transcribed the booklets and lists in *Virginia Revolutionary Public Claims* (Athens: Iberian Publishing Company, 1992). The Commissioner's Books also are on microfilm. The library has a card file of the claims.

The library holds other records relating to the Revolution, including a searchable database with images of the original Letters Received by the Governor, 1776-1784, Journals of the Council of State, and other records of miscellaneous officials charged with managing the war effort and supplying the army. The library holds numerous personal papers, military records, and published works concerning Virginia and Virginians during the war, all listed on the online catalog. Helpful reference works include:

> Boatner, Mark M., *Encyclopedia of the American Revolution*. Mechanicsburg, Pennsylvania: Stackpole Books, 1994.

> Shelby, John E., *The Revolution in Virginia, 1775–1783*. Williamsburg, Virginia: Colonial Williamsburg Foundation, 1988.

> Weisinger, Minor T., *Using Virginia Revolutionary War Records*. Richmond, Virginia: Library of Virginia, 1999.

The library has six searchable databases, available online, related to Revolutionary War service:

> Revolutionary War Bounty Warrants

> Revolutionary War Land Office Military Certificates

> Revolutionary War Public Service Claims

> Revolutionary War Records, Using Virginia

> Revolutionary War Rejected Claims

> Revolutionary War Virginia State Pensions

Another very helpful published guide is Lewis Preston Summers' *Annals of Southwest Virginia, 1769-1800* (Greenville, South Carolina: Southern Historical Press, 1929, Reprinted 1992). In addition to transcribed county records, the book includes a list of veterans of the Revolution; numerous company muster rolls for the French and Indian War, Lord Dunmore's War, Second Cherokee War, and Revolutionary War; lists of soldiers stationed at numerous frontier forts; and, French and Indian War land grants issued by proclamation of the British Crown in 1763.

For service in the War of 1812, see the guide *Soldiers of the War of 1812* (Research Notes Number 19) available on the library webpage. Another useful guide is Stuart Lee Butler's *A Guide to Virginia Militia Units in the War of 1812* (Athens, Georgia: Iberian Publishing Company, 1988).

Two printed volumes of militia muster rolls and payrolls are:

> *Pay Rolls of the Militia Entitled to Land Bounty under the Act of Congress of Sept. 28, 1850* (published 1851)
>
> *Muster Rolls of the Virginia Militia in the War of 1812, Being a Supplement of the Pay Rolls* (published 1852).

Both are also on microfilm and have been published with an index in *Virginia Militia in the War of 1812: From Rolls in the Auditor's Office at Richmond.* (Baltimore, Maryland: Genealogical Publishing Company, 2001).

The most important materials concerning the War of 1812 are the records of the Auditor of Public Accounts. A detailed description of the records is in John S. Salmon and J. Christian Kolbe's *Auditor of Public Accounts Inventory.* Selected entries from the record series include:

> Entry 247, General Militia Records, 1811–1821, muster rolls, payrolls, claims for reimbursement for services and supplies, and payment accounts. The unindexed records are arranged by militia unit and support service.
>
> Entry 248, Account and Receipt Books, 1811–1816, accounts for goods and services, including horses and wagons impressed into service.
>
> Entry 250, List of Certificates Issued for Militia and War of 1812 Expenses, 1807–1808, 1812–1817, list with names, dates, and dollar amounts, arranged alphabetically.
>
> Entry 253, Muster Rolls and Payrolls, 1812–1815, 27 unindexed volumes of lists of militia companies.
>
> Entry 256, Quartermaster's Account Book, 1815, list of payments for claims of goods and services rendered, arranged chronologically.
>
> Entry 257, Register of Claims, 1813–1814, alphabetical list of claimants, with descriptions of goods and services rendered, and amounts claimed.
>
> Entry 258, Register of Furloughs, 1814, one volume of furloughs, giving regiment number, name of soldier, county of residence, and date, length,

and reason for furlough. A second list of discharges gives name of soldier, rank, regiment, county of residence, and date and reason for discharge.

The library also holds other pertinent records, including:

Register of Applications for Appointments in the Force to be Raised for the Defense of the Commonwealth, ca. 1812 (War 13, miscellaneous reel 985), list of applicants, their regiment, county, appointment solicited, and by whom recommended, arranged by the artillery, cavalry, infantry, surgical department, and rifle corps.

Bernard Peyton. Order Book, 20th Regiment, U. S. Infantry, 1812–1814 (Accession 27776), clothing accounts and enlistments. The clothing accounts include the original signature or marks of the soldiers receiving clothing. The enlistments include place of birth, age, height, complexion, hair and eye color, and occupation.

List of Depositions Relating to Slaves and Other Property Plundered by the Enemy During the Late War, 1812 (Accession 36873), list of claimants, county of residence, number of slaves or other property lost, and value or amount claimed.

Claims of Virginia Against the U. S. for War of 1812 Debts (Office of the Second Auditor, entry 17), correspondence, receipts, accounts, and other records relating to Virginia's costs in supporting the war effort.

West Virginia

West Virginia Archives and History
The Culture Center
Capitol Complex
1900 Kanawha Boulevard East
Charleston West Virginia 25305

(304) 558-0220

Because West Virginia was part of Virginia prior to its becoming a state in 1863, the colonial and state records pertinent to the Indian wars fought on its territory are held by the Virginia State Library in Richmond. The West Virginia Archives holds local county records, or microfilmed copies, prior to 1863. The following publications include bibliographies, research guides, and state histories that cover the pertinent Indian wars:

De Hass, Wills, *History of the Early Settlement and Indian Wars of Western Virginia.* Wheeling, West Virginia: H. Hoblitzell, 1851.

Forbes, Harold M., *West Virginia History: A Bibliography and Guide to Research.* Morgantown, West Virginia: West Virginia University Press, 1981.

Hale, John P., *History of the Great Kanawha Valley.* Gauley Bridge, West Virginia: Gauley & New River Publishing Company, 1891, Reprinted 1994.

Hughes, Josiah, *Pioneer West Virginia.* Charleston, West Virginia: Josiah Hughes, 1932.

Johnston, Ross B., *West Virginians in the American Revolution.* Baltimore, Maryland: Genealogical Publishing Company, 1939, Reprinted 2005.

Lewis, Virgil A., *Soldiery of West Virginia in the French and Indian Wars, Lord Dunmore's War, the Revolution, the Later Indian Wars.* (3rd Biennial Report of Department of Archives and History, 1911.)   Baltimore, Maryland: Genealogical Publishing Company, Reprinted 1967.

McGinnis, Carol, *West Virginia Genealogy: Sources & Resources.* Baltimore, Maryland: Genealogical Publishing Company, 1988.

McWhorter, Lucullus Virgil, *The Border Settlers of Northwestern Virginia, From 1768 to 1795, Embracing the Life of Jesse Hughes, and Other Noted Scouts of the Great Woods of the Trans-Allegheny.* Hamilton, Ohio: The Republican Publishing Company, 1915.

North, E. Lee, *Redcoats, Redskins, and Red-Eyed Monsters.* Cranbury, New Jersey: A. S. Barnes and Company, Inc., 1979.

Stinson, Helen S., *A Handbook for Genealogical Research in West Virginia*. South Charleston, West Virginia: Kanawha Valley Genealogical Socity, 1981.

Withers, Alexander Scott, *Chronicles of Border Warfare, or A History of the Settlement by the Whites, of North-Western Virginia, and of the Indian Wars and Massacres in that Section of the State*. Baltimore, Maryland: Clearfield Company, 1895, Reprinted 2007.

Native American Tribes and Archives

Alabama

Echota Cherokee Tribe of Alabama
630 County Rd 1281
P. O. Box 768
Falkville, Al 35622

(256) 734-7337

www.echotacherokeetribe.homestead.com

Recognized by the state, the tribe claims to be descended from remnant Cherokee people who remained in northeastern Alabama when the others were removed to the Indian Territory.

Cherokee Tribe of Northeast Alabama
P. O. Box 66
Grant, Alabama 35747

(256) 426-6344

www.cherokeetribeofnortheastalabama.com

Recognized by the state, the tribe claims to be descended from remnant Cherokee people who remained in northeastern Alabama when the others were removed to the Indian Territory. The tribe has applied for federal recognition.

MOWA Band of Choctaw Indians
1080 West Red Fox Road
Mount Vernon, Alabama 36560

(251) 829-5500

http://www.mowa-choctaw.com/

The MOWA band of Choctaw Indians occupies an area in south Washington County and north Mobile County near the southwest Alabama towns of Citronelle, Mount Vernon, and McIntosh. The band takes their name from the first two letters of Mobile and Washington counties, where members settled, straddling the county line. The group is recognized by the state. The band settled the area in two phases. The first phase consisted of a group of Choctaw, who fought with the Red Sticks during the First Creek War and fled there for safety. The second phase came in the 1830s, when some south Alabama Choctaws avoided forced removal to the Indian Territory.

Piqua Shawnee Tribe
3412 Wellford Circle
Birmingham, Alabama 35226

piquashawnee@gmail.com

www.piquashawnee.com

Recognized by the state, the tribe claims to be descended from remnant Shawnee people who remained in Alabama when the others were removed to the Indian Territory.

United Cherokee Ani-Yun-Wiya Nation
1531 Blount Avenue
P. O. Box 754
Guntersville, Alabama 35976

(256) 582-2333

ucanonline@bellsouth.net

www.ucan-online.org

Recognized by the state, the tribe claims to be descended from remnant Cherokee people who remained in Alabama when the others were removed to the Indian Territory.

Poarch Band of Creek Indians
5811 Jack Springs Road
Atmore, Alabama 36502

(251) 368-9136

http://pci-nsn.gov/westminster/index.html

The only federally recognized tribe in Alabama, this band consists of descendants from several friendly Creek families who were allowed to stay because of their service to the federal government.

Ma-Chis Lower Creek Indian Tribe of Alabama
202 North Main Street
Kinston, Alabama 36453

(334) 565-3207

machis@centurytel.net www.machistribe.net

State-recognized, the tribe claims to be descended from remnant Creek people who remained in Alabama when the others were removed to the Indian Territory.

Southeastern Mvskoke Nation
P. O. Box 296
Midland City, Alabama 36350

(334) 983-3723

Recognized by the state, the tribe claims to be descended from remnant Creek people who remained in Alabama when the others were removed to the Indian Territory.

Cher-O-Creek Intra Tribal Indians
PO Box 717
Dothan, Alabama 36302

(334) 596-4866

Also recognized by the state, this tribe claims to be descended from remnant Creek people who remained in Alabama when the others were removed to the Indian Territory.

Florida

The Seminole Tribe of Florida
6300 Stirling Road
Hollywood, Florida 33024

(800) 683-7800

http://www.semtribe.com/History/

The Seminole Tribe of Florida are federally recognized and consist of descendants of about 300 Seminole who never surrendered and eluded capture during the Seminole Wars.

Miccosukee Tribe of Indians of Florida
Miccosukee Indian Village and Museum
Mile Marker 35
U. S. Highway 41
Tamiami Trail, Miami, Florida 33194

(305) 552-8365

http://www.miccosukee.com/

The federally recognized tribe consists of descendants of about 100 Mikasuki-speaking Creeks who never surrendered and eluded capture during the Seminole Wars.

Georgia

Cherokee of Georgia Tribal Council
110 Cherokee Way
St. George, Georgia 31562

(912) 843-2230

https://www.cherokeeofgeorgia.org/home.html

Recognized by the state, these Cherokee claim to be descended from scattered remnants who remained in Georgia when the others were removed to the Indian Territory.

Georgia Tribe of Eastern Cherokees
P. O. Box 1915
Cumming, Georgia 30028

info@georgiatribeofeasterncherokee.com

http://www.georgiatribeofeasterncherokee.com/

The state-recognized tribe consists primarily of descendants of mixed-blood families who were not removed.

Lower Musckogee Creek Tribe
106 Tall Pine Drive
Whigham Georgia 39897

http://lowermuskogeetribe.com/home.html

The state-recognized tribe maintains the Tama Tribal Town on a small reservation in Whigham, Georgia.

Louisiana

Adai Caddo Indian Nation
Adai Indian Nation Cultural Center
4460 Highway 485
Robeline, Louisiana 71469

(877) 472-1007

http://www.natchitoches.net/attractions/adai-indian-nation-cultural-center/

In 1700, Adai villages extended from the Red River southward beyond the Sabine River, into Texas. The trail connecting the Adai villages became the noted Contraband Trail, between the French and Spanish provinces. The state recognized tribe maintains the cultural center.

Chitimacha Tribe of Louisiana
P. O. Box 661
155 Chitimacha Loop
Charenton, Louisiana 70523

(337) 923-4973

info@chitimacha.gov

http://www.chitimacha.gov/

The tribe is recognized by the federal government and is the only tribe in Louisiana still occupying a portion of their ancestral lands.

Coushatta Tribe of Louisiana
P. O. Box 10
Elton, Louisiana 70532

(337) 584 1560

http://koasatiheritage.org/

The tribe, located in Allen and Jefferson Davis Parishes, is one of four federally recognized tribes of Koasati people. Formerly allied with the Creek, and closely associated with the Alabama tribe, the Coushatta migrated across the Mississippi River after 1763.

Jena Band of Choctaw Indians
1052 Chanaha Hina Street
Trout, Louisiana 71371

http://jenachoctaw.org/

The band, in Catahoula, Grant, and La Salle Parishes, is one of three Choctaw groups recognized by the federal government. The band migrated to Louisiana after the Treaty of Dancing Rabbit Creek, rather than stay in Mississippi or be removed to the Indian Territory.

Four Winds Tribe, Louisiana Cherokee
P. O. Box 127
DeRidder, Louisiana 70634

fourwindscherokee@fourwindscherokee.com

http://www.fourwindscherokee.com/
This Louisiana-recognized tribe is an amalgamation of the Atakapa, who were living in the ungoverned area between French Louisiana and Spanish Texas, and small groups of Cherokee, Choctaw, and Creek families who joined them during Indian removal in the 1830s.

Mississippi

Mississippi Band of Choctaw Indians
101 Industrial Road
Choctaw, Mississippi 39350

(601) 656-5251

http://www.choctaw.org/

The federally-recognized band is composed of descendants of Mississippi Choctaw who refused to remove to the Indian Territory. The band maintains a museum and archives on its reservation.

North Carolina

Eastern Band of Cherokee Indians
88 Council House Loop
P. O. Box 455
Cherokee, North Carolina 28719

(828) 497-7000

https://ebci.com/

The Enrollment Office provides a Cherokee genealogy research service for searching records prior to the 1924 Baker Roll. These records date back to 1835 and enumerate the members of the Eastern Band of Cherokee Indians within the limits of North Carolina, Tennessee, Georgia, and Alabama. The service does not provide aid in determining eligibility for enrollment with the Eastern Band of Cherokee Indians. The tribe is recognized by the federal government.

Occaneechi Band of the Saponi Nation
P. O. Box 356
Mebane, North Carolina 27302

Tribal Grounds and Office
4902 Dailey Store Road
Burlington, North Carolina 27217

(336) 421-1317

obsntribe@gmail.com

http://obsn.org/

A state-recognized tribe, its members are descendants of the Saponi-related people who joined together after the Treaties of Middle Plantation in 1677 and 1680. They were closely allied with the Catawba confederation.

Cherokee Historical Association
564 Tsali Boulevard
Cherokee, North Carolina 28719

(828) 497-2111

http://www.cherokeehistorical.org/

The nonprofit organization operates two cultural attractions, the Oconaluftee Indian Village and the outdoor drama *Unto These Hills*. The Oconaluftee Indian Village is a living, working Cherokee village of the 18th century, demonstrating ancient techniques for survival passed down from generation to generation. *Unto These Hills* is an outdoor drama, highlighting Cherokee history from the first contact with Europeans to the infamous and tragic Trail of Tears.

Coharie Tribal Council
Coharie Tribal Center
7531 North U. S. Highway 421
Clinton, North Carolina 28328

910-564-6909

http://www.coharietribe.org/

This state-recognized tribe is composed of descendants of the Neusiok and Coree people of central North Carolina.

Haliwa-Saponi Indian Tribe
P. O. Box 99
Hollister, North Carolina 27844

(252) 586-4017

info@haliwa-saponi.com

http://haliwa-saponi.com/

The state-recognized tribe is composed of descendants of the Tuscarora, Nansemond & Saponi.

Lumbee Tribe of North Carolina
6984 State Highway 711 West
P. O. Box 2709
Pembroke, North Carolina 28372

(910) 521-7861 or (855) 801-9738

http://www.lumbeetribe.com/

The ancestors of this state-recognized tribe mostly are Cheraw and related Siouan-speaking natives.

Meherrin-Chowanoke Nation
P. O. Box S
Winton, North Carolina 27986

(252) 301-6081

MeherrinChowanokeServices@gmail.com

http://meherrin-chowanoke.com/

The state-recognized tribe claims descent from the Chowanoke, who resided on the reservation established in Gates County in 1677.

Waccamaw-Siouan Tribe
P. O. Box 69
7239 Old Lake Road
Bolton, North Carolina 28423

(910) 655-8778

http://waccamaw-siouan.com/index.html

The state-recognized tribe is composed of descendants of the Waccamaw people who lived in villages along the Waccamaw and Pee Dee rivers in North Carolina.

Oklahoma

Cherokee Nation
W.W. Keeler Tribal Complex
17675 South Muskogee Avenue
Tahlequah, Oklahoma 74464

(918) 453-5000 and (800) 256-0671

http://www.cherokee.org/Home.aspx

Members of this federally-recognized tribe are descendants of the Cherokee who were removed to the Indian Territory.

Cherokee Heritage Center
21192 South Keeler Drive
Park Hill, Oklahoma 74451

(918) 456-6007 and (888) 999-6007

http://www.cherokeeheritage.org/

The Cherokee Heritage Center Archives maintains valuable records of the Cherokee people and makes them available free to the public. The archives holds mainly text-based, primary source records, including collections of government and private documents, photographs, posters, maps, architectural drawings, books, papers, and articles focusing on Cherokee history and culture. Access to the archives is by appointment with the archivist.

United Keetoowah Band of Cherokee Indians in Oklahoma
P. O. Box 746
Tahlequah, Oklahoma 74465

(918) 431-1818

http://www.keetoowahcherokee.org/

Members of the federally-recognized band are composed primarily of descendants of the Cherokee who settled in present-day Arkansas and Oklahoma circa 1817. They were well established before most of the Cherokee were removed from the Southeast to the Indian Territory. The band maintains the John Hair Cultural Center and Museum.

Chickasaw Cultural Center
867 Cooper Memorial Drive
Sulphur, Oklahoma 73086

(580) 622-7130

www.chickasawculturalcenter.com

The center houses the Holisso Research Center, a clearinghouse for the study and research of Chickasaw and other southeastern tribes and houses genealogy and photographic archives. The archives holds the Dawes rolls, muster rolls, annuity rolls, federal census records, historical records, cemetery records, government records, and family files.

Chickasaw Tribal Library
1003 Chamber Loop
Ada, Oklahoma 74820

(580) 310-6477

https://chickasaw.net/Our-Nation/Heritage/Museums/Tribal-Library.aspx

For research, the library has both a genealogist and a cultural research specialist on staff for those wishing to research the Dawes Rolls or general Chickasaw history and culture. Research requests are open to both internal and external entities. The library is home to the Chickasaw Historical Society and currently has both old and new volumes of *The Journal of Chickasaw History and Culture* available for purchase.

Choctaw Nation of Oklahoma
529 North 16th Street
Durant, Oklahoma 74701

(800) 522-6170

https://www.choctawnation.com/homepage

The federally-recognized nation is the government for the tribe, whose members were removed to the Indian Territory in the 1830s. The Old Capitol Museum is located at Tvshka Homma and features exhibits on the history, culture, and family life of the tribe,

Muscogee (Creek) Nation
Highway 75 & Loop 56
Okmulgee, Oklahoma 74447

(800) 482-1979 and (918) 732-7600

http://www.mcn-nsn.gov/

The nation is federally recognized as the government for the descendants of the Creek families relocated to the Indian Territory in the 1830s.

Seminole Nation of Oklahoma
Tribal Complex
630 North Main Street
Seminole, Oklahoma 74868

(405) 382-2743

http://sno-nsn.gov/

The Seminole Nation Museum is located at Wewoka and features exhibits on Seminole culture and history. An adjoining gallery and craft shop features contemporary and traditional Seminole crafts.

South Carolina

Beaver Creek Indians of Orangeburg County, South Carolina
230 Pine Street NW
P. O. Box 699
Salley, South Carolina 29137

(803) 356-4807

http://beavercreekindians.org/index.html

The state-recognized tribe is composed of members who descend from several small mixed-blood bands who settled along the north and south branches of the Edisto River in the Big and Little Beaver Creek area.

Catawba Indian Nation
996 Avenue of the Nations
Rock Hill, South Carolina 29730

(803) 366-4792

info@catawbaindian.net

http://catawbaindian.net/

The Catawba are the only tribe in South Carolina recognized by the federal government. The tribe maintains a cultural center with exhibits featuring the history of the tribe.

Pee Dee Nation of Upper South Carolina
3814 Highway 57 North
Little Rock, South Carolina 29567

(843) 586-9675

staff@peedeenation.org

http://www.peedeenation.org/

Members of this state-recognized tribe descend from the natives who lived along the Pee Dee River and were allies of the settlers in the Tuscarora and Yamasee Wars. The tribal archives include school records, census data, military records, tribal artifacts, photographs, maps, personal letters, church records, birth & death certificates, marriage licenses, as well as an extensive collection of official government documentation dating from the present-day all the way back to the 16th Century.

Sumter Tribe of the Cheraw

http://www.thesumtertribeofcherawindians.org/home.html

Members of the state-recognized tribe descend from seven interrelated families dating from the late 18th century in the area near Sumter, South Carolina.

Pee Dee Indian Tribe of South Carolina
P. O. Box 157
McColl, South Carolina 29570

134 Longer Sand Lane
Bennettsville, South Carolina 29512

http://www.thepeedeeindiantribeofsc.com/

Members of the state-recognized tribe descend from the natives who lived along the Pee Dee River and were allies of the settlers in the Tuscarora and Yamasee Wars.

Santee Indian Nation of South Carolina
208 Foster Mill Circle
Pauline, South Carolina 29374

http://santeebeadman.tripod.com/

Recognized by the state, this historically small tribe was centered around the Santee River, near the modern city of Santee.

Wassamasaw Tribe of Varnertown Indians
P. O. Box 428
Summerville, South Carolina 29484

wassamasaw@hotmail.com

(843) 900-1789

http://s651079524.initial-website.com/

The Wassamassaw descend from remnants of the Catawba, Edisto, and Cherokee, as well as European and African American ancestors, who settled around the Wassamassaw Swamp near Varnertown. South Carolina recognizes the tribe.

The Waccamaw Indian People
591 Bluewater Road
Aynor, South Carolina 29511

(843) 358-6877

https://www.waccamaw.org/

The Waccamaw are descendants of a group of people who lived and farmed in the area of South Carolina now known as Dog Bluff, in Horry County.

Chaloklowa Chickasaw Indian People
501 Tanners Lane
Florence, South Carolina 29554

(843) 380-1481

https://www.facebook.com/pages/Chaloklowa-Chickasaw-Indian-People/489744807842890

The state recognized the Chaloklowa, who claim descent from a group of 50 Chickasaw who moved into South Carolina at the state's request in the 18th century.

Eastern Cherokee, Southern Iroquois & United Tribes of South Carolina
Tribal Enrollment Office
P. O. Box 7062
Columbia South Carolina 29202

(803) 699-0446

http://www.cherokeeofsouthcarolina.com/index.html

The state-recognized organization is composed of an amalgamation of remnants of many different tribes. The ancestors of the Cherokee in the organization mostly are from the Lower Towns.

Virginia

Cheroenhaka (Nottoway) Indian Tribe
P. O. Box 397
Courtland, Virginia 23837

https://www.facebook.com/CheroenhakaNottowayIndianTribe

These state-recognized tribe members are descendants of the Cheroenhaka who lived in the coastal plain of southeastern Virginia.

Chickahominy Tribe
8200 Lott Cary Road
Providence Forge, Virginia 23140

http://chickahominytribe.org/default.html

The state-recognized tribe originally lived in permanent villages along the Chickahominy River. In 1646, a treaty set aside land for them in the Pamunkey Neck. Eventually, continued white encroachment pushed them to the Chickahominey Ridge, between Richmond and Williamsburg.

Eastern Chickahominy Tribe
2895 Mount Pleasant Road
Providence Forge, Virginia 23140

(804) 966-2719

https://www.facebook.com/pg/Chickahominy-Indians-Eastern-Division-146928818713696/about/?ref=page_internal

These Native Americans originally lived in permanent villages along the Chickahominy River. In 1646, a treaty set aside land for them in the Pamunkey Neck. Some of them later migrated to New Kent County, where they continue to live today. Virginia has given them official status.

Mattaponi Indian Reservation
1314 Mattaponi Reservation Circle
West Point, Virginia 23181

mattaponi@mattaponination.com

https://www.mattaponination.com/home.html

Formerly one of the principal tribes of the Powhatan Confederation, this tribe has continued to respect the terms of the 1646 treaty, each year presenting a tribute to the Virginia Governor. In 1658, the state created a reservation for the tribe on the Mattaponi River. The state-recognized tribe maintains a museum featuring their tribal history.

Monacan Indian Nation
P. O. Box 1136
Madison Heights, Virginia 24572

(434) 946-0389

http://www.monacannation.com/

The state-recognized tribe descend from remnants of the original people who lived between the Roanoke and Potomac rivers, in the piedmont region, from the fall line to the Blue Ridge Mountains.

Nansemond Indian Tribal Association
1001 Pembroke Lane
Suffolk, Virginia 23434

http://www.nansemond.org/

This tribe, now recognized by the state, originally lived along the Nansemond River and was part of the Powhatan Confederation.

Nottoway Indian Tribe of Virginia
P. O Box 246
Capron, Virginia 23829

http://nottowayindians.org/home.html

The tribe is recognized by the state and originally lived in the Piedmont region of Virginia. The tribe generally were friendly to the early settlers. After Bacon's Rebellion, they signed the Treaty of Middle Plantation in 1677.

Patawomeck Indian Tribe of Virginia
1416 Brent Street
Fredericksburg, Virginia 22401

(540) 371-4437

http://www.patawomeckindiantribeofvirginia.org/

The state-recognized tribe is comprised of descendants of the few survivors of the 1666 massacre.

Pamunkey Indian Tribe and Reservation
191 Lay Landing Road
Pamunkey Indian Reservation
King William, Virginia 23086

(804) 843-4792

http://www.pamunkey.net/home.html

The Pamunkey were originally part of the Powhatan Confederation. After Bacon's Rebellion, the tribe signed the Treaty of Middle Plantation in 1677. Today, their descendants are a tribe recognized by the state. The tribe maintain a museum and cultural center on their reservation.

Rappahannock Indian Tribe
5036 Indian Neck Road
Saint Stephens Church, Virginia 23148

(804) 769-0260

https://www.facebook.com/rappahannocktribe

Present-day members of the state-recognized tribe are descendants of the allied Rappahannock, Morattico, Portobacco, and Doeg tribes, who merged in the late 17th century.

Sappony
Sappony Tribal Center
4218 Virgilina Road
Virgilina, Virginia 24598

(434) 585-3352

sappony@msn.com

http://www.sappony.org/index.htm

The Sappony, or Saponi, Tribe originated in the Piedmont region of North Carolina and Virginia. In 1714, Virginia Governor Spotswood resettled the tribe to the area around Fort Christanna. The members of the state-recognized tribe are descendants of the people who stayed in the area.

Upper Mattaponi Indian Tribe
P. O. Box 184
King William, Virginia 23086

http://www.uppermattaponi.org/

These members of the state-recognized tribe are descendants of the Mattapony who lived in the upper reaches of the Mattapony River.

The Draper Manuscript Collection

Overview

Lyman Copeland Draper, 1815-1891, was the secretary of the State Historical Society of Wisconsin. Starting in the early 1830s, Draper began corresponding with and interviewing the families of the early settlers of the trans-Allegheny West, encompassing parts of Alabama, Georgia, North Carolina, South Carolina, Pennsylvania, Virginia, and West Virginia, and all of Illinois, Indiana, Kentucky, Ohio, and Tennessee. Draper intended to write and publish a series of biographies of the early settlers and chronicle the various Indian wars. He published ten volumes of research notes and one volume on the Battle of King's Mountain.

The Draper Manuscript Collection includes his correspondence, research notes, transcriptions of original records, interview notes, collected personal papers, newspaper extracts, published sources, and numerous other documents, together comprising the largest source of first-hand accounts of the settlement of the trans-Allegheny West. The State Historical Society of Wisconsin houses the original collection, but microfilm copies are widely held by many libraries with significant historical and genealogical collections.

The collection principally covers the period from the French and Indian War through the War of 1812. Significant strengths of the collection include primary sources for Lord Dunmore's War, Revolutionary War west of the Allegheny Mountains, and the Indian wars prior to circa 1820. Military and other related records are a very large part of the collection.

The Collection

Society staff organized the collection into fifty separate series of publications containing 491 volumes, all arranged by person, subject, and state. Each series is identified by a consecutive capital letter.

A, *George M. Bedinger Papers*, 1 volume

B, *Draper's Life of Boone*, 5 volumes

C, *Daniel Boone Papers*, 33 volumes

D, *Border Forays*, 5 volumes

E, *Samuel Brady and Lewis Wetzel Papers*, 16 volumes

F, *Joseph Brant Papers*, 22 volumes

G, *Brant Miscellanies*, 3 volumes

H, *Daniel Brodhead Papers*, 3 volumes

J, *George Rogers Clark Papers*, 65 volumes

K, *George Rogers Clark Miscellanies*, 6 volumes

L, *Jonathan Clark Papers*, 2 volumes

M, *William Clark Papers*, 6 volumes

N, *William Croghan Papers*, 3 volumes

O, *Daniel and Benjamin Drake Papers*, 2 volumes

P, *Draper's Biographical sketches*, 3 volumes

Q, *Draper's Historical Miscellanies*, 8 volumes

R, *Draper's Memoranda Books*, 3 volumes

S, *Draper's Notes*, 33 volumes

T, *Thomas Forsyth Papers*, 9 volumes

U, *Frontier Wars Papers*, 4 volumes

V, *Georgia, Alabama, and South Carolina Papers*, 1 volume

W, *Josiah Harmar Papers*, 2 volumes

X, *William Henry Harrison Papers*, 5 volumes

Y, *Thomas Spottswood Hinde Papers*, 41 volumes

Z, *Illinois Manuscripts*, 1 volume

AA, *William Irvine Papers*, 2 volumes

BB, *Simon Kenton Papers*, 13 volumes

CC, *Kentucky Papers*, 37 volumes

DD, *King's Mountain Papers*, 19 volumes

EE, *London Documents at Albany*, 1 volume

FF, *The Mecklenburg Declaration,* 3 volumes

GG, *Mecklenburg Declaration Papers*, 3 volumes

HH, *Mecklenburg Declaration Miscellanies*, 2 volumes

JJ, *Newspaper Extracts*, 4 volumes

KK, *North Carolina Papers*, 1 volume

LL, *Paris Documents at Albany,* 1 volume

MM, *Robert Patterson Papers*, 3 volumes

NN, *Pittsburgh and Northwest Virginia Papers*, 10 volumes

OO, *Pension Statements*, 1 volume

PP, *Potter Family Papers*, 1 volume

QQ, *William Preston Papers*, 6 volumes

RR, *Rudolph-Ney Papers*, 10 volumes

SS, *David Shepherd Papers,* 5 volumes

TT, *South Carolina Papers*, 1 volume

UU, *South Carolina in the Revolution Miscellanies*, 2 volumes

VV, *Thomas Sumter Papers*, 24 volumes

WW, *John Cleves Symmes Papers*, 4 volumes

XX, *Tennessee Papers*, 7 volumes

YY, *Tecumseh Papers*, 13 volumes

ZZ, *Virginia Papers,* 16 volumes

No overall complete name index exists for the collection. Some of the volumes include partial indexes compiled by Draper, and separate indexes have been published for eleven portions of the series, including J, U, CC, DD, QQ, SS, TT, UU, VV, XX, and ZZ. The so-called Calendar Series are not complete, every name indexes, but rather include only key names, places, and events. In addition, six of the individual series have been transcribed and published with complete indexes. Those series are:

A, *George M. Bedinger Papers*

V, *Georgia, Alabama, and South Carolina Papers*

Z, *Illinois Papers*

GG, *Mecklenburg Declaration*

NN, *Pittsburgh and Northwest Virginia Papers*

TT, *South Carolina Papers*

ZZ, *Virginia Papers* (volumes 1 through 5 only)

Josephine L. Harper's *A Guide to the Draper Manuscripts* (Madison, Wisconsin: State Historical Society of Wisconsin, 1983) is essential for research in the collection. The guide provides a list of key subjects, events, and persons mentioned in each volume, and following each series is a general index of the subjects, events, and persons. Appendix I is an index to the Revolutionary War pensioners contacted by Draper, citing the series, volume, and page number where the pensioner's papers may be found. Appendix II is an index of the persons who were interviewed, obituary subjects, authors, cartographers, and correspondents who contributed to the collection. Appendix III is a list of the maps contained in the collection. Appendix IV is a list of the microfilmed copy of the collection. The entire collection was microfilmed in 1949 and again in the 1970s. More than ninety libraries have complete sets of the microfilm, many willing to lend single reels via Interlibrary Loan.

The Historical Society published five documentary books from the collection, essentially compilations of selected documents concerning a particular aspect of the Revolutionary War era. The indexed documentaries, presenting the selected materials in chronological order, are

> *Documentary History of Dunmore's War, 1774.*
>
> *The Revolution on the Upper Ohio, 1775-1777.*
>
> *Frontier Defense on the Upper Ohio 1777-1778.*
>
> *Frontier Advance on the Upper Ohio, 1778-1779.*
>
> *Frontier Retreat on the Upper Ohio, 1779-*1781.

Other scholars have compiled documentary histories from the collection, including:

> Enoch, Harry G., *Affair at Captina Creek.* Bowie, Maryland: Heritage Books, 1999.
>
> _____, *In Search of Morgan's Station.* Bowie, Maryland: Heritage Books, 1997.
>
> _____, *The Last Indian Raid in Kentucky.* Bowie, Maryland: Heritage Books, 1997.
>
> Koontz, Louis Knott, *The Virginia Frontier, 1754-1763.* Baltimore, Maryland: Johns Hopkins Press, 1925.
>
> Lobdell, Jared C., *Further Materials on Lewis Wetzel and the Upper Ohio Frontier.* Bowie, Maryland: Heritage Books, 1994.
>
> _____, *Indian Warfare in Western Pennsylvania and Northwest Virginia at the Time of the Revolution.* Bowie, Maryland: Heritage Books, 1992.
>
> _____, *Recollections of Lewis Bonnett, Jr. (1788-1850): And the Bonnett and Wetzel Families.* Bowie, Maryland: Heritage Books, 1991.
>
> McCullough, Edward P., *The Early History of Montgomery County, Kentucky.* Westminster, Maryland: Heritage Books, 2006.

Payne, Dale, *Biographical Sketches of the Pioneers: Their Lives and Adventures*. North Kansas City, Missouri: Technical Communication Services, 2006.

_____, *Narratives of Pioneer Life and Border Warfare: Personal Recollections, Memoirs, and Reminiscences of Indian Campaigns, Captivities, and Pioneer Life on the Eastern Frontier*. Fayetteville, West Virginia: Dale Payne, 2004-2005.

Other Significant Repositories and Sources

National

Family History Library
35 North West Temple
Salt Lake City, Utah 84150

(801) 240-6996

https://familysearch.org/locations/saltlakecity-library

The largest genealogical collection in the world includes more than 2.4 million reels of microfilmed records; 727,000 microfiche; 356,000 books, serials, and other formats; 4,500 periodicals; and, 3,725 electronic resources. The library catalog is searchable online. For a small fee, microfilm may be ordered for viewing at local Family History Centers and numerous cooperating public libraries. Many of their microfilmed records have and continue to be digitized and made available online at no cost.

National Genealogical Society
3108 Columbia Pike, Suite 300
Arlington, Virginia 22204

(703) 525-0050

http://www.ngsgenealogy.org/

NGS publishes two periodicals, *The National Genealogical Society Quarterly* and *NGS Magazine*. They also publish other books of interest, including state by state research guides. Their more than 20,000 books are available through Interlibrary Loan from the St. Louis Public Library.

National Society Sons of the American Revolution Linrary
809 West Main Street
Louisville, Kentucky 40202

(502) 589-1776

NSSAR@sar.org

https://sar.org/

The SAR Genealogical Research Library collection contains over 55,000 items including family histories; local, county, and state records; and, online genealogical databases. The Mary & James S. Craik Special Collections Room also houses the miniature of Dr. James Craik by Charles

Willson Peale, the George Washington book collection, and several artifacts of importance surrounding General Washington's life and early American history.

National Society Daughters of the American Revolution Library
1776 D Street NW
Washington, DC 20006

(202) 628-1776

http://www.dar.org/library

The library collection houses more than 225,000 books, 10,000 research files, thousands of manuscript items, and special collections on Native American, American history, and genealogy. The book collection includes 40,000 family histories and genealogies, many of which are unique or available in only a few other libraries. The library is free and open to the public. The overall collection is strong in the history of the colonial era, Revolutionary War, and 19th century.

The Genealogical Records Committee Reports, more than 20,000 volumes of genealogically significant records collected by local DAR chapters, has been indexed and the index is available online. The American Indian Collection, comprising 2,000 volumes, and the Manuscript Collection are both unique to the library, whose catalog is searchable online.

Midwest Genealogy Center
3440 South Lee's Summit Road
Independence, Missouri 64055

816.252.7228

http://www.mymcpl.org/genealogy

The center is one of the preeminent resources for family history, providing access to 750,000 on-site materials. One strength of the collection is the several databases on genealogy, geography, history, newspapers, and web resources. Another strength is the numerous research guides, all available for download from the website, including a Cherokee Indian Research Road Map, Cherokee Indian Research Step by Step, Native American Research for Five Civilized Tribes, War of 1812 Military Bounty-Land and Pension Pathfinder, and Guide to Military Service & Pension Records.

Thomas Gilcrease Institute of American History and Art
1400 North Gilcrease Museum Road
Tulsa, Oklahoma 74127

918-596-2700

https://gilcrease.org/

The archival collection contains over 100,000 books, manuscripts, documents, and maps ranging from 1494 to the present. The museum also has a substantial collection of manuscripts by Cherokee principal chief John Ross and Choctaw Chief Peter Pitchlynn.

J. Erik Jonsson Central Library
Genealogy Section
1515 Young Street
Dallas, Texas 75201

(214) 670-1433

http://dallaslibrary2.org/genealogy/index.php

The collection is one of the largest genealogical collections in the United States, featuring over 115,000 print volumes, 64,000 microfilm, 89,000 microfiche, 3,000 files of family research and 700 maps/charts. While the collection has a strong emphasis on Texas, it has significant holdings of southern newspapers and a very large and significant array of American military records.

Clayton Library Center for Genealogical Research
5300 Caroline Street
Houston, Texas 77004

(832) 393-2600

http://www2.houstonlibrary.org/clayton/

The center has a research collection containing materials for all 50 states, with 100,000 books, 3000 periodicals, 70,000 reels of microfilm, a large collection of microfiche and micro-cards, and numerous electronic databases. While the collection's primary emphasis is Texas, especially Houston and surrounding area, it is strong for all the southern states. Of particular interest are its holdings of material on the southern colonies, the *Territorial Papers of the United States,* the *American State Papers*, British Colonial Office records, Louisiana colonial records, and the Natchez Trace Collection, 1759-1813. Researchers should know that numerous veterans of the War of 1812 and the various Indian wars migrated to Texas before, during, and following the Texas Revolution.

Genealogy Center
Allen County Public Library
900 Library Plaza
Fort Wayne, Indiana 46802

(260) 421-1225

http://www.genealogycenter.org/Databases/FreeDatabases.aspx

The Genealogy Center has a large collection of books, periodicals, and microfilm. Their *Native American Gateway* is an online resource for those exploring First Nations family history. Information on how to begin such research, links to materials from the National Archives and links to popular data are complemented by a continually updated listing of resources held by The Genealogy Center.

Newberry Library
60 W Walton Street
Chicago, Illinois 60610

(312) 943-9090

https://www.newberry.org/

The library has a large collection of materials on early American history, including colonial records; published state archives; historical and genealogical society papers; state, county and town histories; newspapers and periodicals; missionary accounts; travel literature; diaries, sermons and hymns; Indian captivity narratives; and, historical monographs, complemented by published editions of primary sources, such as the Early American Imprints and Early American Newspapers microfilm series. The British colonial materials include the French and Indian War, Hudson Bay Company, Indian wars, and captivities and treaties. The French colonial materials include a complete set of the Jesuit Relations in original Cramoisy editions and multiple editions of Hennepin and Champlain. The Spanish colonial materials include transcripts from the Archives of the Indes at Seville, Simancus, Madrid, Nacogdoches, and Matamoras. The Revolutionary Era materials include extensive local and family history materials, a nearly complete set of the publications of historical societies, colonial government records, as well as the Ayer and Ruggles collections.

Helpful specific guides to research at the Newberry include:

> Butler, Ruth Lapham, *Checklist of American Revolutionary War Pamphlets in the Newberry Library*. Chicago, Illinois: Newberry Library, 1922.
>
> _____, *For the Study of American Colonial History: The Newberry Library*. William and Mary Quarterly, Volume 2, 1945, pages 286-95.
>
> Johnson, Richard Colles and Cynthia H. Peters, *A Princely Gift: the Rudy Lamont Ruggles Collection of the Newberry Library ... with an Introduction by Lawrence W. Towner*. Chicago, Illinois: Newberry Library, 1986.
>
> Storm, Colton, *A Catalog of the Everett D. Graff Collection of Western Americana*. Chicago, Illinois: Published for the Newberry Library by University of Chicago Press, 1968.
>
> Storm, Colton, *The Everett D. Graff Collection in the Newberry Library*. The Newberry Library Bulletin 5, Number 6, 1960.

Alabama

Alabama Genealogical Society, Inc.
P. O. Box 293921
Samford University
800 Lakeshore Drive
Birmingham, Alabama 35229

http://www.algensoc.org/

In addition to publishing a semi-annual magazine and sponsoring seminars, the society sponsors the First Families of Alabama Certificate Program, which honors those who settled in Alabama before statehood in 1819.

Public Library of Anniston – Calhoun County
108 East 10th Street
Anniston, Alabama 36201

(256) 237-8501

http://publiclibrary.cc/

The Alabama Room Collection holds more than 11,000 printed volumes, 10,000 rolls of microfilm, numerous bound periodicals, vertical file clippings, family files, photographs, paintings, maps, manuscripts, and computer-based research materials. Significant holdings include Calhoun County newspapers from 1827, Calhoun County court records, Calhoun County cemetery records, and the Leonardo Andrea Collection (80 microfilm rolls containing research of South Carolinian professional genealogist, Leonardo Andrea). Other areas of strength include Revolutionary War Pensions and Bounty-land Warrants; American Indian studies; materials relating to the surrounding counties of Cleburne, Clay, Randolph, Talladega and St. Clair; and, the Alabama Virtual Library.

Special Collections & Archives
Ralph Brown Draughon Library
Auburn University
231 Mell Street
Auburn, Alabama 36849

(334) 844-1732

http://www.lib.auburn.edu/specialcollections/

The library features the Alabama Collection, Genealogy Collection, Special Collection, Thesis and Dissertation Collection, and the Treasure Collection. The library also houses the largest collection of Alabama newspapers.

Samford University Library
800 Lakeshore Drive
Birmingham, Alabama 35229

205-726-2011

https://www.samford.edu/library/

The library holds a large collection of books on Alabama history and genealogy and microfilm copies of many county records. The library features the Bledsoe-Kelly Collection, with more than 50,000 manuscript extracts and abstracts of state and local records, church and family records, and related correspondence, and the Brantley Collection, with more than 6,000 books, manuscripts, maps, photographs, and newspapers. Special Collections houses the official archives of the Alabama Baptist Church.

W. S. Hoole Special Collections Library
University of Alabama Libraries and
Williams Americana Collection
Amelia Gayle Gorgas Library
Box 870266
Tuscaloosa, Alabama 35487

(205) 348-6047

https://www.lib.ua.edu/#/home

The Alabama Collection features books on Alabama state and local history and genealogy, as well as copies of all university theses and dissertations. Special Collections also features a large collection of newspapers from Alabama and other southern states. The historical manuscript collection reflects Alabama history and genealogy.

Family and Regional History Program and Library
Wallace State Community College
801 Main Street NW
Hanceville, Alabama 35077

(256) 352-8263

http://www.wallacestate.edu/library

The Family and Regional History program is located on the fifth and sixth floors of the library building. It includes an extensive and growing research collection, concentrating on Alabama and the South. The library is a partner with the Family History Library and, thus has access to their microfilm holdings.

Linn-Henley Research Center
Birmingham Public Library
2100 Park Place
Birmingham, Alabama 35203

(205) 226-3600

The Tutwiler Collection of Southern History and Literature includes more than 56,000 printed volumes, 16,000 rolls of microfilm, and extensive newspaper and periodical collections. One area of strength is microfilm copies of Society of Colonial Wars membership application. The library holds the Birmingham Department of Archives and History, including the J. H. Scruggs, Jr. Collection, containing information on postal roads, steamboats, Creek Indian deeds, probate records, and Savannah, Georgia militia. The archives also features the Hill Ferguson Papers on the history and people of Birmingham, city and county records, and Antebellum Collection of miscellaneous manuscripts, 1820-1859, including slave receipts, diaries, land sales, newspaper clippings, correspondence, registers, and other materials.

Gadsden Public Library
254 College Street
Gadsden, Alabama 35901

(256) 549-4699

http://gadsdenlibrary.org/reference/

The Genealogy and Reference Department houses Gadsden, Etowah County, and state historical items and has an abundance of family history and genealogical research tools, including online databases and computers that are dedicated to genealogical study. Historical newspapers are available on microfilm including the Gadsden Times from 1867 to present. Several interesting programs on local history and genealogy are also held throughout the year. In addition, the Reference section has excellent maps, atlases, federal government documents, and other useful research materials.

Huntsville-Madison County Public Library
915 Monroe Street
Huntsville, Alabama 35801

(256) 532-5940

http://hmcpl.org/specialcollections

The Special Collections Department features a large surname file, with correspondence, clippings, family charts, bible records, and other materials, and an extensive collection of old Alabama newspapers. One strength is its 1812 Territory of Mississippi records. The entire collection focuses primarily on northern Alabama and southern Tennessee.

Mobile Public Library
Local History & Genealogy
753 Government Street
Mobile, Alabama 36602

(251)-208-7093

http://www.mobilepubliclibrary.org/index.php

One strength of the collection is the photocopies of early colonial records of Mobile County. The library features a large collection of southern Alabama county records and other research materials, newspapers, and vertical files on early Mobile settlers.

Florida

Florida State Genealogical Society
P. O. Box 940927
Maitland, Florida 32794

http://www.flsgs.org/

The society publishes *The Florida Genealogist*, organizes webinars, and sponsors the Florida Pioneer Certificate Program for those who descend from a pioneer who settled in Florida prior to statehood in 1845. They also maintain a database of veterans of the War of 1812 and their widows who were buried in Florida.

Florida Historical Society
435 Brevard Avenue
Cocoa, Florida 32922

(321) 690-1971

https://myfloridahistory.org/default

The Society publishes a scholarly quarterly and maintains the Brevard Museum, Rossetter House Museum, and Alma C. Field Library of Florida History.

Alma C. Field Library of Florida History
435 Brevard Avenue
Cocoa, Florida 32922 **USA**

(321) 690-1971

The library collects documentary materials relating to Florida's history and pre-history. They hold over 8,000 bound volumes, a separate collection of rare books, original territorial government publications, as well as early Spanish period narrative histories of Florida. The archival collection consists of over 10,000 print photographs, organized by subject and by county. They house over 1,000 early Florida maps, including a collection of 19th century plat maps, early colonial period maps, county soil surveys, and many others. The Library also has a collection of historic newspapers. Original copies of the Florida State Genealogical Society's Pioneer Descendant certificate program applications are housed at the library. Most materials housed at the library can be searched via the online catalog.

Southern Genealogist's Exchange Society
6215 Sauterne Drive
Jacksonville, Florida 32210

(904) 778-1000

http://www.sgesjax.org/

The library holds a significant collection of material on Duval County and northeastern Florida, some of which is available nowhere else.

Charlton W. Tebeau Library of Florida History
101 West Flagler Street
Miami, Florida 33130 USA

(305) 357-1492

http://www.historical-museum.org/collect/rc.htm

The library holds the archives, books, publications, and documentary collections of the Historical Association of Southern Florida. The collections concentrate on the history of south Florida, including the Everglades. The searchable library catalog is available online.

Hilton-Green Research Room
117 East Government Street
Pensacola, Florida 32501

(850) 595-5840

http://www.historicpensacola.org/education-research/hilton-green-research-room/

The archives contain over 100,000 images that include street scenes, buildings, residences, fortifications, ships, industries, festivals, portraits, and other images of local interest. Other holdings include Pensacola city directories, telephone books, cemetery records, records of the Spanish Land Grants, extensive files of local newspaper clippings, microfilm of early Pensacola newspapers, and bound copies of the *Pensacola Gazette* from 1834-1854. The Lelia Abercrombie Historical Reference Library contains many out of print and hard to find volumes about Northwest Florida. The archives also house a variety of scrapbooks, family correspondence, records from local organizations, business records, and correspondence.

Florida History and Genealogy Library
John F. Germany Public Library, 2nd floor
900 North Ashley Drive
Tampa, Florida 33602

(813) 273-3652

http://www.hcplc.org/hcplc/locations/jfg/genealogy.html

The library is one of the largest in the southeastern United States, with a wide array of print, microform, and electronic resources. The collection has a geographic emphasis on Florida, the southeast region, original Thirteen Colonies, and the states bordering on the Mississippi River. Of particular interest is the large array of databases, online genealogical services, and other online resources.

Julian W. Lowenstein
Archive Center & Genealogy Department
Indian River County Main Library
1600 21st Street
Vero Beach, Florida 32960

(772) 770-5060 x5

http://www.irclibrary.org/genealogy/

The library has more than 35,000 titles, 40,000 microfiche, 6,000 microfilm, eight computers, and wireless access. The collection has a strong emphasis on Florida and the southeastern United States. Of particular note are its Florida History, Microfilm, and Rustin Military Collections.

Jacksonville Public Library Main Branch
303 North Laura Street
Jacksonville, Florida 32202

(904) 630-2665

http://www.jaxpubliclibrary.org/research/collections

The Special Collections Department holds the oldest assemblage of Floridiana in the state. The genealogy collection covers the southeastern United States very well, including biography, genealogy, and history. More than 13,000 books, journals, CDs, and microfilms are searchable from the library website. The library is affiliated with the Family History Library as a Family History Center.

Polk County Historical and Genealogical Library
100 East Main Street
Bartow, Florida 33830-4629

(863) 534-4380

http://www.polk-county.net/boccsite/Our-Community/History-Center/Genealogical-Library/

The library is one of the largest facilities of its type in the region with more than 40,000 items in the collection, including books, microfilm, and periodicals concerning the history and genealogy of the eastern United States.

St. Augustine Historical Society Research Library
6 Artillery Lane
St. Augustine, Florida 32804

(904) 825-2333

http://www.saintaugustinehistoricalsociety.org/research-library/

The Research Library specializes in local history, Florida colonial history, and genealogy. The collection includes maps, photographs, vertical subject files, church records, circuit court cases, city government records, manuscript collections, circuit court records, and biographical files. The online catalog indexes the book collection, manuscript finding aids, the map and photographic collections, *El Escribano, The St. Augustine Journal of History*, and the Society newsletter the *East Florida Gazette*. The library holds the manuscript, *The Patriot War Papers and Patriot War Claims 1812-1846.*

State Library of Florida
R. A. Gray Building
500 South Bronough Street
Tallahassee, Florida 32399

(850) 245-6600

library@dos.myflorida.com

http://dlis.dos.state.fl.us/library/

Published records of Florida, and state government publications, including 700,000 books, magazines, and newspapers; Florida maps and photographs; and, over 200,000 government documents. Significant holdings include more than 2,000 Florida maps, Genealogical Collection, and Native American Collection. The latter collection holds significant material on the Ais, Apalachee, Calusa, Creek, Miccosukee, Seminole, Timucua, and Yamasee tribes.

Volusia County Public Library Daytona Beach Regional
105 East Magnolia Avenue
Daytona Beach Florida 32114

(386) 257-6036

The library has a large history and genealogy collection with emphasis on Florida and the eastern United States. The searchable catalog is available online.

West Florida Public Library
Genealogy Branch
5740 North 9th Avenue
Pensacola, Florida 32504

(850) 494-7373

http://mywfpl.com/

The collection focuses on the southeastern states, supplemented with a large selection of material from the northeastern and central states. Military books are also available. Of special note are its family histories, hereditary society records, and its Native American collection covering the Cherokee, Chickasaw, Choctaw, Creek, and Seminole tribes.

P. K. Younge Library of Florida History
George A. Smathers Library
University of Florida
Gainesville, Florida 32611

352-273-2778

http://www.uflib.ufl.edu/spec/pkyonge/index.html

The library has an extensive collection of Spanish colonial documents on microfilm, including the *East Florida Papers* from the Library of Congress; documents from the Archivo General de Indias, in Seville, collected as part of the John B. Stetson Collection on the Spanish Borderlands; partial and complete legajos about Florida microfilmed by the Archivo General de Indias for use at the University of Florida; and, additional collections of materials gathered by historians working in Spain, the Caribbean, and Mexico.

One significant holding is *Pioneer Days in Florida,* a collection of first-hand accounts from the 19th century. Their collection includes significant holding on antebellum Florida, the Second Seminole War, and the best Florida newspaper collection in the state. Many of the important materials are digitized and available online.

Meek-Eaton Black Archives
Florida A&M University
445 Gamble Street
Tallahassee, Florida 32307

(850) 599-3020

archives@dos.myflorida.com

http://famu.edu/index.cfm?MEBA

The center is one of the largest repositories relating to African-American history and culture in the Southeast. Most of the archival holdings consist of records relating to the history of Africans and African Americans, especially their institutions and organizations, including manuscripts, books, journals, magazines, maps, newspapers, and photographs. Some of the records are unique and not available elsewhere. One significant holding is the Benjamin and Dorothy Holmes Black Church Collection.

University of South Florida Tampa Library Special Collections
4202 East Fowler Avenue
Tampa, Florida 33620

(813) 974-2729

libraryservicesdesk@usf.edu

http://www.lib.usf.edu/special-collections/

The Florida Studies Center Collections contain monographs, maps, manuscripts, photographs, printed ephemera, oral histories, and artists' books relating to Florida's history and culture, especially the Tampa Bay region and its relationship with the Caribbean Basin. The collections center around the themes of immigration, race, and ethnicity, placing them in a global context. Strengths include their collection of published Florida local histories and Hillsborough County records.

University of West Florida Archives and West Florida History Center
John C. Pace Library
11000 University Parkway
Pensacola, Florida 32514

(850) 474-2424

The center has approximately 800 collections totaling about 1.8 million items, 250,000 photographs, and 6,000 maps, personal papers, manuscripts, genealogical and business records, audio and video materials, and other sources of information. Their holdings constitute one of the largest research collections on West Florida, its history, development, and people from earliest settlement to the present. The center also is the archives of the University of West Florida.

Georgia

Georgia Genealogical Society
P. O. Box 550247
Atlanta, Georgia 30355

http://gagensociety.org/

The society publishes a quarterly and holds regular conferences and webinars. The society also is a sponsor of the annual Institute of Genealogical and Historical Research held at the University of Georgia in Athens.

Georgia Historical Society
Research Center
501 Whitaker Street
Savannah, Georgia 31401

(912) 651-2125

http://georgiahistory.com/

Located in historic Hodgson Hall, the center preserves an unparalleled collection on Georgia history, including more than four million manuscripts, 100,000 photographs, 30,000 architectural drawings, 15,000 books, and thousands of maps, portraits, and artifacts. The collection includes an original draft of the U. S. Constitution, records related to the Cherokee Removal and Trail of Tears, and the correspondence of Thomas Jefferson and Andrew Jackson. The manuscript collection includes family papers, military records of every Georgia war, the papers of Georgia's major political leaders, colonial account books, diaries, plantation records, papers of social and cultural organizations, and business records ranging from the 18th through the 20th century.

Atlanta History Center
130 West Paces Ferry Road NW
Atlanta, Georgia 30305

(404) 814-4040

http://www.atlantahistorycenter.com/

The Atlanta History Center has a major library and archive, a history museum, house museum, family farm, book store, and gift shop. While their Kernan Research Center's military history concentrates on the Civil War, particularly the 1864 Atlanta Campaign, they do hold materials on earlier Indian wars.

Heritage Room
Athens-Clarke County Library
2025 Baxter Street
Athens, Georgia 30606

(706) 613-3650 x350

http://www.athenslibrary.org/athens/departments/heritage

The library has a large collection of historical and genealogical materials focusing on Georgia and the other southern states. Their Native American Collection is concentrated on the Cherokee and Creek tribes. Other collection highlights include their series of Subject Guides, including Georgia, Other Genealogy Materials, and the Georgia Vertical Files.

Special Collection Department
Atlanta-Fulton Public Library Central Library
One Margaret Mitchell Square
Atlanta, Georgia 30303

(404) 730-1896

http://www.afpls.org/special-collections-m

The department features Georgia and Southern history and genealogy materials. The Georgia Collection includes books, journals, microfilmed newspapers, maps, ephemera, and vertical files related to Atlanta, Georgia, and southern history. The Genealogy Collection includes books and microfilm relating to genealogy and family history research. The core of the collection addresses research on Georgia families, and provides general guides and how-to resources for genealogists.

Coweta County Genealogical Society Research Library
8 Carmichael Street
Newnan, Georgia 30263

(470) 215-1966

The library is home to a large inventory of historical and genealogical books and publications. It contains books and publications from most, if not all, fifty states. The collection includes many surname books, family history compilations, family folders, historical newspapers, military books, index publications, and miscellaneous historical and reference books, magazines and pamphlets.

DeKalb History Center
Old Courthouse on the Square
101 East Court Square
Decatur, Georgia 30030

(404) 373-1088

http://www.dekalbhistory.org/

The center's collections include a wide variety of materials including subject files, maps, manuscripts, photographs, and rare books. The library focuses on books relating to DeKalb County and the region surrounding Atlanta. Highlights include specific collections of biographical files, maps, special collections, and subject files.

Georgia Salzburger Society
Loest Research Library
2980 Ebenezer Road
Georgia Highway 275
Rincon, Georgia 31326

(912) 754-7001

http://visitebenezer.com/loest-research-library/

The library has a large collection of histories, journals, genealogical records, and church histories, with emphasis on the Salzburgers, early settlers of Effingham County.

Ellen Payne Odom Genealogy Library
Moultrie-Colquitt County Library
204 5th Street, S.E.
Moultrie, Georgia 31768 USA

(229) 985-6540

http://mccls.org/odom_gen.htm

The library has a good collection on American history and genealogy. Of special note are its military, Native American, patriotic organizations, Georgia, Scottish immigration, and Emmett Lucas collections.

Huxford-Spear Genealogical Library
20 South College Street
Homerville, Georgia 31634

(912) 487-2310

https://huxford.com/

The library holds Judge Folks Huxford's extensive collection of family histories from the Wiregrass region of Georgia. The collection holds more than 57,000 research books and other materials, including 16,000 family folders and a large collection of microfilm and microfiche. Of special note is Folks Huxford's *Pioneers of Wiregrass Georgia* (Homerville, Georgia: Huxford Genealogical Society, 2006), a finding list of more than 5,000 sketches with references to over 100,000 related families

Ladson Genealogical Library
125 Church Street
Vidalia, Georgia 30474

(912) 537-8186

http://ohoopeelibrary.org/locations/ladson-genealogical-library/

Their significant manuscript collections include the Leonardo Andrea Collection of South Carolina; Annie Laurie Hill's notes on the Hall, McKinney, Pope and Exum families of Wilkes County, Georgia; the Pauline Young Collection; the files of Mrs. Eugene A. Stanley of Savannah; and, the collection of Mrs. Martha Ann de l'Etoile of Griffin, Georgia. Special collections include the Kitty Ware Wade Collection of historic photographs.

Thomasville Genealogical, History, and Fine Arts Library
135 North Broad Street
Thomasville, Georgia 31792

229-226-9640

http://www.n-georgia.com/thomasville-genealogical-history-fine-arts-museum.html

The library is a major repository of materials for family research with an emphasis on the southeastern states, including Georgia, Virginia, South Carolina, North Carolina, Alabama, Tennessee, Mississippi, Florida, and Kentucky. Some of the resources available include family, state, and county histories, including the Hopkins Collection and the Singletary Collection, and early newspapers.

Washington Memorial Library
Middle Georgia Regional Library
Genealogical & Historical Room
1180 Washington Avenue
Macon, Georgia 31201

Telephone: 478-744-0821

The library's collection includes more than 32,000 volumes and over 24,000 microforms, with emphasis on Georgia, southern states, and original colonies. Significant space is devoted to colonial history and the Revolutionary War. Of special interest is their large collections of family histories, including books, other published material, vertical files, research notes, and other family records.

Hargrett Rare Book & Manuscript Library
University of Georgia Main Library
320 South Jackson Street
Athens, Georgia 30602

(706) 542-3251

The Hargrett Library focuses on Georgia history and culture, holding rare books and Georgiana, historical manuscripts, photographs, maps, broadsides, and university archives and records. Their collections include more than 200,000 books on Georgia history, as well as a large collection of historical maps and old newspapers.

348

Kentucky

Kentucky Genealogical Society
P. O. Box 153
Frankfort, Kentucky 40602

info@kygs.org

https://kentuckygenealogicalsociety.org/

Bluegrass Roots is the society's quarterly journal. They also hold an annual genealogical seminar as well as a series of smaller workshops around the state.

Martin F. Schmidt Research Library
Kentucky Historical Society
100 West Broadway
Frankfort, Kentucky 40601

(502) 564-1792 x4460

khsrefdesk@ky.gov

http://history.ky.gov/library/

The library holds the largest genealogical collection in the state, with more than 16,000 rolls of microfilm, 90,000 books and periodicals, and 30,000 vertical files focused primarily on Kentucky history and genealogy. The Society's Archival Collections of 1,900 cubic feet of manuscripts, 2,000 maps, 8,000 oral histories, 200,000 historic photographs, and 9,100 rare books provide unique resources to researchers. The Library Collections Catalog is available online, as is the Digital Collections Catalog, which includes over 20,000 images of original manuscripts, maps, photographs, and finding aids for a portion of the collections. Images of over 85,000 museum artifacts can be accessed via the Objects Catalog. The library is affiliated with the Family History Library.

Daviess County Public Library
2020 Frederica Street
Owensboro, Kentucky 42301

(270) 684-0211

http://www.dcplibrary.org/genealogy

The library features one of the best genealogy collections in Kentucky, with special emphasis on local and Kentucky history. Of special note are its holdings of local newspapers and Kentucky military records.

Minnie Winder Genealogy & Local History Room
Boyd County Public Library
Ashland Main Branch
1740 Central Avenue
Ashland, Kentucky 41101

(606) 329-0518

http://thebookplace.org/genealogy/

Situated near where Kentucky, Ohio, and West Virginia meet, the library houses the largest genealogical collection in the Tri-State area and Eastern Kentucky. The collection, with more than 6,000 print volumes, 2,500 periodical issues, and over 6,200 rolls of microfilm, has strong coverage of eastern Kentucky and the Tri-State area, emphasizing early migration from Pennsylvania, Virginia, West Virginia, and North Carolina, and including many sources available nowhere else, such as family folders, biographies, genealogies, and pedigrees.

Margaret I. King Library
Department of Special Collections and Archives
University of Kentucky
179 Funkhouser Drive
Lexington, Kentucky 40506

(859) 257-1742

http://libraries.uky.edu/lib.php?lib_id=13

The Department of Special Collections and Archives maintains many collections that lend themselves to the study of family and local history, including the Appalachian Collection, newspapers, church records, genealogical collections, historical manuscript collections, the Draper manuscripts, county and local histories, county, state, and federal records, and a biographical file. A useful guide to the manuscript collection is Thomas D. Clark and Jeanne Slater Trimble's *Guide to Selected Manuscripts Housed in the Division of Special Collections and Archives, Margaret I. King Library, University of Kentucky* (Lexington, Kentucky: University of Kentucky, 1987).

Kenton County Public Library
502 Scott Boulevard
Covington, Kentucky 41011

(859) 962-4070

http://www.kentonlibrary.org/genealogy

The library has extensive statewide, local, and family history materials and in-depth collections for northern Kentucky. One strong holding is the local newspaper index for the years 1835 to 1931. Access to the catalog and the Kenton County Historical Society is available on the website.

Filson Historical Society Library
1310 South Third Street
Louisville, Kentucky 40208

(502) 635-5083

research@filsonhistorical.org

http://filsonhistorical.org/

Formerly known as the Filson Club, the library has a good collection of early Kentucky history and genealogy manuscripts. Their specialty is migration, especially via the Ohio River. The library has several useful online guides, including African American History & Genealogy Sources, Genealogy Research Guide, Jefferson County, Kentucky Cemetery Index, Searching the Online Catalog, and Historic Maps Research Guide.

John Grant Crabbe Library
Special Collections and Archives
Eastern Kentucky University
521 Lancaster Avenue
Richmond, Kentucky 40475

(859) 622-1790

archives.library@eku.edu

http://library.eku.edu/john-grant-crabbe-library

This university library has many records about Kentucky, Virginia, and North Carolina, with an emphasis on Kentucky records. The library website provides numerous guides to research, as well as a searchable catalog.

Lexington Public Library
Kentucky Room
140 East Main Street
Lexington, Kentucky 40507

(859) 231-5520

http://www.lexpublib.org/kyroom

The Kentucky Room contains a wealth of information about Kentucky and Fayette County. The collection features books on all aspects of Kentucky, subject files on Kentucky and Lexington, local newspapers, city directories, maps, and state and local government documents. Of special note are an excellent collection of Lexington newspapers and the Local History Index, an extensive index to newspapers. More detailed information on the collection can be found on the library website.

Pogue Library
Special Collections Department
Murray State University
208 Waterfield Library
Murray, Kentucky 42071

(270) 809-4295 or (866) 774-6612

Specialcollections@murraystate.edu.

http://libguides.murraystate.edu/special_collections_index

The department has significant holdings concerning the history of the Jackson Purchase area of southwestern Kentucky and northwestern Tennessee. The collections include published and printed regional and county histories, manuscript materials, oral histories, and other significantly unique items.

Western Kentucky University Library Special Collections
1444 Kentucky Street
Bowling Green, Kentucky 42101

(270) 745-6125.

library.web@wku.edu

http://www.wku.edu/library/dlsc/index.php

The Kentucky Library Research Collections comprise a unique research center of primary sources for both the university community and general public users. Originally called the "Kentucky Library" with a mission to collect "all things Kentucky," the collection quickly grew to encompass the world, with rare books, photographs, rare periodicals, and specialized research collections in diverse formats dating from the 15th century. The library has significant genealogical records, church histories, oral histories, and biographical files relating to south central Kentucky, early settlers, and the Shakers.

Louisiana

Louisiana Genealogical and Historical Society
P. O. Box 82060
Baton Rouge, Louisiana 70884

http://www.louisianaghs.org/

The society publishes *The Louisiana Genealogical Register*, an eclectic collection of Louisiana records, historical and genealogical articles, queries, announcements, and "how to" advice. They sponsor an annual spring conference in Baton Rouge and fall workshop in different locations around the state. The Society is the official registry of the First Families of Louisiana Certificate Program which recognizes families who settled within the present boundaries of the state on or before December 20, 1803.

Louisiana State Library
760 Third Street
Baton Rouge, Louisiana 70802

(504) 342-4913

http://www.state.lib.la.us/

The library has a comprehensive collection of materials on Louisiana history and genealogy resources, including military records, journals published by state genealogical and historical societies, and family histories. Of note are the Journals and Newspapers, Louisiana Collection, Louisiana Documents, and Louisiana Gumbo. Special materials in the Louisiana Collection include, Acts of the Louisiana Legislature, 1810 to current, historical city directories, maps, historical Louisiana state government publications, documents relating to the Louisiana Historic Standing Structures Survey, documents relating to the Louisiana Works Progress Administration, Louisiana-related federal government documents, newspapers from major Louisiana cities in print, on microfilm, and in electronic format, military service and parish records on microfilm, and vertical files of newspaper articles and ephemeral materials.

Linus A. Sims Memorial Library
Southeastern Louisiana University
1211 SGA Drive
Hammond, Louisiana 70402

(985) 549-3860

http://southeastern.edu/library/

The library holds a significant collection of materials related to Louisiana genealogy and history, with staff prepared research guides.

Historic New Orleans Collection
William Research Center
410 Charter Street
New Orleans, Louisiana 70130

(504) 598-7171

http://www.hnoc.org/

The collection's rare and important holdings are available to the general public, with access to more than 30,000 library items, including books, pamphlets, sheet music, broadsides, theater programs, and periodicals; more than two miles of documents and manuscripts; a microfilm collection; and more than 500,000 photographs, prints, drawings, and paintings.   Rare manuscripts and documents are available in the original and in microform. Among the strengths of the collections are its holdings concerning the Battle of New Orleans, colonial history, maps, military records, people, plantations, and steam boats and steamships. Of special note are its microfilm holdings of Louisiana records from the U. S. National Archives, French National Archives, General Archive of the Indies in Seville, Spain, Cuban National Archives, National Archive of the United Kingdom, and other British archives and libraries.

Louisiana Historical Center Library
400 Esplanade Avenue
New Orleans, Louisiana 70176

(504) 568-8214

The library houses 28,000 items related to various aspects of Louisiana history, the history of the Mississippi Valley, the Gulf Coast, and especially the territory that was part of the Louisiana Purchase. The library contains numerous pamphlets, materials in typescript form, and a great deal of manuscript materials from the period when Iberville settled Louisiana. All of the printed histories of Louisiana are on the shelves ranging from LePage du Pratz, Father Hennepin, B.F. French, Martin, Gayarre, Maringy, to contemporary writers.

The Louisiana Colonial Judicial Records of both the French Superior Council (1714-1769) and the Spanish Judiciary (1769-1803) are important criminal and civil records, the case files often containing a wealth of biographical information about Louisiana's colonial inhabitants ranging from estate inventories, records of commercial transactions, correspondence, copies of wills, marriage contracts, and baptismal, marriage, and burial records. Under Spanish rule, many slaves of Indian ancestry petitioned government authorities for their freedom, usually granted upon proof of native ancestry, and those records are also a part of the collection. Other materials of note are the map, newspaper, and manuscript collections.   The microfilm collections include The Louisiana Notarial Records Collection, Records of The Diocese of Louisiana and the Floridas (1576-1803), Colonial Records of St. Charles Parish (1740-1972), Colonial Records of Avoyelles Parish (1793-1796), Colonial Records of St. Landry Parish (1764-1793), the Pontalba-Almonester-Mero Papers (1792-1796), and 59 reels of dissertations written about Louisiana, 1954-1978.

New Orleans Public Library
219 Loyola Avenue
New Orleans, Louisiana 70140

(504) 596-2612

http://archives.nolalibrary.org/~nopl/spec/speclist.htm

The library's Louisiana Division collects resources relating to Louisiana, New Orleans, and their citizens. Additional areas of concentration are the Mississippi River, the Gulf of Mexico, and the South. Included within the Division's collections are books by or about Louisianans; city, regional, and state documents; and, manuscripts, maps, newspapers, periodicals, microfilms, photographs, and ephemera of every sort. The division also houses the City Archives, the official repository for the records of the New Orleans municipal government (1769-present), and holds on deposit the pre-1927 records of the civil courts and the pre-1932 records of the criminal courts of Orleans Parish. Special Collections include the Rare Vertical File, the Louisiana Photograph Collection, Map Collection, Manuscript Collection, and the Rare Book Collection. Their extensive Genealogy Collection contains books, periodicals and microfilms with emphasis on New Orleans, Louisiana, Southeast United States, Nova Scotia, France, and Spain. An inventory of the records in this important collection is Collin B. Hamer, Jr.'s *Genealogical Materials in the New Orleans Public Library*, New Orleans, Louisiana: Friends of the New Orleans Public Library, 1984.

Orleans Parish Notarial Archives
Civil Courts Building
421 Loyola Avenue, Room B-4
New Orleans, Louisiana 70112

(504) 568-8578

http://www.notarialarchives.org/

Records date from 1735 to July 1970, during the time of Civil Law notarial practice, when notaries archived their own records. The records are arranged the way they were created by notary and then by date. Annual indexes maintained by the notaries are bound into volumes. Because New Orleans was once a French and a Spanish colony, records prior to the Louisiana Purchase (1803) are in French or Spanish. After the Louisiana Purchase, many 19th century records continued to be written in French. While there is no comprehensive index to the records, a companion office to the Notarial Archives, the Conveyance Division, maintains party-name indexes to property transfers back to 1827. The Conveyance indexes are annual, and are divided into "Vendor" and "Purchaser." The Conveyance indexes are extremely useful in accessing notarial records created before August 1970. Other useful research tools include indexes of family records, 1770-1840, created by genealogist Charles R. Maduell, Jr.; a building-contract index, 1767-1970, created by Samuel Wilson and Robert J. Cangelosi, Jr.; and, a corporate-charter index, 1852-1904, all of which are available at the Research Center.

Hill Memorial Library
Louisiana State University
Baton Rouge, Louisiana 70803

(504) 388-6551

http://www.lib.lsu.edu/special/

The library's significant holdings include Louisiana and Lower Mississippi River, manuscript, map, and Louisiana newspaper collections. The Lower Louisiana and Lower Mississippi River Collection includes the papers of individuals and families; records of plantations, merchants and financial institutions; the files of political, social, and labor organizations; as well as the personal papers of many of the most important figures in the political history of the region. Geographically, the collection covers the state of Louisiana and the Lower Mississippi Valley, from Memphis to New Orleans, with notable strength in its holdings related to Natchez, St. Francisville, Baton Rouge, and New Orleans. The collections date to the French and Spanish colonial periods.

A helpful guide to Louisiana libraries is *Resources in Louisiana Libraries: Public, Academic, Special, and in Media Centers* (Baton Rouge, Louisiana: Louisiana State Library, 1971.

Manuscripts & Rare Books Department
Howard-Tilton Memorial Library
Tulane University
7001 Freret Street
New Orleans, Louisiana 70118

(504) 865-5131

http://library.tulane.edu/

The library supports a series of helpful research guides for their collections, including *Early American History: A Guide*, *History Research Guide*, *Louisiana History Manuscripts on Microfilm*, and *Primary Sources: United States & Canadian History: A Guide*.

Le Comité des Archives de la Louisiane, Inc.
P. O. Box 1547
Baton Rouge, Louisiana 70821

http://www.lecomite.org/index.html

Le Comité des Archives de la Louisiane, Inc. is the non-profit genealogical support group for the Louisiana State Archives. *Le Raconteur* is published in March, June, September, and December. Each issue contains a variety of original genealogical and historical articles dealing with topics from around Louisiana. Tables of Contents and Annual Indexes dating back to 1984 are available.

Mississippi

Mississippi Genealogical Society
P. O. Box 5301
Jackson, Mississippi 39216

Info@MSGenSociety.org

http://www.msgensociety.org/index.html

The society publishes a quarterly journal, sponsors annual conferences, and publishes books relative to Mississippi research. One important project is their *Survey of Mississippi Courthouses.*

Mississippi Historical Society
P. O. Box 571
Jackson, Mississippi 39205

(601) 576-6849

mhs@mdah.state.ms.us

http://www.mississippihistory.org/

The society publishes the scholarly *Journal of Mississippi History*, the ongoing *Heritage of Mississippi Series*, and *Mississippi History Now*. Published jointly by the state archives and the University Press of Mississippi, the *Heritage of Mississippi Series* includes James F. Barnett, Jr.'s *Mississippi's American Indians*. *Mississippi History Now* is an electronic publication featuring essays and articles on a variety of subjects, including *Chickasaws: The Unconquerable People, French Colonial Period in Mississippi: A Failed Enterprise, Great Migration to the Mississippi Territory: 1798-1819, Mushulatubbee and Choctaw Removal: Chiefs Confront a Changing World, Natchez Indians,* and *Pushmataha: Choctaw Warrior, Diplomat, and Chief.*

Evans Memorial Library
105 North Long Street
Aberdeen, Mississippi 39730

(622) 369-4601

eml@tombigbee.lib.ms.us

http://tombigbee.lib.ms.us/evans

One of the largest genealogy collections in the South, the Evans Memorial Library holds records of the deep South, including Mississippi and Alabama oral histories, church records, newspapers, maps, military records, Chickasaw Indians, African Americans, fraternal histories, scrapbooks, manuscripts and photos.

357

McCardle Research Library
Old Courthouse Museum
1008 Cherry Street
Vicksburg, Mississippi 39183

(601) 636-0741

http://oldcourthouse.org/mccardle-library/

The library is a center for regional and local genealogy for early Mississippians, including local history, histories of Warren County families, local cemetery records, census records, business directories, civil war manuscripts, maps, marriage records, and tax records.

McCain Library and Archives
University of Southern Mississippi
P. O. Box 5148
Hattiesburg, Mississippi 39406

(601) 266-4345

http://lib.usm.edu/spcol.html

The library's Historical Manuscript Collection holds over 10,000 cubic feet of personal, family, business, church, and organizational records. The Genealogy Vertical Files contain biographical information, family trees, newspaper clippings, correspondence, and other items, under four categories: states, counties, Native Americans, and surnames and locations.

Mitchel Library
Mississippi State University
P. O. Box 5408
395 Hardy Road
Mississippi State, Mississippi 39762

(662) 325-7679

sp_coll@library.msstate.edu]

http://lib.msstate.edu/specialcollections/

Mitchell's Special Collections Department contains manuscripts, rare books, and other unique historical materials documenting the history of Mississippi, the South, and beyond. The materials are preserved and organized for the use of students, faculty, and other researchers, and include correspondence; photographs; films; audio recordings; personal, family, and business records; architectural drawings; maps; newspapers; literary manuscripts; artifacts and memorabilia; and, MSU publications and records. Portions of the collection have been photographed and are accessible through the Digital Collections online.

J. D. Williams Library
University of Mississippi Williams Library
P. O. Box 1848
1 Library Loop
University, Mississippi 38677 USA

(662) 915-7408

archivesdept@olemiss.edu

http://www.libraries.olemiss.edu/uml/archives-special-collections

Located on the third floor of the library, the Department of Archives and Special Collections houses important collections of Mississippiana. Online guides to the special collections include *French Revolution and Napoleonic Materials* (including the Louisiana Purchase and War of 1812), *Mississippi Province & Territory*, and *Native Americans,* and *Wars, excluding Civil War.*

Oklahoma

Oklahoma Genealogical Society
P. O. Box 12986
Oklahoma City, Oklahoma 73157

http://www.rootsweb.ancestry.com/~okgs/

The society publishes the *OGS Quarterly* as well as books and other publications. They teach classes on a variety of topics, aimed at everyone from beginner to professional. Their First Families of the Twin Territories Program is open to all who descend from anyone living in the Oklahoma Territory or Indian Territory prior to statehood in 1907.

Oklahoma Historical Society
800 Nazih Zudhi Drive
Oklahoma City, Oklahoma 73105

(405) 522-5225

http://www.okhistory.org/research/

Excellent collections for Native Americans and Anglo settlers of Oklahoma can be found here. A good guide to family history research at the society is Mary Huffman's *Family History: A Bibliography of the Collection in the Oklahoma Historical Society* (Oklahoma City, Oklahoma: The Society, 1992).

Oklahoma Department of Libraries
200 N. E. 18th Street
Oklahoma City, Oklahoma 73105

(405) 521-2502 or (800) 522-8116

https://libraries.ok.gov/

The Oklahoma Department of Libraries includes two significant areas of interest to genealogists: the Oklahoma Room and the State Archives Division. The Oklahoma Room houses a large book library with county histories, periodicals, indexes, and reference works. The State Archives Division maintains Oklahoma government records and other historical documents. Many original documents and other material are available online at *Oklahoma Digital Prairie* and *Archives.OK.Gov.*

Lawton Public Library
110 S. W. 4th Street
Lawton, Oklahoma 73105

(405) 581-3450

http://www.cityof.lawton.ok.us/library/genealogy.htm

The library holds the largest book collection of Oklahoma genealogies, together with periodicals, maps, biographies, family folders, and a statewide index to all Oklahoma Territory tract books.

Western History Collection
University of Oklahoma Libraries
630 Parrington Oval, Room 452
Norman, Oklahoma 73019

(405) 325-3641

http://libraries.ou.edu/locations/?id=22

Key library collections include transcribed interviews with Oklahomans from the 1930s and more than 200 manuscript collections concerning Native Americans. Kristine L. Southwell's *Guide to Manuscripts in the Western History Collections of the University of Oklahoma* (Norman, Oklahoma: University of Oklahoma Press, 2002) is a helpful research guide to the collections.

A significant part of the Western History Collection is titled *The Indian-Pioneer Papers* which is a collection of interviews done during the Great Depression. Biographical information is given for Indians as well as others. There are about 80,000 entries in 112 volumes in the collection with free online access to both an index and the digitized transcripts of the interviews. The collection also includes original historical manuscripts, county records, Spanish, Indian, military, newspapers, cattle trails, ranching, mining, and oil production records.

Hughes County Historical Society
124 North Broadway
Holdenville, Oklahoma 74848

(405) 379-5124

The collection, originally in the Grace M. Pickens Public Library, holds unique Native American papers relating to the Five Civilized Tribes and their removal to Indian Territory, and a good genealogical research collection.

Oklahoma Territorial Museum Carnegie Library
406 East Oklahoma Avenue
Guthrie, Oklahoma 73044

(405) 282-1889

http://www.okterritorialmuseum.org/LIBRARY.html

The Oklahoma Territorial period is well covered here, including Native Americans, Anglos, intruders, Sooners, homesteaders, and land rush people.

Tulsa Genealogical Society Library
9136 East 31st Street
Tulsa, Oklahoma 74145

(918) 627-4224

http://www.tulsagenealogy.org/library/

This is a large library for Oklahoma research, including family bibles, cemeteries, obituaries, family folders, city directories, plat maps, and indexes.

Museum of the Western Prairie Library
1100 Memorial Drive
Altus, Oklahoma 73521

(580) 482-1044

http://www.okhistory.org/sites/westernprairie

The library holds records of Oklahoma settlers, obituaries, periodicals, books, histories, biographies, including many from Texas and New Mexico.

Miami Public Library
200 North Main Street
Miami, Oklahoma 74354

(918) 541-2292

http://miamipl.okpls.org/genealogy/

This library's collections have an emphasis on the Ozark region of Oklahoma, Kansas, Missouri, and Arkansas, including Native Americans.

Talbot Library and Museum
500 South Colcord Avenue
Colcord, Oklahoma 74338

(918) 326-4532

talbotlibrary@earthlink.net

http://www.talbotlibrary.org/

The library is one of the better genealogical libraries in the state, focusing on Northeast Oklahoma, Northwest Arkansas, and Cherokee genealogy research.

Tulsa City-County Library Genealogy Center
Hardesty Regional Library
8316 East 93rd Street
Tulsa, Oklahoma 74133

(918) 549-7691

genaskus@tulsalibrary.org

http://www.tulsalibrary.org/genealogy-center

The center is one of the larger genealogy collections in Oklahoma, with emphasis on Tulsa and Oklahoma, Arkansas, Kentucky, Missouri, Oklahoma, Tennessee, Texas, and Virginia. A limited amount of research, including Indian roll look-ups, can be conducted by email and letters. See their American Indian Research guide.

Thomas Gilcrease Institute of American History and Art
1400 North Gilcrease Museum Road
Tulsa, Oklahoma 74127

(918) 596-2700

Internet: www.gilcrease.org

The library collection, of more than 100,000 items, includes manuscripts, books, photographs, maps, imprints, and broadsides. Lester Hargrett's *The Gilcrease-Hargrett Catalogue of Imprints* (Norman, Oklahoma: University of Oklahoma Press, 1972) is essentially an annotated bibliography of printed materials in the collection pertaining to the American Indian.

Museum of the Great Plains
601 NW Ferris Avenue
Lawton, Oklahoma 73507

(580) 581-3460

info@discovermgp.org

http://www.discovermgp.org/

Together, the museum's photo collection, archives, and research library contain tens of thousands of images, letters, newspapers, diaries, journals, and books.

North Carolina

North Carolina Genealogical Society
6300 Creedmoor Road, Suite 170-323
Raleigh, North Carolina 27612

http://www.ncgenealogy.org/

The society publishes the quarterly *NCGS Journal* and hosts numerous workshops and webinars. They also have an online index to the Delamar Transcripts of Revolutionary War Petitions, abstracted from the legislative files of the North Carolina General Assembly available at the state archives. They also maintain an online index to the loose estate papers housed at the state archives and accessible at FamilySearch.org.

Federation of North Carolina Historical Societies
4610 Mail Service Center
Raleigh, North Carolina 27699

http://www.ncdcr.gov/about/history/fnchs

The federation is a coalition of historical societies, museums, historic sites, associations, and commissions located throughout the state that are dedicated to preserving and promoting history in North Carolina.

State Library of North Carolina
109 East Jones Street
Raleigh, North Carolina 27699

(919) 807-7460

slnc.reference@ncdcr.gov

http://statelibrary.ncdcr.gov/index.html

The library has a large collection of books, periodicals, and genealogies for North Carolina, including digital databases of family bibles, marriages, deaths, newspapers, and cemetery photos, research guides and county records, including wills, deeds, marriages, court minutes, tax lists, and probate records. The library supports DigitalNC, a website from the University of North Carolina with digitized newspapers, yearbooks, photographs, and other records. North Carolina Digital Collections is a joint project of the state archives and state library, with digital images of numerous records.

Duke University Perkins Library
104 Chapel Drive
Durham, North Carolina 27708

(919) 660-5800

http://library.duke.edu/

Perkins houses the largest manuscript collection in the South, including newspapers, county records, bibles, and journals. Nannie M. Trilley and Noma Lee Goodwin's *Guide to the Manuscript Collections in the Duke University Library* (Durham, North Carolina: Duke University Press, 1947) is an indexed list of 8,000 names of individuals, families, and historical subjects.

Genealogical Society of Old Tryon County
319 Doggett Road
P. O. Box 938
Forest City, North Carolina 28043

(828) 247-8700

info@rutherfordcountync.gov

http://rutherfordcountync.gov/genealogicalsociety

The library holds a large collection of books, periodicals, bible records, obituaries, biographies, and indexes for pre-Civil War people from both North Carolina and South Carolina. The collection's emphasis is on the counties of Rutherford, Polk, and Cleveland, including migration data, 500 family histories, 3,000 genealogy books, and 60 Carolina county heritage books.

Public Library of Charlotte and Mecklenburg County
Robinson-Spangler Carolina Room
310 North Tryon Street
Charlotte, North Carolina 28202

(704) 416-0150

https://www.cmlibrary.org/services/genealogy-history-services

For the southern part of the state, the library collections rival those of the state archives. Emphasis is on the Germans, Highland Scots, and Scots-Irish immigrants to North Carolina, with many references to Quakers moving from Pennsylvania to North Carolina. The collection has good indexes, biographies, family folders, and genealogies.

McEachern Library of Local History
Duplin County Historical Society
314 East Main Street
P. O. Box 130
Rose Hill, North Carolina 28458

(910) 296-2180

The library has the largest collection in North America of family folders for immigrants from Scotland, including the highland Scots who came to the Cape Fear River region of North Carolina.

Olivia Raney Local History Library
4016 Carya Drive
Raleigh, North Carolina 27610

(919) 250-1196

http://www.wakegov.com/libraries/locations/orl/Pages/default.aspx

This library houses a collection of 18,000 items, primarily focused on local and family history with background materials on American, North Carolina, and local history.

University of North Carolina Chapel Hill Libraries
Louis R. Wilson Special Collections Library
200 South Road
Wilson Library Campus Box #3948
Chapel Hill, North Carolina 27515

(919) 962-1172

nccref@unc.edu

http://library.unc.edu/wilson/

The Wilson Library is home to the famed Southern Historical Collection with strengths in plantations, slavery, the Civil War, Civil Rights, communities, family, race relations, and religious communities; the North Carolina Collection of published works on North Carolina and its people and biographical index; the Rare Book Collection; the Southern Folklife Collection; the Manuscript Department collection of personal papers, letters, and diaries of early North Carolina residents; and, the Map Department. In addition to the numerous online guides to research, one should consult Susan Sokol Blosser and Clyde Norman Wilson, Jr.'s *The Southern Historical Collection: A Guide to Manuscripts* (Chapel Hill, North Carolina: University of North Carolina Library, 1970).

Rowan Public Library
201 West Fisher Street
Salisbury North Carolina, 28144

(704) 216-8253

Fax: 704-216-8237

http://www.rowancountync.gov/HOME.aspx

The library has manuscripts, diaries, journals, bible records, and family folders from the crossroads of colonial North Carolina. Emphasis is on "Old Rowan County," including more than 150,000 abstracts in the McCubbins and Jo White Linn Collections and 2,000 family histories.

South Carolina

South Carolina Genealogical Society
Tompkins Memorial Library
104 Courthouse Square
Edgefield, South Carolina 29824

(803) 637-4010

scgs@bellsouth.net

http://www.scgen.org/

The South Carolina Genealogical Society and the Old Edgefield District Genealogical Society have deposited at the Tompkins Memorial Library newspapers; Edgefield County records, such as probate wills and deeds, censuses, and mortality tables; an extensive collection of family histories; and, over 2,000 surname files, which contain bible records, newspaper clippings, letters, lineage charts, and diary excerpts. The collection includes subject files, church histories, and cemetery surveys. The old Ninety Six District is emphasized.

South Carolina Historical Society
100 Meeting Street
Charleston, South Carolina 29401

(803) 723-3225

http://schistory.org/

The library holds colonial immigrant records, biographies, genealogies, and early newspapers. A helpful guide to the manuscript collection is David Moltke-Hansen and Sallie Doscher's "South Carolina Historical Society Manuscript Guide" in the *South Carolina Historical Magazine* (Charleston: South Carolina Historical Society, July 1979). Detailed descriptions of the manuscript collections may be found on the society's website.

South Carolina State Library
1500 Senate Street
Columbia, South Carolina 29201

(803) 734-8666

reference@statelibrary.sc.gov

http://www.statelibrary.sc.gov/

The library holds a large collection of books on South Carolina history and biography, as well as a large collection of newspapers and other genealogical reference works. The library houses the publications of state agencies and state academic institutions in print, electronic, and multimedia formats. Also, the library is a designated depository for federal government records.

Episcopal Diocese of South Carolina Archives
Diocesan House
126 Coming Street
Charleston, South Carolina 29403

(843) 722-4075

http://www.diosc.com/sys/

The surviving original Church of England records dating from South Carolina's colonial period are housed in the archives and have been published in the *South Carolina Historical and Genealogical Magazine*. A descriptive inventory of the records is Margaretta Childs and Isabella G. Leland's "South Carolina Episcopal Church Records" in *South Carolina Historical and Genealogical Magazine,* Volume 84, October 1983, pages 250-63.

Camden Archives and Museum
1314 Broad Street
Camden, South Carolina 29020

(803) 425-6050

archives@camdensc.org

The archives maintains a diverse collection of books, microfilm, maps, files, periodicals, and general reference materials pertaining to the north-central section of South Carolina known as the old Camden District, which today encompasses Clarendon, Sumter, Lee, Kershaw, Lancaster, York, Chester, Fairfield, and northern Richland counties. The South Carolina Daughters of the American Revolution Library and the Colonial Dames XVII Century Library are also located at the archives. As a city department, the archives is home to the City of Camden's historical records.

Charleston County Public Library
68 Calhoun Street
Charleston, South Carolina 29401

(843) 805-6930

http://www.ccpl.org/default.asp

The library has a large number of books, maps, manuscripts, and images covering a wide variety of local history and genealogical topics, in two separate departments. The South Carolina Room has local and regional history and genealogy materials, focusing on the history and genealogy of South Carolina, with a special emphasis on Charleston and the Low Country. The Special Collections Department is an archive of historic manuscripts, books, and visual materials representing Charleston and the surrounding Low Country. Access to the original materials in

Special Collections is by appointment only, but much of the unique manuscript material is available on microfilm or photocopies in the South Carolina Room.

Charleston Library Society
164 King Street
Charleston, South Carolina 29401

(803) 723-9912

http://www.charlestonlibrarysociety.org/

Founded in 1748, the library's Archives and Special Collections consist of more than 14,500 rare books, 5,000 rare and semi-rare pamphlets, 400 manuscript collections, and 470 maps and plats, including collections of correspondence and other personal papers of people of historic note, such as George Washington, John Marshall, Robert E. Lee, Henry Laurens, Charles Cotesworth Pinckney, and John C. Calhoun, and an extensive collection of Southern colonial newspapers, family folders, and genealogies. The library maintains a searchable online catalog of its complete collections.

Francis M. Hipp Reading Room
Special Collections & Archives
Strom Thurmond Institute
Clemson University
230 Kappa Street
Clemson, South Carolina 29634

(864) 656-3031

http://library.clemson.edu/depts/specialcollections/

Most of manuscripts in the Special Collections Library are personal and professional papers of individuals, or records of organizations and business enterprises, usually consisting of unpublished textual documents and may also include photographs, manuscripts, printed ephemera, artifacts, and other items. In some cases, "assembled" collections, intentionally gathered material on a particular subject, are also categorized as manuscript collections. Detailed finding aids to the collections are searchable online.

Darlington County Historical Commission
204 Hewitt Street
Darlington, South Carolina 29532

(843) 398-4710

https://www.facebook.com/DarlingtonCHC/?ref=page_internal

The historical commission offers diverse information for researchers in the fields of history and genealogy pertaining to Darlington County. Among these are courthouse records on the people and lands, agriculture, manufacturing, industry, historical sites, and miscellaneous Revolutionary War records.

Greenville County Library System Hughes Main Library
South Carolina Room
25 Heritage Green Place
Greenville, South Carolina 29601

(864) 242-5000

https://www.greenvillelibrary.org/genealogy-and-local-history

The South Carolina Room in the Hughes Main Library is staffed by experienced genealogists and has an extensive collection of books, manuscripts, microform, periodicals, databases, photographs, maps, and newspapers all searchable in its online catalog.

Orangeburg County Historical Society Library
Salley Archives
1421 Middleton Street
P. O. Box 1881
Orangeburg, South Carolina 29116

(803) 535-0022

ochs@orangeburgh.org

http://www.orangeburgh.org/library-holdings

Holdings include court records, family records, deeds, mortgages, surname folders, church records, cemetery transcripts, books, and documents of local families.

South Caroliniana Library
University of South Carolina
910 Sumter Street
Columbia, South Carolina 29208

(803) 777-3142

http://library.sc.edu/p/Collections/SCL

The library holds an outstanding collection for South Carolina and the South, including manuscripts, genealogies, histories, atlases, and gazetteers. A useful guide to the manuscript collection is Allen H. Stokes's *A Guide to the Manuscript Collection of the South Caroliniana Library* (Columbia, South Carolina: The Library, 1982).

Sumter County Genealogical Center
122 North Washington Street
P. O. Box 2543
Sumter, South Carolina 29151

(803) 774-3901

SumterGenSoc@aol.com

http://sumtercountygenealogicalcenter.org/

The center houses a large collection of books, microfilm, manuscripts, photographs, family folders, biographies, and maps relating to South Carolina history and genealogy. Of special note is the Janie Reville Collection. A helpful guide to other research facilities in the state is John Hammond Moore's, *Research Materials in South Carolina* (Columbia, South Carolina: University of South Carolina Press, 1967).

Tennessee

Tennessee Genealogical Society
7779 Poplar Pike
Germantown, Tennessee 38138

(901) 754-4300

http://www.tngs.org/

The society publishes their quarterly *Ansearchin' News*. They sponsor the Tennessee Ancestry Certificate Program for descendants of persons whose ancestors resided in the area that is now Tennessee at any time from the first settlement in 1769 through the year 1880. (See the following entry.)

Germantown Regional History and Genealogy Center
7779 Poplar Pike
Germantown, Tennessee 38138

(901) 757-8480

http://www.tngs.org/

The Tennessee Genealogical Society uses this facility as its headquarters and repository. The collection emphasizes the Mid-South, Eastern, and Southern States. The Tennessee collection includes genealogy, local history, politics, government, family histories, and personal papers, databases, Tennessee Genealogical Society articles online, bibliographies, biographies, vital records, cemeteries, censuses, church records, city directories, local histories, oral histories, court records, heraldry, immigration records, land records, tax lists, maps, newspapers, military records, periodicals, photographs, research guides, abstracts, indexes, recommended websites, and CDs. Specialized collections include American Indians of the South, DAR records, journals, and diaries.

Tennessee Historical Society
War Memorial Building
305 Sixth Avenue, North
Nashville, Tennessee 37243

(615) 741-8934

info@tennesseehistory.org

http://www.tennesseehistory.org/

The society publishes the scholarly *Tennessee Historical Quarterly* and holds a significant collection of historical manuscripts, other documents, and artifacts housed at the Tennessee State Museum and Tennessee State Library and Archives.

Tennessee State Museum
505 Deaderick Street
Nashville, Tennessee 37243

(615) 741-2692 and (800) 407-4324

museuminfo@tnmuseum.org

http://www.tnmuseum.org/

In addition to a variety of permanent and rotating exhibits, the museum sells numerous books on Tennessee history.

Chattanooga Public Library Downtown
1001 Broad Street
Chattanooga, Tennessee 37402

(423) 757-5317

library@lib.chattanooga.gov

http://chattlibrary.org/local-history

The Local History Collection has the Upper South's largest family folder collection with a strong emphasis on Tennessee and North Carolina. Their holdings include internet genealogy databases, censuses, newspapers, an obituary index, county records, 30,000 books, manuscripts, and genealogical periodicals.

East Tennessee Historical Center
601 South Gay Street
Knoxville, Tennessee 37901

(865) 215-8801

http://www.easttnhistory.org/

The center, home to the East Tennessee Historical Society, also serves as the Knox County Archives. One strength of the center's large historical and genealogical holdings is the original 15,000 applications for First Families of Tennessee project. Another strength is the Calvin M. McClung Historical Collection, with more than 75,000 books, 3,000 printed genealogies, genealogical manuscripts, 19,000 rolls of microfilm, state and local government records, newspapers, and other valuable primary source material.

Kingsport Public Library
400 Broad Street
Kingsport, Tennessee 37660

Reference: (423) 224-2539, Archives: (423) 224-2559

http://www.kingsportlibrary.org/genealogy-and-local-history/

The library holds handbooks and reference guides, local histories, family histories, photographs, cemetery records, newspapers, maps, Revolutionary War records, and Virginia military records.

Memphis Public Library and Information Center
Benjamin L. Hooks Central Library
3030 Poplar Avenue
Memphis, Tennessee 38111

(901) 415-2700

hisref@memphis.lib.tn.us

http://www.memphislibrary.org/research/genealogy/

The Library's Genealogy Collection's strongest area is in microfilmed and indexed Memphis and Shelby County records. They hold a large number of genealogical source books, family folders, county histories, published family histories and magazines with an emphasis on 18th and 19th century southern United States, especially Virginia, North Carolina, Tennessee, Mississippi, and Arkansas. The genealogical holdings include manuscripts, maps, biographies, histories, and directories relating to Memphis, Shelby County, and the mid-South region.

John C. Hodges Library, Special Collections
University of Tennessee
1401 Cumberland Avenue
Knoxville, Tennessee 37996

(423)-974-4480

https://www.lib.utk.edu/special/

Special Collections holds manuscripts, biographies, family histories, local and county histories, federal records, church records, ethnic and American Indians, especially Cherokee and Creek, river traffic information, and outstanding historical reference books. The library's catalog is online and the Tennessee Newspaper Project is available through the catalog.

Nashville Metropolitan Government Archives
3801 Green Hills Village Drive
Nashville, Tennessee 37215

(615) 862-5880

http://www.nashville.gov/Metro-Archives.aspx

The library houses the original Davidson County and Nashville City records. The website has links to web resources and a searchable catalog of the records.

Nashville Public Library
615 Church Street
Nashville, Tennessee 37219

(615) 862-5800

https://library.nashville.org/

The library's Nashville Room maintains the genealogical collection, consisting of indexes to Nashville marriages, Tennessean obituary index, Nashville City Cemetery Index, and Nashville photographs, vertical files of newspaper clippings and family histories, and manuscripts concerning Nashville and Davidson County families.

University of Memphis Library
Special Collections Department
126 Ned R. WcWherter Library
Memphis, Tennessee 38152

(901) 678-8242

http://www.memphis.edu/libraries/special-collections/index.php

The library holds approximately 60,000 books on all aspects of regional history and culture, housed in the Preservation and Special Collections, and is home to the library's most rare and special books that span many different subjects, as well as all the university dissertations and theses prior to 2010.

Paul Meek Library, Special Collections
West Tennessee Heritage Study Center
University of Tennessee at Martin
554 University Street
Martin, Tennessee 38237

(731) 881-7464

speccoll@utm.edu

http://www.utm.edu/departments/special_collections/wthsc.php

The center focuses on the genealogy, history, culture, and family history of Tennessee and its counties, with an emphasis on northwest Tennessee. They also collect newspapers, regional county records, and have federal censuses for Tennessee, 1790–1930. Their WTHSC Index is an important resource.

Virginia

Virginia Genealogical Society
P. O. Box 626
Orange, Virginia 22960

vagensoc@aol.com

http://www.vgs.org/

The society publishes the scholarly quarterly *Magazine of Virginia Genealogy* and hosts an annual conference. They also maintain an online directory of links to Virginia libraries, archives, special collections, and other records repositories.

Virginia Historical Society
428 North Boulevard
Richmond, Virginia 23221

(804) 358-4901

http://www.vahistorical.org/

The library houses a collection of more than ten million documents relating to the history of the Old Dominion and the modern states of Kentucky, Virginia, and West Virginia. The collection includes county records (including wills, deeds, and marriages), military service records, church records, Land Office records, tax records, maps, newspapers, bible records, family papers, and genealogical notes and charts.

Virginia Theological Seminary
Archives of the Bishop Payne Library
3737 Seminary Road
Alexandria, Virginia 22304

(703) 461-1731

AskArchives@vts.edu

https://www.vts.edu/page/resources/seminary-archives

The archives holds many of the original Church of England (now Episcopalian Church) parish registers, vestry books, and manuscripts of colonial Virginia, as well as photos, and the African American Episcopal Historical Collection.

Bristol Public Library
701 Goode Street
Bristol, Virginia 24201

(540) 645-8780

bplref@yahoo.com

http://www.bristol-library.org/

The library has a family folder collection and is a good source of information on the settlers coming from Pennsylvania, Maryland, and northern Virginia along the Great Valley Road into Tennessee, Kentucky, and North Carolina.

Earl Gregg Swem Library
College of William and Mary
P. O. Box 8794
Landrum Drive
Williamsburg, Virginia 23187

(757) 221-3050

sweref@wm.edu

http://guides.libraries.wm.edu/friendly.php?s=genealogy

The library holds the original papers from Jamestown, the Virginia Company, manuscripts, and journals, including numerous genealogical references. The library also is home to the renowned Earl Greeg Swem's *Virginia Historical Index* (Baltimore, Maryland: Genealogical Publishing Company, 1934, 1936, Reprinted 2003). One strength of the library's holdings is its collections of colonial Virginia records, manuscripts, church records, maps, newspapers, periodicals, and other documents.

Germanna Foundation Visitor Center & Library
2062 Germanna Highway
P. O. Box 279
Locust Grove, Virginia 22508

(540) 423-1700

http://germanna.org/resources/genealogy/

The library focuses on the history and genealogy of the original German settlers of Germanna in 1714-1717. Strengths of the collection include a database of descendants, list of original settlers, published genealogies, a DNA project, and other materials.

Handley Regional Library
100 West Piccadilly Street
P. O. Box 58
Winchester, Virginia 22604

(540) 662-9041

archives@handleyregional.org

http://www.youseemore.com/handley/contentpages.asp?loc=69

The Stewart Bell, Jr. Archives Reading Room is jointly operated by the library and the Winchester Frederick County Historical Society. They have a large collection of materials on those who migrated south on the Great Valley Road, starting ca 1732, mostly German and Scots-Irish from Pennsylvania and Maryland, including original manuscripts, newspapers, military records, biographies, family histories, maps, photographs, and county histories.

John D. Rockefeller Jr. Library
P. O. Box 1776
313 First Street
Williamsburg, Virginia 23187

(757) 565-8542

libref@cwf.org

http://research.history.org/library/

The library mainly focuses on the history of the thirteen colonies, Revolutionary War, and early United States. The large holdings include published materials, original manuscripts, photographs, family bibles, and several databases to facilitate research.

Jones Memorial Library
2311 Memorial Avenue
Lynchburg, Virginia 24501

434-846-0501

refdesk@jmlibrary.org

http://www.jmlibrary.org/

The library holds a large collection of historical and genealogical materials, including family folders, and both published and unpublished genealogies, focusing primarily on the early migration from Tidewater Virginia, over the Blue Ridge Mountains, into the Shenandoah Valley.

Mary Ball Washington Museum and Library
8346 Mary Ball Road
Lancaster, Virginia 22503

(804) 462-7280

info@mbwm.org

http://www.mbwm.org/genealogy.asp

The library holds thousands of published records, books, manuscripts, periodicals, and microfilm holdings relating to Lancaster County, the Northern Neck, and Tidewater Virginia. They have a card index to their Virginia and Kentucky books and a large collection of family files.

Esther Murdaugh Wilson Memorial Room
Portsmouth Public Library
601 Court Street
Portsmouth, Virginia 23704

(757) 393-8501

http://www.portsmouth-va-public-library.com/local-history-collection/

The library focuses on the history of Portsmouth, Norfolk County, and the surrounding areas of southeastern Virginia.

Roanoke County Public Library
706 South Jefferson Street
Roanoke, Virginia 24016

(540) 853-2073

virginiaroom@gmail.com

The Virginia Room holds a large collection of history and genealogy materials, with emphasis on the Roanoke Valley and southwestern Virginia, including family folders, books, genealogies, biographies, maps, and photographs. Roanoke sits at the south end of the Great Valley Road, also known as the Great Wagon Road. Here migrants either continued down the Great Wagon Road southward into the Carolinas or turned southwestward heading for Tennessee or Kentucky. Many migrants stayed here for a season or even longer before continuing their journeys.

Albert and Shirley Small Special Collections Library
University of Virginia
P. O. Box 400113
Charlottesville VA 22904

(434) 924-3021

library@virginia.edu

The Special Collections Library has a large collection of Virginia historical and genealogical materials, including colonial records, public and private manuscripts, military records, newspapers, maps, and other records. *Virginia Genealogy: A Guide to Resources in the University of Virginia Library* (Charlottesville, Virginia: University Press of Virginia, 1983) is useful for understanding the large collections and using them effectively.

West Virginia

West Virginia Historical Society
P. O. Box 5220
Charleston, West Virginia 25361

http://freepages.history.rootsweb.ancestry.com/~wvhistorical/index.htm

The society publishes a quarterly magazine. Their webpage offers links to a number of webpages of interest to West Virginia researchers.

Allegheny Regional Family History Society
I.O.O.F. Lodge Building
P. O. Box 1804
Elkins, West Virginia 26241

arhfs@yahoo.com

http://pages.swcp.com/~dhickman/arfhs.html

The library has an online database of articles and pedigrees. They also have cemetery transcripts, obituaries, and allow member queries in their newsletter.

Martinsburg-Berkeley County Public Library
101 West King Street
Martinsburg, West Virginia 25401

304-267-8933

http://www.mbcpl.org/

The library has a good genealogy collection with many sources for the earliest West Virginia settlers.

Parkersburg and Wood County Public Library
3100 Emerson Avenue
Parkersburg, West Virginia 26104

(304) 420-4587

http://parkersburg.lib.wv.us/genealogy.html

The West Augusta Historical and Genealogical Society's collection, housed at the library, includes genealogies, family histories, cemetery transcripts, obituaries and family folders, with an emphasis on northwest West Virginia and parts of southwest Pennsylvania.

West Virginia and Regional History Center
West Virginia University
P. O. Box 6069
1549 University Avenue
Morgantown, West Virginia 26506

(304) 293-3536

https://wvrhc.lib.wvu.edu/

The center houses the largest collection of material on West Virginia history, including 4.5 million manuscript documents, 30,000 books, 15,000 pamphlets, 1,200 newspapers, 100,000 photographs and prints, 5,000 maps, 25,000 microfilms, and oral histories. A helpful guide to the collection is James W. Hess's *Guide to Manuscripts and Archives in the West Virginia Collection* (Morgantown, West Virginia: West Virginia University Library, 1974).

Clarksburg-Harrison Public Library
404 West Pike Street
Clarksburg, West Virginia 26301

(304) 627-2236

http://clarksburglibrary.info/Waldomore/localhistory

The West Virginia Collection is a specialized reference collection devoted to the history of the state. The collection contains census records, cemetery listings, obituaries, cemeteries, local histories, and area family histories, as well as books and periodicals about West Virginia. The collection is maintained with the assistance of the Harrison County Genealogical Society.

Hereditary Societies

Organizations that require their members to be descendants of a particular group commonly are called hereditary societies. Such organizations can be helpful to the researcher in several different ways. First, the subject of one's research may have been documented by a member. Alternatively, his commanding officer or fellow soldier also may have been documented. That documentation may include rare or otherwise obscure records; for example, a transcription or photocopy of a family bible record handed down in a different branch of the family tree. Second, many heredity societies maintain significant libraries, manuscript collections, and museums that may have unique materials found nowhere else concerning one's research subject or the battles in which he participated. Third, many societies publish books, periodicals, scholarly journals, and other publications that may have specific information on the various Indian wars, such as detailed descriptions or first-hand accounts of battles and campaigns. Fourth, some of the societies erect monuments and markers that commemorate both people and places of historical and genealogical interest. Fifth, some societies fund the preservation of historical places and buildings where the subject of one's research may have been. And sixth, the researcher may wish to join a hereditary society to recognize and honor one's ancestor. In short, the programs and activities of the various hereditary societies may be helpful not only in uncovering specific information concerning a participant in an Indian war, but also in learning more about the battles and other aspects of that war.

General Society of Colonial Wars
144 Wapping Road
Portsmouth, Rhode Island 02871

http://www.gscw.org/

The society is an association of state societies that honor and perpetuate the memory and spirit of the men and women who assisted in the establishment, defense, and preservation of the American Colonies, by honoring and perpetuating their memory.

National Society Daughters of Colonial Wars

http://nsdcw.org/

The society is an association of state societies that honor and perpetuate the memory and spirit of the men and women who assisted in the establishment, defense, and preservation of the American Colonies, by collecting and preserving records relative to the American Colonies, promoting historical research and the study of history, and commemorating the events of the American colonial era between 1607 and 1775.

The National Society of the Colonial Dames of America
Dumbarton House
2715 Q Street, NW
Washington, DC 20007

(202) 337-2288

http://nscda.org/

The society is an association of state societies that promotes and preserves colonial history. They preserve, maintain, and operate numerous historic sites and museums. Their websites provide biographies of the member's ancestor, lists of publications, oral histories, and patriotic programs.

Jamestowne Society
P. O. Box 6845
Richmond, Virginia 23230

(804) 353-1226

Jamestowne.society@verizon.net

http://www.jamestowne.org/

Society members are descended from early settlers who lived or held colonial government positions in Jamestown, Virginia prior to 1700, or who invested in its establishment. The society was organized for educational, historical, and patriotic purposes and conducts a range of activities, from visiting early American sites, providing an annual graduate fellowship for research on colonial Virginia prior to 1700, funding the restoration of records, and supporting preservation of colonial sites.

National Society Daughters of the American Colonists
2205 Massachusetts Ave, NW
Washington, DC 20008

(202) 667-3076

http://nsdac.org/

The society is an association of state societies and local chapters dedicated to promoting patriotism; researching, recording, and publishing the history and deeds of the American colonists; commemorating deeds of colonial interest; and, promoting American history in education. The society also places markers at the location of significant colonial events.

National Society Sons of the American Colonists
Registrar General
7501 West 101st Street, Suite 204
Minneapolis, Minnesota 55438

(952) 261-6937

http://americancolonists.org/#

The society is an association of state societies that assists and encourages the preservation of colonial records and historic sites, fosters the continued interest in historical and genealogical research of the colonial era, encourages and supports the growth and development of libraries specializing in genealogical and historical data of the colonial era, publishes on a regular basis a Lineage Book to record the names of members and their ancestral data, and encourages a true and honest respect for the contribution of our ancestors in the establishment of the United States.

National Society Daughters of the American Revolution
1776 D Street NW
Washington, DC 20006

(202) 628-1776

http://www.dar.org/

The society is a service organization for women who are directly descended from a person involved in the United States' struggle for independence. They work to promote historic preservation, education, and patriotism. The organization's membership is limited to direct lineal descendants of soldiers or others of the Revolutionary period who aided the cause of independence. The society maintains a national museum and genealogical library, offers scholarships, collects and preserves historical records, restores and maintains historic sites, and commemorates and memorializes historic events.

National Society Sons of the American Revolution
809 West Main Street
Louisville, Kentucky 40202

(502) 589-1776

NSSAR@sar.org

https://sar.org/

The society promotes patriotism, American history, and education; commemorates and provides memorials to the people and events of the Revolution; collects and preserves historic records; and, identifies and locates the graves of the patriots.

Daughters of the Cincinnati
20 West 44th Street, Suite 508
New York, New York 10036

(212) 991-9945

http://daughters1894.org/

The society, composed of women whose ancestors were officers in George Washington's army and navy during the Revolutionary War, strives to expand and perpetuate the knowledge of the founding of the nation through a range of educational and scholarship programs.

Society of the Cincinnati
2118 Massachusetts Ave NW
Washington, DC 20008

(202) 785-2040

http://societyofthecincinnati.org/

The nation's oldest patriotic organization, founded in 1783 by officers of the Continental Army and their French counterparts who served together in the American Revolution, the Cincinnati promote knowledge and appreciation of the achievement of American independence and fosters fellowship among its members. Dedicated to the principles and ideals of its founders, the modern society maintains its headquarters, library, and museum at Anderson House in Washington, DC.

National Society United States Daughters of the War of 1812
1461 Rhode Island Avenue, NW
Washington, D.C. 20005

(202) 745-1812

contact@usdaughters1812.org

http://www.usdaughters1812.org/home.html

The society is a volunteer women's service organization dedicated to promoting patriotism, preserving and increasing knowledge of the history of the American people by the preservation of documents and relics, marking of historic places, recording of family histories and traditions, celebration of patriotic anniversaries, and teaching and emphasizing the heroic deeds of the civil, military, and naval life of those who molded the government between the close of the American Revolution and the close of the War of 1812. The organization petitions Congress to compile and publish authentic records of men in civil, military, and naval service from 1784 to 1815, and maintains at its National Headquarters in Washington, DC a museum and library of memorabilia of the 1784-1815 period.

General Society of the War of 1812
1219 Charmuth Road
Lutherville, Maryland 21093

http://gsw1812.org/

The General Society is a genealogical society that was founded in 1894 as an umbrella organization for the state societies of descendants of veterans of the War of 1812. The objectives of the society are the collection and preservation of rolls, records, books, and other documents relating to the War of 1812; the encouragement of research and the preservation of historical data, including memorials to patriots of that era in our national history; the caring for the graves of veterans of the War of 1812; the cherishing, maintenance, and extension of the institutions of American freedom; and, the fostering of true patriotism and love of country.

Miscellaneous Libraries, Archives, and Foundations

The Seminole Wars Foundation, Inc.
35247 Reynolds Street
Dade City, Florida 33523

(352) 583-2711

http://www.seminolewars.us/home.html

The foundation preserves sites associated with the wars and publishes books and other materials related to the wars. Starting in 2017, the foundation will sponsor an annual Convocation of Seminole War Historians at St. Augustine.

Santa Cruz Public Library
Genealogical Collection
224 Church Street
Santa Cruz, California 95060

(831) 427-7707 x5794

http://www.santacruzpl.org/elibrary/research/category/5/

The library holds the collection of the Santa Cruz Genealogical Society, the highlight of which is the *Genealogy Clearing House Brayton Collection: Upper South-Eastern States*, covering Kentucky, North Carolina, Tennessee, Virginia, and West Virginia. The collection consists of 560 family group binders, eight binders of pedigree charts, 1,890 correspondence files, and 160 family folders.

Regenstein Library
University of Chicago
1100 East 57th Street
Chicago, Illinois 60637

(773) 702-4685

https://www.lib.uchicago.edu/scrc/modernmss/durrett/

The library's Durrett Collection consists of historical Kentucky and Ohio River Valley manuscripts, comparable in size and content to the Draper Manuscript Collection. The collection contains a wide variety of published and documentary materials on the settlement of Kentucky and the Ohio River Valley. The printed portion of the Durrett Collection includes 20,000 bound volumes; 250 files of pamphlets; 200 volumes of atlases and loose maps; and, 249 newspaper titles. In addition, there were 50,000 pages of handwritten, typed, or photocopied transcripts; magazines; clippings; and photographs, all bearing on the history of the exploration and settlement of the trans-Appalachian west.

The rare and valuable books were separated from the rest of the material, cataloged, and added to the library's Rare Book Collection. Non-rare monographic and serial titles, which constituted the great majority of the material, were cataloged and added to the library's general book collection.

The manuscript material was established as a separate research collection, and incorporated into the holdings of the Department of Special Collections. Among the newspapers are 135 titles published in Kentucky, beginning in 1788 with the *Kentucky Gazette*, the first newspaper established in the state. Other important titles include the *Mirror*, the *Palladium*, the *Guardian of Freedom*, the *Farmer's Library or Ohio Intelligencer*, and numerous campaign newspapers such as *The Patriot* and *The Spirit of '76* from 1826.

The Durrett manuscript collections include a wide array of letters, journals, military reports, business records, legal documents, speeches, sermons, and maps spanning the period from the mid-eighteenth century to the mid-nineteenth century. Among the collections are the personal papers of Mann Butler, Richard H. Collins, George Nicholas, and Joshua Lacy Wilson, all figures with important connections to the Ohio River Valley frontier and its early history. The Durrett manuscripts also include plantation records of Kentucky families. The Durrett Miscellaneous Manuscripts contain individual manuscripts and groups of letters from a range of historical figures who played key roles in the development of the western country, from Thomas Jefferson, James Madison, Alexander Hamilton, and James Wilkinson to Daniel Boone, George Rogers Clark, Isaac Shelby, Harry Innes, and Henry Clay. The manuscripts are divided into the following series:

> Broadsides, Broadsheets, and Circulars
>
> Mann Butler Papers
>
> Richard H. Collins Papers
>
> Reuben T. Durrett Personal Papers
>
> Joel Tanner Hart Papers
>
> Lewis Family Papers
>
> Edmund Lyne Estate Papers
>
> George Nicholas Papers
>
> Joshua Lacy Wilson Papers
>
> Pictures, Maps, and Sketches
>
> Durrett Miscellaneous Manuscripts
>
> Durrett Codices

Historical Society of Western Pennsylvania
Senator John Heinz History Center
Library and Archives
1212 Smallman Street
Pittsburgh, Pennsylvania 15222

(412) 454-6364

library@heinzhistorycenter.org

http://www.heinzhistorycenter.org/libraryArchives.aspx

The library holds the colonial records of the Ohio Company, with reference to land grants and settlers since the 1750s in southwestern Pennsylvania and that portion of Virginia that became West Virginia.

William L. Clements Library
University of Michigan
909 South University Avenue
The University of Michigan
Ann Arbor, Michigan 48109

(734) 764-2347

www.clements.umich.edu

The Manuscripts Division holds the following important collections:

> William Henry Lyttelton Papers, 1730-1806 and 1755-1761: The papers document Lyttelton's career as governor of South Carolina and governor of Jamaica. They primarily relate to his colonial administration of South Carolina and Jamaica, and military engagements with Native Americans on the South Carolina frontier and against the French in the West Indies.

> Edward H. Fitzgerald Journals, 1834-1852: The journals are comprised of two volumes and one document, belonging to a U. S. army officer who served in the Seminole War, the Mexican War, and at several western outposts in California and Oregon. The volumes amount to Fitzgerald's daily journal kept during his service with the navy in the Mediterranean. He wrote sporadic diary entries and poems in Florida during the Seminole War and in Mexico and California.

> Bouquet's Expedition against the Indians, 1764: The expedition against the Indians consists of two orderly books issued by Colonel Henry Bouquet, spanning August-November 1764, during which time he lead a small army into the western Ohio Indian territory to retrieve white captives and to enforce a peace settlement with the Delaware, Mingo, Shawnee, and Wyandot Indians. These volumes contain detailed information on

Bouquet's decisions and actions, and explain how he maneuvered his forces through the wilderness.

Native American History Collection, 1688-1921: The collection contains miscellaneous letters and documents concerning Native Americans in the United States, Canada, and the West Indies, and their interactions with British and American settlers.

Thomas Gage Papers, 1754-1807: The papers consist of the military and governmental correspondence and headquarter papers of General Thomas Gage, officer in the British Army in America (1754-1763) and commander-in-chief of the British forces in North America between 1763 and 1775. The papers include incoming correspondence and copies of letters written by Gage, together with a large quantity of documents related to military administration and manuscript maps of North America. The collection is particularly strong in documenting the British administration of North America after the French and Indian War, interactions with Native Americans, and the years preceding the American Revolution. The Thomas Gage warrants series is described in a separate finding aid.

Swearingen-Bedinger Papers, 1759-1948: Correspondence, Revolutionary War military documents, land and financial documents, and maps pertaining to several generations of the interconnected Swearingen and Bedinger families of present-day Virginia, West Virginia, and Kentucky.

Jeffery Amherst Papers, 1758-1764: The papers consist of 763 items, including correspondence, documents, and military orders of Jeffery Amherst, British commander-in-chief in North America from 1758-1763. Included are Amherst's letters to General Thomas Gage and the papers given to Gage with the transfer of authority in 1763.

Great Britain Indian Department Collection, 1753-1795: The collection is made up of documents, letters, and other manuscripts relating to interactions between government and military officials, Native Americans, and American residents.

General Publications

The following published materials are general in nature, in that they cover multiple wars or states.

Clodfelter, Michael, *Warfare and Armed Conflicts: A Statistical Reference to Casualty and Other Figures, 1618-1991, Volume I, A Note on the Statistics, Introduction, 1618-1899.* Jefferson, North Carolina: McFarland & Company, Inc., 1992.

Cooper, Jerry, *The Militia and the National Guard in America Since Colonial Times.* Research Guides in Military Studies, Number 7, Westport, Connecticut: Greenwood Press, 1993.

Dollarhide, William and Ronald A. Bremer, *America's Best Genealogy Resource Centers.* Bountiful, Utah: Heritage Quest, 1998.

Garrison, Ellen, *Archives in Appalachia: A Directory.* Boone, North Carolina: Appalachian Consortium Press, 1985. The directory covers the mountain regions of Georgia, Kentucky, North Carolina, South Carolina, Tennessee, Virginia, and West Virginia, arranged by state, then by name of repository, each entry providing the archive's name and address, phone number, dates covered by the collection, records in the collection, subjects covered by the collection, and size of the collection.

Haas, Irvin, *America's Historic Battlefields.* New York, New York: Hippocrene Books, 1987.

Higham, Robin, *A Guide to the Sources of United States Military History.* Hamden, Connecticut: Archon Books, 1975.

Horowitz, Lois, *A Bibliography of Military Name Lists from Pre-1675 to 1900: A Guide to Genealogical Sources.* Metuchen, New Jersey: The Scarecrow Press, Inc., 1990.

Huston, Andrew Ross, General Society of Colonial Wars, *Honoring our Colonial History: Tablets, Monuments, and Memorials Placed by the Society of Colonial Wars 1892-2010.* Charleston, South Carolina, Advantage, Inc., 2011.

Ivers, Larry E., *This Torrent of Indians, War on the Southern Frontier, 1715-1728.* Charleston, South Carolina: University of South Carolina Press, 2016.

Miller, Allan R. and Peter Maslowski, *For the Common Defense: A Military History of the United States of America.* New York, New York: The Free Press, 1984.

Ratjar, Steve, *Indian War Sites: A Guidebook to Battlefields, Monuments, and Memorials, State by State, with Canada and Mexico.* Jefferson, North Carolina: McFarland, 1999.

Roberts, Robert B., *Encyclopedia of Historic Forts: The Military, Pioneer, and Trading Posts of the United States.* New York, New York: Macmillan, 1988, 10th Printing.

Sweeney, Jerry K., *A Handbook of American Military History, From the Revolutionary War to the Present.* Boulder, Colorado: Westview Press, 1996.

Whisker, James Biser, *The American Colonial Militia, Volume I, Introduction.* Lewiston, New York: The Edwin Mellen Press, 1997.

_____, *The American Colonial Militia, Volume III, The Pennsylvania Colonial Militia.* Lewiston, New York: The Edwin Mellen Press, 1997.

_____, *The American Colonial Militia, Volume V, The Colonial Militia of the Southern States, 1606-1785.* Lewiston, New York: The Edwin Mellen Press, 1997.

Williams, T. Harry, *The History of American Wars, From 1745 to 1918.* Baton Rouge, Louisiana: Louisiana State University Press, 1981.

Wulff, Matt, *Ranger: North American Frontier Soldier.* Westminster, Maryland: Heritage Books, Inc., 2008.

Reenactment Organizations

The Illinois Regiment, Virginia State Forces

http://www.illinoisregiment.org/

This umbrella organization coordinates the activities of reenactors of the five companies that composed the illustrious Illinois Regiment during the Revolutionary War. The units hold numerous reenactments every summer of the battles in which their namesake units participated.

The Florida Frontier Guards
Seminole War Re-enactors & Living History, 1835-1842

http://floridafrontierguard.com/index.html

Established in 2003, the Florida Frontier Guard is an unincorporated association of independent Seminole War reenactors dedicated to the interpretation of the common soldiers of the volunteer and militia forces who served in Florida during the Seminole Wars.

Florida Frontiersmen, Inc.

Secretary@floridafrontiersmen.com

http://www.floridafrontiersmen.com/

The Florida Frontiersmen is a private club dedicated to preserving the skills of the first pioneers and settlers on the frontier before 1840. In addition to holding competitive monthly black powder events, they host the Alafia River Rendezvous every January.

397